Nelson's Annual

Preacher's Sourcebook

2002 EDITION

Nelson's Annual Preacher's Sourcebook

2002 EDITION

ROBERT J. MORGAN, EDITOR

THOMAS NELSON PUBLISHERS
Nashville

Book design and composition by Mark McGarry,
Texas Type and Book Works, Dallas, Texas

Morgan, Robert J. (ed.)
    Nelson's annual preacher's sourcebook, 2002 edition.

ISBN 0-7852-4700-9

Printed in the United States of America

1 2 3 4 5 6 7—06 05 04 03 02 01

Contents

Classics for the Pastor's Library

Conversations in a Pastor's Study

Helps for the Pastor's Family

Heroes for the Pastor's Heart

Quotes for the Pastor's Wall

Techniques for the Pastor's Delivery

Introduction

I know you're busy, so I'll be quick. Here is a toolchest of ideas, expositional outlines, illustrations, Scripture readings, children's sermons, and articles of encouragement for a year's worth of pulpit work. Think of it as a guidebook or a grab-bag. We'll help with the ideas, but you must provide the prayer, passion, and preaching prowess.

My thanks goes to Phil Stoner and Jim Weaver at Thomas Nelson Publishers for conceiving this project, and to Lee Hollaway for his support, patience, understanding, and editorial guidance. I also appreciate Greg Johnson for his assistance and advice.

A special word of tribute goes to my dear friend,

Dr. Jonathan Thigpen
Preacher, educator, executive, and buddy

who passed away shortly after granting the interview on pages 198–99. To him this book is affectionately dedicated.

Editor's Preface

Planning and "Plunching"

I began my current pastorate when Edward Kennedy was challenging Jimmy Carter for the presidency in 1979. Carter, struggling in the polls, was entangled in a series of international problems, including the Iranian hostage crisis. Kennedy exploited Carter's problems, repeatedly accusing the president of "lurching from crisis to crisis."

That phrase bothered me because, whether the charge pertained to Carter or not, I felt it applied to me. My ministry lunged from one headache to another. I spent too much time putting out fires and too little time fanning the flames of the Spirit. I neither had a long-range plan for my work nor any system for developing one. Pastors as well as presidents can lurch from crisis to crisis and from day to day. Sometimes we lurch from church to church.

Weak leadership merely reacts to its ever-changing circumstances. Wiser leadership charts a course, follows its plan, and responds to the variables accordingly. Feeble leaders are crisis driven, while stronger ones are goal-directed. Prudent pastors do not just minister—they *ad*minister. They are overseers, as well as shepherds, and planning is part of their calling. They pray like Paul, preach like Peter, and plan like Nehemiah, who, in rebuilding Jerusalem's walls, evaluated his situation, formulated his goals, developed his strategy, recruited his team, and implemented his plan.

Solomon said, "A prudent man gives thought to his steps" (Prov. 14:15 NIV). If we fail to plan, we plan to fail. Peter Drucker asserts that effectiveness is more than getting things done right; it is getting things done.

How do we administer without becoming addled ministers? How do we oversee the important without being overwhelmed by the immediate? How do we move from frenzied pandemonium to perceptive planning? That was my dilemma, because in seminary I learned more about alliteration than administration. The letters in front of my name are REV—not CEO. I slowly learned, however, that management proficiency can be acquired. For me, it was learning to plan and "plunch."

Planning

People management is arduous, especially in volunteer organizations such as churches; but I am catching on belatedly. Recently, we erected a scaffolding around our planning processes that furnishes me a framework for leadership.

First, with the help of an ad-hoc committee, our church formulated a mission statement for our constitution.—Our congregation, we realized, exists for this purpose: to extend and strengthen the kingdom for Christ and His glory. All our programs must relate in some way to this; otherwise, we have no basis for planning. The committee clothed these purposes in appropriate terminology, and its report was adopted by the church as our joint statement of mission.

Second, we selected another group of leaders and asked them to invest several months on one question: In view of our mission, what does God want our church to be 15, 10, or 5 years from now?—We examined the needs and the demographics of our community, studied programs and ideas from other churches, prayed, brainstormed and prayed again. After making a list of every program, ministry, or goal we could imagine, we started trimming it. We ended up with seven areas in which we formulated SMART goals: Specific, Measurable, Attainable, Relevant, and Timed. For Christian organizations, goals are a statement of faith.

We made a five-column chart representing the next five years and set our goals into the columns. This became our five-year plan, which, after attaining congregational ownership, was adopted by our church and is now reevaluated and updated annually.

What next? In light of the church's direction, I must continually determine my responsibilities as pastor. Each fall, I spend a partial week praying, thinking, and listing the things I would like to accomplish during the year. Then, as I narrow my list to a few priorities, I state them as goals, chart them on project planners, and scratch them into my 12–month calendar. We ask each of our staff members to do the same in their respective areas of responsibility. This enables us to "manage by objective," fulfilling Peter Drucker's counsel: "What the executive needs are criteria which enable him to work on the truly important. . . . If (he) lets the flow of events determine what he does, what he works on . . . he will fritter himself away."

"Plunching"

Now comes the hard part. How do I stay true to my agenda? "Make whatever grand plans you will," Warren Bennis observed, "you may be sure the unexpected or the trivial will disturb and disrupt them."

On automobile trips, I frequently pull alongside the road to check the map. The same is true in following our church's plan. I need regular respites for aligning my ministry to my map. I took Bob Logan's advice in *Leading and Managing Your Church:* "In order to maintain a living, growing ministry, you must schedule regular planning times. Block off a couple of hours a week for this task. In addition allow a half-day per month, a day per quarter, and a two- to three-day retreat each year for the process of goal setting and planning."

My fall retreat provided the annual two or three days, and it was now the "couple of hours a week" I needed most—a prescheduled, practically inviolable appointment. So I concocted a routine I call "plunch"—a planning lunch—just between the Lord and me. Each Friday, I drive to a little café which doesn't mind my occupying a table for awhile. I order a light lunch, pull out my planning notebook, and work through the following sequence.

First, as I thank the Lord for my food, I ask Him to guide me in planning His work. While Proverbs 14:15 says that a prudent man gives thought to his steps, Proverbs 16:9 reminds us: "In his heart a man plans his course, but the Lord determines his steps" (NIV). We are, said the apostle, coworkers with God.

Next, on my weekly calendar, I block in all of next week's prescheduled, non-negotiable events—meetings, services, weddings, and so on. I reserve personal time for family and hobbies. I also pencil in next Friday's "plunch."

Then, on scrap paper, I create a "Next Week's Options" list. I jot down all the things I conceivably could do next week by consulting:

- The next several months on the church calendar;
- The next several months on my personal calendar;
- My annual pastoral goals;
- My current "to-do" list;
- My project planners.

I usually have about 20 items on my list, but I can only concentrate on three or four during the next seven days. I choose the most important ones, blocking off chunks of time in next week's schedule for them. Robert Logan observes: "Establishing priorities and having a calendar of appointments that reflects them are the only ways to become an effective Christian leader." He suggests that we ask ourselves: "What things, if done well, will result in the greatest amount of growth and health of my ministry? What are the few really important things that need to be done?"

When I have finished "plunching," I have a program for the coming week that includes a tentative schedule for each day and an accompanying "to-do" list with priority items listed at the top.

I enter the following Monday with a plan of action for the week. Even then, of course, there is no guarantee that when each day arrives the anticipated time will be there. Ministers' schedules are notoriously unpredictable. We cannot preschedule births, deaths, irate members, and other upheavals. If I do not plan my week in advance, however, I succumb totally to the "tyranny of the urgent."

Now that our church employs several staff members, I ask them to plan and "plunch," using the techniques described. We monitor their goals each month during a routine staff meeting.

I believe that Christ entered each day with a plan. He didn't go around doing *everything,* but He did go around doing *good.* When His ministry on earth ended, He had finished the work His Father had given Him. He did not lurch from crisis to crisis; He moved from project to project. He was never frenzied, and He avoided pandemonium. He redeemed the time.

We can do the same by planning to "plunch"—and "plunching" to plan. Although we cannot avoid crises, we need not lurch from one to another. We do not have time enough for that. If we are going to redeem the moments given us, we must give thought to our steps, and in doing so, avoid the potholes of pandemonium and the misfortune of missed opportunities.

Why not pull out your calendar or Palm Pilot and schedule a couple of hours near the end of this week, or at the beginning of next week? Make a date to treat yourself to "plunch."

Contributors

Dr. Timothy K. Beougher
Associate Professor, Billy Graham School of Missions, Evangelism, and Church Growth, The Southern Baptist Theological Seminary

A Prayer for Progress (February 3)
Learning to Count (February 10)
How To Be a Star (May 5)
Why Do the Righteous Suffer? (June 9)
The Joy of Giving (June 23)
Encouraging Others (July 14)
A Longing To Get Along (August 18)
Relationships in the Model Church (September 1)
The Power of a Proper Perspective (September 22)
Messages From the Manger (December 8)
Looking Forward By Looking Backward (December 15)
Celebrating Christmas (December 15)

Dr. John A. Broadus (1827-1897)
American Baptist seminary president and preacher

Some Laws of Spiritual Work (February 17)

Dr. Ed Dobson
Pastor, Calvary Church in Grand Rapids, Michigan, and Moody Bible Institute's 1993 Pastor of the Year

Shalom (January 13)
Those Salty Christians (April 14)
The Light of the World (April 14)
When a Prophet Confronts a King (May 26)
Surviving Deep Waters and Dark Nights (July 14)
What Jesus Cannot Do (July 21)
The Temptation of Jesus (September 29)
A Heart for God's Word (October 27)

Dr. John Kennedy (1819-1884)
Pastor, Dingwall Free Church of Scotland

The Secret of the Lord (April 28)

Rev. Kevin Riggs
Pastor, Franklin Community Church in Franklin, Tennessee

The Importance of the Resurrection (March 31)
Go for the God (April 7)
Bloom Where You Are Planted (April 14)
Joining the Army of the Great Unknowns (May 19)
The Most Valuable Asset in the World (June 2)
Ridicule, Revenge, and Retaliation: Handling Criticism (August 11)
Turning Clay into Rock (October 6)
Spiritual Fitness (October 6)
Right Where You Are (October 13)
What a Difference a Week Makes (November 17)

Rev. Charles Haddon Spurgeon (1834-1892)
Pastor, Metropolitan Tabernacle, London

Feeble Faith Meets a Strong Savior (January 20)
It May Be (April 21)
Individual Repentance (September 15)

Rev. Drew Wilkerson
Pastor, Jersey Shore Church of God in Jersey Shore, Pennsylvania

When God Strikes the Match (April 7)
What MOM Stands For (May 12)
A Man Called Jabez (July 7)
Follow the Leader (July 28)
The Imagination of God (August 4)
The Truth Test (August 18)
The ABCs of Body Building (August 25)
The Journey Home (September 8)

Winning Over Worry (September 29)
Green Leaf in Drought Time (October 20)
The Advent Of Grace (December 1)
Have a Hopeful New Year (December 29)

Dr. Melvin Worthington
Executive Secretary, National Association of Free Will Baptists

Willing to Wait (April 28)
Wrapped in Grace (May 12)
Have You Heard? (May 19)
Who Is Wise? (May 26)
Dwindling Devotions (June 9)
Reproved, Reassured, and Regulated (June 16)
Where There Is No Vision (June 30)
Envisioning the Eternal (July 14)
Criteria for Contentment (July 28)
Consider Christ (August 11)
Fashioned in the Fire (September 15)
Complete Christians (September 15)
How Can I Find God's Will for Me? (October 13)
Truths for Today (October 20)
Principles for Prosperity (November 3)
Hidden Help (November 3)
Wisdom in the Night (November 10)
Conceptualizing the Church (November 24)
The Way It Was (December 22)
Formula for Faithfulness (December 29)

All other outlines are from the pulpit ministry of the general editor, Rev. Robert J. Morgan, of The Donelson Fellowship in Nashville, Tennessee. Special appreciation goes to Jerry Carraway, worship leader of The Donelson Fellowship, for his invaluable assistance.

2002 Calendar

January 1	New Year's Day
January 6	**Epiphany**
January 13	
January 20	**Sanctity of Human Life Sunday**
January 21	Martin Luther King Jr. Day
January 26	Australia Day (Australia)
January 27	**Super Bowl Sunday**
February 1	National Freedom Day
February 2	Ground Hog Day
February 3	
February 10	
February 12	Lincoln's Birthday
February 13	Ash Wednesday
February 14	St. Valentine's Day
February 17	**First Sunday of Lent**
February 18	Presidents' Day
February 22	Washington's Birthday
February 24	**Second Sunday of Lent**
March 3	**Third Sunday of Lent**
March 10	**Fourth Sunday of Lent**
	Mothering Sunday (United Kingdom)
March 17	**Fifth Sunday of Lent**
	St. Patrick's Day
March 24	**Palm Sunday / Passion Sunday**
March 28	Passover
	Holy Thursday
March 29	Good Friday
March 31	**Easter**

(all **boldface** dates are Sundays)

April 7	**Daylight Savings Time Begins**
April 14	
April 21	
April 24	Secretaries Day
April 28	
May 5	
May 12	**Ascension Sunday**
	Mother's Day
May 18	Armed Forces Day
May 19	**Pentecost Sunday**
May 26	
May 27	Memorial Day
June 2	
June 9	
June 14	Flag Day
June 16	**Father's Day**
June 21	Summer Solstice
June 23	
June 30	
July 1	Canada Day (Canada)
July 4	Independence Day
July 7	
July 14	
July 21	
July 28	
August 4	**Transfiguration Sunday**
August 11	
August 18	

August 25

September 1

September 2   Labor Day

September 8   **Grandparents' Day**

September 15

September 22

September 29

October 1-31   Pastor Appreciation Month

October 6

October 13

October 14   Columbus Day

                Thanksgiving (Canada)

October 20

October 27   **Daylight Savings Time Ends**

October 31   Reformation Day

                Halloween

November 1   All Saints' Day

November 3

November 5   Election Day

November 10   **Day of Prayer for Persecuted Church**

November 11   Veteran's Day

November 17

November 24

November 28   Thanksgiving

November 30   Hanukkuh

December 1   **First Sunday of Advent**

December 8   **Second Sunday of Advent**

December 15   **Third Sunday of Advent**

December 21   Winter Solstice

December 22   **Fourth Sunday of Advent**

December 25   Christmas

December 29

December 31   New Year's Eve

SERMONS AND WORSHIP SUGGESTIONS FOR 52 WEEKS

JANUARY 6, 2002

Dying for a New Beginning

Date preached:

Scripture: Galatians 2:20 I have been crucified with Christ; it is no longer I who live, but Christ lives in me; and the life which I now live in the flesh I live by faith in the Son of God, who loved me and gave Himself for me.

Introduction: The problem with New Year's Resolutions is they tend to "go in one year and out the next." Well, today I'd like us to consider adopting a Bible verse as a resolution. Some people choose a Bible verse at the beginning of January to set the theme for the coming year. If you could have one verse scripted and framed to hang in your living room for the next 12 months, which would you choose? I'd like to suggest Galatians 2:20

This verse presents three configurations to the Christian life.

1. **The Relinquished Life:** Galatians 2:20 tells us the Christian life is a relinquished life: "I have been crucified with Christ." In receiving Christ, we come to the old rugged cross and gaze upon the dying form of one who suffered there for us. We see his hands nailed fast to the wood. We see the spike in his ankles. We see the blood flowing in streaks down his body, and, deeply moved, we turn aside from the kind of life we once lived and take our stand beneath the cross of Jesus. We die to ourselves and to our sin. We die to the world, the flesh, and the devil, and we identify with the cross of Christ. When James Calvert went as a missionary to the cannibals of the Fiji Islands, the captain of the ship sought to turn him back. "You will lose your life and the lives of those with you if you go among such savages," he cried. Calvert only replied, "We died before we came here."

2. **The Exchanged Life:** "It is no longer I who live, but Christ lives in me." Missionary Hudson Taylor called this the "Exchanged Life." None of us can live the Christian life in our own strength or resist temptation solely by our own will power. Only Christ can successfully live the genuine victorious Christian life—it is, after all, *His* life—and when we come to Him in full surrender, He begins living *His* life *through* us. This involves two levels:

- Christian Living: Christ lives His life through us, producing the Fruit of the Spirit (Gal. 5:20), which represents the character qualities of Christ Himself.
- Christian Service: Christ does His work through us. In Romans 15:18, Paul said: "I will not venture to speak of anything except what Christ has accomplished *through* me" (NRSV). In 2 Corinthians 5:20: "We are ambassadors for Christ, as though God were pleading *through* us." In 2 Timothy 4:17, the apostle said: "But the Lord stood with me and strengthened me, so that the message might be preached fully *through* me."

3. **The Trusting Life:** "...and the life which I now live in the flesh I live by faith in the Son of God, who loved me and gave Himself for me." "This is the victory that has overcome the world—our faith" (1 John 5:4). Romans 1:17 tells us that the Christian life is one of faith from first to last, for the just shall live by faith. Isaiah 26:3–4 says: "You will keep him in perfect peace, whose mind is stayed on You, because he trusts in You. Trust in the LORD forever, for in YAH, the LORD, is everlasting strength." Proverbs 3:5 says, "Trust in the LORD with all your heart."

> *In heavenly love abiding, no change my heart shall fear;*
> *And safe is such confiding, for nothing changes here.*
> *The storm may rage around me, my heart may low be laid;*
> *But God is round about me, and can I be dismayed.*

>>> *sermon continued on following page*

APPROPRIATE HYMNS AND SONGS

I Am Crucified With Christ, John G. Elliott; 1992 BMG Songs, Inc. (Admin. by BMG Music Publishing)/Charlie Monk Music.

Thou Wilt Keep Him In Perfect Peace, Vivian Amsler Kretz; 1934. Renewed 1962 U. K. Amster 1977. Assigned to Singspiration Music (Admin. by Brentwood-Benson Music Publishing, Inc.).

In Heavenly Love Abiding, Anna L. Waring/Felix Mendelssohn; Public Domain.

Here Am I, Brian Doerkson; 1995 Mercy/Vineyard Publishing (Admin. by Music Services).

I Would Be True, Howard Arnold Walter/Joseph Yates Peek; Public Domain.

Conclusion: A. W. Tozer wrote, "If you ask God to give you a special message for the opening year, one that will be made seasonable and real in every exigency of the unknown future, you will be surprised how faithfully He will fulfill His word, and how fittingly the Holy Spirit will speak to you of things to come, and anticipate the real needs and exigencies of your life." Perhaps Galatians 2:20 is that word from God for you today, if you're dying for a new beginning and willing to be "crucified with Christ."

FOR THE BULLETIN

✿ On January 6, 1519, Martin Luther met with Karl von Miltitz, representing Pope Leo X, in an effort to prevent a church schism. Miltitz left the meeting thinking he had accomplished his purpose, but Luther would not be silenced. ✿ January 6, 1739, marks the birth of John Fawcett, author of "Blest Be The Tie that Binds." He was converted at age 16 by George Whitefield and became a Baptist pastor. He wrote his famous hymn after he and his wife could not bear leaving their beloved rural congregation for a famous pastorate in London. ✿ On Sunday, January 6, 1850, the "Prince of Preachers," Charles Haddon Spurgeon, was converted. A snowstorm forced 15–year-old Charles to duck into a Primitive Methodist Church. Only a few people were there, and not even the preacher showed up. A thin-looking man finally stood and read Isaiah 45:22. Spying Charles in the back, he pointed his finger, crying, "Look, young man! Look! Look to Christ!" Charles did look and was saved. ✿ On this day in 1884, Gregor Mendel, Austrian Augustinian monk, biologist and botanist, died. He pioneered the study of biological heredity and laid the mathematical foundation of the science of genetics. ✿ Alexander Whyte, one of Scotland's greatest preachers, died on January 6, 1921. ✿ On this day in 1947 another Scottish preacher, Peter Marshall, became Chaplain of the United States Senate. Two years later, he suffered a heart attack and died. His widow, Catherine Marshall, assuaged her grief by writing his biography, *A Man Called Peter.* She went on to become one of the twentieth century's most gifted authors.

WORSHIP HELPS

Worship Theme:
A new beginning in Christ Jesus.

Call to Worship:
2 Corinthians 5:17: Therefore, if anyone is in Christ, he *is* a new creation; old things have passed away; behold, all things have become new.

Readers' Theater:

Reader 1:   This is the day the LORD has made; We will rejoice and be glad in it.

Reader 2:   And when He had come into Jerusalem, all the city was moved, saying, "Who is this?" So the multitudes said, "This is Jesus, the prophet from Nazareth of Galilee."

Reader 3:   This is My beloved Son, in whom I am well pleased.

All: This is the bread which comes down from heaven.

Reader 1:   This is the day that the LORD has made.

Reader 3:   And it will be said in that day: "Behold, this is our God; We have waited for Him, and He will save us. This is the LORD... We will be glad and rejoice in His salvation."

All: For this is God, Our God forever and ever; He will be our guide even to death.

Taken from Psalm 118:24; Matthew 21:10; Matthew 3:17; John 6:50; Psalm 118:24; Isaiah 25:9; and Psalm 48:14.

Pastoral Prayer:
Consider using Frances Ridley Havergal's hymn, "Another Year is Dawning" for today's prayer. Havergal (1836–1879) wrote several prayers and hymns for New Year's Day. The following was written in 1874 and printed on specially designed cards for her friends:

> *Another year is dawning, dear Master, let it be,*
> *in working or in waiting, another year with Thee.*
> *Another year of progress, another year of praise,*
> *Another year of proving Thy presence all the days.*

STATS, STORIES AND MORE

Crucified With Christ

- I was sitting upstairs reading Romans and I came to the words, "Knowing this, that our old man was crucified with Him...." Knowing this! How could I know it? I prayed, "Lord, open my eyes!" and then, in a flash, I saw.

  —*Watchman Nee, on how he first realized he had been crucified with Christ.*

- When God calls a man, he bids him come and die.

  —*Dietrich Bonhoeffer, German Christian martyred by the Nazis.*

- There came a day when George Mueller died, utterly died! No longer did his own desires, preferences, and tastes come first. He knew that from then on Christ must be all in all.

  — *George Mueller, when asked the secret of his victorious Christian life.*

Dying With Jesus

Dying with Jesus, by death reckoned mine;
Living with Jesus a new life divine;
Looking to Jesus till glory doth shine,
Moment by moment, O Lord, I am Thine
—Daniel W. Whittle

The Exchanged Life

In his book *The Christ Life For Your Life*, F. B. Meyer tells of traveling by train. He saw a man in his compartment reading the famous devotional book, *Imitation of Christ* by Thomas à Kempis. Dr. Meyer said, "That's a grand book." "Yes, it is," replied the passenger.

"But I have found something better," said Meyer, who proceeded to use the illustration of painting a picture. He said, in effect, "What if I saw a beautiful masterpiece in the museum and I wanted a copy for myself? I could try to imitate it, to copy it onto a canvas using my own abilities of imitation. But how different the picture would look if the spirit of the great artist himself could somehow flow into my heart, into my mind, into my body, into my fingers and paint the picture through me."

Christlikeness isn't just a matter of imitating Christ. It is Christ Himself living His life and doing His work through us.

Additional Sermon or Lesson Ideas

The Evening and the Morning

Date preached:

SCRIPTURE: Genesis 1:5

INTRODUCTION: Since 1890, America has celebrated New Year's Day with the fabulous Tournament of Roses Parade from Pasadena. Every inch of every float must be covered with flowers or other natural materials, and an average float requires about 100,000 blossoms. But life itself isn't a "tournament of roses." Each year contains its share of sorrows and troubles. Remember that God often works in reverse. In Genesis 1:5, we find that God moves from evening to morning. Out of the darkness, the light is born. Out of the night comes the dawning. As someone said, "The night is darkest just before the dawn." This is true:

1. In Misery - See the woman with the issue of blood (Matt. 9:20).
2. In Misfortune - See Paul and Silas in prison (Acts 16).
3. In Misunderstanding - See Paul and Barnabas (Acts 15:36ff).
4. In Mistakes - See Elisha's servant (2 Kings 4:38).

CONCLUSION: God never promised us a tournament of roses, but He can turn mornings out of evenings and bring forth roses from compost heaps. Begin the year by entrusting your burdens to Him.

The God of Fresh Starts

Date preached:

SCRIPTURE: Psalm 139

INTRODUCTION: Psalm 139:16 says, "All the days ordained for me were written in your book before one of them ever came to be." At the beginning of another set of 365 days, we can find our bearing by considering:

1. God Knows (vv.1–4).
2. God Dwells (vv. 5–12).
3. God Creates (vv. 13–16).
4. God Loves (vv. 17–18).
5. God Judges (vv. 19–22).
6. God Sanctifies (vv. 23–24).

CONCLUSION: Make this your prayer for the New Year: Search me, O God, and know my heart; try me, and know my anxieties. See if there is any wicked way in me, and lead me in the way everlasting.

JANUARY 13, 2002

SUGGESTED SERMON

Shalom

Date preached:

By Dr. Ed Dobson

Scripture: Mark 5:21–34, especially verse 34 And He said to her, "Daughter, your faith has made you well. Go in peace, and be healed of your affliction."

Introduction: I want to teach you a Hebrew word this morning: shalom. If you wanted to greet someone in Hebrew, you would say, "Shalom." When you leave someone you don't say, "Later, Dude," or all of the American stuff we've come up with. You simply say, "Shalom" —"Peace!" This is the word Jesus used in Mark 5.

Background of Mark 5:21–24: Jesus had been in Capernaum on the western shores of the Lake of Galilee. He had sailed southeast to the Gentile section of Galilee and healed a demoniac. When the people of the region begged Jesus to leave them, He returned to Capernaum. Here he was met by a distraught father, but before He could deal with Jairus' problem, a needy woman sought to touch Him.

Vs. 25: Think about this woman in the context of first-century Judaism. Religious law (see Leviticus 15) had very serious regulations concerning hemorrhaging. The laws of bleeding not only made the woman herself unclean, but whatever and whoever she touched also became unclean. The result was embarrassment, isolation, and religious stigma. Before we think this was too horrible, remember that in biblical times people didn't have the medicines and medical knowledge we have today. But additionally, there was fatigue. Physicians tell us when you lose more blood than you are able to create, you become anemic. This women was tired, fatigued, exhausted.

Vs. 26: The Talmud suggested eleven specific cures for bleeding, such as sitting at a crossroads with a cup of wine, waiting for someone to come from behind to frighten you. This woman had tried every cure and spent all she had on doctors who, at that time in history, were scorned and, in this case, ineffective.

Vv. 27–28: Her touching Christ was an incredible act of courage. According to the law, whoever this woman touched became unclean; yet she reached out to touch the Lord, to touch His robe. "If I can just touch Him," she said to herself, "I know I will be healed."

Vs. 29: Two miracles occurred here: (1) her bleeding stopped; (2) her strength returned instantly.

Vs. 30: When you begin touching people at the point of their need, there is a cost, a drain of spiritual power. Nothing fatigues me like preaching or ministering.

Vv. 31–34: Instead of being irritated, Jesus looked at this poor woman as a father would his daughter. He said: "Daughter, your faith has healed you. Go in Shalom." This is the word I want you to remember. It inferred wholeness of body and soul. It implied living a life in harmony with others, to live with the fullness and the wholeness of all of God's blessings. In Number 6:22, the rabbis believed that the giving of peace was the climax of God's blessings. Here was a woman isolated from her family, friends, and religious community. Jesus looked at her with fatherly compassion and said, "Daughter, go in Shalom. When you go back to your house, you go to your house in peace. When you eat with your family, you eat in Shalom. When you talk, you talk in Shalom. When you hug, you hug in Shalom. Go in Shalom." He was bestowing on her all God's richest blessings (see Isaiah 55:10–12). When Jesus says to you and me, "Go in peace," He is saying, "Go back to your family in harmony. Recognize that once you were

>>> *sermon continued on following page*

APPROPRIATE HYMNS AND SONGS

I Need Thee Every Hour, Annie S. Hawks/Robert Lowry; Public Domain.

I Need Thee Every Hour, David Baker; © 1971 Word Music Group, Inc.

Does Jesus Care?, Frank E. Graeff/J. Lincoln Hall; Public Domain.

All I Need, Lincoln Brewster/Danny Chambers/Israel Houghton; © 1996 Praise on the Rock Music (Admin. by Integrity's Praise! Music, Inc.).

Sweet Shalom, Claire Cloninger/Gary Sadler/Chris Springer; © 1994 Juniper Landing Music (Admin. by Word Music Group, Inc.)/Word Music, Inc./Integrity's Hosanna! Music/Integrity's Praise! Music.

unclean, but now you are clean, you are literally under all of the blessings of God. Go in joy; go with celebration. Go in Shalom."

Conclusion: Where is this Shalom available? Isaiah 9:6 says: "And His name will be called..."

- **Wonderful Counselor.** This woman had sought the advice of rabbis and doctors, to no avail, but Jesus had just the words and power she needed. Perhaps you've been spending a lot of money for help and advice instead of listening to the Lord and His Word.
- **Mighty God.** Only God could have done for her what Jesus did.
- **Everlasting Father.** Jesus said to her, "Daughter...." He is for us a compassionate "Dad."
- **Prince of Peace.** Where can we find this Shalom? Only in Christ, the Wonderful Counselor, the Mighty God, the Everlasting Father, the Prince of Peace. Come to Him today and listen to Him say to you, "Son, daughter—go in Shalom."

FOR THE BULLETIN

❉ On January 13, 1522, Martin Luther, exhausted in his efforts of translating the New Testament into German, wrote a friend that he had undertaken a task beyond his power, and that he now understood why no one had attempted it before. His translation was published later that year. ❉ January 13 marks the death of George Fox, founder of the Society of Friends, or Quakers, in 1691. ❉ Torrential rain on January 13, 1856, kept missionary J. Hudson Taylor confined to a little boat during a preaching tour of China. His diary on that day reads, "The rain was so heavy all day that no one could leave the boats. Thus we enjoyed a delightful day of rest, such as we had not had for some time; and the weather prevented much inquiry being made for us. Had the day been fine we should most likely have been discovered, even if we had not left the boats. As it was, we were allowed to think in peace, and with wonder and gratitude, of the gracious dealings of our God, who had thus led us apart into "a desert place" to rest awhile. ❉ On this day in 1892, Amy Carmichael responded to God's call to be a foreign missionary. ❉ On January 13, 1915, Mary Slessor passed away at age 66, following nearly 39 years of remarkable missionary service in Nigeria. Her last words were, "Do not weep, do not weep; the Lord is taking me home."

WORSHIP HELPS

Worship Theme:

Jesus, the Great Physician, gives us peace.

Call to Worship:

John 14:27: Peace I leave with you, My peace I give to you; not as the world gives do I give to you. Let not your heart be troubled, neither let it be afraid.

Hymn Story:

Annie Sherwood Hawks, 37, a housewife in Brooklyn, New York, looked out her window on a brilliant June morning in 1872. Though busy taking care of her three children, she felt a reassuring sense of God's presence. "I wonder how anyone could live without Him?" she thought to herself. "How could anyone face pain or deep and abiding joy apart from Him?" Almost without thinking about it, she composed a few lines of verse in her mind. She jotted them down quickly between chores, and the next Sunday she handed them her pastor, Rev. Robert Lowry, apologizing for their simplicity. Lowry put the words to music, but neither of them dreamed of how widely their simple little hymn would be sung:

> *I need Thee every hour, Most gracious Lord;*
> *No tender voice like Thine, Can peace afford.*
> *I need Thee, Oh, I need Thee; Every hour I need Thee;*
> *O bless me now, my Savior, I come to Thee.*

Scripture Reading:

The LORD will give strength to His people; The LORD will bless His people with peace. Dominion and fear *belong* to Him; He makes peace in His high places. Is there any number to His armies? Upon whom does His light not rise? Acquaint yourself with Him, and be at peace; Thereby good will come to you. The LORD bless you and keep you; The LORD make His face shine upon you, And be gracious to you; The LORD lift up His countenance upon you, And give you peace. My peace I give to you. Let the peace of God rule in your hearts.

Taken from Psalm 29:11, Job 25:2; 22:21; Numbers 6:24–26; John 14:27; and Colossians 3:25.

STATS, STORIES AND MORE

The Best of Physicians...

"In the 21st century we have a great deal of respect and admiration for physicians because of all of the advances in medicine. But in the first century doctors were not all that well respected. This really doesn't have a lot to do with my sermon, but for the doctors present I thought this would be a blessing to you. I came across the writings of Rabbi Judah who was giving instructions on how fathers ought to teach a trade to their sons: 'Donkey drivers are most of them wicked. Camel drivers are most of them proper folks. Sailors are most of them saintly, but the best of physicians is destined for hell.'"

—Ed Dobson

Drained

"I remember the first marathon I ever ran—Grandfather Mountain Marathon. Mile 17 to mile 26.2 was up the side of a mountain. I was a tad tired when I got to the top. I've done triathlons, I've backpacked, I know the feeling of giving of yourself physically and being drained of physical power. But you know, when I get through preaching today, and tonight I go home and I put my feet up, I am more tired. I can't explain this because preaching doesn't require a lot of energy. I'm not running 26 miles, I'm not backpacking 18 1/2 miles. I'm not doing a triathlon. There is something about spiritual ministry that drains the power out of you."

—Ed Dobson

Hudson Taylor's Spiritual Secret

In their book, *Hudson Taylor's Spiritual Secret,* Dr. and Mrs. Howard Taylor quote this about the famous missionary J. Hudson Taylor: "He was an object lesson in quietness. He drew from the bank of heaven every farthing of his daily income—'My peace I give unto you.' Whatever did not agitate the Savior or ruffle His spirit, was not to agitate him. The serenity of the Lord Jesus concerning any matter, and at its most crucial moment, was his ideal and practical possession. He knew nothing of rush or hurry, of quivering nerves or vexation of spirit. He knew that there is a peace passing all understanding, and that he could not do without it."

Additional Sermons and Lesson Ideas

Photo Album of Christ

Date preached:

SCRIPTURE: Psalm 110

INTRODUCTION: All of us have photo albums in our homes. The Bible is one long photo album of Christ, and two of the most interesting pictures are displayed in Psalm 110. Along with Psalm 118, this messianic Psalm is by far the most frequently quoted in the New Testament.

1. **Christ is Our High King** (vv. 1–3). Here we are allowed to eavesdrop on a conversation between the Father and the Son. Christ is promised kingly victory over His enemies. According to verse 3, it's our privilege to be His volunteers. There is a great difference between the morale of soldiers whose side is losing and those whose side is winning. Our attitude should daily reflect our knowledge of our King.

2. **Christ is Our High Priest** (vv. 4–7). This passage is the link in the biblical information about Melchizedek, whom we meet in Genesis 14 and again in Hebrews 5–7. As our High Priest, Christ...
   - Understands our weakness (Heb. 4:15).
   - Atones for our sins (Heb. 5:1–3).
   - Intercedes for our needs (Heb. 7:25).

CONCLUSION: Just as we keep snapshots of our loved ones in our pocketbooks or billfolds, let's keep these two pictures of Christ in our hearts.

A Many-Splendored Thing

Date preached:

SCRIPTURE: 1 Corinthians 13

INTRODUCTION: The song says, "Love is a Many-Splendored Thing," but in our culture, it's too often splintered instead of splendored. In our society, it's difficult to define, describe, or recognize. But the Bible gives us a 15-splendored description of love in 1 Corinthians 13:

> **Love:** (1) suffers long; (2) is kind; (3) doesn't envy; (4) does not parade itself; (4) isn't puffed up; (5) isn't rude; (6) isn't selfish; (7) isn't easily provoked; (8) thinks no evil; (9) doesn't rejoice in sin; (10) loves truth; (11) bears up; (12) believes; (13) hopes; (14) endures; (15) never fails.

CONCLUSION: To determine the level of your love, take out the word "Love" and insert your own name before reading these verses: "I suffer long; I am kind; I don't envy..." How do you do?

JANUARY 20, 2002

Feeble Faith Meets Strong Savior   *Date preached:*

(Adapted from a sermon by Charles Haddon Spurgeon)

Scripture: Mark 9:14–29, especially verses 23–27 Jesus said to him, "If you can believe, all things *are* possible to him who believes." Immediately the father of the child cried out and said with tears, "Lord, I believe; help my unbelief!" When Jesus saw that the people came running together, He rebuked the unclean spirit, saying to it, "Deaf and dumb spirit, I command you, come out of him and enter him no more!" Then *the spirit* cried out, convulsed him greatly, and came out of him. And he became as one dead, so that many said, "He is dead." But Jesus took him by the hand and lifted him up, and he arose.

Introduction: *U. S. News and World Report* said in a recent issue, "In the United States, 27 million adults and 7.5 million children have a diagnosable mental disorder—more than the combined number of people with cancer, heart disease, and lung disorders." For many, that mental disorder is anxiety, worry, a fretful heart. The man in today's story was in the grips of an understandable anxiety attack, for his son was in crisis. Our greatest worries are often over those we love the most. Perhaps the only good thing we can say about worry is that it sometimes drives us to the Lord. In our story today, it brought this father to Jesus, but once there, his unbelief threatened his receiving of the Lord's help. While worry may sometimes drive us to the Lord, it can so dominate our prayers that we have trouble claiming God's answers by faith. Perhaps this father's case may help us understand our own. Let us note the case carefully and observe...

I. **The Suspected Difficulty** — The father may have thought...
   A. The Disciples Were Incompetent. Despite their bravado, they seemed unable to help. Sometimes other people, despite good intentions, can't relieve our need. Sometimes even our Christian friends in the church appear to be powerless to help.
   B. The Problem Was Hopeless. The boy's disease was fitful, mysterious, and terribly violent. We sometimes forget that the Lord delights to work impossibilities.
   C. The Savior Was Powerless. The man half hinted at this when he said, "Master, if you can do anything...." The people of Isaiah's day grew discouraged in their exile, wondering if God saw their problems or cared

about their cause (Isa. 40:25). Anxiety whispers demonically in our ear, "God doesn't care. The Savior is powerless."

2. **The Tearful Discovery** — "He said with tears..."
   A. His small faith discovered his unbelief. Sometimes we have just enough faith to realize how weak our belief really is. That isn't a great faith, but it's enough to start with. If we have just enough faith to recognize its own weakness, we have a place to start. God has a foothold in our hearts. Sometimes in rock climbing, all you need is the smallest crevice for a foothold or a tiny crack for inserting a finger.
   B. He was distressed at the sight of his own unbelief. Worry and anxiety is tantamount to unbelief, and unbelief is a great sin. It kept the children of Israel out of the Promised Land for 40 years. Unbelief doubts:
      • The power of Omnipotence.
      • The value of biblical promises.
      • The efficacy of Christ's blood.
      • The prevalence of Christ's pleas on our behalf.
      • The very truth of Scripture.
   C. He turned his thoughts in that direction, no longer saying, "Lord, help my child!" but, "Lord, help my unbelief!"

>>> *sermon continued on following page*

APPROPRIATE HYMNS AND SONGS

O For a Faith That Will Not Shrink, William H. Bathurst/Carl G. Glaser; Public Domain.

My Faith Has Found a Resting Place, Lidie H. Edmunds/Andre Grety; Public Domain.

My Faith Still Holds, William J. Gaither/Gloria Gaither; © 1972 William J. Gaither ARR UBP of Gaither Copyright Management (Admin. by Gaither Copyright Management).

That's What Faith Must Be, Michael Card; © 1988 Birdwing Music (a div. of EMI Christian Music Publishing)/Mole End Music (Admin. by EMI Christian Music Publishing).

God Will Make a Way, Don Moen; © 1990 Integrity's Hosanna! Music (c/o Integrity Music, Inc.) (Admin. by Integrity Music, Inc.).

3. **The Intelligent Appeal** — The poor father cried to Jesus...
   A. On the basis of faith. "Lord, I believe...." Can you come to Christ today with even a small amount of faith? Isaiah 42:3 says, A bruised reed shall he not break, and the smoking flax shall he not quench."
   B. With confession of sin. "...my unbelief." Chronic anxiety represents the sin of unbelief, a serious sin needed repentance.
   C. To One who knows how to help in this matter. "...help!" And Jesus did help. And Jesus does help. And Jesus will help.

Conclusion: If you're worried about a loved one or about some other life-difficulty, come to Jesus with any case, and in every case. Come with your little faith, for in this matter He can help as no other can.

FOR THE BULLETIN

✻ Decius Trajan, Emperor of Rome, executed Fabian, Bishop of Rome, on January 20, 250. ✻ January 20, 1669, is the birthday of Susanna Wesley. ✻ On this date in 1828, early American evangelist David Marks preached all day and retired to bed exhausted. Just past midnight, he felt so ill he thought he was going to die. Marks grew joyous at the prospect of heaven. But suddenly, thinking of sinners bound for hell, he seemed to hear a whisper: "Will you still go and warn them?" Weeping, Marks replied, "Yes, Lord, I will go and warn them as long as it shall be Thy will." His recovery began instantly, adding years to his evangelistic labors. ✻ On January 20, 1858, missionaries Hudson and Maria Taylor were married. ✻ During the Revival of 1905, a Day of Prayer was proclaimed in Denver, Colorado, on Friday, January 20. So many people flocked to churches and theaters for prayer that most of the city's stores and schools closed. The impact of the revival was felt for months. ✻ Eliza Davis served many years as the first black woman from Texas to go to Africa as a missionary. At age 65 she was recalled by her denomination, the National Baptist Convention, for retirement. But two years later, Eliza raised her own support and returned to Africa to serve another 25 years. On January 20, 1979, she celebrated her 100th birthday. ✻ On January 20, 1987, Terry Waite, the Archbishop of Canterbury's envoy in Lebanon, was kidnapped. He was not released until November, 1991.

WORSHIP HELPS

Worship Theme:
We must learn to turn our problems into prayers, choose worship over worry, and overcome fear by faith.

Call to Worship:
Psalm 56:3–4: "Whenever I am afraid, I will trust in You. In God (I will praise His word), in God I have put my trust; I will not fear."

Applicable Scripture Readings:
Philippians 4:4–9
Matthew 5:20–34
Jeremiah 7:7–8

Pastoral Prayer:
Almighty God, we are easily frightened, quickly shaken, and often anxious about our lives and about those we love. Yet You have said, "Fret not," and "Fear not," and "Faint not." Forgive us for so easily fretting, fearing, and fainting. Forgive us for being slow of heart in trusting You as we should. Help us, O Lord, to cast our burdens upon You, and teach us to say, "Lord, I believe." We offer You our sons, daughters, fathers, mothers, brothers, sisters, and friends. Bless each of them, Lord, and make us a part of the blessing. In Jesus' name. Amen.

KidsTalk

Here's an idea for helping the children to memorize Psalm 56:3: "Whenever I am afraid, I will trust in You." Using powerpoint, a hand-held marker board, or a portable blackboard, put the ten words (including textual reference) on the board. Have the children read it with you. Then erase one word. Have them read it, inserting the word from their memories. Erase another word, and so forth, until, on the eleventh time through, the children are saying the verse totally from memory.

STATS, STORIES AND MORE

Someone Once Said . . .

"Worry is a small trickle of fear that meanders through the mind until it cuts a channel into which all other thoughts are drained."

—*Anonymous*

"Worry is a destructive process of occupying the mind with thoughts contrary to God's love and care."

—*Norman Vincent Peale*

"Worry is putting question marks where God has put periods."

—*John R. Rice*

"Worry is the interest we pay on tomorrow's troubles."

—*E. Stanley Jones*

"Worry pulls tomorrow's cloud over today's sunshine."

—*Chuck Swindoll*

From *U.S. News and World Report*

Half of all people will have at least one serious mental disorder during their lifetime, according to the National Institute of Mental Health, and nearly 1 in 3 will experience a significant mental problem—such as depression, phobia, panic disorder, or anxiety—in any given year.

You Know It's Going to Be a Rotten Day When:
- You call Suicide Prevention and they put you on hold.
- You see a *60 Minutes* news team waiting in your office.
- You turn on the morning news and they're showing emergency routes out of the city.
- Your twin sister forgets your birthday.
- Your car horn gets stuck as you follow a group of Hell's Angels on the freeway.
- The bird singing outside your window is a buzzard.

Some Important Verses on Anxiety:

"Why are you fearful, O you of little faith?" (Matt. 8:26).

"Do not worry about tomorrow" (Matt. 6:34).

"Don't worry about anything; instead, pray about everything" (Phil. 4:6 TLB).

Additional Sermons and Lesson Ideas

A Neglected Corner

Date preached:

SCRIPTURE: Ephesians 1:13–14; 4:30; 2 Corinthians 1:21–22; and 2 Corinthians 5:5

INTRODUCTION: The "sealing" of the Holy Spirit is a neglected corner of truth, but it is important enough to be mentioned four times in Scripture.

In antiquity people used seals to authenticate documents (Jer. 32:10), and archaeologists have discovered more than 1,200 seals from Old Testament times. In trusting Christ as Savior, we are marked with a seal, the Holy Spirit. This is:

1. **A Mark of Ownership:** Buyers of timber in the forests of Asia Minor would select trees which would be felled, stamped them with the buyer's seal, and floated them downstream. At the port in Ephesus, the markings would iden- tify the logs. God stamps us with His seal, indicating ownership.

2. **An Imprint of Identity:** In biblical times, everyone's unique seal, when pressed into wax, imprinted his identity. Charles Wesley wrote in "Hark! The Herald Angels Sing": "Adam's likeness now efface; Stamp Thine image in its place."

3. **A Bond of Security:** Both Daniel's lions' den and Christ's tomb were sealed by royal decree. When we come to Christ, we are sealed with the Holy Spirit, implying security.

4. **A Deposit of Inheritance:** The Holy Spirit's presence in our heart is a down payment on the future blessings, like a child who has inherited a fortune but until he comes of age lives on an allotted amount.

CONCLUSION: The presence of the Holy Spirit within Christians is one of our greatest comforts and strengths.

What's Your Address?

Date preached:

SCRIPTURE: John 15:1–4

INTRODUCTION: The word "abide" means "to live" or "to dwell." In the *New King James Version*, this word occurs 36 times, giving us several addresses for the Christian. We are to abide:

- In God's tabernacle (Ps. 15:1 and 61:4).
- Under the shadow of the Almighty (Ps. 91:1).
- Among the wise (Prov. 15:31).
- In God's Word (John 8:31).
- In sound doctrine (2 John 9).
- In Christ (John 15:4–10; 1 John 2:27–28; and 4:13).

CONCLUSION: Philippians 3:20 tells us our citizenship is in heaven. When asked for your heavenly address, here are your answers. Here is where we are to truly feel at home.

Thomas Watson

It was tough being an evangelical pastor in 17th century England.

As the government see-sawed between Catholic and Protestant-leaning monarchs, the Puritans and Dissenters were hounded, hunted down, and harried out of the land. In 1662, a series of Parliamentary acts further plagued the Puritans. The Act of Uniformity, for example, required all English ministers to either use the government-sanctioned *Book of Common Prayer* in their services or leave their pulpits. As a result, on August 17, 1662, two thousand ministers preached their farewell sermons and were expelled from their churches.

Among them was Thomas Watson.

I wish we knew more about Watson, for he is among the most readable and quotable of the Puritans. His writings brim with practical, biblical

---

Discontent is an ungrateful sin, because we have more mercies than afflictions; and it is an irrational sin, because afflictions work for good. . . . The devil blows the coals of passion and discontent, and then warms himself at the fire."

THOMAS WATSON

---

truth. He could grasp doctrine like J. I. Packer, craft a sermon like John Stott, and turn a phrase like Vance Havner.

His date and place of birth are unknown to us, and little information has survived about his upbringing. We know that in 1646, following his training at Cambridge, he married a minister's daughter and the two of them moved to the city of London, where Thomas became rector of the parish of St. Stephen's, Walbrook.

There the popularity of his sermons was excelled only by the renown of his deeply moving, extemporaneous prayers. Crowds came, souls were converted, and his influence spread through London and across England. His ministry at St. Stephens continued, with brief interruptions (he was once thrown into the Tower of London for his political views), until the aforementioned Act of Uniformity in 1662.

Ejected but not dejected, he continued teaching and preaching in barns, homes, kitchens, and wooded groves, quietly and always at risk. After the Declaration of Indulgence restored his freedom to minister in 1672, he publicly resumed preaching in the great hall of a friend's mansion.

His failing health finally forced his removal to the village of Barnston, where he died in 1686 while engaged in prayer.

If you've never read any of the Puritans, *Gleanings from Thomas Watson* is an excellent starting place. It's an assortment of irresistible, pithy truths culled from Watson's writings, first compiled and published in 1915 by Central Bible Truth Depot in London. It has recently been reprinted by Soli Deo Gloria Publishers.

Here are some samples from my own underlined and dog-eared copy:

- "True grace holds out in the winter season. That is a precious faith, which, like the star, shines brightest in the darkest night."
- "Other physicians can only cure them that are sick, but Christ cures them that are dead. He doth not only cure them but crown them. Christ doth not only raise from the bed, but to the throne. He gives the sick man not only health but heaven."
- "The world is fading not filling."
- "If God be our God, He will give us peace in trouble. When there is a storm without, He will make peace within. The world can create trouble in peace, but God can create peace in trouble."
- "Who would have thought to have found adultery in David, and drunkenness in Noah, and cursing in Job? If God leave a man to himself, how suddenly and scandalously may sin break forth in the holiest men of the earth! 'I say unto all, Watch.' A wandering heart needs a watchful eye."
- "Prayer delights God's ear, it melts His heart, it opens His hand: God cannot deny a praying soul."
- "The world is but a great inn, where we are to stay a night or two, and be gone; what madness is it so to set our heart upon our inn, as to forget our home."

Charles Spurgeon called Watson "one of the most concise, racy, illustrative, and suggestive" of those who made the Puritan age the "Augustan period of evangelical literature."

I wouldn't call Watson "racy"—he was, after all, a Puritan—but he has certainly become one of my favorite authors. I hope you'll make his acquaintance, too. ✿

JANUARY 27, 2002

Power Surge

Date preached:

Scripture: Ephesians 1:15–23, especially verses 19–23 ...and what *is* the exceeding greatness of His power toward us who believe, according to the working of His mighty power which He worked in Christ when He raised Him from the dead and seated *Him* at His right hand in the heavenly *places,* far above all principality and power and might and dominion, and every name that is named, not only in this age but also in that which is to come. And He put all *things* under His feet, and gave Him *to be* head over all *things* to the church, which is His body, the fullness of Him who fills all in all.

Introduction: Recently when my CD player died, I asked a friend to look at it. "I think the needle is broken," I told him. "CD players don't have needles," he said, laughing. "They use laser beams to read songs encoded on the disk. The eye on yours is dusty." He cleaned it and the problems disappeared. In his prayer for the Ephesians, Paul asked God to enlighten their eyes so they could better understand the message encoded in His Word, especially the "exceeding greatness of His power." What is God's power like? We see it displayed in:

- **Nature.** The hymnist speaks of "Thy power throughout the universe displayed." Have you ever marveled at the power of God in a thunderstorm?
- **Answered prayer.** James 5:16 says, "The effective, fervent prayer of a righteous man avails much."
- **Changed lives.** "Therefore if anyone is in Christ, he is a new creation; old things have passed away; behold, all things have become new" (2 Cor. 5:17).
- **Daily victory.** When you see a Christian living above the circumstances (rather than under them), you can credit the uplift of God's power (Isa. 40:30–31; 41:10).
- **Christian ministry.** Jesus said, "You shall receive power when the Holy Spirit has come upon you; and you shall be witnesses to Me" (Acts 1:8).

Most of us don't fully appreciate and appropriate God's power in our lives. Paul devotes the last paragraph of Ephesians 1 to describing this divine power as:

1. **Resurrection Power:** verses 19–20 says: "...the working of His mighty power which He worked in Christ when He raised Him from the dead...." How often we've stood by a casket and wanted to touch the body lying there and restore it to life. We can't do it, but God can reverse the death process. The same power that raised Christ from the grave is available to change our lives, to answer our prayers, to resolve our difficulties, to give us immortality.

2. **Exaltation Power:** "and seated Him at His right hand in the heavenly places...." After Christ's resurrection, He ascended and sat at the Father's right hand. If we had a telescope powerful enough to peer into the highest heaven, we would see Christ now seated on the throne, exalted in layers of light, surrounded by His angels, enveloped with glory. The power that exalted Christ is available to change our lives, to answer our prayers, to give us daily strength.

3. **Lordship Power:** "far above all principality and power and might and dominion, and every name that is named, not only in this age but also in that which is to come." Christ is higher than the angels, greater than the demons, wider than the universe. He rules in the affairs of men and directs history toward its pre-appointed end. That Lordship power of Jesus Christ is the same power available to meet our needs.

4. **Headship Power:** "...and gave Him to be head over all things to the church, which is His body, the fullness of Him who fills all in all." Christ is the boss

>>> *sermon continued on following page*

APPROPRIATE HYMNS AND SONGS

All Hail the Power of Jesus' Name, Edward Perronet/Oliver Holden/John Rippon; Public Domain.

How Great Thou Art, Stuart Hine; © 1941, 1953, 1955, Stuart K. Hine. Renewed 1981 Manna Music, Inc.

Firm Foundation, Nancy Gordon/Jamie Harvill; © 1994 Integrity's Hosanna! Music/Integrity's Praise! Music (Admin. by Integrity Music, Inc.).

God Is Able, Chris Machen/Robert Sterling; © 1988 Word Music, Inc./Desert North Music/Two Fine Boys Music (Admin. by Word Music, Inc.).

Great and Mighty Is the Lord Our God, Marlene Bigley; © 1984 Sound III, Inc./Universal-MCA Music (Admin. by Universal-MCA Music Publishing).

of His church, the senior pastor, the archbishop, the great shepherd. He's our great High Priest. And the work that He does in this world, He does through His church. The parts of my body are useless unless directed by my brain. Christ is our Head, we are His body. Our only job is to obey His commands.

Conclusion: Are you living in the supernatural power of Jesus Christ? That power is measured by His resurrection, His exaltation, His Lordship, and His Headship. And that is available to change your life, to answer your prayers, to resolve your difficulties, and to give you everlasting life.

FOR THE BULLETIN

❃ Robert Murray McCheyne, born in 1813, was a Scottish minister and disciple of the godly Andrew Bonar. He was a sickly man and died very young, but the spiritual quality of his life and ministry live to this day. On January 27, 1842, he sat down with pen and paper to reply to a young boy named Johnnie who was anxious about his soul. McCheyne began: "I was very glad to receive your kind note, and am glad to send you a short line in return, although my time is much taken up. You are very dear to me, because your soul is precious; and if you are ever brought to Jesus, washed and justified, you will praise Him more sweetly than an angel of light. I was riding in the snow today where no foot had trodden, and it was pure, pure white; and I thought again and again of that verse: 'Wash me, and I shall be whiter than snow.'" ❃ On January 27, 1880, U. S. Patent No. 223,898 was granted to Thomas Alva Edison for his electric lamp. ❃ January 27, 1908, Charles M. Alexander, evangelistic gospel song leader and associate of D. L. Moody and R. A. Torrey, made up his mind to join Wilber Chapman in evangelistic campaigns around the world. The two worked together until Alexander's death in 1920 and are considered one of the most effective evangelistic partnerships of the twentieth century. ❃ The Russians liberated Auschwitz concentration camp on January 27, 1945, where the Nazis had murdered 1.5 million men, women and children, including more than one million Jews. ❃ On January 27, 1980, Christian Adventist leader Vladimir Shelkov, 84, died in the Soviet labor camp of Tabaga where temperatures often dropped to eighty degrees below zero. He had spent 23 years in such labor camps because of his faith in Christ.

WORSHIP HELPS

Worship Theme:
The exceeding greatness of God's Power.

Call to Worship:
"For I am not ashamed of the gospel of Christ, for it is the power of God to salvation for everyone who believes, for the Jew first and also for the Greek" (Rom. 1:16).

Responsive Reading:

Leader: Then Jesus returned in the power of the Spirit to Galilee, and news of Him went out through all the surrounding region.

People: But Jesus, knowing their thoughts, said, "Why do you think evil in your hearts? For which is easier, to say, 'Your sins are forgiven you,' or to say, 'Arise and walk'?

Leader: But that you may know that the Son of Man has power on earth to forgive sins"—then He said to the paralytic, "Arise, take up your bed, and go to your house." And he arose and departed to his house.

People: Now when the multitudes saw *it*, they marveled and glorified God, who had given such power to men.

Leader: Then the sign of the Son of Man will appear in heaven, and then all the tribes of the earth will mourn, and they will see the Son of Man coming on the clouds of heaven with power and great glory.

All: But you shall receive power when the Holy Spirit has come upon you; and you shall be witnesses to Me.

Taken from Luke 4:14; Matthew 9:4–8; 24:30; Acts 1:8

Benediction:
Dismiss us now, O Lord, in Your Name. Send us forth in your strength. Keep us in Your care. For Thine is the kingdom, the power, and the glory forever. Amen.

STATS, STORIES AND MORE

Someone Once Said...
"The older I get, the greater power I seem to have to help the world; I am like a snowball —the further I am rolled the more I gain."
—*Susan B. Anthony, U.S. social reformer, suffragist (1820–1906).*

Power Over Nature
Missionary Bertha Smith once lived in an ox stall in China while evangelizing a particular area. The flies almost drove her crazy, especially at mealtimes. Finally she prayed: "Lord, I am one of your spoiled children. All my life I have been accustomed to screened houses and clean food. I just can't eat with those flies all over my food. Down in Egypt you had flies to come and go at Your word. You are the same today and You are ready to work the same way if my situation demands it. Now please do one of two things for me: either take the flies away, or enable me to eat and not mind them."

From that moment, not a fly flew into that ox stall for the remaining days Bertha was there.

Resurrection Power
Josh McDowell entered university looking for a good time and searching for happiness in life. He tried going to church, but found religion unsatisfying. He ran for student leadership positions, but was disappointed by how quickly the glamour wore off. He tried the party circuit, but he woke up Monday mornings feeling worse than ever.

Noticing a group of students engaged in Bible study, he became intrigued by the radiance of one of the young ladies. He asked her the reason for it. She looked him in the eye and said, "Jesus Christ." Josh accepted their challenge to intellectually examine the claims of Christ, and after much research, he admitted that he couldn't refute the body of proof supporting Christianity.

One of the major factors in his conversion was his inability to ignore the historical resurrection of Jesus Christ, a point he made later to a student at the University of Uruguay who asked him, "Professor McDowell, why can't you intellectually refute Christianity?"

"For a very simple reason," replied McDowell. "I am not able to explain away an event in history — the resurrection of Jesus Christ."

Additional Sermons and Lesson Ideas

Things to Remember When You Don't Like Yourself   *Date preached:*
SCRIPTURE: Romans 12:3–6

INTRODUCTION: Socrates was once asked why Alcibiades, a brilliant leader who had traveled around the world, was such an unhappy man. "Because wherever he goes," said Socrates, "Alcibiades takes himself with him." Do you have the same problem?

1. **Satan's Two Traps**
   A. **Feeling superior:** "...not to think of himself more highly than he ought to think."
   B. **Feeling inferior:** Low self-esteem is inverted pride, a preoccupation with self. It stems from a world dominated by the theory of evolution, the media, competition, technology, and the breakdown of the home.
2. **God's Three Truths**
   A. **God made us part of His body:** "...we, being many, are one body in Christ" (v. 5).
   B. **He made us part of His body with many others:** "... and individually members of one another" (v. 5).
   C. **He made us a gifted part of His body:** "Having then gifts differing according to the grace that is given to us..." (v. 6).

CONCLUSION: It's a command to obey: Think soberly about yourself.

Great Is Thy Faithfulness   *Date preached:*
SCRIPTURE: "But God is faithful..." (1 Cor. 10:13).

Introduction: Has someone recently let you down? All of us are occasionally hurt or disappointed by another—and sooner or later, we all disappoint someone else. But God will never disappoint, deceive, or disillusion us. He is faithful, and His faithfulness is:

1. Infinite. (Ps. 36:5).
2. Established (Ps. 89:2).
3. Incomparable (Ps. 89:8).
4. Unfailing (Ps. 89:3).
5. Everlasting (Ps. 119:90).
6. Great (Lam. 3:23).
7. Unconditional (2 Tim. 2:12).
8. Worthy of our Trust (Heb. 10:23).

Conclusion: A. W. Tozer wrote in *The Knowledge of the Holy*, "Men become unfaithful out of desire, fear, weakness, loss of interest, or because of some strong influence from without. Obviously none of these forces can affect God in any way.... The tempted, the anxious, the fearful, the discouraged may all find new hope and good cheer in the knowledge that our Heavenly Father is faithful."

FEBRUARY 3, 2002

"A Prayer for Progress"

Date preached:

By Dr. Timothy Beougher

Scripture: Philippians 1:9–11 And this I pray, that your love may abound still more and more in knowledge and all discernment, that you may approve the things that are excellent, that you may be sincere and without offense till the day of Christ, being filled with the fruits of righteousness which *are* by Jesus Christ, to the glory and praise of God.

Introduction: The *Virginia Medical Monthly* told of a married woman with three children. After her husband died, she began dressing like a twenty-year-old and joined in her children's parties. As the children grew older, their mother seemed to grow younger. Psychiatrists call it "personality regression." She slipped backward one year every three or four months. At 61, she acted like a 6-year-old. She was sent to a sanitarium where she insisted on playing with toys and babbling like a child. Then she became a 3-year-old, spilling her food, crawling, and crying "Mama." Backward still farther to the age of one, she drank milk curled up like a tiny baby. Finally, she went back over the line and died.

The same thing can happen to Christians (1 Cor. 3:1; Heb. 3:12). In today's text, we see that the believers in the city of Philippi had demonstrated growth in their spiritual lives, but Paul prayed for more progress.

1. **Prayer for a Growing Love** (v. 9). The Greek language has three words for love: *Eros* (romantic love), *phileo* (brotherly love), and *agape* (a self-giving love). People can love with *phileo* and *eros* on their own, but the *agape* of God is quite distinctive. Paul prayed for this love to "abound"—not a one-time overflowing, but a continual activity (Rom. 5:5). This is an others-centered love. It looks for needs in the lives of others and seeks to meet those needs with no thought of returned favors. This love is also characterized by knowledge and discernment. Many people today want to focus on love with no discernment. From their perspective, love means tolerance, accepting anyone and everything, like the song that says, "If loving you is wrong, I don't want to be right." But love must be based on truth, and that leads to the need for...

2. **Prayer for a Deeper Discernment** (v. 10). Paul understood the struggles we face in our choices. He wanted believers to evaluate the things of life cor-

rectly. Many things in life have no ultimate value, and the Bible reminds us that to find the real worth of things, we must weigh them in the light of eternity and approve the things that are excellent. There must be an ultimate standard to follow, one not to be found in the varied philosophies of mankind, but arrived at only through a knowledge of God's Word (Heb. 4:12). Genuine love, when making a decision, asks:

- Does the Bible speak against it? (Ps. 119:9–11)
- Will it glorify God? (1 Cor. 10:31)
- Will it harm me physically or spiritually? (1 Cor. 6:12)
- Could it cause another to stumble? (Rom. 14:21)
- Would I make that choice if Jesus were standing right here?

3. **Prayer for Righteous Character** (vv. 10–11). Paul prayed that his friends would be without offence until the day of Christ, filled with the fruits of righteousness. This is an Old Testament picture (Ps. 1; Jer. 17:8). God wants a bumper crop of righteousness in our lives. This is not self-generated or self-produced fruit; it come through power Christ provides (John 15:5). Its purpose: "...the glory and praise of God." That was Paul's goal, and it should be ours. Matthew 5:16 says, "Let your light so shine before men, that they may see your good works and glorify your Father in heaven." Is that your desire?

>>> *sermon continued on following page*

APPROPRIATE HYMNS AND SONGS

I Am Thine, O Lord, Fanny J. Crosby/William H. Doane; Public Domain.

Jesus, Draw Me Close, Rick Founds; © 1990 Maranatha Praise, Inc. (Admin. by The Copyright Company).

I'd Rather Have Jesus, Rhea F. Miller/George Beverly Shea; © 1922, 1950 Renewed 1939, 1966 Word Music Inc. (a div. of Word Music Group, Inc.) (Admin. by Word Music Group, Inc.).

Let Us Search and Try Our Ways, Jack Hayford; © 1978 Rocksmith Music (Mandina/Rocksmith Music).

Once to Every Man and Nation, James Russell Lowell/David Stanley York; © 1951 Theodore Presser Company.

Conclusion: This morning God's Word sets a standard for each of us in several areas. Since these principles are in the setting of a prayer, it reminds us to pray for these characteristics to be realities in the lives of others. Have you ever wondered how you should pray for someone else? Ever found yourself just saying, "Lord, bless this person," because you weren't sure what to pray for? Paul gives us a model in this "Prayer for Progress." An added benefit of praying this prayer is that we already know God likes it! Pray these things for your children, your parents, for your friends, for your fellow church members—and don't forget to pray it for yourself. Make up your mind to prayerfully grow in the grace and knowledge of our Lord Jesus Christ.

FOR THE BULLETIN

✹ February 3, 865, marks the death of Anskar, the "Apostle to the North." Anskar (or Ansgar) was a French Benedictine monk who gave himself to missionary service, planting the gospel in Scandinavia. ✹ Rev. John Rogers spent his last Sunday, February 3, 1555, quietly in Newmarket Jail where he had been interred for preaching the gospel. Rogers was a convert of William Tyndale and Miles Coverdale, whom he had met in Antwerp. Returning to England, Rogers had become a proponent of the Reformation, hence his imprisonment during the reign of Queen Mary. On Monday morning, February 4, 1555, the jailer's wife woke him with a rumor that his death was imminent. Later that morning, he was led to the stake and burned to ashes, leaving behind a wife and eleven children. ✹ On this day in 1675, King Charles II of England revoked the Declaration of Indulgence. John Bunyan was among those arrested. His writings from prison (including *Pilgrim's Progress*) immortalized him and spread the message of Christ around the world. ✹ February 3, 1816, is the birthday of the English preacher, F. W. Robertson, whose sermons, published posthumously, made him better known after his death than while he was living. ✹ On Thursday, February 3, 1898, George Truett, the new, young pastor of the First Baptist Church of Dallas, Texas, went quail hunting with the city's police chief, J. C. Arnold. Somehow Truett's gun discharged, killing Arnold. In the days to follow, Truett nearly lost his mind from anguish. But at length, he had a dream in which he saw Jesus saying to him, "You are my man from now on." Truett eventually returned to the pulpit to become one of the most power preachers of the twentieth century. ✹ On February 3, 1913, the sixteenth amendment to the constitution was ratified, giving the U.S. Government the power to impose and collect income taxes.

Worship Theme:
We must grow in the grace and knowledge of Jesus Christ, maturing, developing, and progressing for His glory.

Call to Worship:
"but grow in the grace and knowledge of our Lord and Savior Jesus Christ. To Him *be* the glory both now and forever. Amen" (2 Peter 3:18).

Scripture Reading:
We should no longer be children, tossed to and fro and carried about with every wind of doctrine, by the trickery of men, in the cunning craftiness of deceitful plotting, but, speaking the truth in love, grow up in all things into Him who is the head—Christ. The righteous shall flourish like a palm tree, he shall grow like a cedar in Lebanon. Those who are planted in the house of the LORD shall flourish in the courts of our God. Therefore, laying aside all malice, all deceit, hypocrisy, envy, and all evil speaking, as newborn babes, desire the pure milk of the word, that you may grow thereby, if indeed you have tasted that the Lord is gracious.

Taken from: Ephesians 4:14–15; Psalm 92:12–13; 1 Peter 2:1–3.

Benediction:
Now may the God of patience and comfort grant you to be like-minded toward one another, according to Christ Jesus, that you may with one mind *and* one mouth glorify the God and Father of our Lord Jesus Christ (Rom. 15:5–6).

Kids Talk

Show pictures of yourself as a baby and ask the children if they can recognize who it is. Show them pictures of yourself as a child, as a young person. Explain that you were once their size, but God created us so that we grow (Luke 2:52). Tell the children that God also wants us to grow in love, in knowing His Word, and in serving Him. End with a prayer for the children modeled after Philippians 1:9–11.

STATS, STORIES AND MORE

"If Loving You Is Wrong . . ."
"We're gonna love our whole life long / 'Cause baby, if it feels so right /
How can it be wrong?"
—*sung by Elvis Presley.*

"What looked so wrong a moment before, just now it feels so right"
—*sung by Jesse Winchester.*

"So much love in my life / I can't get enough of your touch / Feels so
right"
—*sung by Mariah Carey.*

"It feels so right now / hold me tight / Tell me I'm the only one"
—*sung by the Beatles.*

"It can't be wrong, when it feels so right"
—*sung by LeAnn Rimes.*

The Pews at First Baptist
Timothy Beougher tells of a friend named Chuck who, traveling through
Texas, spent Saturday night in Dallas to attend First Baptist Church and
hear Dr. W. A. Criswell. He arrived early to get a good seat. Behind him a
woman began muttering, "I've been a member of this church forty years
and I've sat in that pew every Sunday of my life! Who do those kids think
they are to take MY pew!" Chuck wanted to tell her, "I can't believe you've
sat in this pew, close to the pulpit, and listened to the preaching of George
Truett and W. A. Criswell for 40 years and still act like that!"
    But he remained quiet.

Channels Only
James Montgomery Boice tells of Lawrence of Arabia visiting Paris after
World War I with some Arab friends. He showed them around Paris, but
what fascinated them most was the faucet in their hotel room. They spent
hours turning it on and off; they thought it was wonderful. All they had to
do was turn the handle, and they could get all the water they wanted.
    When time came to leave, Lawrence found them in the bathroom trying
to detach the faucet. They explained, "It is very dry in Arabia. What we need
are faucets. If we have them, we will have all the water we want." Lawrence
had to explain that the effectiveness of the faucets lay in their connection to
the pipeline.
    Are you connected to God's pipeline? Is His love flowing through you?

Additional Sermons and Lesson Ideas

Putting Christ Back into Christ-ian

Date preached:

SCRIPTURE: Psalm 40:1–8

INTRODUCTION: The word Christian means Christ-like, but Ruth Graham wrote, "The very term 'Christ-like' is confusing. Like Him in what way? His ability to heal? To cast out demons? To raise the dead?" Quoting Psalm 40, Ruth concluded, "I think basically what is meant by the term 'Christ-like' has got to do with His attitude toward His Father's will." Psalm 40 is a messianic Psalm, and verses 6–8 (quoted in Hebrews 10) tell us that Christlikeness means:

1. **Ears that are open** (v. 6). Jesus heard what His Father was saying. He knew the Old Testament. One scholar determined that 10 percent of His daily conversation consisted of quotes from the Old Testament.
2. **A Life that is available** (v. 7). Like Isaiah's "Here am I, send me."
3. **A Heart that is yielded** (v. 8). Not just willing, but delighting, to do His will.

CONCLUSION: Consecrate me now to Thy service, Lord, by the power of grace divine; / Let my soul look up with a steadfast hope, and my will be lost in Thine.

The "Be Strongs" of Scripture

Date preached:

SCRIPTURE: 2 Timothy 2:1

INTRODUCTION: Fatigue, stress, disappointment, and the troubles of life can leave us like the person of whom it is said in Proverbs 24:10: "If you faint in the day of adversity, Your strength is small." When Paul told Timothy, "Be strong," he was giving us the last of the Bible's 35 commandments that include those two words. Let's study this theme through Scripture:

- Deuteronomy 11:8
- Deuteronomy 31:6–7, 23, with Joshua 1:6, 7, 9, 18
- Joshua 10:25
- 1 Kings 2:2 with 1 Chronicles 22:13 and 28:10–13
- 2 Chronicles 32:7–8
- Daniel 10:19 with 11:32
- 1 Corinthians 16:13
- Ephesians 6:10

CONCLUSION: Isaiah 40:31 promises that, even in difficulty, those who wait on the Lord shall renew their strength.

Trends in Preaching

An Interview with Dr. Michael Diduit
Executive Vice-president of Union University
and Editor of *Preaching Magazine*

Can you spot any major trend occurring in the world of preaching today? A quantum shift in the way preaching is done?

Over recent years there has been this move toward the new homiletic with an emphasis on narrative, on preaching for a post-modern era. What I'm beginning to see is a recognition of weaknesses in that kind of preaching. It is preaching adapted to a culture that doesn't believe anything; so I'm seeing a shift away from induction and narrative as the basic form of the sermon. Not an elimination of those elements, but a recognition that prepositional truth is important, too. In strong evangelical churches, there is a renewed emphasis on solid biblical exposition which employs narrative as a tool, but doesn't use it as a consistent framework for the sermon itself.

What impact has the seeker movement had on preaching?

It has caused us to recognize the importance of the language we use. It's very easy for preachers to fall into jargon, to use the "inside lingo" that, frankly, occurs in any field. If you put two insurance agents in the same room, they'll start using terms the rest of us won't fully understand. But it's easy for us in the pulpit to fall into a jargon that doesn't necessarily communicate to the person in the pew, much less to the person in the street. Beyond that, one of the excellent trends that has come from the seeker movement is the recognition of the importance of application. How do I take these biblical principles and put them into practice? Rick Warren is a good example of that. He is not an expository preacher. He is a biblical preacher, and he preaches biblical sermons. But a traditional expositor will draw the outline of his message from the text. Rick finds the point of the text and builds on the application. Every major point is built on application. We who are more traditional expositors can apply this by being much more application-centered in the way we deal with our passage.

Has the seeker movement had any negative influence on preaching?

Sometimes there has been a tendency to adapt not just our communication method to the culture, but the message itself. We live in a post-modern era. It's very important to recognize that Christianity is rooted in historical, objective truth. We must be careful that we don't adapt the message itself into an inadequate worldview. We can adapt our methods, but not our message. Every good preacher today has to be a cross-cultural communicator.

Are sermon series becoming more or less popular?

More popular. Even within the very conservative expository settings, we are seeing sermon series being shorter and more thematic. There are still those who preach through books in the Bible, and some do it very effectively. But many preachers are taking a topic such as prayer or discipleship and developing strong biblical expositions from numerous passages rather than just moving through a single book such as Ephesians.

Do you practice your sermons aloud before you step in the pulpit?

I do. Some don't like to do that, but I'm finding more and more who talk through their sermons in advance. Some preachers like to go into their pulpit on Saturday night and mouth their sermon aloud. Sometimes when I hear myself saying certain words, I realize it isn't sounding just right. I can hear my mistakes in advance and correct them.

Do you ever go into the pulpit feeling ill-prepared?

I've never met a preacher who hasn't. One hopes those times are few and far between. But there are times when we must pray, "Dear God, I'm more aware than ever that it's all up to you." Apart from the Holy Spirit, preaching is just like dry cinder, dry wood. But when the Holy Spirit touches a sermon, it's like pouring gas over it and striking a match. No matter how well-prepared or ill-prepared I am, I want to go into the pulpit with an awareness that preaching is the work of the Holy Spirit. ✸

FEBRUARY 10, 2002

Go Fish
Date preached:

Scripture: Matthew 4:18–22, especially vv. 18–20 And Jesus, walking by the Sea of Galilee, saw two brothers, Simon called Peter, and Andrew his brother, casting a net into the sea; for they were fishermen. Then He said to them, "Follow Me, and I will make you fishers of men." They immediately left *their* nets and followed Him.

Introduction: One of the questions I'd like to ask the Great Physician, were it possible, is why our variety of Christianity is not more contagious. Why are we not winning more of our friends, relatives, and associates to Christ? Why are we not better witnesses? According to surveys by George Barna, only about half (53 percent) of born again Christians feel a sense of responsibility to tell others about their faith. In other words, nearly half of us don't think it's our personal responsibility to share our beliefs with those who don't know Christ.

One day as Jesus walked by the lakeshore He thought about the symbolism of the Sea of Galilee. It was a large, lovely lake, ringed by villages, nestled in the hollow of the hills, but Jesus saw more than blue water and bobbing boats. To His perceptive mind that lake represented the world. Watching the boats floating in the water, he thought of the local churches He would establish in the world. As He saw fisherman, He thought of His followers. The nets represented His evangelistic appeal, claiming souls for eternal life. Coming upon some fishermen that day, Jesus issued the first invitation in the New Testament: "Follow Me, and I will make you fishers of men."

1. **We're To Be Followers of Christ.** Jesus spoke much about our following Him. The word "follow" occurs 92 times in the Gospels (NKJV).
    *   "He who does not take his cross and follow after Me is not worthy of Me" (Matt. 10:38).
    *   He told the rich young ruler, "If you want to be perfect, go, sell what you have and give to the poor, and you will have treasure in heaven; and come, follow Me." (Matt. 19:21)
    *   He evangelized Levi the tax-collector with just two words: "Follow Me" (Luke 5:27).
    *   "I am the light of the world. He who follows Me shall not walk in darkness, but have the light of life" (John 8:12).

- "My sheep hear My voice, and I know them, and they follow Me" (John 10:27).
- His last words to Peter were similar to His first words: "If I will that he remain till I come, what *is that* to you? You follow Me" (John 21:22).

Following Christ means we make Him Lord of our daily lives, seek out His promises and claim them, seek out His commands and obey them, and offer ourselves as living sacrifices for Him (Rom. 12:1–2).

2. **We're To Be Fashioned By Christ.** "… and I will make you." The parallel account (Mark 1:17) says: "I will make you to become…." As we follow Christ, He makes us to become. He begins to carve us into His type of people. A school teacher who was bypassed for a promotion went to her administrator and complained, "I have twenty years of experience, and you promoted someone who had only been teaching five years." The administrator replied, "No, you don't have twenty years of experience. You have one year of experience twenty times. You're still teaching the same things and in the same way you did your first year. You haven't grown in your profession." Christ wants us to grow, to develop, to become effective representatives of Himself.

3. **We're to be Fisherman for Christ.** "…I will make you fishers of men." Some years ago the New York Fire Department had a great parade. Included were buses loaded with people from all walks of life. The sign said: "All of these were saved by our Fire Department from burning buildings." In Paul's letters, he said that those he had won to Christ were his crown and joy, his trophies of grace.

>>> *sermon continued on following page*

APPROPRIATE HYMNS AND SONGS

Christ for the World We Sing, Samuel Wolcott/Felice De Giardini; Public Domain.

I'll Tell the World That I'm a Christian, Baynard L. Fox; © 1958, 1986 Fox Music Publications (a div. of Fred Bock Music Company, Inc.) (Admin. by Fred Bock Music Company, Inc.).

Jesus Shall Reign, Isaac Watts/Gerrit Gustafson; © 1990 Integrity's Hosanna! Music (Admin. by Integrity Music, Inc.).

Carry the Light, Twila Paris; © 1989 Ariose Music (Admin by EMI Christian Music Publishing)/Mountain Spring Music.

Song for the Nations, Chris Christensen; © 1986 Integrity's Hosanna! Music.

Conclusion: How can we be better witnesses for Christ?

- Ask God to give you a burden for a handful of people who need to be saved, and begin praying for them.
- Live a consistent Christian life, letting others see the hope within you.
- Be ready when asked to give a reason for that hope (1 Peter 3:15).
- Seize opportunities for inviting others to church. If you invite enough people, some will come. And if enough come, some will be saved.

FOR THE BULLETIN

❂ On February 10, 754, Emperor Constantine V called an iconoclastic council in Constantinople. The 330 bishops denounced artists who made pictures of the Savior, saying that the Eucharist alone presents the proper image of Christ. ❂ John Wesley fell on ice-covered London Bridge, on February 10, 1751, and was carried to the home of nurse Mary Vazeille. During his recuperation, he proposed to her. "I groaned all day, and several following ones," his brother Charles wrote. "I could eat no pleasant food, nor preach, nor rest, either by night or by day." John and Mary's marriage, unfortunately, was not a happy one. ❂ A. B. Earle, author of "Bringing in the Sheaves," was a well-known evangelist who began preaching in 1830 at age 18. During the next 50 years he preached 19,780 times, with 150,000 people professing Christ. On February 10, 1859, Earle, dedicating himself anew to Christ, wrote: "This day I make a new consecration of my all to Christ. Jesus, I now forever give myself to Thee; my soul to be washed in Thy blood and saved in heaven at last; my whole body to be used for Thy glory; my mouth to speak for Thee at all times; my eyes to weep over lost sinners." ❂ February 10, 1859, is the birthday of the famous missionary to China, Jonathan Goforth.

Kids Talk

If you have a fishing rod, reel, net, or gear, bring it to church and show the children (watching out, of course, for the hooks). Perhaps give them a casting demonstration. Share with them Jesus' words about being fishers of men, and suggest ways (or have the children suggest ways) in which they can bring their friends to church or help win them to Christ.

Worship Theme:
Follow Christ and Become His Witness

Call to Worship:
"Now then, we are ambassadors for Christ, as though God were pleading through us: we implore you on Christ's behalf, be reconciled to God" (2 Corinthians 5:20).

Applicable Scripture Readings:
Deuteronomy 32:1–4
Acts 1:1–8
1 Peter 3:13–17

Responsive Reading:

Men: O Zion, You who bring good tidings, Get up into the high mountain; O Jerusalem,

Women: You who bring good tidings, Lift up your voice with strength, Lift it up, be not afraid; Say to the cities of Judah, "Behold your God!"

Men: "The Spirit of the Lord God is upon Me, Because the LORD has anointed Me to preach good tidings to the poor; He has sent Me to heal the brokenhearted, To proclaim liberty to the captives, And the opening of the prison to those who are bound.

Women: Behold, on the mountains the feet of him who brings good tidings, Who proclaims peace!

Leader: Then the angel said to them,

Everyone: Do not be afraid, for behold, I bring you good tidings of great joy which will be to all people. For there is born to you this day in the city of David a Savior, who is Christ the Lord.

Taken from Isaiah 7:9; 61:1; Nahum 1:15; Luke 2:10–11.

STATS, STORIES AND MORE

According to George Barna . . .

- One out of three adults (33 percent) is unchurched. A proportion that represents 65–70 million adults in America (2000).
- The highest proportion of unchurched is in the Northeast (44 percent), compared to 33 percent in the West, 32 percent in the Midwest and 26 percent in the South (2000).
- Nine out of ten American adults (86 percent) cannot accurately define the meaning of the "Great Commission." Seven out of ten adults have no clue what "John 3:16" means (1994).

Traveling with Watchman Nee

In his biography of Watchman Nee, Bob Laurent tells of a time Nee took his friend Shepherd Ma on a tour of China, traveling in a Model T Ford with full gasoline cans and donated Bibles. Along the way, Nee told Shepherd this story about missionary Thomas Chalmers.

Chalmers was an overnight guest in a home where a highly-educated agnostic was present. The two men took to each other and spent the evening talking about world affairs, then both retired to their separate bedrooms. Minutes later, Chalmers heard a thud. Racing over, he discovered his new friend's body on the floor. As others gathered in the room of the deceased, Chalmers said, "Had I known that this would happen, I would not have spent the last two hours chatting about so many things. I would have pointed him to eternal things. But, alas, I have not used even five minutes to speak to him of the salvation of his soul.... Now it is too late."

More From Watchman Nee:

"[Winning souls] is something you cannot outgrow; it is a lifetime undertaking."

"We need to be joined to the Holy Spirit so that the living water may flow through us. But let me also say that the channel of life has two ends: One end is open toward the Holy Spirit; but the other end is open toward men."

"Beloved, there are two big days in the life of a believer: the day on which he believes in the Lord—and every day after that when he leads someone to faith in Christ."

Additional Sermons and Lesson Ideas

How to Relax

Date preached:

SCRIPTURE: Psalm 131

INTRODUCTION: People today are spinning with stress, filled with fear, scrambling to hang onto things they can't ultimately keep. They should read Psalm 131, one of the shortest chapters in the Bible. Charles Spurgeon said, "[It] is one of the shortest Psalms to read, but one of the longest to learn."

1. **We Must Quit our Striving by trusting God from the outset with life's concerns** (v. 1). "LORD, my heart is not haughty...neither do I concern myself...." Some try to be gods for their own lives, but David said, "Lord, my heart isn't so proud that I presume to know what's best for me. That's your concern."
2. **We Must Quiet our Souls by trusting God with the outcome of life's concerns** (vv. 2–3). "Calmed and quieted" are similar Hebrew terms that mean "leveled." Both words are used to describe the sea after the passing of a storm.

CONCLUSION: The lesson of Psalm 131: God is weaning us from things that are temporary so that we might enjoy things that are eternal. Quit struggling, quiet your soul, and hope in the Lord, both now and forever.

Learning to Count

Date preached:

By Dr. Timothy Beougher

SCRIPTURE: Philippians 3:1–10

INTRODUCTION: A study in Chicago schools found that many children couldn't perform simple arithmetic without a calculator. Christians also need to learn to count. The word "count" in our text means to evaluate or to consider.

1. **Count it All Joy** (vv. 1–3). We must beware the kill-joys of the Christian life: false teachers, false teaching, dogs, evil workers, legalists.
2. **Count it All Loss** (vv. 4–8). The verb "I counted" indicates Paul made a conscious decision to repudiate his religious heritage and accomplishments.
3. **Count it All Gain** (vv. 8–11). Nothing else matters but gaining Jesus Christ, being found in Him.

CONCLUSION: Look at your own ledger sheet—what are you writing under gain? Under loss? "Nothing in my hand I bring, simply to Thy cross I cling."

FEBRUARY 17, 2002

SUGGESTED SERMON

On A Hill Far Away

Date preached:

Scripture: Genesis 22:1–19, especially v. 14 And Abraham called the name of the place, The-LORD-Will-Provide; as it is said *to* this day, "In the Mount of the LORD it shall be provided."

Introduction: When we board an airliner, we're asked to show a photo ID. For security reasons, the airlines don't take us at our word. They want proof that we're who we claim to be. Jesus' critics demanded proof of His identity, thus He showed them His "photo ID." He told them His portrait was on every page of the Old Testament. "If you believed Moses, you would believe Me; for he wrote about Me" (John 5:46). Where did Moses write of Jesus? One place is Genesis 22. The young man Isaac is a remarkable prototype of Jesus Christ. Everything about Isaac in this passage points to his being a type or illustration of Christ. Everything about him reminds us of the Lord Jesus, and those who carefully study Genesis 22 find a remarkable series of parallels between Isaac and Immanuel:

1. **Both Isaac and Jesus were sons of promise.** The angel had announced to Abraham that he and Sarah would bear a son. Likewise, the birth of Christ was announced beforehand by an angel to Mary and Joseph. Even the very names of these boys were given before conception.

2. **Both were born miraculously.** God "tinkered" with a woman's womb to cause a supernatural conception in both cases.

3. **Both Isaac and Jesus were called the only begotten sons of their fathers.** (John 3:16; Heb. 11:17).

4. **Both Isaac and Jesus had fathers who were willing to sacrifice their sons "on a hill far away."** According to 2 Chronicles 3:1, Mount Moriah is in Jerusalem. The range of mountains where Abraham built his altar would later become the very spot where Christ would die for the sins of the world. That's why Genesis 22 keeps emphasizing the particular site of the mountain chosen by God (vv. 2, 3, 9, 14). "In the Mount of the LORD it shall be provided."

5. **Both Isaac and Jesus carried the wood up the hill on their own backs.** It was the wood on which they were to be sacrificed.

6. **Both were to be offered as a burnt offering for sin.**

7. **Both willingly allowed themselves to be placed on the wood they had carried on their backs to the top of the mountain.** Both became obedient unto death.

8. **Both Isaac and Jesus were "dead" for three days.** In Jesus' case, it was a literal death. In Isaac's case, it was figurative, but it was a figure the biblical writers didn't want us to miss. According to Genesis 22:3, Moriah was three days' journey for Abraham. During those three days, he grieved for his son as one lost. According to Hebrews 11:17, figuratively speaking, Abraham received Isaac back from the dead on the third day.

9. **Both, being raised up, were given a bride selected by their fathers through whom all the world would be blessed.** With Isaac, it was Rebekah. With Christ, it is His bride, the church.

Conclusion: How would you answer this question: What biblical figure was a son of promise, and both his birth and his name were announced in advance? He was conceived miraculously is his mother's womb. He was the only begotten son, yet his father was willing to sacrifice him as a burnt offering on a hill far away. He carried the wood on which he was to be sacrificed on his own back,

>>> *sermon continued on following page*

APPROPRIATE HYMNS AND SONGS

And Can It Be, Charles Wesley/Thomas Campbell; Public Domain.

Blessed Redeemer, Avis B. Christiansen/Harry Dixon Loes; © 1921 Renewed 1949 Harry Dixon Loes. Assigned to Singspiration Music (Admin. by Brentwood-Benson Music Publishing, Inc.).

My Savior's Love, Charles H. Gabriel; Public Domain.

I Stand Amazed, Dennis Jernigan; © 1991 Shepherd's Heart Music, Inc. (Admin. by Word Music Group, Inc.).

When Praise Demands a Sacrifice, Sue Smith/Russell Mauldin; © 1990 John T. Benson Publishing Co. (Admin. by Brentwood-Benson Music Publishing, Inc.).

and he went submissively. He was "dead" for three days, then arose. Being raised up, he took a bride selected by his father, through whom all the world would be blessed.

Two thousand years before Calvary, we have the gospel story given to us in advance through a preview, a prototype. Yet Isaac himself could never have actually provided purification for sins, for he was a sinner just as we are. Two millennia later and two millennia ago, God became a man, went to the cross, and there, shedding His blood, bridged the gulf between His own holiness on the one hand, and you and me on the other. On the mountain of the Lord, it was provided.

Will you believe it? Will you receive it? "He came unto his own, and his own received him not. But as many as received him, to them gave he power to become the sons of God, *even* to them that believe on his name" (John 1:11–12).

FOR THE BULLETIN

❋ On February 17, 1600, Italian philosopher and mathematician, Giorgano Bruno, whose theories anticipated modern science, was betrayed to the Inquisition and burned as a heretic in Rome. ❋ On February 17, 1688, James Renwick, 28, was martyred at the Grassmarket in Edinburgh. Renwick, a Scottish Covenanter, had preached through the "mosses, muirs, and mountains" of Scotland, until his arrest. On the morning of his death, Renwick said grace over breakfast, praying, "O Lord, Thou hast brought me within two hours of eternity, and this is no matter of terror to me, more than if I were to lie down in a bed of roses." ❋ On February 17, 1739, George Whitefield, denied a pulpit, preached for the first time in the open air near Bristol, England, to coal miners. ❋ On February 17, 1795, the London Missionary Society (as it was later known) was organized by 34 men at the Castle and Falcon public house in London. ❋ On this day in 1850, schoolteacher James Garfield traveled by sleigh to a church meeting where he was so impressed with the gospel that he shortly made a profession of faith. He became a preacher with the Disciples of Christ before entering politics, and later became the only minister to serve as President of the United States (unordained, in keeping with the practice of the Disciples of Christ). ❋ On February 17, 1977 Uganda Radio announced the death of Anglican Archbishop Janani Luwum. He had been arrested by Idi Amin's soldiers, tortured, then shot through the heart.

WORSHIP HELPS

Worship Theme:
"Amazing Love! How can it be that Thou, my God, shouldst die for me!"

Call to Worship:
"In Him we have redemption through His blood, the forgiveness of sins, according to the riches of His grace" (Eph. 1:7).

Poem to Use in Pastoral Prayer:
I know this cleansing blood of Thine
Was shed, dear Lord! for me;
For me, for all—oh! Grace Divine!
Who look by faith to Thee.
(author unknown)

Scripture Reading from John 19:
And He, bearing His cross, went out to a place called the Place of a Skull, which is called in Hebrew, Golgotha, where they crucified Him, and two others with Him, one on either side, and Jesus in the center. Now Pilate wrote a title and put it on the cross. And the writing was:

JESUS OF NAZARETH, THE KING OF THE JEWS.

Then many of the Jews read this title, for the place where Jesus was crucified was near the city; and it was written in Hebrew, Greek, and Latin....

After this, Jesus, knowing that all things were now accomplished, that the Scripture might be fulfilled, said, "I thirst!" Now a vessel full of sour wine was sitting there; and they filled a sponge with sour wine, put it on hyssop, and put it to His mouth. So when Jesus had received the sour wine, He said, "It is finished!" And bowing His head, He gave up His spirit.

Benediction:
"To Him who loved us and washed us from our sins in His own blood, and has made us kings and priests to His God and Father, to Him be glory and dominion forever and ever. Amen" (Rev. 1:6).

STATS, STORIES AND MORE

Christ in the Old Testament
"Prophecy is a species of miracle...."
—*George Park Fisher*

"Prophecy is a miracle of utterance."
—*A. T. Pierson*

"No miracle which He wrought so unmistakably set on Him the seal of God as the convergence of a thousand lines of prophecy in Him, as in one burning focal point of dazzling glory. Every sacrifice lit, from Abel's altar until the last Passover of the Passion week, pointed as with flaming fingers to Calvary's cross."
—*A. T. Pierson*

"The apostles throughout the New Testament appealed to two areas of Christ's life to establish His Messiahship. One was the resurrection and the other fulfilled messianic prophecy. The Old Testament written over a 1,500 year period contains several hundred references to the coming Messiah. All these were fulfilled in Christ."
—*Josh McDowell*

Holding High the Cross
In his book, *Kingdoms in Conflict,* Charles Colson tells of a time when Prime Minister Jaruzelski ordered crucifixes removed from classrooms throughout Poland, just as they had been banned in factories, hospitals, and other public institutions. This provoked waves of anger all across Poland, and the government relented, insisting that the law remain on the books, but agreeing not to press for removal of the crucifixes, particularly in the schoolrooms.

But one zealous Communist school administrator in Garwolin decided that the law was the law. So one evening he had the crucifixes removed from lecture halls where they had hung since the school's founding in the twenties. A group of parents entered the school and hung more crosses. The administrator promptly had these taken down.

The next day two-thirds of the school's students staged a sit-in. When heavily armed riot police arrived, the students were forced into the streets. They marched, crucifixes held high, to a nearby church where they were joined by 2,500 others from nearby schools for a morning of prayer. Soldiers surrounded the church. But the pictures of students holding crosses high above their heads flashed around the world.

Additional Sermons and Lesson Ideas

Some Laws of Spiritual Work

Date preached:

Based on an outline by John A. Broadus

SCRIPTURE: John 4:32–38

INTRODUCTION: Ever grow tired of doing good? Jesus was faint in John 4, so the disciples went to purchase food. When they returned, they were astonished at the change in Him. He was sitting up, face animated, eyes kindled. He told them, "I have food to eat of which you do not know." From this passage with its images, we may discover several laws of spiritual work.

1. **Spiritual work is refreshing to soul and body** (v. 34). If we love spiritual work, it will kindle our souls.
2. **There are seasons in the spiritual sphere, of sowing and reaping, just as in farming** (v. 35).
3. **Spiritual work links the workers in unity** (v. 36).
4. **Spiritual work has rich rewards** (vv. 36–38).

CONCLUSION: God will reward all we do, and all we try to do, and all we wish to do. O blessed God! He will be our reward forever and ever.

More Than Enough

Date preached:

SCRIPTURE: John 10:10

INTRODUCTION: God uses the word "abundant" to describe His blessings to us, a word that means, "more than enough." In Christ, we have more than enough:

- **Mercy.** "The LORD is...abundant in mercy" (Num. 14:18; see also Neh. 9:27, Ps. 86:5; 15; 1 Peter 1:3).
- **Kindness.** "God... abundant in kindness..." (Neh. 9:17; see also Jonah 4:2).
- **Justice.** "He is excellent... in abundant justice" (Job 37:23).
- **Redemption.** "With Him is abundant redemption" (Ps. 130:7).
- **Pardon.** "He will abundantly pardon" (Isa. 55:7).
- **Answered Prayer.** "Him who is able to do exceedingly abundantly above all that we ask ..." (Eph. 3:20).
- **Grace.** "The grace of our Lord was exceedingly abundant..." (1 Tim. 1:13).
- **The Holy Spirit.** "The Holy Spirit, whom He poured out on us abundantly..." (Titus 3:5).
- **Our entrance into heaven.** "An entrance will be supplied to you abundantly into the everlasting kingdom of our Lord and Savior Jesus Christ" (2 Peter 1:11).

CONCLUSION: Our response to abundant life should be abundant rejoicing (Phil. 1:26).

Augustine's *Confessions*

Reading Augustine's *Confessions* isn't a picnic, but it *is* a feast. In the modern sense of the term, this is history's first autobiography; and even after 1,600 years, it remains one of the most fascinating and encouraging books on the shelf.

Aurelius Augustine was born in North Africa in A.D. 354. Patricius, his father, was a pagan, but his mother, Monica, was a devout Christian. Writing in his mid-forties, Augustine recounts his brilliant, bespotted life from birth to conversion. The *Confessions* is composed in the form of a prayer consisting of 13 chapters, or "books." The first nine chapters record the story of his life and conversion to Christ. The last four are philosophical and theological in nature and are, while rich, somewhat less gripping.

If you make up your mind to plow into *Confessions*, here's what you'll find:

Honesty. Augustine remembers his father seeing him at age 16 in the public baths. Noting that Augustine had sailed into puberty, Patricius promptly went home and told Monica she'd soon be a grandmother. Monica earnestly begged her son not to commit fornication. But, "these appeared to me but womanish counsels, which I would have blushed to obey." The teenager was soon head-over-heels in love with sex. "Fool that I was, I foamed in my wickedness as the sea and, forsaking Thee, followed the rushing of my own tide, and burst out of all Thy bounds. . . . The madness of lust held full sway in me."

Brilliance. When he wasn't in bed or at the theater ("stage plays captivated me"), the young Augustine was hitting the books, devouring the Latin classics, studying Cicero, and developing his considerable gifts in rhetoric. "In that unstable period of my life, I studied the books of eloquence, for it was in eloquence that I was eager to be eminent." The student soon became a teacher himself, lecturing in the universities of Carthage, Rome, and Milan, rubbing shoulders with the most influential men of his age.

Relevance. If you don't think a 21st century reader can relate to a fourth century North African, just consider this: Not only was Augustine caught up in sex, entertainment, and education—he became involved in an eastern cult. He joined the Manicheans—about as "new age" a group as any you'll find today. "Nearly nine years passed in which I wallowed in the mud of that deep pit and in the darkness of falsehood."

Simplicity. Though brilliant, Augustine knew how to serve truth on simple platters. For example, he explains human depravity by recounting how he and his friends once stripped a neighbor's pear tree of its fruit, thereby robbing the man of his livelihood. Why did he do it? "I stole those simply that I might steal, for, having stolen them, I threw them away. My soul gratification in them was my own sin."

Encouragement. For over three decades, Monica prayed for her wild and wayward son. She followed him to Carthage, to Rome, and on to Milan, weeping, pleading, and assaulting heaven with perpetual missiles of prayer. "Thy hands, O my God, in the hidden design of Thy providence did not desert my soul; and out of the blood of my mother's heart, through the tears she poured out by day and by night, there was a sacrifice offered to Thee for me, and by marvelous ways Thou didst deal with me." And at last, Augustine, under deep conviction, retreated to a friend's villa in Milan. He wanted to become a Christian, but didn't want to relinquish his immorality. "I was still tightly bound by the love of women." While wrestling with these things in the garden, Augustine suddenly heard a nearby child singing, "Take up and read!" There was a book laying nearby, and "I snatched it up, opened it, and in silence read the paragraph on which my eyes first fell: 'Behave properly as in the day, not in carousing and drunkenness, not in sexual promiscuity and sensuality, not in strife and jealousy. But put on the Lord Jesus, and make no provision for the flesh to fulfill its lusts' (Romans 13:13–14). I wanted to read no further, nor did I need to. For instantly, as the sentence ended, there was infused into my heart something like the light of full certainty and all the gloom of doubt vanished away.... Then we went to my mother and told her what happened, to her great joy. We explained to her how it had occurred—and she leaped for joy triumphant; and she blessed Thee, who art able to do exceedingly abundantly above all that we ask or think."

Shortly after, Monica died, saying her life's work was over. But her son's work was only beginning. St. Augustine went on to shape all subsequent Christian history, writing over 1,000 works (including 242 books), and giving us this remarkable account of a prodigal son and his praying mother. ✻

FEBRUARY 24, 2002

Date preached:

Making the Most of Your Nervous Breakdown

Scripture: 1 Kings 19:1–21, especially verses 1–3a And Ahab told Jezebel all that Elijah had done, also how he had executed all the prophets with the sword. Then Jezebel sent a messenger to Elijah, saying, "So let the gods do *to me,* and more also, if I do not make your life as the life of one of them by tomorrow about this time." And when he saw *that,* he arose and ran for his life....

Introduction: The *Wall Street Journal* recently ran a front page story on the subject of nervous breakdowns, saying "The nervous breakdown, the mysterious affliction that has been a staple of American life and literature for more than a century, has been wiped out by the combined forces of psychiatry, pharmacology, and managed care. But people keep breaking down anyway." According to *USA Today's* weekend magazine, anxiety disorders are the Number 1 mental health problem in the United States, costing Americans more than $42 billion a year in doctor bills and workplace losses. In the Bible, the prophet Elijah once had a "nervous breakdown." By studying his experience we can learn how God deals with us when we're overwrought and overstrained.

The Lord wrote a sevenfold prescription for Elijah. The same therapy will work for us.

1. **Sleep and nourishment** (vv. 4–8). Elijah was exhausted, for he had combated paganism for three years, waged a vigorous war on Mt. Carmel against the prophets of Baal, prayed with exceeding earnestness, and had run a virtual marathon back to Jezreel. When we're exhausted, we have less control over our emotions. Depression descends more easily. Worry grips us more doggedly. Temptations catch us unawares. Verses 4–8 tell of how God provided sleep, bread, and water for Elijah under the broom tree.

2. **Angelic help** (vv. 5–7). The Lord sent an angel to care for Elijah. Hebrews 1:14 says that angels are ministering spirits sent to serve those who inherit salvation. Many times, according to intimations in the Bible, angels minister to us though we're unaware of it.

3. **Ventilation** (vv. 9–10). God allowed Elijah to repeatedly ventilate his frustrations. When we can express our feelings to a good friend or to the Lord, it helps reduce our swirling emotions to tangible thoughts and words. We can identify them and begin to get them "out of our system."

4. **God's still, small voice** (vv. 11–13). The ultimate answer to life's downturns is rediscovering God's infallible Word. Elijah needed a gentle word of reassurance, a gentle whisper. The same whisper comes to us as we open the Scripture. Golfer Tom Lehman gave his life to Christ in high school when a friend invited him to a Fellowship of Christian Athletes meeting. After college, Tom worked hard to enter the PGA Tour, and in 1991 was named the Ben Hogan Tour Player of the Year. But in 1995, his doctors discovered pre-cancerous colon polyps, and surgery was required. Tom and his wife got down on their knees and committed the matter to God, and the Lord gave him Joshua 1:9 to strengthen him during the crisis: *Be strong and of good courage; do not be afraid, nor be dismayed, for the LORD your God is with you.*

5. **A renewal of purpose** (vv. 14–17). The Lord gave Elijah a set of new assignments. Nothing helps us overcome discouragement like rediscovering our purpose in life and setting to work at what God has called us to do.

6. **Reassurance** (v. 18). Things are never as bad as they appear where God is concerned. Elijah had twice insisted that he was the only surviving worshiper of God. The Lord told him there were 7000 others.

>>> *sermon continued on following page*

APPROPRIATE HYMNS AND SONGS

O Breath of Life, Bessie Porter Head/Joel Blomquist; Public Domain.

The Lord's My Shepherd, I'll Not Want, from the Scottish Psalter, 1650/Arr. From William Havergal by Lowell Mason; Public Domain.

Revive Us Again, William P. Mackay/John J. Husband; Public Domain.

The New 23rd, Ralph Carmichael; © 1969 Bud John Songs, Inc. (Admin. by EMI Christian Music Publishing).

All Things Are Possible, Darlene Zschech; © 1997 Darlede Zschech (Hillsong) (Admin. by Integrity Music, Inc.).

7. **A Friend** (vv. 19–21). The Lord provided the solitary Elijah with a friend, Elisha, to share the load. A healthy life keeps its friendships in good repair.

Conclusion: Are you overwhelmed, stressed, discouraged, depressed? God wants to renew your strength and to restore your soul. The way He revived Elijah is the pattern He wants to use to revive your spirit, too.

FOR THE BULLETIN

❂ On this day in A.D. 303, a general persecution of Christians was unleashed in the Roman Empire by edict of Diocletian. The historian Eusebius saw churches razed, Scriptures burned, and pastors torn to pieces in the amphitheater. ❂ On February 24, 1208, Francis of Assisi attended Mass in the church of Saint Mary of the Angels. As Matthew 10:9 was read, Francis was deeply moved. Shortly thereafter, inspired by that verse, he began his itinerant ministry. ❂ James Mitchell, Scottish preacher, was tortured for his faith on February 24, 1676. Mitchell's right leg was inserted into a device designed to crush the leg by using an iron wedge and mallet. Mitchell fainted following the ninth blow. ❂ February 24, 1811, is the birthday of Daniel Payne, first African-American university president in the United States. Payne, sixth bishop of the African Methodist Episcopal Church, helped establish Union Seminary and Wilberforce University in Ohio. ❂ On February 24, 1812, missionary Henry Martyn finished the Persian translation of the New Testament. ❂ Amanda Smith (1837–1915) was a black scrub woman and ex-slave who began accepting invitations to preach as a Methodist holiness evangelist throughout the South, traveling alone by train, her belongings rolled in a carpetbag. Her fame leaped the Atlantic, and she was called to England for meetings, then to India, then to Africa. She organized women's bands, young people's groups, temperance societies, children's meetings. She adopted homeless youngsters and started an orphanage near Chicago. Amanda Smith died on February 24, 1915. ❂ On February 24, 1945, Olympic hero and missionary Eric Liddell was buried at Weihsien internment camp.

WORSHIP HELPS

Worship Theme:
The Scripture gives us God's methods and means for accomplishing renewal in our hearts.

Call to Worship:
"Bless the Lord, O my soul, And forget not all His benefits... Who satisfies your mouth with good things, So that your youth is renewed like the eagle's" (Ps. 103:2, 5).

Applicable Scripture Readings:
Isaiah 40:28–31
Psalm 23:1–6

Responsive Reading from Psalm 23 and Isaiah 40:

Leader: The Lord is my shepherd; I shall not want. He makes me to lie down in green pastures; He leads me beside the still waters. He restores my soul.

People: He gives power to the weak, And to those who have no might He increases strength.

Leader: Even the youths shall faint and be weary, And the young men shall utterly fall,

People: But those who wait on the Lord Shall renew their strength; They shall mount up with wings like eagles, They shall run and not be weary, They shall walk and not faint.

Kids Talk

Show the children a rechargeable flashlight with weak power reserves. Ask them what's wrong. Why is the light so dim? Tell them that God calls us to be lights. He wants our faces to be bright. He wants us to light up the lives of others by telling them about Christ. In order to be bright-eyed and strong ourselves, we need God's strength every day. Plug the flashlight into an extension cord, or show them another that has been recently recharged. Explain how prayer, Bible study, and church attendance recharges us each day. If you have time, mention Elijah as an example.

STATS, STORIES AND MORE

Someone Once Said:
"Inside myself is a place where I live all alone, and that's where you renew your springs that never dry up."
—*Pearl Buck*

"We must always change, renew, rejuvenate ourselves; otherwise we harden."
—*Johann Wolfgang von Goethe*

Stats from *USA Today:*
- Anxiety disorders affect at least 19 million people aged 18–54 each year, according to the National Institute of Mental Health (from *USA Today Weekend,* August 22–24, 1997, pp. 4–5).
- 4 million Americans endure a constant state of fretfulness called generalized anxiety disorder (from *USA Today Weekend,* August 22–24, 1997, pp. 4–5).

Sleepless in America
"[Americans] accumulate sleep debt like penny-ante gamblers racking up IOUs. Each weekday night they get an hour and six minutes less, on average, than the eight hours that sleep experts recommend, each weekend night half an hour less. By the end of the year, they are short 338 hours—two full weeks—of rest. They are the great unslept, somnambulating through life on the verge of sleep bankruptcy. Like sleepwalkers, they are dangerously unaware of the risks to their health."
—*U.S. News and World Report (Cover story, 10/16/2000).*

Angelic Help
In her book *Evidence Not Seen,* missionary Darlene Deibler Rose tells of being awakened one evening by noises in her house. She was in an isolated area of the Dutch East Indies, and, thinking the noises were from rats, she sprang from the bed to chase them away. Suddenly she found herself face-to-face with a bandit who, with one fluid movement, drew his machete and held it in a striking position. Darlene impulsively rushed him, and he suddenly turned and fled, the missionary hot on his heels. Suddenly Darlene stopped in her tracks. "Lord," she said, "what a stupid thing for me to do." Immediately Psalm 34:7 came to mind: "The angel of the Lord encamps all around those who fear Him." She later learned from her gardener that the bandit had fled because "of those people you had there—those people in white who stood about the house."

Additional Sermons and Lesson Ideas

Not in Small Print
Date preached:

SCRIPTURE: Luke 14:26, 27, 33

INTRODUCTION: Many modern Christians don't think of using the term "disciples" to describe themselves. Yet Jesus never put the terms of discipleship in small print in the contract. Three times in Luke 14 He warned that unless we make certain commitments in life, we cannot be His disciples. To Bible teacher F. B. Meyer (1847–1929), that meant three things:

1. **Separation** (Luke 14:26). Jesus warned us that following Him may involve separation from loved ones, from hearth and home. He must come before family ties and human affection.
2. **Crucifixion** (Luke 14:27). Jesus said, "whoever does not bear his cross and come after Me cannot be My disciple." Dietrich Bonhoeffer said, "When God calls a man, he bids him come and die."
3. **Renunciation** (Luke 14:33). All we have must be gladly yielded when Christ asks for it.

A Sermon in One Chapter
Date preached:

SCRIPTURE: Isaiah 59

INTRODUCTION: Isaiah 59 is a powerful chapter, a sermon within itself, containing three great points.

1. **Our Sinfulness** (Isa. 59:1–8). The word *separation* may be the cruelest in the world. Nothing pulls at our hearts like separation. The Bible teaches that a thick iron plate, extending into infinity in all directions, separates us from the God who created this universe and who made us in His own image. Engraved on it is the word *iniquity*.
2. **Our Helplessness** (Isa. 59:9–15). Whereas verses 1–8 tell us about our sinfulness, verses 9–15 tells us about our helplessness. Something within us craves for love and permanence. But left to ourselves, we can't seem to find these things.
3. **God's Graciousness** (Isa. 59:16–21). God himself provided for our deliverance and salvation through Jesus Christ, and it was because Christ was utterly righteous that He was enabled to do this. This is the gospel in a nutshell. We are doomed and hopeless sinners; but God, in Whom no sin can ever abide, became a purely righteous Man who offered Himself a sacrifice of atonement for our deliverance and salvation.

MARCH 3, 2002

Your Hope-filled Future

Date preached:

Scripture: 1 Peter 1:3–5 Blessed be the God and Father of our Lord Jesus Christ, who according to His abundant mercy has begotten us again to a living hope through the resurrection of Jesus Christ from the dead, to an inheritance incorruptible and undefiled and that does not fade away, reserved in heaven for you, who are kept by the power of God through faith for salvation ready to be revealed in the last time.

Introduction: In November of 2000, baseball player Darryl Strawberry, plagued by drug addictions, jail time, and cancer, stood before a judge in Tampa and confessed, "I'm an addict, I go out and use drugs. I figure the drugs may kill me." He continued, "Life hasn't been worth living for me, that's the honest truth.... I basically wanted to die. At the time, I would rather just go ahead and kill myself. I couldn't kill myself because of the fact of my five children. I started to look at them and that wouldn't be fair to them for me to kill myself that way."

We all go through certain "dark nights of the soul" when life is potholed with pain. Simon Peter had such a night. The friend he denied three times had been crucified, and his own heart shattered. He must have been thinking back at those days as he picked up his quill and began his letter with the words of our text. We can observe four great truths from 1 Peter 1:3:

1. **A Great Mercy.** The passage begins by describing God's abundant mercy. "Mercy" is compassionate treatment for those who don't deserve it or who can't afford it. The two blind men in Jericho cried, "Have mercy on us, O Lord." The Canaanite woman in Matthew 15 cried, "Have mercy on me, O Lord, Son of David!" The ten lepers in Luke 17 cried, "Jesus, Master, have mercy on us!" The publican in Luke 18 said, "God, be merciful to me a sinner!" Warren Wiersbe puts it this way: "Grace is what God gives me that I don't deserve; mercy is what God doesn't give me that I do deserve." Have you cried out to God for mercy?

2. **A New Birth.** "Blessed be the God and Father of our Lord Jesus Christ, who according to His abundant mercy *has begotten us again.*" A painter on a Paris sidewalk set up his easel, opened his paints, and started to paint a picture called "Life." He noticed pigeons in the park, tulips blooming along the

Champs-Elysees, and the bustle of people on the street. But he messed up his painting. His colors weren't true and his perspective was poor. Looking at his work with disfavor, he threw it away. He took another canvas and started "Life" all over again. Jesus allows us to do that through the new birth.

3. **A Living Hope.** Some people go through life *moping* around. Some by *groping* for answers. Some by *coping* as well as they can. The Christian responds by *hoping*, and not just empty positivism, but a durable optimism grounded in God's promises. Christians are optimistic about: (1) The here and now; and about (2) The "by and by."

4. **A Risen Lord.** "...has begotten us again to a living hope through the resurrection of Jesus Christ from the dead." Our burdens are swallowed up by the empty tomb, and our tomorrows are as bright as the flash of His resurrection victory.

Conclusion: During one difficult period when things appeared especially bleak, the reformer Martin Luther was seen tracing two words on the table with his fingertip: *Vivit, vivit!* —"He lives, He lives!" And because Christ lives, we can live abundantly today and eternally tomorrow, a life that is both forgiven and forever. So lift up your hearts, focus on your Lord, put on a smile, and say: Blessed be the God and Father of my Lord Jesus Christ, who according to His abundant mercy has begotten me again to a living hope through the resurrection of Jesus Christ from the dead.

APPROPRIATE HYMNS AND SONGS

O God Our Help in Ages Past, Isaac Watts/William Croft; Public Domain.

Teach Me Thy Way, O Lord, Benjamin Mansell Ramsey; Public Domain.

Surely Goodness and Mercy, John W. Peterson/Alfred B. Smith; © 1954 Singspiration Music (Admin. by Brentwood-Benson Music Publishing, Inc.).

Everlasting Hope, Chrissy Cymbala; © 1991 Word Music Group, Inc.

Hope in God, Dennis Jernigan; © 1994 Shepherd's Heart Music, Inc. (Admin. by Word Music Group, Inc.).

KidsTalk

Pull out a handkerchief to show the children. Ask, "What can you learn about me from my handkerchief?" Have them suggest answers. You might have a cold, you might sweat a lot, etc. Ask, "When I use my handkerchief like this, what does it mean?" Pretend to cry and wipe your eyes. "Now, when I use my handkerchief like this, what does it mean?" Wave it over your head like a banner or tie it to a dowel and wave it like a flag. Say, "Sometimes we have to wipe our eyes. We sometimes cry. But usually, we should have our handkerchiefs up in the air celebrating life, for God wants us to be happy people.

FOR THE BULLETIN

● On March 3, 1547, the Council of Trent began affirming the seven sacraments of the Roman church, all of them, it said, necessary for salvation: Baptism, Confirmation, the Eucharist, Penance, Extreme Unction, Orders, and Matrimony. The Protestant view of two divine ordinances — baptism and the Lord's Supper — was rejected. ● Alexander Graham Bell, inventor of the telephone, was born on March 3, 1847. ● Missionary Mary Paton died of tropical fever on March 3, 1859, four months after arriving on the island of Tanna with her husband, John. The couple's baby boy died shortly afterward, and John was forced to leave the island with no apparent results. John Paton later remarried and became a world-renowned missionary. A son from his second marriage eventually resumed the work on Tanna and won that island for Christ. ● On Friday, March 3, 1871, Frank W. Boreham was born in Tunbridge Wells, England. His birth was accompanied by the sound of peeling bells, blasting rockets, and salvoes of artillery, for that day Europe was celebrating the end of the Franco-Prussian war. In time, F. W. Boreham became a powerful pastor, preacher, and writer, the author of numerous devotional books which are now considered classics. ● On March 3, 1931, *The Star Spangled Banner* was adopted as America's national anthem. Its author, Francis Scott Key, was an evangelical Christian who taught a Bible class for children and until his death served as vice-president of the American Sunday School Union and was an outspoken witness for Christ.

WORSHIP HELPS

Worship Theme:
Praise God who has given us a living hope through the resurrection of Christ.

Call to Worship:
1 Peter 1:3: Praise be to the God and Father of our Lord Jesus Christ. In God's great mercy he has caused us to be born again into a living hope, because Jesus Christ rose from the dead (NCV).

Applicable Scripture Readings:
John 3:1–8
Psalm 86:1–7
1 Peter 1:22–25

Responsive Reading from Titus 2:11–14:

Leader:	For the grace of God that brings salvation has appeared to all men...
People:	Teaching us that, denying ungodliness and worldly lusts, we should live soberly, righteously, and godly in the present age...
Leader:	Looking for the blessed hope and glorious appearing of our great God and Savior Jesus Christ...
People:	Who gave Himself for us, that He might redeem us from every lawless deed and purify for Himself His own special people, zealous for good works.

STATS, STORIES AND MORE

Someone Once Said:
"Our prayer and God's mercy are like two buckets in a well; while the one ascends the other descends."
—*Mark Hopkins, U.S. Educator (1802–1887)*

"Life with Christ is an endless hope, without Him a hopeless end."
—*Anonymous*

"The biggest fact about Joseph's tomb was that it wasn't a tomb at all—it was a room for a transient. Jesus just stopped there a night or two on his way back to glory."
—*Herbert Booth Smith*

New Beginning
Joe McUtchen preaches the gospel each Wednesday night at Safehouse, an urban ministry in Atlanta. A drug addict named Willy began attending and responding to the message. Seeing his progress, Safehouse placed Willy in a Christian rehab program in Tampa. Some months later, Willy called Joe. "Joe, when I got here they asked me about my addictions, and they helped me through withdrawals. They talked to me about God. When they found out I used to be a master chef, they called around and got me a job at the Ritz-Carlton. In my rehab program I learned that I should do everything with all my heart, like I was doing it for God. Now I'm head chef at the Ritz-Carlton. I'd like to come back to Safehouse some Wednesday and give my testimony."

"That'd be great, Willy," said Joe. "And while you're here, Judy and I would like for you to stay with us. No need to pay for a room."

There was a pause on the line, then Willy said, "That's not necessary, Joe. When I come to Atlanta, there's already a room waiting for me. I'll be staying at the Ritz."

Lyle Schaller on "Hope"
In his book, *44 Ways to Increase Church Attendance*, church growth guru Lyle Schaller suggests that growing churches must offer a note of hope. "Perhaps the most common characteristic of churches that are attracting increasing numbers of people today is not where the minister is on the theological spectrum or the denominational affiliation, but on what people hear and feel during the worship experience. [People need] a note of hope."

Additional Sermons and Lesson Ideas

Sweeter Than Honey
Date preached:

SCRIPTURE: Psalm 19:10; Psalm 119:103

INTRODUCTION: Traveling in Scotland, Charles Spurgeon found an old, worn Bible. He thumbed through it and noticed a small hole where a worm had eaten its way from cover to cover. "Lord," exclaimed Spurgeon, "make me a bookworm like that." We need that prayer, too, for most Christians are poor Bible students, but daily Bible study provides three qualities to our lives:

1. **Fellowship with the Savior.** Prayer and the Bible are our channels of communication with the Lord.
2. **Food for the Soul.** The Bible does for our hearts what food does for our bodies—it nourishes, strengthens, satisfies, and actually *becomes* us, for "we are what we eat."
3. **A Formula for Success.** We can find this formula at the beginning, middle, and end of the Bible
   A. Joshua 1:8
   B. Psalm 1:1–3
   C. James 1:5

As we read God's words and thoughts, chewing on them, meditating, digesting and assimilating them into our own minds, we begin increasingly to think as God does, and His thoughts are always successful.

Evening Song
Date preached:

SCRIPTURE: Psalm 3

BACKGROUND: The heading for this Psalm gives us a tragic background—the rebellion of David's son Absalom. That evening David found himself:

- Hated by his subjects
- Hunted by his son
- Haunted in his spirit

Under those conditions, he composed Psalm 3. Its eight simple verses fall into four stanzas of two verses each, having to do with:

1. **His Soul** (vv. 1–2). David's soul was cast down. Many considered his circumstances hopeless.
2. **His Shield** (vv. 3–4). In this situation, David remembered that God was a shield completely encircling him.
3. **His Sleep** (vv. 5–6). Surrounded by such a God, David was able to lay down and sleep unafraid.
4. **His Salvation** (vv. 7–8). Salvation, not just from our sins but from our circumstances, belongs to the Lord. No one ever cares for us like Jesus.

MARCH 10, 2002

By Grace Through Faith
Date preached:

Scripture: Ephesians 2:1–10, especially verses 8–9 For by grace you have been saved through faith, and that not of yourselves; it is the gift of God, not of works, lest anyone should boast.

Introduction: In the mid-1500s, when Peter Gabriel began preaching Reformation truth in the reeds and thickets throughout Holland, it was announced there would be a great service outside Amsterdam on July 14, 1566. Authorities shut the city gates, but people swam the canals or forced their way out in the early hours when the milkmaids left for the fields. Thousands gathered. Gabriel announced his text—Ephesians 2:8–10—and preached for four hours, but nobody minded. They hadn't heard the gospel in a thousand years, and they were hungry for its message. Gabriel's sermon that day helped establish the Reformation in Holland. Today's sermon won't last four hours, but it's from the same text. Listen to it as if you were hearing it for the first time in a thousand years.

The theme of the passage is salvation by grace through faith (vv. 5, 8). In church language, we say, "I got saved on such and such a date." The word means, "to rescue from danger, to deliver." Some years ago, there was a flash flood in Tennessee. A woman recovering from hip surgery was confined to bed. The flood occurred at night, and the waters swept into her house. Unable to save herself, she was in danger of drowning in her own bed until the paramedics arrived and rescued her. We are sinners; we can't save ourselves. We need a divine paramedic to rescue us from drowning in the floodtides of God's wrath. When we trust Jesus Christ as our personal Savior we are saved.

1. **Human Condition** (vv. 1–3). Verses 1–3 describe the hopelessness of our human condition.
    - Dead in our sins (v. 1). Most of our politicians, business leaders, educators, journalists, and work associates are dead. This world is being run by people who are spiritually and eternally dead.
    - Walking according to the course of this world (v. 2; see Matt. 7:13–14).
    - Following the prince of the power of the air (v. 2), Satan, whose

demonic hosts fill the air and pollute the atmosphere.

- Following the spirit now at work in the disobedient (v. 2).
- Gratifying the cravings of the flesh (v. 3).
- Objects of wrath (v. 3).

2. **Divine Motivation** (v. 4). "But God, who is rich in mercy, because of His great love with which He loved us…"
   - His Rich Mercy
   - His Great Love

3. **Eternal Salvation** (vvs. 5–9).
   - God makes us alive in Christ.
   - He seats us with Christ in heavenly realms.
   - He will show us the incomparable riches of His grace. Paul wrote this while imprisoned in Rome, but he had the attitude of someone living in heavenly realms.

Conclusion: When Charles Spurgeon was a teen, he was asked to preach at his grandfather's church in Suffolk. His train was late, so Grandfather Spurgeon began the sermon, preaching from Ephesians 2:8–9. There was a commotion at the door, and in walked Charles. "Here comes my grandson," exclaimed the old man. "He can preach the gospel better than I can, but you cannot preach a better gospel, can you, Charles?" Charles replied, "You can preach better than I can. Please go on." The grandfather refused, but he explained to Charles where he was in his sermon. The younger preacher stepped to the pulpit and took over

>>> *sermon continued on following page*

APPROPRIATE HYMNS AND SONGS

Amazing Grace, John Newton/Edwin Excell/John P. Rees; Public Domain.

Grace Alone, Scott Wesley Brown/Jeff Nelson; © 1998 Maranatha! Music.

Wonderful Grace of Jesus, Lillenas/Haldor; Public Domain.

All That Thrills My Soul Is Jesus, Thoro Harris; © 1931 Mrs. Thoro Harris. Renewed 1959 Nazarene Publishing House-Lillenas (Admin. by The Copyright Company).

Behold the Lamb, Dottie Rambo; © 1979 John T. Benson Publishing Company (Admin. by Brentwood-Benson Music Publishing, Inc.).

just where his grandfather had left off. After a few minutes, the grandfather interrupted, wanting to preach a little more. Then he sat down again, and Charles resumed, with his grandfather sitting behind him, saying, "Good! Tell them that again, Charles. Tell them that again." Ever after, Charles Spurgeon said that whenever he preached from Ephesians 2, he could hear his grandfather whispering, "Tell them that again, Charles. Tell them that again."

Maybe you've heard this truth before, but I'm glad to tell you again: By grace are we saved through faith. Perhaps you are dead in your sins, following the ways of the world, gratifying the cravings of your sinful nature, an object of wrath. God in His great love and rich mercy, wants to raise you from the dead, seat you with Himself in the heavenly reams, and show you the incomparable riches of his grace in Christ Jesus. Will you come to Him today?

FOR THE BULLETIN

❂ This is "Mothering Day" in the United Kingdom, the British version of "Mother's Day." ❂ Balthasar Hubmaier, one of the foremost leaders of the Austrian Anabaptists, was burned at the stake as a heretic in the public square of Vienna on March 10, 1528. Three days later his faithful wife was drowned in the Danube. Hubmaier was called "one of the purest spirits of the Reformation." ❂ On or about March 10, 1554, Nicholas Ridley, bishop of London, along with Thomas Cramner, archbishop of Canterbury, and Hugh Latimer, were taken from their cells in the Tower of London to Oxford University to debate Reformation truth with the professors there. From there, the three heroes were sent to the common prison at Barcardo and later executed. ❂ A foul-mouthed, lascivious sailor was terrified when a storm struck his ship on March 10, 1748. "Almost every passing wave broke over my head," he wrote. "I expected that every time the vessel descended into the sea, she would rise no more. I dreaded death...." He survived the storm, and shortly afterward, John Newton discovered God's amazing grace. ❂ The U.S. government issued paper money for the first time on March 10, 1862. ❂ George Mueller was a German who, following a life of sin and imprisonment, became a far-famed Christian, opening orphanages in England and doing evangelistic work around the globe. His efforts procured millions of dollars for Christian causes, but when he died on this day in 1898 (age 93), his possessions were valued at $800.

WORSHIP HELPS

Worship Theme:
God, who is rich in mercy and great in love, has saved us by grace through faith.

Call to Worship:
"Not by works of righteousness which we have done, but according to His mercy He saved us, through the washing of regeneration and renewing of the Holy Spirit, whom He poured out on us abundantly through Jesus Christ our Savior" (Titus 3:5–6).

Readers' Theatre:

Both:	But now the righteousness of God apart from the law is revealed, being witnessed by the Law and the Prophets.
Reader 1:	Even the righteousness of God, through faith in Jesus Christ, to all and on all who believe.
Reader 2:	For there is no difference; for all have sinned and fall short of the glory of God, being justified freely
Reader 1:	by His grace
All:	through the redemption that is in Christ Jesus
Reader 1:	whom God set forth as a propitiation by His blood, through faith...
Both:	that He might be just and the justifier of the one who has faith in Jesus.

Taken from Romans 3:21 and following

Pastoral Prayer:
Our God and Almighty Father, we are self-deceived and self-deceiving people, thinking we're here in our Sunday dress when, according to your Word, all our righteousness is as filthy rags. Teach us our sinfulness in the light of your holiness, but we also ask you to teach us your love in the light of our sinfulness. Amazing love! Amazing grace! O Lamb of God, we come.

"Children of Wrath"

"Children of wrath" is a Hebrew idiomatic phrase meaning we are under the sentence of wrath, facing the wrath of God. This doesn't mean that God is mad at us in an immature or juvenile sort of way. It refers to God's right and necessary response to objective moral evil. In John, chapter 3, we have the wonderful 16th verse, but we forget that the last verse of that chapter says: "He who believes in the Son has everlasting life; and he who does not believe the Son shall not see life, but the wrath of God abides on him."

The *Hindenburg* was a German airship that arrived in America on May 6, 1937, after cruising across the Atlantic. It was coming in for a landing at an airfield in New Jersey at 7:25 at night, and it was a thrilling sight, three football fields in length, held aloft by 7 million cubit feet of hydrogen. It could fly 84 miles an hour. It was luxurious, with a dining salon, lounges, and staterooms. Gigantic Nazi swastikas were painted on its tail fins. Hundreds of people gathered to watch it land. Suddenly a lapping tongue of fire appeared near the stern, and within a few seconds the *Hindenburg* exploded in a huge ball of fire, falling tail first with flames shooting out the nose. In one moment, the wonder and excitement and beauty was turned to fire and terror and destruction.

Without Christ all of us are passengers aboard the *Hindenburg*. We may be enjoying ourselves to the fullest, but we don't realize that the next moment is going to bring us to judgment.

Amazing Grace

"What is grace? I know until you ask me; when you ask me, I do not know."

—*St. Augustine*

"As heat is opposed to cold, and light to darkness, so grace is opposed to sin."

—*Thomas Benton Brooks*

"Grace is but glory begun, and glory is but grace perfected."

—*Jonathan Edwards*

"Grace is free, but when once you take it you are bound forever to the Giver."

—*E. Stanley Jones*

"What but Thy grace can foil the tempter's power?"

—*Henry Francis Lyte in "Abide with Me"*

Additional Sermons and Lesson Ideas

Christ's Cure for Anxious Care

Date preached:

SCRIPTURE: Matthew 6:19–34

INTRODUCTION: Jesus must have understood what worriers we are, because He began and ended His ministry on that theme. In His closing address, the Upper Room Discourse in John 13–16, He told us, "Let not your hearts be troubled" (14:1). He opened His ministry in the same way, in the Sermon on the Mount, saying, "Do not worry..." (Matt 6:25). In this passage, He suggests six steps for overcoming anxious care.

1. **Give yourself fully to Him** (vv. 19–24).
2. **Rejoice in the wonder of each new day** (vv. 25–26).
3. **Admit the futility of worrying** (v. 27).
4. **Remember the loving care of the Almighty** (vv. 28–29).
5. **Trust His faithfulness** (v. 30).
6. **Live one day at a time** (vv. 31–34).

CONCLUSION: Whatever is controlled by the Lord Jesus is patrolled by Him. Whatever is surrendered to His keeping is surrounded by His care. If He feeds the birds and clothes the flowers, He will surely take care of you.

When You Can't Sleep

Date preached:

SCRIPTURE: Job 7:4

INTRODUCTION: Sleeping disorders are nothing new. Several Bible characters also had bouts with insomnia, including Job (Job 7:4), Nebuchadnezzar (Dan. 2:1), Jacob (Gen. 31:40), David (Ps. 6:6), and the lover in Song of Songs (3:1). Sleeplessness can lead to:

1. **Sin.** As with David when he rose in the night and looked on Bathsheba (2 Sam. 11, see also Ps. 36:4).
2. **Study.** Esther 6:1. How often do Christians arise in the night, sleepless, and open their Bibles! (Ps. 1:2; Ps. 119:148; Ps. 63:6).
3. **Service.** (Ps. 141:1; 2 Cor. 11:27). Many a note of encouragement has been penned at midnight.
4. **Singing.** Songs in the night (Acts 16:25; Ps. 42:8, 77:6, 119:62).
5. **Supplication.** (Is. 26.9; Luke 6:12, Lam. 2:19; Dan. 6:18, Ps. 77).

Storytelling in Sermons

An Interview with
Professional Storyteller Steven James

There seems to be a renewed interest in storytelling today.

Storytelling has become big business in the United States. There are more than a thousand storytelling festivals every year throughout the country, and story books (like Chicken Soup) are very popular. People who study communication patterns have found that our country is very image-centered; we listen to stories through images, through movies, television plots. So, yes, we're in a renaissance period of storytelling. This is showing up in the pulpit. Since the 1970s there have been a series of homiletical books that emphasize narrative preaching, image-rich preaching.

How can a pastor tap into this?

One thing I would say is that Jesus told stories, and He didn't always explain them. Part of the power of stories is that they speak for themselves. Sometimes the more you explain a story the less its impact. Trust the power of the stories, and sometimes let the story be the point instead of letting it make the point.

How long should a story be in a sermon?

Sometimes they can be very short and sometimes they can be the entire message. Some of the most effective sermons use a technique known as story-stacking.

Story-stacking?

Jesus didn't typically give three-point sermons. He pretty much preached one-point sermons. He would choose a topic and then stack stories one on top of the other. We call this story-stacking. Each story gives an aspect of the truth, but no story gives all the information in itself. So each of the stories reflects a particular facet of the overall truth, and by stacking the stories together, you present comprehensive teaching. Jesus did this on the subject of the kingdom of God in Matthew 13. He did it with the Second

Coming in Matthew 25. He did it with the lost items in Luke 15. There are even some similar patterns in the Sermon on the Mount. In this type of presentation, you just pile on images, one after another, allowing each image or story to convey an aspect of the overall message.

Where can a pastor find good stories?

In finding stories for my own use, I follow the acronym LIFE. The L stand for Literature. Are there stories that I have read that will work for this sermon? I stands for Imagination. Are there stories I can make up, like parables? The F is for Folklore. Are there stories that people are telling today (contemporary folk tales) or ancient folk tales that will suit my purposes? Then there's Experience. Have things happened in my own life that I can share? Of course, I search the Scriptures, too, looking for parallel stories to include from God's Word.

Would you recommend a pastor write out his sermons and practice his stories aloud?

I would say the second part. Practice the stories out loud. What I encourage people to do is to make notes, but not necessarily to write the story out, for there's the danger they will then try to recite it from memory or to read it, and that isn't good as an extemporaneous delivery. Practice the story several times out loud, telling it different ways until you feel comfortable. Then, if you need to write it down, do so. ✿

MARCH 17, 2002

God's Poems

Date preached:

Scripture: Ephesians 2:8–10, especially verse 10 For we are His workmanship, created in Christ Jesus for good works, which God prepared beforehand that we should walk in them.

Introduction: Writing in the magazine *Challenge,* Tibor Scitovsky, professor emeritus of economics at Stanford University, suggests that high school and youth gang shootings may be caused, in part, by boredom. "What makes those teenagers become so violent in the first place?" he asks. "I suspect that their motivation could well be boredom." He thinks the affluence of our society has fostered too much leisure, and that the fragmentation of the home has left children without proper oversight. The ensuing boredom induces much mischief. God doesn't want His people to be bored.

- "For we are God's masterpiece. He has created us anew in Christ Jesus, so that we can do the good things he planned for us long ago" (NLT).
- "For we are God's workmanship, created in Christ Jesus to do good works, which God prepared in advance for us to do" (NIV).

In Ephesians 2:1–9, Paul insists we are not saved by doing good works. Now, in verse 10, he tells us how important good works are in their proper place. We set about doing good works, not *in order to be saved,* but *because we are saved.* We aren't saved *by* good works, but *for* good works. "Works" is not the condition of our salvation, but the consequence of it.

There are three grammatical phrases in this verse, separated by two commas:

1. **For we are His workmanship.** The Greek word for "workmanship" is ποίημα (*poy´-ay-mah*), from which we get our English word "poem." It means something that is composed or constructed, something that is made. It occurs one other time in the New Testament, in Romans 1:20, referring to God's making of the universe. God is an artisan with two works of which He is unusually proud—His universe and His people. We are thereby "under construction." He is perfecting that which concerns us (Ps. 138:8). He who has begun a good work in us will carry it on to completion (Phil. 1:6).

2. **Created in Christ Jesus for good works.** The importance God attaches to good works is seen in the following verses:
   - Matthew 5:16
   - Acts 9:36
   - 1 Timothy 6:18
   - Titus 2:6, 14 and 3:8, 14
   - Hebrews 10:24
   - 1 Peter 2:11

We get the idea from these verses that by "good works" the Bible means charitable deeds and acts of kindness, not merely sermons, sunday School lessons, and songs. Random acts of kindness make Christianity tangible to the unsaved world. William Penn wrote: "I expect to pass through life but once. If therefore there be any kindness I can show or any good thing I can do to any fellow-being, let me do it now, and not defer or neglect it, for I shall not pass this way again."

3. **Which God prepared beforehand that we should walk in them.** God prepared these good deeds in advance for us to do. Some commentators believe Paul is speaking here in a general way, telling us that God wants us to walk through life doing good works. But as it is translated in several versions, it sounds

>>> *sermon continued on following page*

APPROPRIATE HYMNS AND SONGS

Come Into His Presence, Lynn Baird; © 1983 Integrity's Hosanna! Music (Admin. Integrity Music, Inc.).

Blessed to Be a Blessing, Scott Wesley Brown/Dwight Liles/Niles Borop/Claire Cloninger; © 1988 BMG Songs, Inc. (Admin. by BMG Publishing)/Pamela Kay Music (Admin. by EMI Christian Music Publishing)/Niles Borop Music (Admin. by Integrated Copyright Group, Inc.)/Ariose Music (Admin. by EMI Christian Music Publishing)/Word Music, Inc. (a div. of Word Music Group, Inc.); (Admin. by Word Music Group, Inc.).

How Clear Is Our Vocation Lord, Fred Pratt Green/C. Hubert H. Parry; © 1982 Hope Publishing Co.

I Would Be Like Jesus, James Rowe/Bently D. Ackley; Public Domain.

Little Is Much When God Is In It; Dwight Brock/Mrs. F. W. Kittie Louise Suffield; © 1969 Stamps-Baxter Music (Admin. by Brentwood-Benson Music Publishing, Inc.).

more specific than that. Perhaps God, in His eternal omniscience and sovereignty, has planned out the specific work in advance He desires for us to do. That shouldn't be too surprising. Sometimes we make out lists of assignments for our children, as do teachers for their students.

- Jeremiah's work was assigned before his birth (Jer. 1:1–2).
- Paul was set apart from his mother's womb to take the gospel to the Gentiles (Gal. 1:15).
- Every day of my life was recorded in your book. Every moment was laid out before a single day had passed (Ps. 139:16 TLB).

Conclusion: Christians should never be bored, for God has specific work for each of us to do. We aren't saved by doing work, but we do works because we're saved. Perhaps you're saying, "I don't have a clue as to what God wants me to do. How do I find out?" Remember that "good works" are often tantamount to acts of kindness done in the name of Christ. Just look around for someone you can help or encourage, for an opportunity to do something kind for someone with no thought of a favor in return. Be a blessing to someone today, and brighten the corner where you are.

FOR THE BULLETIN

❋ St. Patrick was born in A.D. 373, along the banks of the River Clyde in what is now called Scotland. When he was 16, raiders kidnapped and enslaved him in Ireland. There Patrick submitted his life to Christ and afterward escaped and returned home. But Patrick couldn't get his Irish captors from his mind. One night, he dreamed of an Irish man begging him to come evangelize Ireland. It wasn't an easy decision, but Patrick, about 30, said his good-byes and returned to his former captors with the Latin Bible under his arm. As he evangelized the countryside, multitudes came to listen. He later wrote, "For I am very much God's debtor, who gave me such grace that many people were reborn in God through me and afterwards confirmed, and that clerics were ordained for them everywhere, for a people just coming to the faith." He died, according to tradition, on this day in A.D. 461. ❋ On March 17, 1513, affable young Giovanni de' Medici was consecrated to the priesthood, having already been named pope. As Pope Leo X, he revived the sale of indulgences to finance the building of the Church of St. Peter's in Rome, sparking the Reformation under Martin Luther. ❋ March 17, 1780 is the birthday of Thomas Chalmers, powerful leader of the Free Church of Scotland and one of the greatest preachers of his age.

WORSHIP HELPS

Worship Theme:
As those saved by grace, we should be kind, letting our good works bring glory to God.

Call to Worship:
"Enter into His gates with thanksgiving, And into His courts with praise. Be thankful to Him, and bless His name. For the LORD is good; His mercy is everlasting, And His truth endures to all generations" (Ps. 100:4–5).

Scripture Reading:
"Remind them to be subject to rulers and authorities, to obey, to be ready for every good work, to speak evil of no one, to be peaceable, gentle, showing all humility to all men. For we ourselves were also once foolish, disobedient, deceived, serving various lusts and pleasures, living in malice and envy, hateful and hating one another. But when the kindness and the love of God our Savior toward man appeared, not by works of righteousness which we have done, but according to His mercy He saved us, through the washing of regeneration and renewing of the Holy Spirit, whom He poured out on us abundantly through Jesus Christ our Savior, that having been justified by His grace we should become heirs according to the hope of eternal life.

This is a faithful saying, and these things I want you to affirm constantly, that those who have believed in God should be careful to maintain good works. These things are good and profitable to men" (Titus 3:1–8).

Kids Talk

Tell the children the story of Dorcas from Acts 9:36–43. Ask the children to guess about some of the "good works" and "charitable deeds" that she did. Perhaps she made and gave a robe to a child who didn't have enough clothes. Perhaps she set an extra plate at the table for a stranger. Then ask the children if they can think of any ways in which they can be kind to someone during the coming week. End with Ephesians 4:32: "And be kind to one another."

STATS, STORIES AND MORE

Someone Once Said . . .

"Kindness is a language the blind can see and the deaf can hear."

—*Anonymous*

"Life is not made up of great sacrifices and duties but of little things: in which smiles and kindness given habitually are what win and preserve the heart."

—*Sir Humphrey Davy, English chemist (1778 - 1829)*

"You cannot do a kindness too soon, for you never know how soon it will be too late."

—*Ralph Waldo Emerson*

Proverbs From Around the World

"One kind word can warm three winter months."

—*Japanese Proverb*

"Write injuries in sand, kindnesses in marble."

—*French Proverb*

"With a sweet tongue of kindness, you can drag an elephant by a hair."

—*Persian Proverb*

Small, but Long

Kindness usually consists of small things, but simple acts of kindness may be long remembered. Christopher Williams still remembers when he was serving with the Marines in Kaneohe Bay, Hawaii. Receiving news that his father had passed away, he rushed to get home. "The only thing nice I had to wear [to the funeral]," he said, "was my dress blues. I wanted to get a fresh haircut."

The barbershop in Mokapu Mall was crowded, but, needing to get to the airport, Williams explained his situation to one of the barbers, a lady named Nhanh Pham. She moved the Marine to next in line and gave special attention to his haircut. When he started to pay her, she told him the haircut was free. Not only that, but she gave him money the other barbers in the shop had collected while he'd been there. They wanted to make sure Williams could buy flowers for the funeral.

Because of the kind gesture, the barbers were later presented a certificate of commendation from Willams' commanding officers in the Marine Corps.

What kindness have you done this week for which the Lord could present you with a certificate of commendation?

Additional Sermons and Lesson Ideas

A Hurt Only God Can Heal

Date preached:

SCRIPTURE: 1 Samuel 2:1–10

INTRODUCTION: The prophet Samuel, a man of prayer, learned the art of prayer from his mother. Out of the 37 verses about Hannah in the Bible, 23 describe her at prayer. In chapter 1, she took a hurt only God could heal and turned it into a prayer only God could hear. In chapter 2, she offered praise only God deserved.

1. **God Satisfies the Soul** (v. 1). Contrast with her story in chapter 1. When everything seems against us, we find God alone satisfies our souls.
2. **God Rectifies the Score** (vv. 2–5). Hannah left her enemies with the Lord.
3. **God Fortifies the Saved** (vv. 6–9a). In prayer, we gain new strength.
4. **God Glories the Son** (vv. 9b-10). This is a prophecy about Christ, and it's the first time in Scripture He's given the title Messiah. The virgin Mary later used this prayer as a basis for her own Magnificat.

CONCLUSION: Learn to turn hurts only God can heal into prayers only He can hear.

The Trinity As Seen in Three Birds

Date preached:

SCRIPTURE: Isaiah 40:9: "Behold your God"

INTRODUCTION: One of the most interesting observations about the Trinity was made by the British divine, Dr. Geoffrey King. God, he once said, has identified Himself with three birds in the Bible, each one teaching us something of His care and concern for us.

1. **God the Father is Like an Eagle.** He majestically cares for us (Ex. 19:4; Deut. 32:11; Isa. 40:31).
2. **God the Son is Like a Hen.** He longs to guard and protects us like a hen her chicks (Matthew 23:37).
3. **God the Holy Spirit is Like a Dove.** He wants to descend on us with power and purity (Matthew 3:16).

CONCLUSION: How creative is our God. How wonderfully He wants to show us Himself in simple ways even a child can understand. Let Him bear you up. Let Him shelter your soul. Let Him impart power and purity to your life.

MARCH 24, 2002

Everyone Loves a Parade

Date preached:

Scripture: Matthew 21:1–17, especially verses 7–16 They brought the donkey and the colt, laid their clothes on them, and set Him on them. And a very great multitude spread their clothes on the road; others cut down branches from the trees and spread them on the road. Then the multitudes who went before and those who followed cried out, saying: "Hosanna to the Son of David! 'Blessed is He who comes in the name of the LORD!' Hosanna in the highest!"

Then Jesus went into the temple of God and drove out all those who bought and sold in the temple, and overturned the tables of the money changers and the seats of those who sold doves. And He said to them, "It is written, 'My house shall be called a house of prayer,' but you have made it a 'den of thieves.'"

Then the blind and the lame came to Him in the temple, and He healed them. But when the chief priests and scribes saw the wonderful things that He did, and the children crying out in the temple and saying, "Hosanna to the Son of David!" they were indignant and said to Him, "Do You hear what these are saying?"

And Jesus said to them, "Yes. Have you never read, 'Out of the mouth of babes and nursing infants You have perfected praise'?"

Introduction: Everyone loves a parade—especially children. I remember one of my first parades, a Christmas parade in my hometown with the bands and floats and characters. My dad hoisted me onto his shoulders so I can get a better look through the crowds. The atmosphere in Jerusalem on Palm Sunday was much like that. Lots of children probably sat atop their father's shoulders. Others were running here and there, peeping through legs, pushing and shoving for a good view of the most famous and controversial person in Palestine who was passing by on a four-legged convertible.

As Matthew tells the story, he punctuates it with Old Testament quotations. There are no less than five of them:

- About the donkey (Zech. 9:9).
- The cry of the crowds (Psalm 118:26).
- His entrance into the temple (Isaiah 56:7).
- The nature of His house (Jeremiah 7:11).
- From the lips of children (Psalm 8:2).

These five Scriptures were all fulfilled in one tumultuous parade, and they seem to outline the course of our Christian experience:

1. **Christ Enters our Lives.** He wants to enter our lives just as He entered Jerusalem on that bright springtime day. He comes riding on the Holy Spirit, and it's a grand event. Before football coach Tom Landry died, he shared his testimony many times. As a youngster he had said, "If I can just be part of a championship team, I would have everything." As a high school player, he said, "If I can just play college football. . . ." As a college player, he said, "If I can just go on to professional football. . . ." As a professional player, he said, "If I could just be on a championship team. . . ." He reached every goal, but he said, "Everything and every accomplishment left me the same way after the enthusiasm wore off." Until He met Christ. "I found out for the first time," he said, "what Jesus meant when He said, 'I have come that they might have life, and have it more abundantly.'"

2. **He Induces Thanksgiving.** As He enters our lives, we want to shout, "Hosanna! Praise! Glory to God in the Highest!"

3. **He Cleanses Us and Makes Us People of Prayer.** The first thing Jesus did, having entered Jerusalem, was this: He went straight to the heart of the

>>> *sermon continued on following page*

APPROPRIATE HYMNS AND SONGS

All Glory, Laud and Honor, Theodulf of Orleans, translated by John M. Neale/Melchior Teschner; Public Domain.

Hosanna, Loud Hosanna, Jenette Threlfall/From Gesanbuch der Herzogl, Wurtemburg, 1784; Public Domain.

In the Name of the Lord, Sandi Patty/Phil McHugh/Gloria Gaither; 1986 William J. Gaither, Inc./Sandi's Songs Music (Admin by Gaither Copyright Management)/River Oaks Music Company (a div. of EMI Christian Music Publishing).

We Will Glorify, Twila Paris; © 1982 Singspiration Music (Admin. by Brentwood-Benson Publishing, Inc.).

Shout to the Lord, Darlene Zschech; © 1993 Darlene Zschech (Hillsong) (Admin. by Integrity Music, Inc.).

city—the temple—and began throwing things out. He does the same with us, going right to the center of our souls. He overturns, renovates, and rearranges our lives. He says, "Your life is a den of iniquity. I want to make it into a house of prayer."

4. **He Draws Forth Our Praise.** Matthew reminds us at the end of this passage that from the lips of children and infants God has ordained praise.

Conclusion: This Palm Sunday is a wonderful day to let this process begin with you. Perhaps you feel your life is as confused as the bedlam in the courtyard of Jerusalem's temple. Jesus wants to ride into your life, give you a "Hosanna," overturn some habits, teach you to pray, and He desires your praise. Come to the one about whom it was said, "Hosanna! Blessed is He who comes in the name of the Lord! Hosanna in the highest!"

FOR THE BULLETIN

❋ In the eleventh century, two rival popes were locked in battle, Victor IV at the Vatican, and Alexander III at Anagni, Italy. A church council decided in favor of Victor and excommunicated Alexander. On March 24, 1160, Alexander issued a counter-excommunication, creating a conflict that divided Europe for years. ❋ When England's king, John Lackland, objected to the pope's choice for archbishop of Canterbury, England was placed under an interdict on March 24, 1208. The conflict was among the debacles that weakened the king, forcing him to sign the Magna Carta at Runnymede in 1215. ❋ On this day in 1603, Queen Elizabeth I died. James VI of Scotland acceded to the throne as James I, uniting the thrones of Scotland and England, and authorizing a new English translation of the Bible. ❋ Today is the birthday of the blind hymn writer, Fanny Crosby, born in 1820. Her 8,000 songs include: "Rescue the Perishing," "Blessed Assurance," "To God Be the Glory," and "All the Way My Savior Leads Me." ❋ On March 24, 1874, as Philip Bliss sang his own song, "Almost Persuaded," at an evangelistic campaign, he was deeply moved. The next day he surrendered to full-time Christian service. Three years later Bliss, 38, perished in a train wreck in Ohio, leaving behind such hymns as "Hallelujah, What a Savior," "Jesus Loves Even Me," and "Wonderful Words of Life," and the music for "It Is Well With My Soul." ❋ March 24, 1904 is the birthday of Malcolm Muggeridge.

Worship Theme:
When Jesus enters our lives, He changes our habits and attitudes, but He brings joy and praise.

Call to Worship:
"Hosanna to the Son of David! 'Blessed is He who comes in the name of the LORD!' Hosanna in the highest!" (Matt. 21:9).

Responsive Reading:

Leader:	Save now, I pray, O LORD;
People:	O LORD, I pray, send now prosperity.
Leader:	Blessed is he who comes in the name of the LORD! We have blessèd you from the house of the LORD.
People:	God is the LORD, And He has given us light;
Leader:	Bind the sacrifice with cords to the horns of the altar.
People:	You are my God, and I will praise You; You are my God, I will exalt You.
Everyone:	Oh, give thanks to the LORD, for He is good! For His mercy endures forever.

Taken from Psalm 118:25–29.

Pastoral Prayer:
Eternal God, we praise You today with the word *Hosanna!* Blessed is He who came in the name of the Lord. Blessed is our Lord Jesus, born in the straw of Bethlehem, raised in the mountains of Galilee, slain on the cross of Calvary. May this be a holy week for us, and may this hour of worship be pleasing to You as we lift up our hands and our heads and our hearts. In Jesus's name, Amen.

Benediction:
Keep us safe through this day, O Lord. Keep us safe through this week until we again return to praise Your Name in the assembly of the saints. Amen.

The Meaning of "Hosanna!"

The word "Hosanna" is only found in the Gospel accounts of Palm Sunday (Matt. 21; Mark 11; John 12). It is a transliteration of the Hebrew and the Aramaic, meaning "save now, we pray," but, as used by the crowds on Palm Sunday, it was more praise than prayer. The Hebrew version of the word, found in Psalm 118:25, was originally a cry for God's help, but in the Gospels, as a cry of joy or a shout of welcome by the Palm Sunday crowds, it indicates they saw in Him the fulfillment of their messianic hopes.

All Glory, Laud, and Honor

As the 700s rolled into the 800s, the greatest man in the world was Charlemagne, King of the Franks and Holy Roman Emperor. Having gained control of most of Western Europe, he set himself to reform the legal, judicial, and military systems of his empire. He established schools and promoted Christianity; and in his capital, scholars and saints gathered from across Europe.

Among them was Theodulf. He was about fifty years old in A.D. 800, and he possessed an established reputation as churchman, poet, and scholar. Charlemagne made him Bishop of Orleans in Spain, and Theodulf traveled widely, taking part in the great events of the empire. Upon the death of the Alcuin, Charlemagne's "Secretary of Education," Theodulf advanced to that position. Unfortunately, Theodulf's fortunes died when Charlemagne did. Accused by the new emperor of treason, he was imprisoned in the monastery of Angers. He stoutly maintained his innocence and was pardoned in 818; but he died shortly afterward and was buried on September 19, 821.

Theodulf of Orleans is best remembered, however, for his beautiful hymn *Gloria, Laus et Honor*, which has been sung every Palm Sunday for over a thousand years in churches around the world. It was reportedly written during his imprisonment:

> *All glory, laud, and honor*
> *To Thee, Redeemer, King,*
> *To whom the lips of children*
> *Make sweet hosannas ring:*
> *Thou art the King of Israel,*
> *Thou David's royal Son,*
> *Who in the Lord's name comest,*
> *The King and blessed one!*

Additional Sermons and Lesson Ideas

The Way of the Cross

Date preached:

SCRIPTURE: Matthew 27:35–50

INTRODUCTION: This week, thousands of pilgrims will journey to Jerusalem, to the Via Dolorosa. Others will hike down the steep, narrow street that leads from the Mount of Olives to Gethsemane, the traditional Palm Sunday walk. I'd like for us to take a pilgrimage this morning, too.

1. **Gethsemane.** Here we learn about yielding to the Lord's will in prayer.
2. **Gabbatha.** Here, at the pavement where Christ was condemned, we learn of suffering.
3. **Golgotha.** Here we see the full measure of God's love.
4. **The Grave.** The disciples buried not only their Lord, but their hope, their courage, their future.
5. **The Garden.** Here in the garden tomb we see our Risen Lord. If Christ can conquer death, He can meet every other need we face.

CONCLUSION: During this Holy Week, fix your thoughts on Jesus. Walk where He walked, and feel His presence near.

Advance Information

Date preached:

SCRIPTURE: Luke 24: 25–27

INTRODUCTION: Our faith in Christ isn't based on wishful thinking, nor does it consist of blind leaps. Jesus provided "many infallible proofs," including fulfilled Old Testament prophecy. Every phase of our Lord's passion was predicted. Some examples:

- Betrayed by a friend (Ps. 41:9; 55:12–14).
- Sold for 30 pieces of silver, thrown on the floor of a temple and later given to a potter (Zech. 11:12–13).
- Accused by false witnesses (Ps. 109:2).
- Silent before accusers (Isa. 53:7).
- Mocked and Beaten (Isa. 50:6; 53:5).
- Pierced in hands and feet (Ps. 22:16).
- Crucified with thieves (Isa. 53:9, 12).
- Ridiculed (Ps. 22:7).
- Garments gambled away (Ps. 22:18).
- Agonized by thirst (Ps. 22:15).
- No bones broken (Ex. 12:46; Num. 9:12; Ps. 34:20).
- Pierced (Ps. 22:16; Zech. 12:10).
- Buried with the rich (Isa. 53:9).

CONCLUSION: God told us *before* it happened, so that we might believe *after* it happened. Put your faith in Christ today, who loved you and gave Himself for you.

MARCH 31, 2002

The Easter Outlook

Date preached:

Scripture: Matthew 28:1–8 Now after the Sabbath, as the first day of the week began to dawn, Mary Magdalene and the other Mary came to see the tomb. And behold, there was a great earthquake; for an angel of the Lord descended from heaven, and came and rolled back the stone from the door, and sat on it. His countenance was like lightning, and his clothing as white as snow. And the guards shook for fear of him, and became like dead men.

But the angel answered and said to the women, "Do not be afraid, for I know that you seek Jesus who was crucified. He is not here; for He is risen, as He said. Come, see the place where the Lord lay. And go quickly and tell His disciples that He is risen from the dead, and indeed He is going before you into Galilee; there you will see Him. Behold, I have told you."

So they went out quickly from the tomb with fear and great joy, and ran to bring His disciples word.

Introduction: In his farewell address to the nation just before leaving office, President George Washington included this sentence: "Let us with caution indulge the supposition, that morality can be maintained without religion." But a recent survey, conducted by the non-partisan, New York based agency, Public Agenda, found that 58% of all Americans say that it is not necessary to believe in God to be moral or have good values. We've entered a post-Christian consciousness in which people want to have a spiritual dimension to their lives, but don't want to be tied down to a Christian theology. On this Easter, we uphold the reality of the bodily resurrection of Christ from a Jerusalem grave. It is only the resurrection of Christ that gives us a foundation for morality, spirituality, and even rationality (1 Cor. 15:12–19). More than that, it is Easter that gives us our distinctively Christian outlook on life. What impact did Easter make on the women who made their way to the tomb in Matthew 28? What did it do for them? How did it change them? And how can we have the same experience today? Easter gives us:

1. **Steady Nerves.** "Do not be afraid." Many of us are subconsciously dominated by fear, worry, and anxiety. According to current statistics, anxiety disorders are the number one mental health problem in the United States. One study

showed that the odds of developing an anxiety disorder have doubled in the past four decades (World Health Organization). These women were nervous and afraid, but the first syllables of the Easter message was: "Do not be afraid." Because of Easter, we can have steady nerves.

2. **Awestruck Minds.** "For I know that you seek Jesus who was crucified. He is not here; for He is risen, as He said. Come, see the place where the Lord lay." Imagine how thunderstruck were these women, full of wonder and amazement. Evangelist Gipsy Smith used to say, "I've never lost the wonder." A fan once startled Mark Twain by telling the famous author, "I wish I had never read *Huckleberry Finn*." With a scowl, the great humorist asked the reason for such a remark. "So that I could have the pleasure again of reading it for the first time," came the reply. Come to the empty tomb and wonder at the Easter miracle as though you were hearing it for the first time.

3. **Open Mouths.** "And go quickly and tell His disciples that He is risen from the dead." A message this great demands sharing. If you were to win a million dollars or be honored in a special way, you'd want to share the news with your closest friends. Notice how brief was the turnaround time between hearing and telling. These women went immediately to share their news.

>>> *sermon continued on following page*

APPROPRIATE HYMNS AND SONGS

Christ Arose, Robert Lowry; Public Domain.

Christ the Lord Is Risen Today, Charles Wesley; Public Domain.

Celebrate Jesus, Gary Oliver; © 1988 Integrity's Hosanna! Music (Admin. by Integrity Music, Inc.)

Easter Song, Anne Herring; © 1974 Latter Rain Music (Admin. by EMI Christian Music Publishing).

Christ Is Risen, Graham Kendrick; © 1989 Make Way Music (Admin. by Music Services).

4. **High Hopes.** "And indeed He is going before you into Galilee; there you will see Him." One of the greatest things about the resurrection of Christ is the certainty it gives us of seeing our Lord again. He has gone before us into the heavens; there we shall see Him, just as He has told us (Acts 1:11).

Conclusion: This is a day for joy! for a total life change! for a different perspective! Because of our living Christ we can face life with steady nerves, awestruck minds, loosened mouths, and high hopes. He is risen! He is risen indeed!

FOR THE BULLETIN

❧ On March 31, 1492, Ferdinand and Isabella, unable to convert Jews to Christianity by force, signed an edict giving them three months to leave Spain. Stripped of homes and possessions, 140,000 Jews streamed to borders and ports, leaving the land that had been their home for 1,500 years. The last Jew reportedly left on August 2, the traditional anniversary of the destruction of the First and Second Temples, the saddest day in Jewish history. Ironically, the very next day, August 3, 1492, Christopher Columbus sailed from Spain to discover the New World. ❧ In 1631, John Donne, one of the most remarkable preachers of the 17th century, died on this day. Here is a sample of one of his sermons: "The whole life of Christ was a continual Passion; others die martyrs but Christ was born a martyr. He found a Golgotha even in Bethlehem, where he was born; for to his tenderness then the straws were almost as sharp as thorns after, and the manger as uneasy at first as his cross at last. His birth and death were but one continual act, and his Christmas Day and his Good Friday are but the evening and morning of one and the same day." ❧ March 31, 1860 is the birthday of evangelist Rodney (Gipsy) Smith. He was born in a Gypsy tent near Epping Forest, England, and received no education. Converted to Christ at age 15, he became a world-famous evangelist until his death in 1947.

Worship Theme:
Christ is risen from the dead!

Call to Worship:
"To you first, God, having raised up His Servant Jesus, sent Him to bless you, in turning away every one of you from your iniquities" (Acts 3:26).

Responsive Reading:

Leader: And we are witnesses of all things which He did both in the land of the Jews and in Jerusalem, whom they killed by hanging on a tree.

People: Him God raised up on the third day, and showed Him openly, not to all the people, but to witnesses chosen before by God, even to us who ate and drank with Him after He arose from the dead.

Leader: And He commanded us to preach to the people, and to testify that it is He who was ordained by God to be Judge of the living and the dead.

People: To Him all the prophets witness that, through His name, whoever believes in Him will receive remission of sins.

Everyone: And God both raised up the Lord and will also raise us up by His power.

Taken from Acts 10:39–42, 1 Corinthians 6:14.

Pastoral Prayer:
Almighty God, we serve a Risen Savior! We worship a Living Lord, and we come to You in His name today, full of thanksgiving and praise, adoration and dedication, singing and praying with joy in our hearts that Jesus Christ our Lord is risen from the dead. May we feel His presence near. May we see Him with our hearts. May we feel Him with our souls. May we trust Him with our needs. May we share Him with our mouths. Grant us, Lord, to see His empty tomb today, and may that emptiness fill our hearts. In Jesus' name we pray. Amen.

STATS, STORIES AND MORE

Easter People
"Do not abandon yourselves to despair. . . . We are the Easter people and hallelujah is our song."
—*Pope John Paul II*

"The Easter message tells us that our enemies, sin, the curse, and death, are beaten. Ultimately they can no longer start mischief. They still behave as though the game were not decided, the battle were not fought; we must still reckon with them, but fundamentally we must cease to fear them any more."
—*Karl Barth*

"Easter is the truth that turns a church from a museum into a ministry."
—*Warren Wiersbe*

That's a Good One!
According to William J. Bausch, in the Greek Orthodox tradition the day after Easter was devoted to telling jokes. The idea was that in the resurrection of Jesus Christ, God was playing a great cosmic joke on the devil. In devoting the Monday after Easter to joke-telling, they were reveling in the fact that, on Easter Sunday, God had the last word.

In Search of a Model
In his autobiographical account, *A Song of Accents*, famous missionary Dr. E. Stanley Jones tells about a layman, a newspaperman, a mutual friend, who was called upon to conduct a funeral service. Being an exact man, he wanted to do it properly and in the best Christian tradition. So he turned to the New Testament as the original source and example of how Jesus conducted a funeral. And he found that Jesus didn't conduct funerals at all. All He dealt with were resurrections.

A Positive Example
The French mathematician Auguste Comte was talking about religion one day with the Scottish essayist Thomas Carlyle. Comte suggested they start a new religion to replace Christianity, based on positive thinking and mathematical principles. Carlyle thought about it a moment and replied, "Very good, Mr. Comte, very good. All you will need to do will be to speak as never a man spoke, and live as never a man lived, and be crucified, and rise again the third day, and get the world to believe that you are still alive. Then your religion will have a chance to get on."

Additional Sermons and Lesson Ideas

Angel at the Tomb
Date preached:

SCRIPTURE: Matthew 28:1–10

INTRODUCTION:

1. **The Angel's Mission** (vv. 1–4). This angel had the ability to materialize, to make the earth quake, and to roll away a massive stone as if it were a marshmallow. Hebrews chapter 1 tells us that angels are ministering spirits sent to serve those who inherit salvation.
2. **The Angel's Message** (vv. 5–7). The word "angel"—*angelos*—means messenger. And what a message!
3. **The Angel's Master** (vv. 8–10). The angel was simply the advance messenger for the Risen Christ, the head over all principalities and powers.

CONCLUSION: The reason Christ died is so that we might live, and the reason He rose again is that we might serve a Risen Savior.

The Importance of the Resurrection
Date preached:

by Kevin Riggs

SCRIPTURE: 1 Corinthians 15:1–22

INTRODUCTION: The most important truth taught in the Bible is the bodily resurrection of Jesus Christ. Without the resurrection there is no Christianity and what we believe is mere philosophical rhetoric taught by a man who was either crazy, a liar, or both.

1. **Without the resurrection we have no faith** (vv. 3–4; 12–17). Without the resurrection Paul says our faith is "useless" and "futile." If Christ wasn't raised, the witnesses of the resurrection gave false testimonies and there is no basis for faith.
2. **Without the resurrection we have no forgiveness of sins** (v. 17). The holiness and love of God was seen on the cross, but forgiveness and grace were seen in the empty tomb. If Christ would not have raised from the dead, He could not have forgiven sins.
3. **Without the resurrection we have no future** (vv. 18–19). If Jesus was not raised from the dead, those who have died before us would be lost and perishing and would have no hope. Without hope for a future there is no meaning for today.
4. **Because of the resurrection we have life** (vv. 20–22). Because of the resurrection you and I can have both eternal and abundant life.

CONCLUSION: But now Christ is risen from the dead! It's high time we began living in the light of that reality.

SPECIAL OCCASION SERMON

A Communion Sermon

Date preached:

Scripture Reading: John 1:29

Introduction: Though the Bible was written over a period of 1,500 years in 66 installments by over 40 authors in three languages, it all meshes together perfectly, every part and parcel of it revolving around one theme and one person: Jesus Christ. Even Genesis—the first book of the Bible—gives us lessons about Jesus Christ. It is there that we begin a "crimson cord" of truth that stretches all the way to the final chapters of Scripture, telling us of the virtues of the Lamb of God.

1. **The Lamb Is Necessary—Genesis 3:21 and 4:1–4.** When God first placed Adam and Eve in the Garden they were so innocent and pure that even clothing was unnecessary. They were naked and not ashamed. When they sinned against God, they became self-conscious. Their thoughts flew to lust, and they became aware that the children they bore through their sexual union would be infected with a sinful nature. And so they made for themselves garments of fig leaves. But by their own efforts, they could never cover up or wash away the guilt and shame that they felt. And so the Lord killed an innocent animal and made garments for them from the skin of that animal. Arthur Pink, in his book on Genesis, says that this is the first gospel sermon, preached by God, not in words but in symbol and action. From this one simple verse, we can learn four things about salvation: (1) It is of God alone. We can never cover our guilt by our own efforts; (2) it is accomplished by the death of an innocent substitute; (3) it is accomplished by the shedding of blood (Heb. 9:22); and (4) it is accomplished by the slaying of a spotless lamb. We aren't told in Genesis 3 that the animal slain was a lamb, but the follow-up story regarding Abel's sacrifice in chapter 4 implies it.

2. **The Lamb Is Provided—Genesis 22:8, 13, 14.** God demanded that Abraham offer Isaac as a sacrifice on Mt. Moriah, the Mountain of the Lord. This mountain is later identified in Scripture as Mt. Zion (2 Chron. 3:1). It is possibly the very mountain on which Jesus Christ would later be crucified.

There Abraham was told that God alone would provide salvation on that mountain, that He would provide the Lamb.

3. **The Lamb Is Slain—Exodus 12:1–7, 13.** The story of the Passover Lamb and the immortal words of verse 13 ("When I see the blood, I will pass over you"), is one of Scriptures most powerful "types of Christ."

4. **The Lamb Must Be Perfect—Leviticus 22:21.** Without spot or blemish.

5. **The Lamb Is Identified as a Suffering Savior—Isaiah 53.** "He was led as a lamb to the slaughter" (v. 7).

6. **The Lamb Is Jesus!—John 1:29.** Notice John's dramatic way of introducing the Messiah. He doesn't say, "Behold the King of kings and Lord of lords." He says, "Behold The Lamb. . . ."

7. **The Lamb Is to Be Proclaimed to the Nations—Acts 8:31–35.** In one of the first missionary stories in church history, Philip used Isaiah 53 to tell the official from Ethiopia about the Lamb of God.

8. **The Lamb Is to Be Trusted for Salvation—1 Peter 1:18–21.**

9. **The Lamb Is to Be Worshiped—Revelation 5:6–10.** We see the biblical song of the Lamb reach a crescendo in the Book of Revelation, with the angels of God gathered around the Lamb in rapturous worship.

Conclusion: Last of all, the Bible ends with a warning about the Lamb's Book of Life (Rev. 21:27). The Lamb is keeping a book, and in it are the names of all those who come to God by faith in Him. There is no other way. This is the crimson thread that progressively unrolls throughout Scripture, from Genesis to Revelation, pulling all the books together around one master theme: God loves us, we disobeyed Him, and He redeemed us through the blood of the Lamb.

> *Just as I am, without one plea,*
> *But that Thy blood was shed for me,*
> *And that Thou bidst me come to Thee,*
> *O Lamb of God, I come! I come!*

APRIL 7, 2002

SUGGESTED SERMON

When God Strikes the Match

Date preached:

By Rev. Drew Wilkerson

Scripture: 2 Timothy 1:1–12, especially verse 6–8 Therefore I remind you to stir up the gift of God which is in you through the laying on of my hands. For God has not given us a spirit of fear, but of power and of love and of a sound mind. Therefore do not be ashamed of the testimony of our Lord, nor of me His prisoner, but share with me in the sufferings for the gospel according to the power of God.

Introduction: Someone once said, "There are many things in life that will catch your eye, but only a few will catch your heart. Pursue those." For example, consider Tiger Woods. In a recent magazine article, Tiger said, "Don't mistake my ability to focus for misery. I'm having a great time on the course." But he describes his concentration as "really intense." The book, *Lessons from the Top,* says: "No trait is more noticeable in the leaders on our list than the passion they share for their people and their companies. Quite simply, they love what they do." When we talk about passion, we aren't talking about a brand of perfume or about the steamy nature of an explicit television show or novel. We're talking about a burning drive God places within us to change the world. We're talking about the motivation we feel to go about His work. When passion burns inside us, we focus on life more easily and effectively. In 2 Timothy, Paul helps us identify four action steps that identify and intensify passion.

Action Step 1: Reach Up To God (vv. 1–4). Everyone wants to be connected to something, but many people today are plugging their lives into dead wall sockets. Paul understood that the spiritual life pulsating within him was given to him by God alone, and he wanted Timothy (and you and me) to share in it. Paul was an apostle (sent) of Jesus Christ according to the will of God and according to the promise of life that he had found in Christ Jesus. He had experienced God's grace, mercy, and peace. All those graces were like lumps of coal fueling the passion for his life's work.

Action Step 2: Reach Inside Yourself (v. 5). Helen Keller said, "Life is either a daring adventure or nothing." Timothy had been raised in a Christian home.

His mother and grandmother had laid a solid foundation in his life, a sincere faith. If we're going to be passionate in life we must decide to stop being the victim and become the victorious winner God has ordained us to be. We must trust Him with a confident, inner faith in His plans for us (Jer. 29:11). When we allow the seeds of God's Word to germinate and grow within us, when we walk by daily faith thereby, we will have all the resources we need. Paul was simply reminding us that in Christ we have the necessary foundation to be what God has called us to be.

Action Step 3: Reach Down to Others (vv. 6–7). Paul urged Timothy to fan into flame the gift he had been given by God. It was essential that Timothy obey because countless numbers of others needed to be touched by his ministry, just as he had been touched by Paul's. When a Christian is transformed by Christ and empowered by the Holy Spirit, the fire of passion ignites. Paul didn't want Timothy to become discouraged, for he believed in this young man. So did God. Now it was time for Timothy to reach down to others and make the message of the gospel come alive.

Action Step 4: Reach Out to the World (vv. 8–12). Paul was not ashamed of the gospel. His purpose and passion were to reach the lost and to inspire Timothy to do the same. Passion knows no boundaries when God is leading us. We are appointed as heralds and apostles and teachers and sharers of the gospel.

>>> *sermon continued on following page*

APPROPRIATE HYMNS AND SONGS

All Hail the Power of Jesus' Name, Edward Perronet/John Rippon/James Ellor; Public Domain.

Be Thou My Vision, Eleanor Hull/Mary E. Byrne; Public Domain.

In Your Presence O God, Lynn DeShazo; © 1994 Integrity's Hosanna! Music (Admin. by Integrity Music, Inc.).

Set My Soul Afire, Eugene M. Bartlette; © 1965 Albert E. Brumley and Sons (Admin. by Integrated Copyright Group, Inc.).

A Heart for You, Walt Harrah; © 1986 Maranatha Praise, Inc. (Admin. by The Copyright Company).

Conclusion: To be set on fire, we must let God kindle the blaze. What is your passion? Are you ready to partner with God and make a difference in life? Fred Shero said, "Success is not the result of spontaneous combustion. You must set yourself on fire." Those words are true with one minor change: "Success is not the result of spontaneous combustion. You must first allow God to set you on fire." Life is worth living when we reach up, reach in, reach down, and reach out. Life is worth living when we let God strike the match.

FOR THE BULLETIN

❀ On April 7, 1163, the bones of the great theologian and churchman Anselm (who had died in 1109) were brought at last into the chapel of St. Peter and St. Paul at Canterbury Cathedral. Later that year Thomas à Becket asked Pope Alexander III to initiate Anselm's canonization. ❀ In Florence on April 7, 1498, Savonarola's close friend, Fra Domenico, was to walk between two rows of wood which had been soaked with oil and were to be set afire. Crowds gathered from across Italy, but Savonarola delayed and was afterward executed on the same public square where the ordeal by fire was to have occurred. ❀ St. Francis Xavier, Spanish Jesuit missionary, was born on April 7, 1506. One of the best known Roman Catholic missionaries, he brought Christianity to Japan and India. It was on his birthday, April 7, 1541, when he set out for the regions beyond, sailing from Lisbon for Portuguese India. ❀ "Truly mine is no common source of grief," wrote John Calvin on April 7, 1549, in a sad letter to his friend, Peter Viret. "I have been bereaved of the best companion of my life." Calvin was mourning for his wife, Idelette, who had passed away only a few days before. ❀ April 7, 1763, marks the death of William Grimshaw, the "Whitefield" of the countryside in eighteenth century England. ❀ On April 7, 1901, missionary James Chalmers set out along the New Guinea coast on his last missionary expedition. He was murdered and eaten by cannibals on the island of Goaribari.

WORSHIP HELPS

Worship Theme:
Stir up the gift of God which is in you (2 Tim. 1:6).

Responsive Reading:

Leader: If we trust in the Lord we need not fear. We can be sure that
            He is guiding us and leading us.

People: We will delight in You, O Lord. We will obey you and believe
            that you will ignite Your passion within our hearts.

Leader: Commitment will not be easy but necessary. Commitment
            will be the key that unlocks the storehouse of God's bless-
            ings.

People: May we partner with You, O God, to do greater things than
            we could imagine or believe. May Your righteousness shine
            within us so that other people will see You through us and
            in us.

Taken from Psalm 37

Benediction:
Grace, mercy, and peace from God the Father and Christ Jesus our Lord
(2 Tim. 1:2).

Kids Talk

Plug an appliance like a hair dryer into a power strip that is not plugged into the wall. Ask the child why it won't work. Then plug the power strip into the outlet and ask one of the children to turn the dryer on. Ask them how it works. Explain that the dryer cannot get hot unless it is plugged into the right source of power. We are the same. When we are passionate about something, we are "hot." We must therefore be "plugged into" Jesus Christ.

STATS, STORIES AND MORE

Someone Once Said . . .

"I think passion is the critical variable. It has taken me a long time to come around to that, but if a pastor does not have passion for a mission, you can forget the rest."

—*Lyle Schaller*

"We're face-to-face with our destiny. And we must meet it with a high, resolute courage. For ours is a life of action, of strenuous performance, of duty. Let us live in the harness of striving mightily. Let us run the risk of wearing out rather than rusting out."

—*Teddy Roosevelt*

"Do it no matter what. If you believe in it, it is something very honorable. If somebody around you or your family does not understand it, then that's their problem. But if you do have a passion, an honest passion, just do it."

—*Mario Andretti, auto racer*

"Find something you're passionate about and keep tremendously interested in it."

—*Julia Child*

"Lord, the task is impossible for me but not for Thee. Lead the way and I will follow. Why should I fear? I am on a royal mission."

—*Mary Slessor*

The Passion Play

When the Black Plague skirted the village of Oberammergau, Germany, during the Thirty Years' War, the grateful citizens vowed that every ten years they would perform a play to honor the passion of Christ. The first Passion Play was presented on Pentecost in 1634, on a stage in a cemetery above the fresh graves of the plague victims. In A.D. 2000, the Oberammergau villagers presented the passion play for the 40th time Although the text and music have been adopted to modern times, few other components have changed over the more than 360 years since the play's first performance. The over 2,000 actors and workers are all native Oberammergau villagers.

Has Christ done something so special for you that every day your life is a Passion Play for His glory?

Additional Sermons and Lesson Ideas

Go for the God

Date preached:

By Kevin Riggs

SCRIPTURE: Philippians 3:12–14

INTRODUCTION: This passage tells us to strive for God's best in our lives, like an Olympic runner striving for the gold.

1. **Never think you've reached perfection** (v. 13). Paul had not taken hold of: (1) complete knowledge of Christ; (2) sinless perfection; (3) finishing all God had called him to do. We must therefore (1) continue learning all we can about Christ; (2) never think we're above sinning; (3) continue working.
2. **Never quit progressing** (v. 13). Forget the past and strain toward what's ahead. We can learn from the past, but dwelling on the past may keep us from moving forward.
3. **Never stop pressing** (v. 14). To "press toward" means to persevere and endure till the end. As an Olympic runner presses toward the finish line, so you are to keep focused to the finish line of the Christian faith.

CONCLUSION: We often scatter ourselves too thin. Learn to downsize. Focus on the one thing God wants you to do, and press toward that goal.

The Fugitive

Date preached:

SCRIPTURE: 1 Samuel 21:10—22:1a and Psalm 34:4–10

BACKGROUND: If you've ever had a day in which everything went wrong, you should become familiar with this passage. Murphy's Law had kicked into David's life, even forcing him to hide in the hometown of the slain giant, Goliath himself (compare 1 Sam. 21:10 with 1 Sam. 17:4). David was very low, feigning insanity as his only hope of escape. But notice (from the heading of Psalm 34) that it was on this occasion that David wrote Psalm 34 with its opening notes of praise. We, too, can turn our problems into praise when we remember:

1. **God Relieves Our Fears** (v. 4). He can deliver us from every one of them.
2. **He Brightens Our Faces** (v. 5). We look to Him and are radiant, as Moses was in Exodus 34.
3. **He Defeats Our Foes** (vv. 6, 7). "The Prince of Darkness grim, we tremble not for him."
4. **He Provides Our Food** (vv. 8–10). He is meeting every need.

CONCLUSION: Next time you have a bad day, try turning your problems into prayers and your sighs into songs.

CLASSICS FOR THE PASTOR'S LIBRARY

Hudson Taylor's Spiritual Secret

It's time to put down that best-seller and spend a few days re-reading *Hudson Taylor's Spiritual Secret*. What? You haven't read it the first time? Well, clear your reading schedule and plow in. Discovery House Publishers has a new edition, revised and edited by Gregg Lewis, that brings this highly readable but deeply impacting classic back to life.

Hudson Taylor's Spiritual Secret is just as its name implies, a biography of the great pioneer missionary to China, J. Hudson Taylor, that focuses on the spiritual lessons learned throughout a dramatic lifetime—how to trust God, how to handle grief, how to stay calm amid crises, how to harvest souls, how to "move man, through God, by prayer alone." It tells an epic story, complete with shipwrecks, riots, romance, grief, and, as the preface says, "a setting as broad as the world, and a plot with as many up and down struggles as any first-rate novel."

Taylor was born in England in 1832, and converted as a teenager through his mother's insistent praying. After spending time studying medicine and theology, he sailed for China under the banner of the China Evangelization Society, arriving in Shanghai in 1854, where he shocked fellow missionaries by adopting Chinese dress and pressing toward the interior of China.

From the beginning, Taylor refused to engage in fund-raising, convinced that God Himself would provide the needed resources. This approach brought him repeatedly to his knees, but God never failed him. In time, Taylor established China Inland Mission (now OMF International), which, upon his death in 1905, had 849 missionaries and 125,000 Chinese Christians.

I've found every chapter of *Hudson Taylor's Spiritual Secret* rich reading, but the core of the book involves a time in 1869 when Taylor was on the brink of physical and emotional collapse. Political problems in both China and England, coupled with the demands of his growing missions family, had driven him to anxiety and exhaustion.

A letter from fellow missionary John McCarthy turned the tide. The secret to inner victory, said McCarthy, is realizing that "the Lord Jesus received is holiness begun; the Lord Jesus cherished is holiness advancing; the Lord Jesus counted upon as never absent would be holiness complete."

McCarthy wrote, "Abiding, not striving nor struggling; looking off to Him, trusting Him for present power. . . . This is not new, yet 'tis new to me. . . . How then to have our faith increased? Only by thinking of all that Jesus is and all He is for us. . . . Not a striving to have faith . . . but a looking off to the Faithful One seems all we need."

Hudson Taylor read those words in a little mission station at Chinkiang on an autumn Saturday in 1869, and ". . . as I read, I saw it all. I looked to Jesus; and when I saw, oh how the joy flowed."

John 15 took center stage in his life as he realized the joy of abiding in Christ. He later wrote: "As to work, mine was never so plentiful or so difficult; but the weight and strain are now gone. The last month has been perhaps the happiest in my life; and I long to tell you a little of what the Lord has done for my soul."

The authors of *Spiritual Secret* are Dr. and Mrs. Howard Taylor. The bulk of the writing was by the latter, Geraldine Taylor, the missionary's daughter-in-law, herself a missionary to China. As a young missionary, her letters home were so vivid and personal that, unknown to her, they were published. Their reception led Hudson Taylor to ask her to compile a history of CIM, and this became her first book.

In the years that followed, she brought Chinese missions to readers all over the world through her histories, biographies, and devotional books. Readers today may find her style a bit slow-going. Gregg Lewis calls it "an uncomfortable mixture of early twentieth-century camp meeting preaching and Victorian English Comp 101." But I've never found her books all that difficult, and I treasure my little collection. If you can find them (several are still in print), check out:

Borden of Yale '09 — The life of William Borden
Behind the Ranges — The life of J. O. Fraser
The Triumph of John and Betty Stam
One of China's Scholars — The story of Pastor Hsi
Guinness of Honan — The life of Mrs. Taylor's brother, G. Whitfield Guinness, missionary physician to China
Margaret King's Vision — The story of a woman who advocated women's issues in China and who died while serving with China Inland Mission

Dr. and Mrs. Taylor also wrote a longer, two-volume biography of J. Hudson Taylor, but by all means, start with *Hudson Taylor's Spiritual Secret*. You may find out, as I did, that it contains more than one secret of the victorious Christian life, and they are secrets we badly need to learn. ❀

APRIL 14, 2002

SUGGESTED SERMON

Those Salty Christians

Date preached:

By Dr. Ed Dobson

Scripture: Matthew 5:13–16, especially verse 13 "You are the salt of the earth; but if the salt loses its flavor, how shall it be seasoned? It is then good for nothing but to be thrown out and trampled underfoot by men."

Introduction: The recently-ended Winter Olympics in Salt Lake City acquainted us with the Great Salt Lake of Utah, the largest inland body of salt water in the Western Hemisphere and one of the most saline inland bodies of water in the world. The Bear, Weber, and Jordan rivers carry more than 1.1 million tons of salts annually into the lake. The total dissolved mineral accumulation in the lake basin is some 5 billion tons. In a sense, that lake is an illustration of the church in this world. According to Matthew 5:13, we should be known for our saltiness.

    Context: This passage about the "salt of the earth" comes immediately after the Beatitudes (the Beautiful Attitudes) in verses 3–10. The context tells us that if we live out these Beautiful Attitudes and if we withstand the ensuing persecution referred to in verses 11 and 12, we will be God's Great Salt Sea. In ancient times, salt was used:

1. **As a Preservative.** Homes didn't have refrigerators or freezers, so families would store their meat and perishables in salt, which resisted normal, natural decay. The world around us is in decay (Rom. 8:21), and Jesus has placed us here as a powerful influence in arresting the decay around us. For example in 1 Corinthians 7:12–16, in writing about marriage, Paul counsels believers married to non-believers to stay in the relationship (if possible) because their faith will have a positive, sanctifying influence on the home. You can have a preserving influence even in your own marriage and children.

2. **As a Flavoring.** Believers should be known not only for arresting decay, but for contributing in positive and flavorful ways to life around us. Colossians 4:6 says, "Let your speech always be with grace, seasoned with salt, that you may know how you ought to answer each one."

3. **As an Important Ingredient in Sacrifices.** In Mark 9:49, 50, Jesus said, "For everyone will be seasoned with fire, and every sacrifice will be seasoned with salt. Salt is good, but if the salt loses its flavor, how will you season it? Have salt in yourselves, and have peace with one another." He was referring to Leviticus 2:13: "And every offering of your grain offering you shall season with salt; you shall not allow the salt of the covenant of your God to be lacking from your grain offering. With all your offerings you shall offer salt." As Old Testament saints brought their offerings to the tabernacle and temple, God required one ingredient to be added—salt. Why? According to Jewish tradition, on the second day of creation God separated the lower waters from the higher waters. Jewish tradition claims that the lower waters were upset with God because they wanted to be closer to Him like the higher waters, so God made an agreement with them. Salt was to be added to every offering. Hence, as they boiled the ocean water for salt for the offerings, the water would convert to steam and ascend to heaven, closer to God. We should be the means for bringing people closer to God.

Conclusion: But Jesus added a warning: "But if the salt loses its flavor, how shall it be seasoned? It is then good for nothing but to be thrown out and trampled underfoot by men." In ancient times, when salt was mixed with other substances it diluted or neutralized its nature. We must never become diluted by the stuff of this world. We must guard against letting sin compromise our

>>> *sermon continued on following page*

APPROPRIATE HYMNS AND SONGS

Change Me, God, Fred F. McKinnon/Kathy Leonard; © 1997 HPP Publishing Company.

Salt and Light; Amy Grant/Wes King; © 1992 Age to Age Music, Inc. (Admin. by The Loving Company/Locally Owned Music, Inc.).

We Are Your Church, Andy Park; © 1988 Mercy/Vineyard Publishing (Admin. by Music Services).

Let Others See Jesus in You; B. B. McKinney; © 1924. Renewed 1952 Broadman Press (Admin. Genevox Music Group).

The Trees of the Field, Stuart Dauermann/Steffi Geiser Rubin; © 1975 Lillenas Publishing Company (Admin. by The Copyright Company).

power, arrest our influence, or weaken our testimony. Salt must be pure, otherwise it is trampled underfoot. In ancient times, when someone left the Jewish faith they became a heretic and were disowned by the synagogue. If they later repented, before they were officially received and forgiven, they would lie across the door of the synagogue and invite everyone coming into the synagogue to trample them, to step on them, symbolizing that when we depart from the purity of our commitment to God, we end up trampling the reputation of God. In a world of decay, Christians are preservatives. In a world of bland modernity, we are the flavoring. In a world of low waters, we help people ascend to God. But we must remain pure and pungent, uncorrupted and uncompromised. Are you worth your salt?

FOR THE BULLETIN

✿ Georg Frideric Handel, organist and composer, died on April 14, 1759. Handel was best known for *Messiah*, which he wrote in 23 days. "Whether I was in the body or out of the body when I wrote it, I know not," he later said, trying to describe the experience. ✿ April 14, 1802, is the birthday of Horace Bushnell, 19th century Congregational minister and the author of *Christian Nurture*. ✿ Abraham Lincoln was shot by John Wilkes Booth on this night in 1865. He died the next day. ✿ On April 14, 1912, the *Titanic* struck an iceberg. ✿ As the ship sank, Charles Herbert Lightoller of the White Star Line was trapped in a funnel running down to a boiler room. Psalm 91:11 came to his mind: "He shall give His angels charge over you, to keep you in all your ways." Suddenly, an explosion from the boiler shot him to the surface where he was rescued. ✿ Colonel Archibald Gracie also went down with the ship. But during those moments, his wife, asleep in New York, awoke with a sudden impression to pray. After his remarkable rescue, Gracie wrote: "I know of no recorded instance of Providential deliverance more directly attributable to . . . prayer." ✿ John Harper, pastor of Walworth Road Church in London, was on his way to preach at Moody Church in Chicago. He perished in the sinking of the Titanic, but several months later an unnamed man in Hamilton, Canada, told of being converted to Christ in the waters of the North Atlantic due to Harper's shouting to him the words of Acts 16:31.

Worship Theme:
God means to impact the world through His people.

Call to Worship:
"Let the heavens rejoice, and let the earth be glad; let the sea roar, and all its fullness; let the field be joyful, and all that is in it. Then all the trees of the woods will rejoice before the LORD" (Psalm 96:11, 12).

Encouragements for Singing:
"For it to be a hymn, it is needful, therefore, for it to have three things—praise, praise to God, and these sung."
—*Augustine*

"Music is the handmaiden of theology."
—*Luther*

"Sing lustily and with a good courage. Beware of singing as if you were half dead or asleep."
—*John Wesley*

"Is not Jesus Christ the sweetest of all singers? Is not Jesus Christ in the midst of the congregation, gathering up all the notes which come from sincere lips, to put them into the golden censer, and to make them rise as precious incense before the throne of the infinite majesty?"
—*Charles Spurgeon*

"Come, Thou Fount of every blessing, Tune my heart to sing Thy grace."
—*Robert Robinson*

Pastoral Prayer:
Our Lord, Ever-Present Overseer of Heaven and Earth, You know the ways of this world, and You see the thoughts and intents of our hearts. Forgive our sins. Purify us, and make us more like Christ. And use us, Lord, use even us, just as You will, and when, and where. Make us the salt of the earth and the light of the world. Help us to not only brighten the corner where we are, but may all the world be blessed by our presence in this world and by our involvement in worship this day. We pray in Jesus' name, Amen.

STATS, STORIES AND MORE

From the Sermons of Charles H. Spurgeon

- One wise man may deliver a whole city; one good man may be the means of safety to a thousand others. The holy ones are "the salt of the earth," the means of the preservation of the wicked. Without the godly as a conserve, the race would be utterly destroyed.

- If all the professed Christians who live in London really walked as Christ walked, would not the salt have more effect upon the corrupt mass than the stuff which is now called salt seems to have? We preach here in the pulpit; but what can we do unless you preach yonder at home? It is you preaching in your shops, in your kitchens, in your nurseries, in your parlors, in the streets, which will tell on the masses. This is the preaching—the best preaching in the world, for it is seen as well as heard.

- Lord, revive Thy work in my soul, that my conversation may be more Christlike, seasoned with salt, and kept by the Holy Spirit.

The 2 Percent Solution

Ruth Bell Graham once told of an incident that occurred in a totalitarian country where the official church existed only under government oversight. In this case, the state secretary for church affairs was a medical doctor as well as a brilliant pastor. One day he was called before high officials who wanted him to be more repressive of Christians.

"I know you gentlemen wish to interrogate me," he began. "But first, may I say something? You know I am a medical doctor. As a doctor I know the importance of salt in the human body: it should be maintained at about 2 percent. If it is less, a person gets sick. If it is eliminated altogether, he will die. Now, Jesus Christ has said Christians are the salt of the earth."

Then he paused. "That is all. And now, gentlemen, what is it that you wish to say to me?"

He was dismissed without further comment.

Out of the Shaker

Salt in the shaker does no good. We need to get together and sing, praise, and open God's Word. When the salt gets together there is fellowship in the shaker, but our real purpose is only fulfilled when we're shaken out of the container and into the community.

Additional Sermons and Lesson Ideas

The Light of the World

Date preached:

By Ed Dobson

SCRIPTURE: Matthew 5:13–16

INTRODUCTION: Lamps come in different shapes and sizes, as large as the sun, as small as a penlight. But every light has certain commonalties.

1. **A light is meant to be seen.** Israeli villages were built on ridges to be seen at night, set aglow by small oil lamps. In Matthew 5, Jesus was not talking about massive lights, but about little lamps to light the world.
2. **A light is for guiding others.** It should give light to everyone in the house.
3. **We are lamps, not the light.** Jesus shines through us as we let others see our good works and glorify our Father.

CONCLUSION: Jesus is warning us here against believing that the world is basically good, and our job is to improve it. He also warns us against believing the world is basically bad, therefore we should have nothing to do with it. The world is dark, but we are His lights. Don't underestimate your influence.

Bloom Where You Are Planted

By Kevin Riggs

Date preached:

SCRIPTURE: 1 Corinthians 7:17–24

INTRODUCTION: Many Christians wish they were someone else or somewhere else. Paul teaches us here that no matter where a person is, or what we can or can't do, God can use us. The key word is acceptance.

1. **Accept Your Calling** (vv. 17, 22, 24). God has placed you where you need to be, with unique talents and abilities, with spiritual gifts for His glory. Instead of wishing for another calling, accept the one already assigned.
2. **Accept Your Character** (v. 18). It isn't circumcision or uncircumcision, but whether or not you keep God's commandments. Be all you can be for Him. Don't try to be something you cannot.
3. **Accept Your Condition** (vv. 21–23). If your circumstance changes, great. If not, serve God anyway, no matter what condition you find yourself in (Phil. 4:11). Don't quit because things aren't the way you desire. God has put you where you are to serve Him now. Bloom where you're planted.

APRIL 21, 2002

SUGGESTED SERMON   *Date preached:*

Five Ways To Improve Your Marriage

Scripture: Song of Songs 1:15–16

> THE BELOVED
> Behold, you are fair, my love!
> Behold, you are fair!
> You have dove's eyes.
> THE SHULAMITE
> Behold, you are handsome, my beloved!
> Yes, pleasant!
> Also our bed is green [verdant].

Introduction: Our text expresses the love of a husband and wife for each other. In his eyes, she is beautiful, with eyes like doves. In her eyes, he is the most handsome man in the world. Their love is rich and real, and their marriage bed is verdant. This is God's ideal. Here are five ideas for fashioning your marriage to be like that:

1. **Express Affection.** Dr. Nathaniel Branden is a California psychologist whose advice about marriage has appeared in national magazines. When asked, "Are there specific ways in which couples who remain happily in love behave differently from couples who don't?" he replies that couples who stay in love never take their relationship for granted; they express affection for each other every day in various ways:
   - They frequently say, "I love you."
   - They are physically affectionate, holding hands, hugging, cuddling.
   - They express their love sexually.
   - They verbalize their appreciation and admiration.
   - They share their thoughts and feelings, learning to self-disclose what's on their minds and hearts to each other, confiding in each other.
   - They convey their love materially, giving little gifts to each other.
   - They create time alone together.

2. **Act Like You Love Each Other.** There may be days when we don't feel as much love. But psychologists tell us that if we act *as if* we feel a certain way, sooner or later we'll actually begin feeling that way. William James said: "By

regulating the action . . . we can indirectly regulate the feeling." Tony Compolo wrote: "I challenge those who come to me for marriage counseling this way: If you do what I tell you to do for an entire month, I can promise you that by the end of the month, you will be in love with your mate. Are you willing to give it a try? When couples accept my challenge, the results are invariably successful. My prescription for creating love is simple: Do ten things each day that you would do if you really were in love. I know that if people do loving things, it will not be long before they experience the feelings that are often identified as being in love."

3. **Avoid "Platonic" Friendships with Members of the Opposite Sex.** Most affairs begin as innocent relationships which, without anyone's realizing it, begin to develop a life of their own. While we can't isolate ourselves from the opposite sex, we need to keep tight boundaries. It's dangerous to find yourself telling a member of the opposite sex something that you wouldn't want your spouse to know, to find yourself wanting to spend time with a member of the opposite sex besides your husband or wife, and to find yourself alone with a member of the opposite sex. Have personal rules, and avoid being drawn into relationships that may divert your emotional energy and attention from your marriage.

4. **Have Your Devotions.** At the marriage of Queen Elizabeth II to the Duke of Edinburgh in 1947, the Archbishop of Canterbury, Geoffery Francis Fisher, said: "The ever-living Christ is here to bless you. The nearer you keep him, the nearer you will be to one another." The couple that prays together stays together.

>>> *sermon continued on following page*

APPROPRIATE HYMNS AND SONGS

A Christian Home, Barbara Hart/Jean Sibelius; © 1965, 1986 Singspiration Music (Admin. by Brentwood-Benson Music Publishing, Inc.).

Bind Us Together, Bob Gillman; © 1977 Kingsway's Thankyou Music (Admin. by EMI Christian Music Publishing).

Family Song, Steve Hampton; © 1978, 1985 Scripture in Song (a div. of Integrity Music, Inc.) (Admin. by Integrity Music, Inc.).

In Our Households, Heavenly Father, Marie J. Post/Dale Grotenhuis; © 1987 CRC Publications.

We Are a Family, David Holsinger; © 1989 Master Song Music.

5. **Draw Strength From Each Other.** A sailor during World War II was dumped into the ocean when his ship sank. As he floundered in the water, weighed down by clothing and equipment, he spotted another sailor also struggling to stay afloat. He grabbed him and held on for dear life. Later, he was very ashamed, knowing he could have pulled his partner under. Sometime later, he bumped into this man and was astonished when the second man said, "I want to thank you for keeping me from sinking. You held me up until we were rescued." The sailor understood they had held up each other. Healthy couples learn to cling to each other in times of stress, holding each other up, allowing problems to draw them together rather than pull them apart.

Conclusion: Make up your mind to be a marathoner in marriage, to run with patience the race that is set before you, loving your husband or wife, looking unto Jesus—the author and finisher of our faith—and of our family.

FOR THE BULLETIN

❀ On April 21, 847, Rabanus Maurus became archbishop of Mainz. A pupil of Alcuin, he went on to became a famed educator himself and a commentator of Scriptures. ❀ The theologian Anselm died on April 21, 1109. He was Archbishop of Canterbury and one of the founders of medieval scholasticism. ❀ On the morning of April 21, 1142, Peter Abelard, French philosopher and theologian, died. His reputation was marred by theological controversy and by his love affair with Héloise and its unsavory aftermath. ❀ On Easter Sunday, April 21, 1538, John Calvin, defying a governmental order against preaching in Geneva, ascended to the pulpit of St. Pierre. He was banished, but returned in 1541 and ministered there until his death in 1564. ❀ April 21, 1783, is the birthday of Reginald Heber, author of the missionary hymn, "From Greenland's Icy Mountains." ❀ George Mueller's first orphans' home opened on April 21, 1836, with 26 orphan girls. ❀ D. L. Moody was converted on April 21, 1855, in the back of a shoe store in Boston through the efforts of his Sunday school teacher, Edward Kimball. ❀ Dr. A. W. Tozer was born April 21, 1897. ❀ On April 21, 1992, Ngugen Lap Ma, head pastor of the Southwestern Region for the Evangelical Church in Vietnam, was placed under house arrest, charged with being "number one person against Communism." Along with his wife and ten children, he was sentenced to internal exile without a hearing or trial.

WORSHIP HELPS

Worship Theme:
Our life relationships (especially in marriage) should reflect the love and unity of Christ.

Call to Worship:
"Therefore by Him let us continually offer the sacrifice of praise to God, that is, the fruit of our lips, giving thanks to His name" (Heb. 13:15).

Meditation for the Offering:
Proverbs 3:9 says, "Honor the LORD with your possessions, and with the firstfruits of all your increase." When Solomon wrote that, most of his subjects were farmers. If he were writing today, he might say: "Honor the Lord with your money, and with the first part of your regular income." The next verse contains a related promise: "So your barns will be filled with plenty, and your vats will overflow with new wine." Or as we might put it today: "So God will meet all your needs." As we worship the Lord this morning, let's honor Him, not just with our prayers and praises, but with our pocketbooks and purses, with our money, and with the first part of our income. And He will meet all the needs of our lives.

Responsive Reading:

Leader:	"Every commandment which I command you today you must be careful to observe, that you may live and multiply, and go in and possess the land of which the LORD swore to your fathers.
Men:	And you shall remember that the LORD your God led you all the way these forty years in the wilderness, to humble you and test you, to know what was in your heart, whether you would keep His commandments or not.
Women:	He humbled you, allowed you to hunger, and fed you with manna which you did not know nor did your fathers know, that He might make you know...
All:	...that man shall not live by bread alone; but by every word that proceeds from the mouth of the LORD.

Taken from Deuteronomy 8:1–3.

STATS, STORIES AND MORE

Current Statistics
- 25 percent of all adults have experienced at least one divorce during their lifetime.
- Born-again Christians are slightly more likely than non-Christians to go through a divorce, with 26 percent of Christians and 22 percent of non-Christians having gone through a divorce some time in their lives (Barna, 1999).

A Sure Cure?
In his book *The Fine Art of Friendship,* Ted W. Engstrom tells of a man named Joe who was so upset with his wife that he decided on divorce. But before serving her the papers, he made an appointment with a psychologist with the specific purpose of finding out how to make life as difficult as possible for his wife.

The psychologist said, "Well, Joe, I've got the perfect solution. Starting tonight, treat your wife as if she were a goddess. Change your attitude 180 degrees. Start doing everything in your power to please her. Listen to her when she talks about her problems, help around the house, take her out to dinner on weekends. Pretend she's a goddess. Then, after two months of this wonderful behavior, just pack your bags and leave her. That should get to her!"

That night Joe implemented his plan. He couldn't wait to do things for her. He brought her breakfast in bed, had flowers delivered to her for no apparent reason, took her on romantic weekends. They read books to each other at night, and Joe listened to her as never before. He kept this up for the full two months. After the allotted time, the psychologist gave Joe a call at work. "Joe," he asked, "how's it going? Did you file for divorce? Are you a happy bachelor once again?"

"Divorce?" asked Joe in dismay. "Are you kidding? I'm married to a goddess. I've never been happier in my life!"

No Good Thing
A young preacher's wife stood up in a marriage retreat and began nervously to share her testimony. She said, "The Bible promises in Psalm 84:11, 'No good thing will [the Lord] withhold from those who walk uprightly.' Well, my husband is one of those 'no good things'!"

Additional Sermons and Lesson Ideas

It May Be

Date preached:

Based on an observation by Charles Spurgeon

SCRIPTURE: Various

INTRODUCTION: Charles Spurgeon said, "There is a 'may be' about all temporal things," and he observed that those "may be's" can motivate us for action. "In spiritual things," he said, "we may draw encouragement from the faintest sign of hope when it proceeds from God."

1. A "May Be" Encouraged Caleb to Seize the Hill Country. "It may be that the LORD will be with me" (Josh. 14:12).
2. A "May Be" Led Jonathan to Attack the Philistines. "It may be that the LORD will work for us" (1 Sam. 14:6).
3. A "May Be" Cheered David When Absalom Rebelled. "It may be that the LORD will look on my affliction" (2 Sam. 16:12).
4. A "May Be" Strengthened Hezekiah During the Siege of Jerusalem. "It may be that the LORD your God will hear" (2 Kings 19:4).
5. A "May Be" Prompted Jeremiah to Preach His Message to Judah. "It may be that... everyone will turn from his evil way." (Jer. 36:7).

CONCLUSION: Be hopeful by nature. Be naturally optimistic. The Lord has a way of turning "may be's" into realities for His children.

What Mean These Stones?

Date preached:

SCRIPTURE: Joshua 4:1–7

INTRODUCTION: After crossing the Jordan River, Joshua took time to erect a monument to remind the Israelites of the events of that day. The Bible uses the word "remember" 164 times (NKJV). It is very important to keep our own story, our testimony, fresh. Remembering what God has done for us in the past:

1. Rouses Our Reverence (Isa. 46:8, 9). When we count our blessings we crown the Blesser.
2. Challenges Our Children (Ex. 12:26; Josh. 4:21, 22).
3. Fortifies Our Faith (Deut. 7:17, 18). When we forget His power, we forfeit His power.

CONCLUSION: Take every good opportunity to share with others, especially with your children and grandchildren, how God has led you and what he has done in your life (Mark 5:19). Consider leaving a written record of God's grace to you, to be passed down to future generations.

APRIL 28, 2002

The Secret of the Lord

Date preached:

By Dr. John Kennedy

Scripture: Psalm 25:14 The secret of the Lord is with those who fear Him.

Introduction: The older versions of the Bible use the word "peculiar" to describe Christians. Some of us are certainly peculiar, but I hope all of us are peculiar in the biblical sense—special, different, unique, people of singular character and exclusive privileges. Into our souls Christ infuses life; into our ears He whispers secrets. Fearers of God are favorites of God; and as such we are a peculiar people.

1. **Christians differ from others because they fear the Lord.**

    A. Those who fear the Lord are quickened souls, once dead in sin, but now alive to God, "quickened together with Christ." There are Godward movements in our hearts. We have crowned Him King of our hearts.

    B. Those who fear must be near to God. We were once "far off," but have been brought near by the blood of Jesus. The Spirit thus guides us to the throne of grace—not as rebels who dread the king's approach or as strangers who have never visited a sovereign, but as courtiers and children who are already in the palace. Only His loving children and His loyal servants can honor the Lord as a Father and fear Him as a Master.

    C. In approaching God on His throne, we mingle reverence of His glory with hope in His mercy. This is a combination only found where the true fear of God is. The same view of God that inspires hope also produces reverential fear. The glory of God, as seen in the cross, commands our admiration as well as our trust. It is at once solemnizing and encouraging. It bears us down while it draws us near. It breaks our heart as surely as it cheers it.

    D. They who fear the Lord seek to do His will. That the Lord may be pleased and glorified is the end to which we aspire. We cannot be happy without respecting all God's commandments (Ps. 119:6). It is then in reverent obedience that those who fear the Lord may expect His secret to be with them.

2. **True Christians differ from others because with them is "the secret of the Lord."** This means more than that we have the Bible in our hands. The Bible contains the complete revelation of the will of God, but many who have the Bible in their hands don't have the fear of the Lord in their hearts. Those who fear the Lord have received, not the spirit of the world, but the Spirit which is of God, to know the things freely given to them of God. Thus we are "peculiar." The Lord shines the gospel light on us, and He also shines into our hearts the light of the knowledge of His glory in the face of Christ (2 Cor. 4:6). His Spirit guides us into daily lessons about His promises, presence, and power. In the process we are changed into the image of Christ, from glory to glory, by the Spirit of the Lord (2 Cor. 3:18).

A. He acquaints us with His everlasting purpose to save us.
B. He reveals intimations of His will while we pray, providing inner peace regarding problems and opportunities.
C. He gives us secret burdens for others for whom we should plead, often suggesting the case of a particular individual to the mind of one who is pleading at the footstool of mercy. With it may come a suggested portion of Scripture to plead on their behalf.

>>> *sermon continued on following page*

APPROPRIATE HYMNS AND SONGS

Arise, My Soul, Arise, Charles Wesley/Lewis Edson; Public Domain.

Christ Is King of All Creation, Graham Kendrick; © 1991 Make Way Music (Admin. by Music Services).

Glorious Things of Thee Are Spoken, John Newton; Public Domain.

Baruch Hashem Adonai, Dawn Rogers/Tricia Walker; © 1982 Word Music, Inc.

O Master, Let Me Walk With Thee, Washington Gladden/Henry Percy Smith; Public Domain.

D. He reassures us by reminding us of His providential governance over our lives and over history. We watch and walk with God while others live without Him in the world. We speak with Him about His doings, while others are dumb and deaf before Him.

Conclusion: The Lord shares His secrets with those who fear Him, imparting wisdom and peace in difficult times. He gives them guidance during times of decision. He gives reassurance as needed. Fear the Lord. Let His Word be precious, and use it for the ends for which it is given. Aspire for a clearer view of its wonders, a simpler faith in its truth, a ravishing sense of its sweetness, and a deeper experience of its power. Be guided by its light, molded by its form, fed by its manna, and cheered by its comforts, fearing Him and learning His secrets day by day.

FOR THE BULLETIN

❀ April 28th is the traditional date ascribed to the nighttime visit of Nicodemus to Jesus in John 3. ❀ On April 28, 1545, French troops destroyed the Waldensian towns of Merindol and Cabieres, along with 28 nearby villages. Over 4,000 people were slaughtered. Many of the survivors fled to Geneva where Calvin interceded for them. ❀ On April 28, 1564, John Calvin, dying, summoned Geneva ministers to his house to speak with them a final time. He began, "Brethren, after I am dead, persist in this work, and be not dispirited; for the Lord will save this Republic and Church from the threats of the enemy. Let dissension be far away from you, and embrace each other with mutual love." He told them of times in his own ministry when he feared he would be unfruitful. "But," he said, "proceeding in this work, I at length perceived that the Lord had truly blessed my efforts. Do you also persist in this vocation." The ministers were reduced to tears as they departed his room. ❀ On April 28, 1910, Dr. Henry Harris Jessup died in Syria after 54 years of missionary service. He had been called to missions at age 20 while leading a missionary meeting. After having spoken on missions a few minutes, he urged those present to consider going overseas themselves. He suddenly felt hypocritical speaking like that when he himself had been unwilling to go. Not long afterward, he made up his mind and in June, 1854, he sailed for Syria.

WORSHIP HELPS

Worship Theme:
Those who cultivate intimacy with Christ experience His love and grow
in His wisdom.

Call To Worship:
"But ye are a chosen generation, a royal priesthood, an holy nation, a
peculiar people; that ye should shew forth the praises of him who hath
called you out of darkness into his marvellous light" (1 Peter 2:9 KJV).

Reader's Theater:

Reader 1:   There is a God in heaven who revels secrets....

Reader 2:   He reveals deep and secret things;

Reader 1:   He knows what is in the darkness, and light dwells with
Him.

Reader 2:   The perverse person is an abomination to the LORD, but His
secret counsel is with the upright.

Reader 1:   Who is the man that fears the LORD? Him shall He teach in
the way He chooses. He himself shall dwell in prosperity,
and his descendants shall inherit the earth.

Reader 2:   The secret of the LORD is with those who fear Him.

Reader 1:   In the time of trouble He shall hide me in His pavilion; in
the secret place of His tabernacle He shall hide me; He shall
set me high upon a rock.

Reader 2:   He who dwells in the secret place of the Most High shall
abide under the shadow of the Almighty.

*Taken from Daniel 2:28; Daniel 2:22; Proverbs 3:32; Psalm 25:12–14; Psalm 27:5;
Psalm 91:1.*

Benediction:
Dismiss us with Your love, O Lord. Bless and keep us, our Father, and
may God be with us till we meet again.

STATS, STORIES AND MORE

Dr. John Kennedy

Today's suggested sermon is a classic outline by Dr. John Kennedy of Dingwall, Scotland, who died on this day in 1884 at age 64 while on his way home from Italy where he had been convalescing. On that bleak Monday, his friend, Rev. W. S. McDougall penned in his diary, "My beloved friend and nearest brother-minister, Dr. Kennedy of Dingwall, died at Bridge of Allen, on Monday, 28th April 1844. The desolation caused by this bereavement cannot be recorded. Not only are his beloved wife and daughter stricken and prostrate, but the whole Highlands mourn." Kennedy was born in 1819, the fourth son of a minister, but his youth was spent in pleasure-seeking, and he was greatly attracted to the stage. Then one day in 1841, he was told of his father's death. Crushed with grief and deeply convicted of his sins, he offered his life to Christ and became one of the most powerful 19th century Highland preachers in Scotland.

The Fear of God

Have you ever been to Niagara Falls or the Grand Canyon? When you're close to the edge of the falls, enveloped by the thunder and spray of 6 million cubic feet of water bursting over the falls every minute, or when you stand at the rim of the canyon and a sense of dizzying awe overwhelms you as you step back from the edge of that vast expanse and bottomless gorge—that is somewhat akin to the "fear of God." It isn't an unhealthy fear, but an overwhelming sense of God Himself. A. W. Tozer defined it as "astonished reverence." William Anderson, in his book *The Faith That Satisfies*, wrote, "I was really surprised to find more than 300 references in the Old Testament that speak of the fear of the Lord.... The fear of the Lord is reverential trust and hatred of evil, and there you have the whole thing."

Kids Talk

Tell the children you have a secret. Keep giving them hints until they guess it. Tell them that God also has some secrets, but that He shares them with His children in the Bible. For example, Romans 8:28 is a great secret for God's people. He makes all things work together for good for those who love Him.

Additional Sermons and Lesson Ideas

Willing to Wait

Date preached:

By Dr. Melvin Worthington

SCRIPTURE: Psalm 37:7

INTRODUCTION: Who started the rumor that we measure spirituality by excitement, enthusiasm, emotionalism and energy? The Bible suggests that sometimes spirituality is measured by quietness and by the willingness to wait on God.

1.   **The Admonition.** First, waiting implies *submission to God's Word.* Second, it involves *submission to God's will.* Rather than murmurs or complaints, there should be a silent and quiet acquiescence to His will. It also requires *submission to God's ways.*

2.   **The Assurance.** Waiting on God results in *prosperity* (Lam. 3:25, 26), divine *protection* (Prov. 20:22), divine *power* (Isa. 40:31), and divine *perception* (Ps. 25:3–5). Divine *peace* surrounds those who wait patiently for the Lord (Job 14:14; Ps. 52:9).

3.   **The Accomplishments.** Waiting on the Lord hones personal *discipline, development* and *dependence* on the Lord. Human abilities are insufficient to accomplish the Lord's work.

CONCLUSION: Perhaps you have a situation about which you've grown impatient. God may be trying to teach you the secret of Psalm 37:7.

What Is Jesus Doing Right Now?

Date preached:

SCRIPTURE: Hebrews 4:14

INTRODUCTION: If we had a telescope capable of peering into the highest heaven, what would we see Jesus doing right now. What is His present ministry?

1.   **He Is Ruling from His Heavenly Throne.** (Eph. 1:20, Mark 16:19, Phil. 2:9; 1 Peter 3:22). Wesley wrote: "Jesus the Savior reigns / The God of truth and love; / When He had purged our stains / He took His seat above."

2.   **He Directs and Empowers His Church.** (Matt. 16:18, Acts 1:1, 2; Rom. 15:18).

3.   **He Is Interceding for Believers.** (Rom. 8:34, 1 John 2:1, Heb. 2:17, 18, 7:25).

4.   **He Is Preparing a Place for Us.** (John 14:1–3).

5.   **He Is Receiving the Souls of Those Who Die in Christ.** (Acts 7:54–59).

6.   **He is Being Praised by Angels.** (Rev. 5).

CONCLUSION: If Christ is doing all this for you in heaven, what are you doing for Him on earth?

Preaching Without Notes

In January, 1875, New York Pastor Richard Storrs delivered a series of three lectures to the students of Union Theology Seminary, which were later published under the title *Preaching Without Notes*. These lectures, while reflecting the speech patterns of their day, are still pertinent for today's preachers. Here is a digest of Storrs' three lectures as condensed from his book.

First Lecture

This matter of speaking freely to a public assembly without notes is eminently one in regard to which every man must learn for himself; and no one can make his own method a rule for another. Still, we learn from others and perhaps something I say may be of service to you. To lay a foundation for my remarks I will state rapidly what my experience in the matter has been. I began my education by studying for the bar; and was at one time quite familiar with the Boston courtrooms. Mr. Webster was there, in the intervals between the sessions of the Senate. Mr. Choate was there, and Mr. Benjamin R. Curtis in the prime of his force and career. All these attorneys, of course, were in the habit of speaking constantly without notes before the full Bench or to the jury. I could not see, therefore, why a minister—however limited in faculty and in culture in comparison with these eminent men—should not do that before his congregation. And when my plans in life were changed under the impulse of God's Spirit and I devoted myself to ministry, I determined if possible to fit myself to do this, and to preach without reading. It seemed to me this was the more apostolic way. I could not learn that Paul pulled out a Greek manuscript and read it with infirm eyes when he addressed the women at Philippi or even on Mars Hill. It seemed that to speak to men without notes, out of a full and earnest mind, was now as then the most natural way to address them. I was distinctly and deliberately determined, if it was in my power, to learn to speak thus, and not to either read my sermons or write them out and commit them to memory.

At the time, such a method of preaching was not looked upon with favor. I got some practice in the debating society; but on the whole I lost rather than gained in this regard in Seminary. And when I came out, I was hardly as eager or well fitted to preach without notes as I should have been earlier. My conviction of the subject remained, however.

My first settlement in ministry was near Boston. I was 24. But the congregation was not helpful to my plans regarding this method of preaching. In a church capable of holding 600, we had 75. They were affectionate, but the majority were cultured and critical hearers who had been trained under the Boston pulpits in which ministers read their sermons. They were exacting in their demands for precision and elegance of literary form, and were uneasy when I rose without notes. I tried to combine the advantages of both methods: to have notes before me, a some-

It seemed that to speak to men without notes,

out of a full and earnest mind, was now as then the

most natural way to address them.

—RICHARD STORRS

what full skeleton of my discourse, and then to be at liberty, in the intervals, to avail myself of any suggestions that might come. But I found this the poorest method, and the whole sermon became a series of jerks. The intervals were not long enough between my prepared heads to allow the mind to get freely, vigorously at work. So I gave up the plan and started reading my sermons.

When I was called to Brooklyn, I went determined to carry out my plan of preaching without notes. I was 25. My first sermon there was without notes, and was an absolute failure. I had made too much preparation, had written out heads, subheads, and even some paragraphs in full in order to be certain beforehand to have enough material.

The result: I was all the time looking backward, not forward, in preaching. I was trying to remember prearranged trains of thought and particular forms of expression instead of trusting to the impulse of the subject. My verbal memory has always been the weakest part of my mental organization. I hardly trust myself to quote a sentence from any writer without having it before me. I had wholly overloaded this verbal memory. It was a flop, and I sank down into my chair wishing I were Pharaoh when the Red Sea went over him.

I went back to the reading of manuscript sermons. But after a while the old feeling revived. From time to time, through the week, I would address various groups, and I always did so without notes. I wished I could have the same experience on Sundays. At last, after 16 or so years, I began to feel a growing sense of the oppressiveness of routine. It seemed to me my mind was in danger of drying up, that it needed a positive change. I thought of changing churches, but it was impractical. So I determined to begin presenting subjects to the congregation without immediate help from a manuscript. This involved changes in my whole way of working, both before preaching and in it.

At the same time, while our church edifice was being reconstructed, my congregation was thrown for many months into the Academy of Music, and the attenders became more diverse. To have tried to hold their attention while reading from a manuscript was impossible. Inserting a manuscript between them and myself would have been like cutting the telegraph wires and putting a piece of paper into the gap. So I gave up the manuscript on the spot and thenceforth preached morning and evening without any notes. I have never written my sermons since.

I now write only a brief outline of the discourse, covering usually one or two sheets of common notepaper, and have no notes before me in the pulpit—not a line, not a catchword. Here are some general suggestions:

Never begin to preach without notes with any idea of saving yourselves work. There *is* relief from the nervous fatigue that comes from using the pen, and there is a release from confining deskwork. A man who writes his sermon becomes so wearied with it that he can hardly rally to deliver it. One who trains his mind to work without the pen finds after awhile that he can meditate his discourses while he is walking, while he is doing errands, while he is sitting in the parlor waiting for a friend. The whole plan of a sermon will sometimes shape itself suddenly in his mind. Thoughts come to him more and more freely at odd moments. But on the other hand, whatever of time and force is saved must only be more carefully devoted to the complete conscious mastery of the subject so that he knows it thoroughly, has searched it through, is vitally charged with it, and has it fully and vividly in mind. Also, one must expect a degree of mental excitement and of consequent mental exhaustion in uttering his sermon without notes.

Always be careful to keep up the habit of writing, with whatever skill, elegance, and force you can command. It will enlarge and refine your vocabulary and keep you from using cheap and common words. Reading puts rich words into our hands, but only careful writing fixes them in our minds. So write, not sermons necessarily, but essays, articles, etc. You will need the constant discipline of such writing to enable you to form sentences rapidly and securely. Writing also trains one to systematize his thoughts. We must discipline our minds by use of the pen that the thoughts which subsequently rise to our lips may be sound and clear.

Be perfectly frank with your people in regard to this matter of your method of preaching. Let them know that you design to preach without notes and without memorizing the sermon. And give them the reasons.

Discharge your mind of the sermon when once you have preached it; otherwise you will be in danger of repeating preceding trains of thought, recurring phrases. You must keep the mind fresh and hospitable for new subjects, keep it all the time alert. Each sermon must have its own vitality.

Never be discouraged by what seems comparative failure. It is not impossible that what seems to you to be failure may appear quite otherwise to your people. Your business is to do the best you can in the preaching of the gospel, and let that suffice. If you feel you have failed, never get discouraged or morbid.

Do no violence to your own nature. If you find, after sufficient conscientious trial, that you (do not function well without notes), use the pen without reluctance. Some men can never acquire complete self-possession in presence of an audience so as to be at ease and in vigor. I have never believed it the best plan for all ministers to preach without notes. I only think it is better for some. Preaching is as great a work as ever is given to men on earth: to bring divine truths with earnest utterance, to human souls. Whether you do your work with or without notes, do it courageously, earnestly, with devotion.

Second Lecture

I propose to present to you certain specific conditions of success in the work of preaching without notes: physical, mental (this lecture), moral, spiritual (next lecture). Undergirding all: A serious, devout, intelligent, inspiring conviction of the divine origin and authority of the gospel and of its transcendent importance to men.

The first condition of success in preaching is *physical vigor, kept at its highest attainable point.* The intellectual man is always in the best condition for effective, vigorous, sustained mental effort when his physical vigor is most nearly at its height. The mind takes vigor from the body. Sound, sufficient sleep; good, simple, wholesome food; clear, crisp morning air; a brisk walk, a swim beyond the breakers—it sets the very soul in a glow. We must maintain, as far as possible, full health of body if we would discourse to men on the themes of the gospel without help of manuscript. A weak man is apt to screech in his utterance, while the strong man speaks easily, naturally, without any push of his voice by the will. We are responsible to God Himself who has given us our bodies as instruments through which the mind is to work. Force, buoyancy, elasticity, vigor will come to the mind from sound and energetic physical force.

The second condition of success in preaching is *keeping your mind in a state of habitual activity, alertness, energy.* Your thoughts need to come rapidly when you speak, so keep the mind up to its highest point like a battery fully charged. Some times, of course, our mind seems to work better than at others, when a moment will do for us what previous hours had failed to accomplish. How do we keep the mind in the best condition for grandest service? There are many ways, but I will mention only two:

- Reading, intently and rapidly, gives a general celerity to the whole mental movement. Read widely: history, science, philosophy, poetry, law, metaphysics. Only eschew fiction, or use it with great moderation. As a general rule, it doesn't help, serving only as a laxative or anesthetic. And do not read to the point of weariness. Absorb and assimilate as much as you can, but never undertake to carry the burden of multitudes of things to be afterward remembered.

- Conversation, too, with equal minds, is of immense and constant service in refreshing and replenishing the mind. Conversation trains the mind to think rapidly and to formulate thought with facility and success.

The third condition of success in preaching is *Be careful that the plan of your sermon is simple, natural, progressive, easily mastered, and is thoroughly imbedded in your mind.* If there is any secret in regard to speaking freely without notes it is this: that the reflective forces of the mind are to be kept strictly in abeyance, not to be called on for any service—that the spontaneous, suggestive, creative powers may have unhindered play. Nothing, if possible, should be left to be recalled at the time of speaking by a distinct act of memory. It is indispensable that the main plan of the sermon be from the start so plainly in view that it comes up of itself, as it is needed, and does not require to be pulled into sight with any effort. To this end, it must be simple, obvious, natural. If possible, let it be so arranged that one point leads naturally to another, and when the treatment of it is finished, leaves you in front of that which comes up next. By such a progressive arrangement of thought you are yourself carried forward. How?

—by a strictly textual division of the subject;
—by topical division of the subject.

The plan of a discourse, if one is to present it without help from a manuscript, should be so absolutely mixed up with his mind that he cannot forget it. One may often profitably spend more time, therefore, on the principal arrangement of the subject and its proper distribution than on all the collateral and auxiliary details. It may not be apparent to the congregation. It is not always best to have the frame of a sermon like the frame of a Swiss cottage, all shown on the outside. But it must be there and give symmetry to all the details. Once you have the main part of the sermon fully in mind, do not be too solicitous about the minor things and let not the thoughts become engaged to too many details. If you do, you will be as one walking with a thousand minute weights attached to him, each one small but their aggregate amount overwhelming.

The fourth condition of success in preaching is *After care of your physical health, energy of mind, and a carefully mastery of the general plan of the sermon, it is necessary to have command of sufficient subordinate trains of thought to aid you in unfolding and impressing the subject.* Have images in mind, illustrations. As you think through your subject, jot down stories, passages in literature, historical examples, Scripture analogies, scenes in nature, personal experience. When you go through your subject again on Saturday night, some of these will return to your mind and others will not. Glance at your notes, then go and preach; and in the pulpit some of what you had previously approved will almost certainly come to mind as you are preaching. Give it as it comes. Never stop to recall any thing which you are only vaguely conscious of. Have plenty of thought beforehand in your mind, but let them come to your lips as they will; and if they don't come never go back to them.

Third Lecture

The moral and spiritual conditions of success in preaching without notes are:

First: One should have a distinct and an energetic sense of the importance of that particular subject on which he is to preach. The special truth which you are to treat has importance in itself and may be the instrument for accomplishing the work. Engage your mind in it for the time, as if no other subject existed. Then when you have preached it, discharge it from your thoughts, taking another in its place. Treat each subject, as it occurs, amply, cordially, eagerly, with enthusiasm, with the whole force of your mind. Whatever your subject be, let it be for the time the one engrossing subject of your mind. A sermon that is read without having been reabsorbed in the mind never has vital virtue in it—manuscripts yellow with time, unable to convert a mouse. But if you throw your whole enthusiasm for a time into the subject your are treating, when you are abroad or at home, there will be reward.

Second: One should, from the very beginning of his discourse, have in view a definite end, of practical impression, which his discourse is to make and leave on the minds before him. He must speak for a purpose, and the purpose must propel and govern the sermon. Without it he will be like the ship tossing on the waves, hither and yon, in the darkness of a fog. Pursue the converging of all subordinate thoughts into one grand thought, to be pressed upon the hearer until secured. Hither and thither, northward, southward, run the brooks, yet ever meeting and mingling into one as they draw toward the gap until the thousand trickles become a torrent. So all the collateral thoughts, arguments, illustrations of a sermon, when bearing upon a single end of moral impression, combine their forces, rush together at last in a common channel, and strike with heavy impact on the mind.

Third: Have in view individual hearers in the congregation. The rays of light get heating power by being focused through a lens and made to converge on one point. So a man's mental action becomes intense, penetrating, effective, as it contemplates a definite effect on personal minds. Like a lawyer trying to persuade a jury of twelve. our preaching should have persons always in view, not merely subjects. Here is a skeptic in your audience, there a person bothered by disturbing thoughts, another is indifferent, others are sinners waiting to be converted, sufferers to be soothed, tempted to be warned, poor to be cheered, rich who must be taught to be generous.

Fourth: Always carry with you into the pulpit a sense of the immense consequence which may depend on your full and faithful presentation of the truth. An instinctive skill is gained only by earnest, continuous, conscientious work with an awareness of the personal, specific results which may depend on the work. Remember, therefore, when you go into the pulpit, that there may be minds before you in the assembly at critical points in their progress to which your words will give an impulse in one direction or another forevermore.

Fifth: Remember always to carry with you into the pulpit a sense of the personal presence of the Master. Where two or three are gathered together, He is in the midst. Here, in this room, this hour, is the Master. The thought of Christ beside us will absolutely expel our mind from all fear of man.

Finally: Be careless of criticism and expect success. You will meet with criticism. You will learn to preach in the pulpit. You cannot learn to preach in the seminary any more than you can learn to swim by stretching out yourselves upon the table. But remember that half the criticism you hear, and nearly all the praise, is intrinsically worthless. Do not be dismayed by any criticism; but forget it, if unjust, and reap from it, if just, whatever of personal benefit you can. And always, gentlemen, expect success, though not necessarily in fame and wealth. Paul, the greatest of human preachers, did not appear to achieve large success: a few scattered and small congregations in the various Greek cities, with error, impurity, dissension among them, the old paganism still in part poisoning their life. But out of his labors and those of his companions, Christendom has come. Out of the work of each minister come consequences of good, immense if unseen. ✿

Quotes for the Pastor's Wall

❝ Oh, if ministers only saw the inconceivable glory that

is before them, and the preciousness of Christ, they

would not be able to refrain from going about, leap-

ing and clapping their hands for joy, and exclaiming,

"I am a minister of Christ! I am a minister of Christ. ❞

—Gardiner Spring

MAY 5, 2002

SUGGESTED SERMON

How To Be A Star

Date preached:

By Dr. Timothy Beougher

Scripture: Philippians 2:14–18, especially verses 14, 15 Do all things without complaining and disputing, that you may become blameless and harmless, children of God without fault in the midst of a crooked and perverse generation, among whom you shine as lights in the world.

Introduction: Ed McMahon was best known as Johnny Carson's sidekick, but he has more recently hosted "Star Search," a program where aspiring actors and musicians perform before a live audience, hoping for stardom. In Philippians 2, Paul tells us how we can become stars. It has nothing to do with musical ability or acting skills, but everything to do with how we live. According to verse 15, God wants us to be lights in the world, or, as in some translations, "stars in the universe." The word "lights" refers to heavenly luminaries. How, then, do we shine as stars?

1. **Conquer Complaining** (v. 14a). Most of us tend to be negative, and some are so negative they even have negative blood! One commentator said, "I've been around Christians long enough to know that telling us not to complain is a like telling us not to breathe. It is so commonplace to grumble." Yet we're commanded to do all things without grumbling, to do everything without complaining. How can we do that?

   A. **Recognize complaining as a sin.** Grumbling/murmuring was one of the fundamental sins that kept the Israelites out of the Promised Land. It is a variety of rebellion against God (1 Cor. 10:10, 11), a questioning of His wisdom in running the universe, a doubting of His care.

   B. **Acknowledge that complaining is a problem for you.** In the words of the hymn, "It's not my brother, not my sister, but it's me, O Lord, standing in the need of prayer."

   C. **Recognize that God uses difficulties to change us**. We don't always change when we see the light, but we usually do when we feel the heat.

We tend to grumble when things get difficult, but we should recognize that God uses difficulties in life to mature us (James 1:2–4).

D. **Work on your heart attitude** (Matt. 12:34).

2. **Avoid Arguing** (v. 14b: ". . . and disputing"). The word "disputing" implies a questioning mind. It suggests an arrogant attitude by those who assume they're always right. Arguing with others in the body of Christ is disruptive. That's why Paul spent the first part of chapter 2 on humility. "To dwell above, with saints we love, that will be grace and glory; / But to live below with saints we know, now that's a different story!" Why avoid arguing? Verse 15 says: ". . . that you may become blameless and harmless, children of God without fault in the midst of a crooked and perverse generation." Over the centuries, Christians have related to the world in 4 ways:

A. **Total separation**. Monastery; no contact.
B. **Total immersion**. Lots of contact, but no impact.
C. **Split adaptation**. Sunday-only Christian; "hypocrite."
D. **Transformation**. "in but not of the world." With God's help (v. 13), it is possible to conquer complaining and avoid arguing, that we prove blameless and innocent, above reproach, in a fallen world.

3. **Recover Rejoicing** (v. 17, 18). The "drink offering" was a libation poured out completely as part of the ritual of sacrifice. It pictures complete consecration. Observe Paul's response to suffering. He is writing from a prison cell, yet refuses to let his circumstances dictate his attitude. Joy and rejoicing ring through his book. >>> *sermon continued on following page*

APPROPRIATE HYMNS AND SONGS

O For a Heart to Praise My God, Charles Wesley/Carl G. Glaser; Public Domain.

I Am Thine, O Lord, Fanny Crosby, William H. Doane; Public Domain.

Humble Thyself in the Sight of the Lord, Bob Hudson; © 1978 Maranatha! Music (Admin. by the Copyright Company).

We Come to Humble Ourselves, Brian Doerksen; © 1990 Mercy/Vineyard Publishing.

Refiner's Fire, Brian Doerksen; © 1990 Mercy/Vineyard Publishing.

Conclusion: How do we have the perspective and power to do all this? Verse 16 tells us to focus on the Word! Memorize verses on problem areas. If you struggle with complaining, learn Philippians 2:14. When you begin to complain, the Holy Spirit will use that verse to help you.

Our culture is so negative that when it sees someone positive, that person shines like the North Star on a dark night. A complaining Christian is a poor witness. A disputing church is a poor witness. Rejoicing Christians and joyful churches are powerful witnesses. Jesus said they are like a city on a hill which cannot be hidden—it can be seen from great distances. A church should stand out in a community as a beacon. There are two kinds of Christians: those who "whine" and those who "shine." Are you seeking to let your light shine to others around you? Then conquer complaining. Avoid arguing. Regain rejoicing.

FOR THE BULLETIN

❋ The Fifth Ecumenical Church Council began meeting at Constantinople on May 5, 553, to deal with the "Three Chapters," three teachers considered sympathetic to Nestorius. ❋ On May 5, 1415, the Council of Constance unanimously condemned the writings of John Wycliffe and demanded that John Hus recant of his "heresy" in public. Hus refused and was burned at the stake July 6. ❋ The sermons of Savonarola so electrified Florence that on May 5, 1498—on pretext of danger from the plague—the city council forbade all preaching in the city. The great preacher remained silent until Christmas Day. ❋ May 5, 1813 is the birthday of the Danish philosopher Soren Kierkegaard. ❋ Thomas Coke, a short, stocky Welshman, was a High Churchman strongly opposed to Dissenters until he read the sermons and journals of John Wesley. He was so moved that he traveled to London and was led to Christ by one of Wesley's lay preachers. When he returned to his church in Somersetshire parish with the message of new life, his congregation drowned out his voice by ringing the church bells while he spoke, and he was soon dismissed. He went on to become one of Wesley's greatest leaders, crossing the Atlantic 18 times in the advance of Methodist missions. On a missionary voyage to Ceylon he was found dead in his cabin, May 5, 1814, "with a placid smile on his face." He was buried in the Indian Ocean. ❋ May 5, 1818 is the birthday of Karl Marx.

Worship Theme:
Humble Christians best reflect God's glory.

Call To Worship:
"Draw near to God and He will draw near to you. Cleanse your hands, you sinners; and purify your hearts, you double-minded.... Humble yourselves in the sight of the Lord, and He will lift you up" (James 4:8–10).

Appropriate Scripture Readings:
Exodus 17:1–7
1 Corinthians 10:1–11

Offertory Story:
In writing of her years in China, missionary Bertha Smith told of a time when Dr. Wiley Glass, missionary educator, was kneeling during a prayer meeting service at a large church in China. Mr. Wang, the church treasurer, was kneeling nearby. Suddenly the Chinese, overcome with emotion, cried out, "Lord, have mercy on me! I've stolen! I'm a thief! I have stolen from God!"

In astonishment, Dr. Glass said, "Not you, Brother Wang; surely not you! All these years you have been such a trustworthy, devoted deacon, faithful trustee of the seminary, and upright Christian gentleman. You just could not have taken money from the church treasury!"

Brother Wang regained control of himself enough to say, "I have not paid my tithe to the Lord! According to His Word, I have stolen it from Him!" The Chinese keep accurate household and personal accounts. Wang counted up his tithe from the time he became a Christian, more than twenty years before, subtracted from it the total contributed to the church, and sold some land to pay the balance. What a flame he afterward became for the Lord.

Benediction:
As we leave this place, Lord, remind us of the truth of that old song that says "Little is much, if God is in it. Labor not for wealth or fame. There's a cross, and you can win it, if you'll go in Jesus' name." Amen.

STATS, STORIES AND MORE

Someone Once Said . . .

"And the muttering grew to a grumbling; and the grumbling grew to a mighty rumbling; and out of the houses the rats came tumbling."
—*Robert Browning in "The Pied Piper of Hamelin"*

"Any fool can criticize, condemn and complain—and most do."
—*Dale Carnegie*

Attitude

Two buckets, one an optimist and the other a pessimist, talked by the well. "There has never been a life as disappointing as mine," said the latter. "I never come away from the well full but what I return empty again." The optimistic bucket replied: "Mine is a happy life! I never come to the well empty but what I go away again full."

Illustrations from Timothy Beougher

- In his book *The Total Man,* Dan Benson tells of experts who studied tape-recorded conversations from different homes over a period of time. They found ten negative comments for every one positive one. If someone recorded our conversations for a week, what would we find?
- Did you hear about the husband who criticized his wife every morning? If she fixed scrambled eggs, he wanted poached; if she poached them, he wanted scrambled. One morning she scrambled one egg and poached the other. He glared at the plate and said, "Can't you do anything right? You scrambled the wrong one!"
- That reminds me of the woman who was asked, "Do you ever wake up grumpy?" She replied, "No, I usually let him wake up on his own."

You've Done Nothing But Complain

A monk joined a monastery and took a vow of silence. After five years his superior called him and gave him permission to speak two words. The monk said, "Food bad." After another five years the monk again had opportunity to voice two words. This time, he said, "Bed hard." Another five years went by. When asked if he had anything to say, he responded, "I quit."

"Well, you might as well," said his superior. "You've done nothing since you've been here but complain."

Additional Sermons and Lesson Ideas

Axle Grease
Date preached:

SCRIPTURE READING: Acts 4:23–31

INTRODUCTION: When the Egyptians chased the Israelites into the Red Sea, the Lord made their chariot wheels come off so they had difficulty driving (Ex. 14:25). Something similar happens in church work without the axle grease of prayer. The prayer of these early Christians was:

1. **Needed** (Acts 4:18–23). Times this perilous require churches that know how to pray.
2. **Vocal** (v. 24). I often pray silently, but there is something wonderful about audible prayer.
3. **United** (v. 24).
4. **Reverent** (v. 24). "Lord, You are God, who made heaven and earth...."
5. **Scriptural** (vv. 24–26). The early church wove their prayers from the threads of previously given Scripture, in this case from Psalm 2.
6. **Confident** (vv. 29, 30).
7. **Answered** (v. 31).

CONCLUSION: Begin a daily prayer list for your church. Pray for the pastor and staff, for our missionaries, our finances, our outreach, our ministries. Pray that we will all be filled with the Holy Spirit and speak the Word with boldness.

What's Wrong with Entertainment?
Date preached:

SCRIPTURE: Psalm 119:37

INTRODUCTION: Anyone who has turned on their television recently or attended a movie knows two facts: Americans are increasingly caught up in the entertainment culture, and entertainment is increasingly vile, profane, obscene, and explicit. It...

1. **Pollutes Our Children.** We're concerned about pollution in our rivers and streams, but the devil has found an almost irresistible tool to poison the spiritual lives of an entire generation of children.
2. **Warps Our Morals.** J. Oswald Sanders wrote, "The mind is the battleground on which every moral and spiritual battle is fought." See Romans 16:19.
3. **Wastes Our Time.** Christians should not spend hour after hour watching television day and night. We have a higher calling. We are here for a nobler purpose.
4. **Cheapens Our Thoughts.** Philippians 4:8 tells us that our thought and minds should dwell on eight things: What is true, noble, just, etc.

CONCLUSION: Make Psalm 119:37 your prayer and post it prominently near your television.

MAY 12, 2002

SUGGESTED SERMON

What MOM Stands For

Date preached:

By Rev. Drew Wilkerson

Scripture: Luke 1:30–35, especially verses 30 and 31 Then the angel said to her, "Do not be afraid, Mary, for you have found favor with God. And behold, you will conceive in your womb and bring forth a Son, and shall call His name JESUS.

Introduction: According to a survey by *Ladies Home Journal*, 85 percent of women say that motherhood is the best thing that ever happened to them. What's the greatest part? Twenty-one percent say it's watching their kids grow. A category called "Everything" came in second (18 percent), followed by kids' "unconditional love" (14 percent). But 70 percent of all mothers consider motherhood incredibly stressful. It was certainly stressful for Mary. She was the mother of no ordinary boy, but she was a mother still, with all of the concerns, hopes and dreams of any mother for her children. She had found favor with God, was a recipient of His grace, and therefore could say, "My spirit has rejoiced in God my Savior" (v. 47). Yet at times a sword pierced her soul. The calling of motherhood is not an easy one, but Mary demonstrated how to be an effective parent, living a life in His favor and grace. From varied scenes in her life we can see three attributes every godly mother needs.

1. **Models.** A godly mother is a model to follow. Luke 1:26–35 reveals the divine dialogue of God's plan for this young "mother-to-be." At first it must have been hard for Mary to understand God's plan for her life, but she was faithful. Though she struggled to understand, she depended on God moment by moment. This is exactly what God wants mothers to do today. Moms are still the significant caregivers. They have an awesome responsibility to nurture these gifts from God we call kids. Although overwhelming at times, parenthood was never meant by God to be undertaken alone. He is our strong ally. Ruth Bell Graham said, "As a mother, my job is to take care of the possible and trust God with the impossible." Godly mothers are models who trust and who can be trusted.

2. **Optimists.** A godly mother hangs on to an optimistic attitude. In John 2:1–11, a wonderful scene unfolds between a mother and a son. Moms believe their kids can do anything. How true this was of Mary's son, Jesus! The wine had run out at the wedding feast. Mary apparently had some responsibility at the wedding, so she asked her firstborn for help. She didn't know what Jesus would do, but she knew he would do the right thing, and she told the servants to follow His directions. She believed in Him, and this is an attribute children desperately need from their parents today. Psychologist Martin Seligman of the University of Pennsylvania has demonstrated that children's attitudes are more shaped by their mothers than by those of anyone else. "The mother's level of optimism and the child's level were very similar," he wrote in his book *Learned Optimism*. "This was true of both sons and daughters.... If a child has an optimistic mother, this is great, but it can be a disaster for the child if the child has a pessimistic mother."

3. **Mainstays.** In John 19:25–27 and Acts 1:12–14, Mary demonstrates one outstanding attribute—she was a mainstay of the faith. At the foot of the cross when the world had turned its back on Jesus and in the Upper Room when the world thought Jesus was dead, Mary was firm in her reliance on God. A mainstay is the supporting line extending from the mainmast of a ship. It is the chief support of the mast and crucial to the ship's ability to set sail. This is a beautiful description of Mary. She was a mainstay of faith for her son, His followers and the early church. This is also a beautiful picture of all godly mothers. Without faith, it is impossible for a mother to please Him

>>> *sermon continued on following page*

APPROPRIATE HYMNS AND SONGS

Faith of Our Mothers, A. B. Patten/Henri F. Hemy; Public Domain

My Mother's Gentle Love, Ron Hamilton; © 1988 Majesty Music, Inc.

Prayer for Families, Claire Cloninger, Margaret Moody; © 1991 Word Music Group.

Thank You for Mothers, Ken Young; © 1993 Hallel! Music Exec.(Admin. by LCS Music Group, Inc.).

Would You Bless Our Homes and Families? Walter Farquharsen/Ron Klusmeier; © 1974 Worship Arts.

(Heb. 11:6). Their faith in God makes mothers a source of continual strength for their children.

Conclusion: The greatest and most unselfish substance in the world is the love of a mother for her child. Mary was a model to follow, an optimist at all times, and a mainstay of faith. Mary was a godly MOM, and every mother who partners with God can be a light of inspiration to her children as well.

Kids Talk

Interview a few of the children and ask them what they like best about their moms. Ask if any of them are giving their moms a Mother's Day present. What is it? Ask, "What is the wisest thing your mother ever told you?"

FOR THE BULLETIN

Piolius, a third-century Christian in Smyrna, who was arrested and tortured for his faith, died a martyr on May 12, 250. ❀ The cornerstone for the first Methodist building was laid on May 12, 1739. The "New Room," in Bristol, England, housed John Wesley's office and bedroom. Here the great evangelist taught, wrote, and counseled. ❀ On May 12, 1789, William Wilberforce, Christian and abolitionist hero, delivered his first Parliamentary speech against slavery. ❀ William Carey published his book, *An Enquiry into the Obligations of Christians,* on May 12, 1792. This 87–page book became a classic in Christian history that deserves a place alongside Luther's Ninety-five Theses in its influence. It led to the formation of a missionary society that sent Carey to India, launching the modern era of missions. ❀ Florence Nightingale, English nurse and founder of the modern nursing profession, was born in Italy on May 12, 1820. ❀ Samuel Morris was born as Kaboo of the Kru tribe in the Ivory Coast. After being kidnapped by a rival tribe, Kaboo escaped to America where he enrolled in Taylor University under the name Samuel Morris. His influence was extraordinary, and he seemed to possess unusual spiritual power. His sudden death at Taylor on May 12, 1893, inspired a generation of students to go to the mission field. ❀ On May 12, 1945, Warren Wiersbe was converted at a Youth for Christ rally in which Billy Graham preached. ❀ A. W. Tozer passed away on this day in 1963.

Worship Theme:
Our faith in God makes us strong on behalf of others.

Call to Worship:
"My soul magnifies the Lord, And my spirit has rejoiced in God my Savior" (Luke 1:46, 47).

Responsive Reading:

Leader: Who can find a virtuous wife? For her worth is far above rubies. The heart of her husband safely trusts her.... She does him good and not evil.... She opens her mouth with wisdom, and on her tongue is the law of kindness. She watches over the ways of her household.... Her children rise up and call her blessed.

People: Charm is deceitful and beauty is passing, but a woman who fears the Lord, she shall be praised.

Service Ideas:
Place a pre-arranged surprise phone call through the public address system from a son or daughter serving overseas in the military with Mother's Day greeting. Put together a video of children in the Sunday school classes telling the church what they like best about their mothers. Have an older saint prepare and deliver a short testimony on "ways in which my mother shaped my life."

A Mother's Day Prayer Based on Psalm 90:
Lord, as we thank you for our mothers, we ask You to be their dwelling place, reminding them that from everlasting to everlasting You are God. Teach them to number their days, to seize each moment, to avail themselves of every opportunity to trust You and encourage us. Teach them to satisfy their children early with Your love, that these youngsters may rejoice and be glad all their days. Bless our mothers. Let Your beauty be upon them. And establish Thou the work of their hands.

STATS, STORIES AND MORE

According to a survey by the *Ladies Home Journal*:

- About a third of all mothers spend ten or more hours per day with their children; another 47 percent devote four to nine hours daily. Eighty-two percent consider at least half of their parenting hours "quality time."

- Almost every mother polled (98 percent) says she has a close relationship with her children.

- Ninety-nine percent say their fondest hope for their children is for them to be good people. They'd also like their kids to someday have happy marriages (97 percent), successful careers (79 percent) and children of their own (75 percent). Just 19 percent want their offspring to be rich.

- No mother feels she's doing everything perfectly. Three quarters wish they could give their children more guidance and advice. Sixty-nine percent said they'd also like to give their kids more attention. And nearly 80 percent of moms with full-time jobs wish they could give more of both.

Someone Once Said:

"I did not have my mother long, but she cast over me an influence which has lasted all my life. The good effects of her early training I can never lose. If it had not been for her appreciation and her faith in me at a critical time in my experience, I should never likely have become an inventor. I was always a careless boy, and with a mother of different mental caliber, I should have turned out badly. But her firmness, her sweetness, her goodness were potent powers to keep me in the right path. My mother was the making of me."

—*Thomas Edison*

Doing Dishes

After dinner one Mother's Day a mother was washing the dishes when her teenage daughter walked into the kitchen. Horrified to see her mother at the sink, she exclaimed, "Oh, mother, you shouldn't have to do dishes on Mother's Day." The mother was touched by this seeming thoughtfulness and was about to take off her apron and give it to her daughter, when the daughter added, "They'll keep till tomorrow."

Additional Sermons and Lesson Ideas

Wrapped in Grace

Date preached:

By Dr. Melvin Worthington

Scripture: Titus 2:11–15

Introduction: All God's gifts come wrapped in grace, but there are different kinds of grace for our different needs. According to this passage, there is:

1. **Saving Grace** (v. 11). God the Father *planned* our redemption, God the Son *purchased* it, and God the Spirit *performs* it within us. Grace has its *source* in the heart of God; its *scope* encompasses all human beings, and its *sufficiency* meets every need.
2. **Schooling Grace** (vv. 12, 13). The grace of God teaches us to *leave* the old life, to *live* the new life, and to *look* for the return of the Lord Jesus Christ.
3. **Sanctifying Grace** (v. 14). Grace sanctifies or sets us apart from sin and keeps us pure in this present world.
4. **Serving Grace** (v. 15). God's grace enables us to faithfully serve the Lord Jesus Christ.

Conclusion: Whatever need you have today, the answer comes wrapped in God's amazing grace.

Blessed

Date preached:

Scripture: Ruth 4:14–22

Introduction: Milton Berle said, "You know you're getting older when it takes more time to recover than it did to tire out." And Vance Havner once quipped, "The first half of our lives we are romantic. The last half we are rheumatic." But our golden years can also be the most blessed. In Ruth 4, Naomi had come full circle, back to Bethlehem, back to a young and growing family, back to a place of blessing. She was no longer young, but old. The blessings given her by the women in Ruth 4 were partially fulfilled in her grandson Obed, but not completely fulfilled until the time of Obed's future descendant, Jesus Christ. From this passage, we learn that this great descendant was:

1. **The Son of Thrilling Significance.** "may his name be famous in Israel."
2. **The Savior for Dying Sinners.** "a restorer of life."
3. **The Sustainer of Aging Saints.** "a nourisher of your old age."

Conclusion: Naomi's experience was later described perfectly in Isaiah 46:4—Even down to old age, our God will sustain us. When your life comes full circle, rejoice. There are blessings of age about which youth knows nothing.

MAY 19, 2002

SUGGESTED SERMON

Joining the Army of the Great Unknowns

By Kevin Riggs   *Date preached:*

Scripture: Nehemiah 11:1–36

Introduction: Tennessee, the sixteenth state of the union, earned its nickname, "Volunteer State," during the 1800s when America was involved in wars of expansion. Tennesseans volunteered in large numbers during the War of 1812, the Texas Revolution, the Seminole Wars, and the Mexican War. The state became known as a state where people would "volunteer" and fight for what they believed. For every famous volunteer like Davy Crockett and Sam Houston, there were thousands of others who sacrificed without any notoriety or fanfare. Like those countless, unknown volunteers, most people live their lives in obscurity. Few become famous during their lifetime, and fewer remain famous after they are gone. After all, God has called us to be faithful, not famous.

Context: After Nehemiah rebuilt the wall around Jerusalem, his next task was to convince people to move inside the walls, into the "inner city." What took place in Nehemiah 11 was the first "urban development plan" in history. Nehemiah 11 is a listing of names of people who were necessary for the success of the city, but unknown to anyone else. Three groups moved into the city: (1) Leaders (v. 1). (2) Draftees (v. 1). (3) Volunteers (v. 2). This last group deserves attention. The Hebrew word *volunteered* means to impel, or to incite from within. These volunteers symbolize God's army of the great unknowns, the kind of solid people who fill every good and thriving church, people who toil behind the scenes without any credit, with no other desire than to serve. These volunteers teach us a simple truth: *God calls us to be faithful, not famous.* Five unknowns from Nehemiah 11 serve as our example.

1. **Seraiah** (v. 11). Seraiah was in charge of the day-to-day operations of the temple. He was the one who made sure everything was in place and everyone had what they needed. Who are the Seraiahs in our church? Who are those who take care of the little things that go unnoticed by most people? Who are those who give of their time without asking anything in return? Where would your church be without them?

2. **Shabbethai and Jozabad** (v. 16). These two guys were the temple's building and grounds workers. They did whatever was necessary to keep the facilities in tip-top condition. Who are the Shabbethais and Jozabads in our church? Who are those who do whatever is necessary to keep things in good condition? If something breaks, they fix it. If something needs to be moved, they move it. Where would our church be without them?

3. **Mattaniah** (v. 17). Mattaniah was the temple's prayer warrior and chief encourager. While others complained, he prayed and gave thanks. Who are the prayer warriors and chief encouragers in our church? Isn't it time to tell them "thank you"? Where would our church be without them? And should you join their ranks?

4. **Uzzi** (v. 22). Uzzi lead the people in worship each week. He removed barriers and brought people into God's presence. Who are the Uzzis in our church? Who are those who remove barriers so people can worship? Who are those who prepare Sunday school lessons, work in the nursery, or help in Children's Worship? Without their sacrifice it would be hard to concentrate and worship God. Where would our church be without them?

Conclusion: Are you willing to volunteer—to be moved by God from deep within—to serve Him wherever needed, for no recognition? Are you willing to serve God in complete anonymity? God called us to be faithful, not famous, and that means three things.

>>> *sermon continued on following page*

APPROPRIATE HYMNS AND SONGS

Rise Up, O Men of God, William P. Merrill/William H. Walter; Public Domain.

As a Volunteer, W.S. Brown/Charles H. Gabriel; Public Domain.

Find Us Faithful, Jon Mohr; © 1987 Jonathan Mark Music ARR UBP of Gaither Copyright Management/Birdwing Music (Admin. by EMI Christian Music).

Come, All Christians, Be Committed, Eva B. Lloyd/James H. Wood; © 1958 Renewed 1986 Broadman Press ARR (Admin. by Genevox Music Group).

The Body of Christ, Peter Beers; © 1996 Abundant Life Music Company.

- God has given you unique gifts to be used for Him.
- Nothing you do for God will go unnoticed by God.
- More important than people knowing who you are is people knowing who God is.

Outside Washington, D.C., in Arlington National Cemetery, is the Tomb of the Unknown Soldier. This monument represents the millions of Americans who have given their lives in defense of our nation. Every one of us owes a debt of gratitude to this great army of the unknowns. God is looking for a few good men and women who will serve Him and sacrifice all they have for His honor and His glory. He is looking for a few good people who not interested in making a name for themselves, but interested in making the name of Christ known. Will you volunteer for a tour of duty?

FOR THE BULLETIN

❋ During the great persecution under Emperor Decius, two Armenian brothers, Parthenius and Calocerus, were slain for the sake of the gospel, in Rome on May 19, 250. Their necks were reportedly broken by an red-hot iron bar. Their tombs are still visible today. ❋ The educator and statesman Alcuin died on May 19, 804. He was ecclesiastical and educational advisor to Charlemagne. ❋ The English preacher and educator, Dunstan, died on May 19, 988. He was revered as one of England's greatest saints until overshadowed by Thomas à Becket. May 19th is known as St. Dunstan's Day on the western church calendar. ❋ On May 19, 1558, King Philip II's Spanish Armada set sail from Lisbon on its ill-fated attempt to conquer England and overturn Protestantism there. ❋ On May 19, 1662, following the restoration of the monarchy, Charles II broke his promises to England by re-enacting the Act of Uniformity, which went into operation later in the year, forcing hundreds of Puritan and Dissenting pastors from the pulpits. Nonconformists were "hunted like criminals over the mountains; their ears were torn from their roots; they were branded with hot irons; their fingers were wrenched asunder by the thumbkins; the bones of their legs shattered; women were scourged publicly through the streets." ❋ On May 19, 1914, Pastor V. P. Kisil was in a prayer service at his church in the province of Yekaterinoslav in the Soviet Union when a well-known Orthodox extremist named Rakhno entered the room, ran toward the pastor, and stabbed him through his heart.

WORSHIP HELPS

Worship Theme:
All we do should be done as unto the Lord, knowing that from the Lord we receive a reward, for we serve Christ (Col. 3:23, 24).

Call To Worship:
"Prepare your hearts for the LORD, and serve Him only. Serve the Lord with gladness! Serve wholeheartedly, as if you were serving the Lord, not men, because you know that the Lord will reward everyone for whatever good he does" (1 Sam. 7:3; Ps. 100:3; Eph. 6:7–9).

Offertory Prayer:
You've given us so many ways to serve You, O Lord, so many opportunities to extend Your work and to strengthen Your Kingdom. Thank you for including among them the service of giving. Now use every penny, every dollar, every check, every cent. Use every heart, every generous spirit. May we give heartily as unto You, knowing that You love a cheerful giver. Amen.

Scripture Reading:
"Yet now be strong, Zerubbabel," says the LORD; "and be strong, Joshua, son of Jehozadak, the high priest; and be strong, all you people of the land," says the LORD, "and work; for I am with you," says the LORD of hosts.... Whatever your hand finds to do, do it with your might.... And whatever you do, do it heartily, as to the Lord.... As each one has received a gift, minister it to one another, as good stewards of the manifold grace of God. If anyone speaks, let him speak as the oracles of God. If anyone ministers, let him do it as with the ability which God supplies, that in all things God may be glorified through Jesus Christ, to whom belong the glory and the dominion forever and ever. Amen. (Haggai 2:3–4; Eccl. 9:10; Col. 3:23; 1 Peter 4:10–11).

STATS, STORIES AND MORE

One Out of Four

According to the Barna Research organization, nearly 1 out of 4 adults volunteer some of their free time to help a church in a typical week.

Famous or Faithful?

"Fame is a pearl many dive for and only a few bring up. Even when they do, it is not perfect, and they sigh for more, and lose better things in struggling for them."

—*Louisa May Alcott*

"Don't confuse fame with success. Madonna is one; Helen Keller is the other."

—*Erma Bombeck*

"Fame is like a shaved pig with a greased tail, and it is only after it has slipped through the hands of some thousands, that some fellow, by mere chance, holds on to it!"

—*Davy Crockett*

What Are We Doing?

There is a story that when the English architect, Sir Christopher Wren, was directing the building of St. Paul's Cathedral in London, some workers were interviewed by a journalist who asked, "What are you doing here?"

The first said, "I'm cutting stone for three shillings a day."

"I'm putting ten hours a day in on this job," said another.

The third replied, "I'm helping Christopher Wren build the greatest cathedral in England for the glory of God."

Missed Opportunities

In his autobiography, *Just As I Am,* Billy Graham tells of chatting with President John Kennedy at the 1963 National Prayer Breakfast. Graham had the flu, and after his short talk, he wanted to return to his hotel. The president asked him to ride back to the White House with him. "Mr. President, I've got a fever," replied Billy. "Not only am I weak, but I don't want to give you this thing. Couldn't we wait and talk some other time?" It was a cold day and Graham was shivering without his overcoat. So he and President Kennedy parted ways. They never met again. Not long afterward, Kennedy was assassinated. "His hesitation at the car door, and his request, haunt me still," Graham recalls. "What was on his mind? Should I have gone with him? It was an irrecoverable moment."

Additional Sermons and Lesson Ideas

Have You Heard?
Date preached:

By Dr. Melvin Worthington

SCRIPTURE: Matthew 13:1–9, 18–23

INTRODUCTION: Whether in children's picture books, epic movies, or long novels, people love stories. One of Jesus' favorite stories was the Parable of the Sower in which He explains how people respond to His message

1. **The Aim** (vv. 1, 2). Good hearing is as essential as good heralding. This parable discloses the four ways people can respond when the gospel is preached.
2. **The Analogy** (vv. 3–9). Here we have the sower, the seed, the soils and the spoiler. The same seed yielded variously, according to the character and preparation of the soils.
3. **The Application** (vv. 18–23). Only when we hear with the proper heart attitude does the seed of the gospel penetrate our wills and produce practical results in both belief and behavior.

CONCLUSION: What kind of soil is your heart?

How To Relax
Date preached:

SCRIPTURE: Psalm 46:1

INTRODUCTION: There are reportedly over 10,000 counseling techniques in use today, and hundreds of thousands of words have been written or spoken to help people cope with the stresses of life. None of them are more powerful than Psalm 46:1.

1. **God Is Our Security.** "God is our refuge." The Hebrew word "refuge" meant a place of safety. Isaiah and Job used it to describe a shelter from the storm. The songwriter talked of being "hidden in the hollow of God's blessed hand."
2. **God Is Our Strength.** "God is our refuge and strength." See Habakkuk 3:19; Nehemiah 8:10; Isaiah 41:10; Psalm 27:1; Ephesians 3:16; and Philippians 4:13.
3. **God Is Our Savior.** "a very present help in trouble." He not only redeems our souls, He redeems our sorrows and our situations in life.

CONCLUSION: We can only relax emotionally and physically when these truths encase our souls, when we remember that "the LORD of hosts is with us; the God of Jacob is our refuge" (v. 11).

Discouragement in Ministry

An "Interview" with Charles Haddon Spurgeon

Pastor, Metropolitan Tabernacle, London

Mr. Spurgeon, today you'll be speaking to thousands of people. How does that make you feel?

I have to speak today to myself; and whilst I shall be endeavoring to encourage those who are distressed and down-hearted, I shall be preaching to myself, for I need something which shall cheer my heart—why I can not tell, wherefore I do not know, but I have a thorn in the flesh, a messenger of Satan to buffet me; my soul is cast down within me, I feel as if I had rather die than live; all that God hath done by me seems to be forgotten, and my spirit flags and my courage breaks down. I need your prayers.

How can the "victorious" Christian have such feelings?

Fits of depression come over the most of us. Our work, when earnestly undertaken, lays us open to attacks in the direction of depression. Discouragement creeps over my heart and makes me go with heaviness to my work.

I know you've had some health problems. Does your physical condition contribute to depression?

Most of us are in some way or other unsound physically. There can be little doubt that sedentary habits have a tendency to create despondency. Mental work tends to weary and to depress, for much study is a weariness of the flesh. To sit long in one posture, pouring over a book, or driving a quill, is in itself a taxing of nature; but add to this a badly ventilated chamber, a body which has long been without muscular exercise, and a heart burdened with many cares, and we have all the elements for preparing a seething cauldron of despair.

When are you most likely to be depressed?

How often, on Lord's day evenings, do we feel as if life were completely washed out of us!

When else?

I must mention the hour of great success. When at last a long cherished desire is fulfilled, when God has been glorified greatly by our means, and a great triumph achieved, then we are apt to be faint. When I first became a pastor in London, my success appalled me; and the thought of the career which it seemed to open up, so far from elating me, cast me into the lowest depth. Who was I that I should continue to lead so great a multitude? I hope I was not faithless, but I was timorous and filled with a sense of my own unfitness. I dreaded the work.

How do you overcome depression?

Brother, what an all-sufficient promise that is—"I will help Thee." Why, it matters not what God has given us to do; if He helps us we can do it. Give me God to help me, and I will split the world in halves. I thought but yesterday, "I have an opportunity for serving God, but I am too weak for it." And then it struck me, Do the cherubim and seraphim ever say that? Do they ever for a moment say, "I have not strength enough to do it!" No. He would meekly bow his head and say, "He that commanded the deed will enable me to perform it." And so must the Christian say, "My God, dost Thou command? It is enough: 'tis done. Thou never didst send us to warfare at our own charges, and Thou wilt never do so; Thou wilt help us, and be with us to the end." Before we can do much, then, we must know our own weakness, and believe God's strength.

Do you have any advice for ministers who might be discouraged right now?

Be not dismayed by soul-trouble. Count it no strange thing, but a part of ordinary ministerial experience. Cast not away your confidence. Cast thy burden of the present, along with the sin of the past and the fear of the future, upon the Lord, who forsaketh not His saints. Continue with double earnestness to serve your Lord when no visible result is before you. ✸

MAY 26, 2002

When a Prophet Confronts a King

By Dr. Ed Dobson   *Date preached:*

Scripture: Mark 6:14–28, especially verses 17–24 Herod himself had sent and laid hold of John, and bound him in prison for the sake of Herodias, his brother Philip's wife; for he had married her. Because John had said to Herod, "It is not lawful for you to have your brother's wife."

Therefore Herodias held it against him and wanted to kill him, but she could not; for Herod feared John, knowing that he was a just and holy man, and he protected him. And when he heard him, he did many things, and heard him gladly.

Then an opportune day came when Herod on his birthday gave a feast for his nobles, the high officers, and the chief men of Galilee. And when Herodias' daughter herself came in and danced, and pleased Herod and those who sat with him, the king said to the girl, "Ask me whatever you want, and I will give it to you." He also swore to her, "Whatever you ask me, I will give you, up to half my kingdom."

So she went out and said to her mother, "What shall I ask?"

And she said, "The head of John the Baptist!"

Introduction: Our nation and world may be in moral decline, but just consider the political and moral quagmire facing John the Baptist in Mark 6.

1. **The Story:** This is a story recorded in Matthew, Mark, and Luke. Here in Mark's account, we see...

   - **Mark 6:14–16.** If polls and focus groups had existed in Christ's time, this is what they would have revealed about the popular opinion of Jesus and of John. It had been nearly four centuries since the last prophets had been sent by God, and the Jewish people thought that perhaps John and Jesus were prophets. Perhaps John was the forerunner, Elijah, who had been predicted in the last paragraph of the Old Testament.

   - **Verse 17–20.** We have dysfunctional families today, but few as strange as Herod's messed-up family. Herodias, the daughter of Aristobulus, one of the sons of Herod the Great, married her uncle Philip. Herod

Antipas, the ruler in Mark's account, was the half brother of Philip. Though married to another, he lived out of wedlock with Herodias. John the Baptist rebuked him for it, and therefore Herodias nursed a grudge.

- **Verses 21–29.** The dancing of Herodias' daughter was so provocative that Herod offered the girl whatever she wanted. When she and her mother requested John's head, the king was distressed (the same word is used of Jesus in the Garden of Gethsemane), but he sent an executioner, and John's head came back on a platter.

2. **The Lesson:** John the Baptist and King Herod are the antitheses of each other. Herod, part of the Roman empire, had his palaces, soldiers, authority, and prestige. John the Baptist was kind of an ancient hippie out in the desert, just preaching, calling the Pharisees snakes and vipers. He preached about sin and repentance and the coming kingdom. When he had an opportunity to talk to the king, he didn't try to convince Herod to believe in anything. He said, "Let me tell you something. You married your brother's wife. That's not right." John spoke the truth. Our temptation is to stop short of declaring all the truth for fear of offending someone, but John was committed to giving all of the truth to all the people all of the time. John was also a man who lived the truth. Even Herod acknowledged him as righteous and holy. Herod was attracted to John and to John's message. He loved listening to the truth, enjoyed conversing about the truth, was puzzled by the truth.

>>> *sermon continued on following page*

APPROPRIATE HYMNS AND SONGS

Come, Holy Ghost, Our Hearts Inspire, Charles Wesley; Public Domain.

The Solid Rock, Edward Mote/William B. Bradbury; Public Domain.

The Solid Rock, Don Harris; © 1992 Integrity's Hosanna! Music.

Teach Me Thy Way, O Lord, Harvey Loland; © 1980 Sound III, Inc./Universal/MCA Music (Admin. by MCA Music Publishing).

Because We Believe, Nancy Gordon/Jamie Harvill; © 1996 Mother's Heart Music/Integrity's Praise! Music (Admin. by Integrity Music, Inc.).

He respected and feared the one who delivered the truth. But in the final analysis, he rejected the truth. We come on Sunday, open our Bibles, take notes, listen to the truth, and maybe on the way home we even talk about the truth, but the question is: what are you doing with the truth?

Conclusion: Why did Herod reject the truth? Was it his love for sin? Was it pride? Was it pressure from his wife? He knew the truth, but never got to the point of repentance and confession. Sin can cause us to walk out and deny the truth. Pride can cause us to walk out and reject the truth. The pressure of family and peers and friends can cause us to walk out and ignore the truth. What is it that stands as your obstacle on the road to obedience?

FOR THE BULLETIN

❋ In A.D. 596, Pope Gregory I, burdened for the English, sent a missionary team headed by Augustine to Great Britain. They were well-received by King Ethelbert and Queen Bertha, and Christianity was planted on the British Islands. Augustine is often called the "Apostle to the English." On a tomb in Canterbury are these words: "Here rests the Lord Augustine, first archbishop of Canterbury, who being formerly sent hither by the blessed Gregory, bishop of the city of Rome, and by God's assistance supported with miracles, reduced King Ethelbert and his nation from the worship of idols to the faith in Christ, and having ended the days of his office in peace, died on the 26th day of May, in the reign of the same king." ❋ Today marks the death of another early British Christian, the Venerable Bede, father of English history and theology. His *Ecclesiastical History of the English Nation* is meticulously accurate, setting a standard for subsequent historians. Spring of 735 found Bede translating the Gospel of John into Anglo-Saxon. By early morning, May 26, 735, only one chapter remained, and Bede, knowing time was short, worked furiously. By evening the translation was finished and Bede sat on the floor of his small room singing, "Glory be to the Father, and to the Son, and to the Holy Ghost." Finishing the hymn, he passed quietly into the presence of the Lord. ❋ On May 26, 1521, the Edict of Worms outlawed Martin Luther and his followers, following his Papal excommunication in April. ❋ Nickolaus von Zinzendorf was born on May 26, 1700.

WORSHIP HELPS

Worship Theme:
God wants us to hear, accept, and live the truth of His Word.

Call to Worship:
"I will praise You, O Lord, among the peoples; I will sing to You among the nations. For Your mercy reaches unto the heavens, and Your truth unto the clouds" (Ps. 57:9, 10).

Story Behind "The Solid Rock":
One day in 1834, a 34–year-old carpenter and furniture maker in London named Edward Mote was walking to work. He had recently opened his own shop, and that gave him a little more control over his schedule. He liked to whittle away a few minutes here and there on his hobby of writing articles and poems. On this particular day, a phrase came to mind as he walked, and as soon as he arrived at his shop, he gave instructions to his employees before closeting himself inside his office to develop his poem which he titled, "Gracious Experience of a Christian." By the end of the day, he had four verses. On the following Sunday, as he visited a friend whose wife was near death, he quoted the poem. It was so well received that he later had a thousand copies printed. It has since become one of our favorite hymns, reminding us that only Christ and His Word provide a foundation of truth. All other ground is sinking sand.

Benediction:
Grant Lord, that we, in the words of St. Paul, would speak the truth in love. And may our lives complement the truth, not contradict it. May the quality and depth of our lives be such that when others think of us they think of You. It's so easy to enjoy and be puzzled by the truth and to remain unchanged. So grant, Lord, that we'd be open to the truth of Your Word, that we would respond to the truth of Your Word, and that we would obey. Dismiss us now in Your blessing and in the name of Jesus who is the way, the truth and the life. Amen.

STATS, STORIES AND MORE

Holy Boldness

- "The children of Israel went out with boldness" (Ex. 14:8).

- "In the day when I cried out, You answered me, and made me bold with strength in my soul" (Ps. 138:3).

- "The wicked flee when no one pursues, but the righteous are bold as a lion" (Prov. 28:1).

- "Now some of them from Jerusalem said, "Is this not He whom they seek to kill? But look! He speaks boldly, and they say nothing to Him. Do the rulers know indeed that this is truly the Christ?" (John 7:25, 26).

- "Now when they saw the boldness of Peter and John, and perceived that they were uneducated and untrained men, they marveled. And they realized that they had been with Jesus" (Acts 4:13).

- "And when they had prayed, the place where they were assembled together was shaken; and they were all filled with the Holy Spirit, and they spoke the word of God with boldness" (Acts 4:31).

Modern Martyrs

John the Baptist was only one of thousands who have died for speaking the truth. The last 100 years have been the bloodiest in Christian history. There were reportedly more martyrs in the 20th century than in all the previous nineteen combined. The Global Evangelism Movement reports the average number of people martyred for their faith each year is 160,000. There are currently an estimated one million people in prison for religious reasons. World Evangelical Fellowship shares that more people have died in circumstances related to their faith in that century than in all the 20th-century wars combined. Among them was Roy Pontoh, 15, who was among 150 members of Bethel Church in Indonesia attending a retreat on January 20, 1999, when a Muslim mob attacked. Roy was asked, "Are you a Christian?" Armed only with his Bible, the teenager proudly replied, "I am a soldier of Christ." The attacker then cut Roy's hand with a sword and asked again, "Are you a Christian?" Once again, young Roy bravely replied, "I am a soldier of Christ." Angrily, the Muslim attacker stabbed Roy in the stomach and killed him.

Additional Sermons and Lesson Ideas

Who Is Wise?
By Dr. Melvin Worthington

Date preached:

SCRIPTURE: Proverbs 9:10; 16:16; James 1:5; 3:13–18

INTRODUCTION: The word "wisdom" occurs over 200 times in the Bible. The search for wisdom is godly. The source of wisdom is God. James challenges us to pray for wisdom and gives a portrait of the kind of wisdom we need for life's circumstances.

1. **The Pursuit of Wisdom** (James 1:5). As we ask for it, God gives sufficient wisdom for every need.
2. **The Portrait of Wisdom** (James 3:13–18). James identifies two types of wisdom and thoroughly tests both. Earthly wisdom produces a spirit of ambition and contention. Heavenly wisdom originates with God and is pure, peaceable, gentle, easy to be entreated, full of mercy and good fruits.

CONCLUSION: Take seriously God's command to seek wisdom, and evaluate your life by the characteristics of James 3.

The Gospel in a Thimble

Date preached:

SCRIPTURE: Genesis 3:21

INTRODUCTION: Erma Bombeck once called guilt "the gift that keeps on giving." God doesn't want you to bear a weight of guilt through life, and beginning in Genesis 2, He started doing something about it. When Adam and Eve disobeyed God, their sin made them SELF-conscious. They tried to "cover up" with fig leaves and to deal with sin by their own efforts. When God covered them with the skins of a slain animal, we see "the first Gospel sermon preached by God, not in words but in symbol and action" (Arthur Pink). It tell us:

1. Salvation is of God, not through our own efforts.
2. Salvation involves the death of an innocent substitute.
3. Salvation involves the shedding of blood.
4. Salvation involves the slaying of a spotless lamb. While we aren't told that the animal in Genesis 3:21 was a lamb, the next paragraph features a lamb. Abel's sacrifice from his flock was acceptable and began a sequence of Scriptures on the Lamb that stretches through Isaiah 53, John 1:29, 1 Peter 1:19, and on to Revelation 5, 21 and 22.

CONCLUSION: We have no answer for guilt apart from the Lamb of God. Let His blood make you whiter than snow.

SPECIAL OCCASION SERMON

A Missions Sermon

Date preached:

Scripture Reading: Psalm 96

Introduction: On Saturday night, May 29, 1819, a 36-year-old minister named Reginald Heber was talking with his father-in-law, also a minister, about the next day's worship service. The theme was global evangelism. The older man said that he had a good missionary message but needed a suitable conclusion. "Will you write a poem," he said, or words to that effect, "a few lines with which to end my message?" Reginald retired to the corner of the room and, in a few moments, wrote the words that were to make him known as the writer of one of the most famous missionary hymns in Christian history:

> *From Greenland's icy mountains, from India's coral strand,*
> *Where Africa's sunny fountains roll down their golden sand,*
> *From many an ancient river, from many a palmy plain,*
> *They call us to deliver their land from error's chain.*

"From Greenland's Icy Mountains," however, is not our oldest or most famous missionary hymn. There is an even older hymn, one that is infinitely better. We can say that Psalm 96 is arguably the oldest missionary hymn in existence. Notice these phrases: "Sing to the LORD, all the earth . . . Declare His glory among the nations . . . among all peoples . . . families of the peoples [nations] . . . all the earth. . . . Say among the nations, 'The LORD reigns.'" This is the Great Commission a thousand years before Christ spoke it in Matthew 28. Notice the simple words here that constitute our marching orders.

1. **Sing—Verses 1–2a.** Scientists using satellite dishes are picking up "music" from the stars, a melodious humming or vibrating that travels through space. Likewise, the atmosphere around us is God's equivalent to a symphony orchestra. The crickets and frogs on a spring night, the sound of the wind whistling through the trees, the sound of a bubbling brook or of the waves of the ocean swelling and breaking against the coast—it's like an ever-performing concert. How beautifully the birds sing, especially as the dawn breaks and the sun rises! Someone wrote:

This is my Father's world,
And to my listening ear,
All nature sings and round me rings
The music of the spheres.

In this passage we're told that all the earth is to sing praises to the Lord, and as we go forth with God's message, it should be with music playing on our "insides"—psalms, hymns, and spiritual songs (Eph. 5:19).

2. **Proclaim—Verse 2b.** We're to "proclaim the good news of His salvation from day to day." This involves personal evangelism, reaching our friends, relatives, associates, and neighbors with the gospel. We aren't just to go across the sea; we're to go across the street.

3. **Declare—Verse 3.** "Declare His glory among the nations, His wonders among all people." According to missiologist Ralph Winter, only one percent of the world's population knew Jesus Christ as personal Lord and Savior in the 15th century. Today, according to studies done by Dawn International, that figure is at 11.1 percent—and growing. Out of a worldwide population of six billion, there are some 680 million evangelical Christians in the world today. The rate of increase is estimated by DAWN at around 7 percent per year.

4. **Give—Verse 7.** "Give to the LORD, O families of the peoples, give to the LORD glory." We have marching orders telling us to warn the world around us to bow down and acknowledge the Lord.

5. **Worship . . . Tremble—Verse 9.** *All people that on earth do dwell, / Sing to the Lord with cheerful voice; / Him serve with fear, His praise forth tell, / Come ye before Him and rejoice.*

6. **Say—Verse 10.** "Say among the nations, 'The LORD reigns.'" Those three words, "The Lord reigns," are characteristic of this portion of the Psalms, and they are so very powerful. *Jesus shall reign where'er the sun / Doth its successive journeys run. / His kingdom spread from shore to shore / Till moons shall wax and wane no more.*

Conclusion: Sing! Proclaim! Declare! Give! Worship! Say! Those are our marching orders. When missionary Hudson Taylor was seeking to establish his China Inland Mission, he spoke to 2,000 ministers from across Scotland. He began his address by telling of an experience he had while traveling from Shanghai to Ning-po aboard a Chinese boat. Among his fellow passengers had been a Chinese man who was educated in England and went by the name Peter. Hudson talked with him and acquainted him with the teachings of Christ, but Peter had not yet made a personal commitment to Christ. The two men talked extensively. One day as the boat approached a particular city, Hudson went to his cabin, preparing to go ashore to preach and distribute literature. Suddenly he heard a splash, followed by a cry of alarm. Rushing to the deck, he didn't see his new friend Peter. "He went down over there," said the captain of the boat, showing no signs of alarm. Hudson jumped into the water and began swimming toward the sight, but he couldn't locate Peter. Just then he spotted some nearby fishermen with a dragnet. "Come!" Hudson cried to them. "Come and drag over here. A man is drowning!"

"Vah bin," the fishermen replied. "It is not convenient."

"Come quickly, or it will be too late," Hudson pleaded.

"We are busy fishing."

"Never mind your fishing. Come at once and I will pay you well."

"How much will you give us?" the fishermen wanted to know.

"Five dollars. But hurry."

"Too little!" they called back. "We won't come for less than thirty."

"I don't have that much with me, but I'll give you all I have."

"How much is that?" they asked.

"I don't know," shouted Hudson. "About fourteen dollars."

They finally brought their net over, and the first time they passed it through the water they dragged up the missing man. But it was too late. Peter was dead. As Hudson told that story, a wave of indignation swept over the audience, but the missionary looked at them and said, "We condemn those heathen fisherman. We say they are guilty of the man's death—because they could easily have saved him, and did not do it. But what of the millions whom we leave to perish . . .eternally? What of the plain command, 'Go into all the world and preach the gospel to every creature'?"

The Bible tells us to sing . . . to proclaim . . . to declare . . . to give . . . to worship . . . and to say among the nations: "The Lord reigns." That's missions. That is our mandate. And those are our marching orders.

Amanda Smith

Solomon wrote, "Whatever your hand finds to do, do it with your might" (Eccl. 9:10), a sentiment Paul echoed in Colossians 3:23: "And whatever you do, do it heartily, as to the Lord and not to men."

Perhaps no one worked harder than Amanda Smith, a trait learned from her father. Amanda was born into slavery in Maryland on January 23, 1837. Her father, Samuel Berry, worked tirelessly to free his children. He made brooms by day, then walked miles to work in the fields until one or two o'clock in the morning. Returning home, he slept for an hour or two; then he was up again. Thus he eventually purchased freedom for every member of his family.

Amanda grew up committed to Christ. Her mother and grandmother were full of faith, and the Methodist revivals sweeping the area profoundly affected her. She labored in the kitchen, earning a reputation for Maryland biscuits and fried chicken. She also became known as the area's best scrubwoman. When her sister Frances accidentally destroyed her freedom papers, Amanda worked hard to re-purchase them. She often stood at her washtub from six in the morning until six the next morning, then worked for hours at her ironing board. When overcome by fatigue, she would lean her head on the window ledge and sleep a few moments till the need passed.

She somehow found time for witnessing, and her power as an evangelist gained notice. She began accepting invitations and was soon in demand as a Methodist holiness evangelist. She evangelized as far south as Knoxville, Tennessee, and as far west as Austin, Texas. She traveled alone by train and with simplicity, her belongings rolled in a carpetbag. Her fame leaped the Atlantic, and she was called to England for meetings, then to India, then to Africa. She organized women's bands, young people's groups, temperance societies, children's meetings. She adopted homeless youngsters and started an orphanage near Chicago.

She was called "God's image carved in ebony."

Though never ordained, she brought many to Christ through her preaching. She said, "The thought of ordination never entered my mind, for I had received my ordination from Him who said, 'Ye have not chosen Me, but I have chosen you, and ordained you, that ye might go and bring forth fruit'" (John 15:16 KJV). ✿

JUNE 2, 2002

Double, Double, Toil and Trouble   *Date preached:*

Scripture: 1 Samuel 28:3–20, especially verses 5–7 When Saul saw the army of the Philistines, he was afraid, and his heart trembled greatly. And when Saul inquired of the LORD, the LORD did not answer him, either by dreams or by Urim or by the prophets. Then Saul said to his servants, "Find me a woman who is a medium, that I may go to her and inquire of her." And his servants said to him, "In fact, there is a woman who is a medium at En Dor."

Introduction: Our planet is a spiritual battle zone, blanketed with spiritual forces, both good and evil. God's people are surrounded by angels who are ministering spirits sent to serve those who inherit salvation. But there is also an invisible army of evil angels, of demons and evil spirits, enveloping this world. In our text today, we pay a visit to the most famous witch in history, and we see a man who should be walking with Jehovah reduced to double, double, toil and trouble. What had brought Saul to this?

1. **His Charisma Was Obvious.** As a young man, Saul's charisma was an obvious asset to his leadership opportunities. "There was not a more handsome person than he among the children of Israel. From his shoulders upward he was taller than any of the people" (1 Sam. 9:2). Think of the hottest young hunk in the movies, and you'll have a picture of Saul. The Lord made him perfect for the role for which he had been born. God makes us all the way He wants us to be for what He wants us to do. "We are His workmanship, created in Christ Jesus for good works, which God prepared beforehand that we should walk in them" (Eph. 2:10).

2. **His Calling Was Noble.** "Samuel took a flask of oil and poured it on his head, and kissed him and said: 'Is it not because the LORD has anointed you commander over His inheritance?'" (1 Sam. 10:1). The Lord planned to use Saul in an important way, just as He has a purpose for your life. What if we had to go through life without purpose? Aldous E. Huxley said, "Sooner or later, one asks even of Beethoven, even of Shakespeare... 'Is this all?'" God has set eternity in our hearts, and we instinctively feel we are made for a significant

reason. When we commit ourselves to Christ, God promises to use us to accomplish His will in the world.

3. **His Career Was Promising.** In 1 Samuel 11, the young king saves the city of Jabesh Gilead, then freely pardons critics, winning the respect and admiration of all the people.

4. **His Character Was Flawed.** The story of Saul could have been one of most uplifting stories of the Bible, but it quickly headed south because his character was flawed. An advisor to former president Bill Clinton was Dick Morris, who suddenly resigned from the White House due to a sex scandal. In the Detroit newspaper, Morris explained, "I started out being excited working for the president. Then I became arrogant, then I became grandiose, and then I became self-destructive." He said he had "a fundamental flaw in my character, a fundamental weakness in my personality, a fundamental sin, if you will. I'm prone to being infatuated with power and believing that the rules don't apply to me." That describes Saul perfectly. What exploits he might have accomplished, what victories he might have won, what history he might have made if only he had been a better man. We must never tolerate ongoing sin in our lives, must never rationalize our weaknesses or sweep our iniquities under the rug. God is *Jehovah M'Kaddesh*—the God who sanctifies.

>>> *sermon continued on following page*

APPROPRIATE HYMNS AND SONGS

Onward, Christian Soldiers, Sabine Baring-Gould/Arthur Seymour Sullivan; Public Domain.

Stand Up, Stand Up For Jesus, George Duffield, Jr./George J. Webb; Public Domain.

Holy, Holy, Holy, John B. Dykes/Reginald Heber; Public Domain.

Holy, Holy, Holy, Gary Oliver; © 1991 CMI-HP Publishing (Admin. by Word Music Group, Inc.).

Let God Arise, Elizabeth Bacon; © 1970 Sound III, Inc./Universal-MCA Music (Admin. by Universal-MCA Music Publishing).

5. **His Crown Was Lost.** On the last full day of his life, Saul was despairing and despondent, frightened and unfocused. He had lost his relationship with the Lord, his mentor was dead, and his archenemies were encircling him. In extreme distress, he turned to the occult and consulted the witch of En Dor. His ending was among the most tragic of the Bible.

Conclusion: The Lord loves you and wants to do something special with your life. But inner corruption, outward compromise, and spiritual neglect can drain away your confidence and steal away your crown. The witch of En Dor is not your friend. Stay away from her. Commit yourself without reservation to Christ. Draw near to God, and begin living a life worthy of the calling you have received.

FOR THE BULLETIN

❋ In A.D. 177, a mob in Lyons, France, seized a group of Christians including a little girl named Blandina and Bishop Pothinus, who was over 90. The Christians were tortured, scourged, thrown to beasts, and their ashes thrown into the river. Their deaths have been commemorated on June 2nd throughout church history. ❋ On June 2, 455, Gaiseric, King of the Vandals, entered Rome without resistance. The city was in panic, the imperial troops had mutinied, and Emperor Maximas had been killed. Leo, Bishop of Rome, met Gaiseric at the city gate, begging him not to burn the city. Gaiseric nodded, then galloped off, shouting behind him, "Fourteen days' looting!" The city was sacked. ❋ On June 2, 597, England's King Ethelbert was converted under the preaching of Augustine. ❋ Nicholas, a young man from Greece, undertook a pilgrimage to Rome in the 1090s. As he traveled about, he cried, "Lord, have mercy!" Crowds followed him, repeating the chant. Nicholas fell ill in Trani, Italy, and died there on June 2, 1094. His simple cry for mercy had such an impact that the city built the Cathedral of St. Nicholas the Pilgrim, constructed between 1056 and 1186, which stands to this day. ❋ On June 2, 1846, twice-widowed Adoniram Judson married Emily Chubbuck, who proceeded to write a popular biography of her husband's second wife, entitled, *The Memoir of Sarah B. Judson.*. ❋ On June 2, 1979, Pope John Paul II arrived in Poland in the first visit by a Pope to a communist country, hastening the fall of the Iron Curtain.

WORSHIP HELPS

Worship Theme:
God is holy and pure and will not tolerate inner corruption, outward compromise, and spiritual neglect among His people.

Call to Worship:
"I ... beseech you to walk worthy of the calling with which you were called, with all lowliness and gentleness, with longsuffering, bearing with one another in love. ... There is one body and one Spirit, just as you were called in one hope of your calling; one Lord, one faith, one baptism; one God and Father of all, who is above all, and through all, and in you all" (Eph. 4:1–6).

Applicable Scripture Readings:
Deuteronomy 18:9–14; Matthew 5:17–20; 1 Peter 1:13–16

A Prayer by John Donne (1573–1631), noted English preacher:
O Lord ... Thou hast set up many candlesticks, and kindled many lamps for me; but I have either blown them out, or carried them to guide me in forbidden ways. Thou hast given me a desire of knowledge, and some means to it, and some possession of it; and I have armed myself with Thy weapons against Thee. Yet, O God, have mercy upon me, for Thine own sake have mercy upon me. Let not sin and me be able to exceed Thee, nor to defraud Thee, nor to frustrate Thy purposes. But let me, in spite of me, be of so much use to Thy glory, that by Thy mercy to my sin, other sinners may see how much sin Thou canst pardon.

Kids Talk

Show the children one of your shirts, and tell them the story that Dr. V. Raymond Edman used to tell of the Scotsman who had a dress shirt he wore only on special occasions. After he had used it several times he would question its cleanness and possibly take it to the window for better light. His wife's words were very wise, "If it's doubtful, it's dirty." Tell the children to remember that saying, for it will help them make moral choices later on.

STATS, STORIES AND MORE

Witchcraft

Witches have been a regular feature of modern entertainment, with everything from the Wicked Witch in the *Wizard of Oz* to the everyday housewife on *Bewitched* to the popular family program *Sabrina the Teenage Witch*. Even apart from stage and screen, there is a resurgence of serious witchcraft around the world. I found thousands of web sites on the Internet devoted to witchcraft. In the US today there are an estimated 80,000 people practicing white magic, and every high school in the nation is said to have its own witch. In France, an estimated two hundred million dollars is spent each year on witches and sorcerers. CNN recently did a major story on a coven of witches and wizards who used their supernatural powers to try to change Moscow's weather, with the backing of the city government. The nation of Haiti is totally given over to witchcraft and voodoo, having been dedicated to Satan in 1791. Africa today is filled with its witchdoctors who still hold sway over entire tribes and nations.

The Witch of Endor

One of the most famous restaurants in Canada is in Maple Ridge, British Columbia. It's a pub, and it takes its name from an old public house in 18th Century London. The name is *The Witch of Endor*. If you are a patron of the opera you might know of a director named Travis Preston. One of his most famous productions is entitled *Saul and the Witch of Endor*. If you attend a music festival featuring works written by George Frideric Handel, you might hear his oratorio about Saul and the Witch of Endor.

If you visit the great art museums of Europe, you'll see many paintings labeled "Saul and the Witch of Endor" by artists from all periods of history. If you are a fan of Mark Twain, you may know that he has a short story entitled "Curious Relic for Sale" about the Witch of Endor.

Regret, Remorse, Repentance

- *Regret* is being sorry—mentally (King Saul, for example).

- *Remorse* is being sorry—mentally and emotionally (like Judas).

- *Repentance* is being sorry—mentally, emotionally, and volitionally (like Simon Peter, among others).

Additional Sermons and Lesson Ideas

The Most Valuable Asset in the World

Date preached:

By Kevin Riggs

SCRIPTURE: Romans 15:14–16:27

INTRODUCTION: People are the most valuable asset in the world. Your friends are the only "things" you can take to heaven with you. By noticing what Paul said about his friends gives us three traits about friendship.

1. **A Few of Paul's Friends.**
   - **Phoebe.** She served in the church by ministering to others (16:1, 2).
   - **Andronicus and Junia.** A husband-and-wife missionary team (16:7).
   - **Rufus.** Church tradition believes it was Rufus's father who carried Jesus' cross (Mark 15:21) and also suggests Rufus was black (16:13).
   - **Gaius.** A wealthy business leader (16:23).
   - **Erastus.** A politician (16:24).
   - **Tertius and Quartus.** Tertius's name means "third" and Quartus's name means "fourth." These two men were born slaves and were numbered instead of named (16:22, 23).
2. **Traits of a True Friend.** Paul's friends were rich, poor, black, white, Jew, Gentile, men, women, married, singled, slaves, free.
   - A true friend is one who admonishes (15:14–16).
   - A true friend is supportive (15:23–29).
   - A true friend prays (15:30–33).

CONCLUSION: What kind of friend are you?

I Have Sinned, But . . . ?

SCRIPTURE: Luke 15:21

Date preached:

INTRODUCTION: Three of the most difficult words to say are, "I have sinned." But saying them isn't enough. Genuine repentance means saying them with conviction and with a willingness to change our hearts and our habits, with God's help.
   - Pharaoh said, "I have sinned," but he didn't mean it (Ex. 9:7 and 10:16).
   - Balaam said, "I have sinned," but it wasn't lasting (Num. 22:34).
   - Achan said, "I have sinned," but it was too late (Josh. 7:20).
   - Saul said, "I have sinned," but not with humility (1 Sam. 15:24, 30; 26:21).
   - Judas said, "I have sinned," but he didn't repent (Matt. 27:4).

CONCLUSION: The Bible does give us examples of those who with real contrition say, "I have sinned." Consider these two and imitate them:
   - **King David** (2 Sam. 12:13, 24:10; Ps. 51:4).
   - **The Prodigal Son** (Luke 15:18, 21).

HEROES FOR THE PASTOR'S HEART

Jabez

Mary Redfern lived in the small English village of Haddon in Derbyshire. Her mother was bedfast, and all the care for her eight younger siblings fell onto Mary's shoulders. One day in 1769, she heard a commotion in the street. A little man was preaching before a crowd in the open. His name was John Wesley.

Soon after, Richard Boardman, one of Wesley's evangelists, came preaching. He had recently lost his wife, and his demeanor was tender and poignant. He spoke from 1 Chronicles 4:9 about Jabez, "the most respected son in his family." Mary was deeply moved and never forgot the story of Jabez. She moved to Manchester, married, and named her first-born Jabez. And when Wesley preached in Manchester's Oldham Street Church Mary brought little Jabez. The great evangelist touched the child and blessed him.

Little did he know he was blessing his future successor.

Young Jabez Bunting often heard Wesley preach, and he developed a great love for the gospel. As a lad he would walk miles to hear preaching, returning to deliver his own little sermons to long-suffering sisters, using his father's shirts as ministerial robes. When 19 he preached his first official sermon in Sodom, near Manchester, and shortly thereafter he was ordained to the ministry.

Jabez quickly advanced in Methodism, but he often proved hardheaded and strong-willed. When he rose to leadership following Wesley's death, he ruled with a strong hand. His slogan was: "Methodism hates democracy as it hates sin." One of several controversies occurred on September 9, 1825, when the Brunswick Chapel opened in Leeds, England. A dispute arose over whether an organ should be installed. Many members opposed it, but Bunting and the leaders installed it anyway. The organ, it was later said, cost 1,000 pounds and 1,000 Methodists.

Jabez was called the Pope of Methodism. But he preached a clear gospel and brought Methodist theological training and world missions into their own. His influence lasts to this day. ❋

Quotes for the Pastor's Wall

66 There are no sins God's people are more subject to than unbelief and impatience; they are ready, either to faint through unbelief, or to fret through impatience. When men fly out against God by discontent and impatience, it is a sign they do not believe "that all things work together for good, to them that love God." Discontent is an ungrateful sin, because we have more mercies than afflictions; and it is an irrational sin, because afflictions work for good. . . . The devil blows the coals of passion and discontent, and then warms himself at the fire. 99

—Thomas Watson on Fretting and Fainting

JUNE 9, 2002

SUGGESTED SERMON

Dwindling Devotion

Date preached:

By Dr. Melvin Worthington

Scripture: Revelation 2:1–7, especially verses 2–5 "I know your works, your labor, your patience, and that you cannot bear those who are evil. And you have tested those who say they are apostles and are not, and have found them liars; and you have persevered and have patience, and have labored for My name's sake and have not become weary. Nevertheless I have this against you, that you have left your first love. Remember therefore from where you have fallen; repent and do the first works, or else I will come to you quickly and remove your lampstand from its place—unless you repent."

Introduction: Churches are busy places today, but therein lies a pitfall. The active, aggressive and assertive church faces the danger of becoming so consumed by programs that its love for the Lord diminishes. Any church that becomes growth-centered, gift-centered, goal-centered, group-centered, going-centered or giving-centered may forget to be Christ-centered. Some Christians and churches want Jesus present; others want Him prominent. But He will have the pre-eminent place or none! Efficiency and enthusiasm are cold, deadly words when first love is sacrificed on the altar of get-it-done. Christ is pictured as being in the midst of His church, as the one who is holding the seven stars in His right hand. He is in charge of them. He guides and guards them. He walks in the midst of the seven golden candlesticks. He observes what is going on. He habitats the seven golden candlesticks, which represent the church. Christ knows perfectly the true condition of the church at Ephesus, and of this one. He sees what is not visible to the human eye. Consider the following truths in the letter to the church at Ephesus.

1. **Christ's Inventory** (vv. 1–3, 6). Christ commends the church for its progressiveness—they were an active and aggressive group. He commends it for its perseverance—they stayed with the work. He commends the church for its patience—in spite of attempts by advocates of error, they patiently tested the error and maintained a firm endurance amid those who sought to draw them away from Christ. Christ commends them for their purity—they refused to tolerate those in their midst who were evil. Christ further com-

mends their perception—they lived with those who claimed to be apostles, saw through their masks, and called them liars.

2. **Christ's Indictment** (v. 4). But the Lord charged the Ephesian church with dwindling devotion. They had not changed their doctrine, their deeds or their deportment. This church had a serious defect that was not visible to the human eye. It is possible to display right doctrine and right deeds in order to hide a defective heart.

3. **Christ's Instructions** (v. 5). Christ counseled the church to remember from whence they had fallen, to remember how it once was. "Nothing is better adapted to affect a backsliding Christian or a backsliding church," wrote one commentator, "than to call to distinct recollection the former condition—the happier days of piety." Christ counsels them to repent. Repent means to change one's mind or purposes, thus affecting their conduct. They are counseled to repeat the first works. These works refer to those that were done when the church was first established, to engage at once in doing what they did in the first and best days of their piety. Let them read the Bible as they once did. Let them pray as they once did. Let them go about their Christian duties as they once did.

>>> *sermon continued on following page*

APPROPRIATE HYMNS AND SONGS

My Jesus, I Love Thee, William R. Featherston/Adonirom J. Gordon; Public Domain.

All Creatures of Our God and King, St. Francis of Assisi/William H. Draper; Public Domain.

All My Days, Bill Batstone/Bob Somma; © 1990 Maranatha Praise, Inc. (Admin. by The Copyright Company).

More and More Like Jesus, Kevin Thompson; © 1982 Integrity's Hosanna! Music (Admin. by Integrity Music).

My Tribute, Andrae Crouch; © 1971 Bud John Songs, Inc. (Admin. by EMI Christian Music Publishing).

4. **Christ's Incentive** (v. 7). Without repentance, Christ declared that He would personally come and disband their church. That's tough language and straight talk. The eye of Jesus is marking every declension. And as our love declines, His anger burns. There is a limit to His forbearing meekness. Those who continue to offend Him shall be without defense and stranded helplessly in the path of His fury when judgment strikes. Those who would not leave their first love—Christ Himself—must post a daily quiet time when they regularly meet the Lord by perusing the scriptures, praying in the Spirit and putting away sin. He who will not love Christ supremely soon discovers that he cannot love Christ at all!

Conclusion: Perhaps you have solid beliefs and sturdy morality. But deep inside, are you head-over-heels in love with Christ? If not, repent of it, and rekindle your love for Him today.

FOR THE BULLETIN

❀ On June 9, 68, Emperor Nero, 30, under whose rule Peter, Paul, and a multitude of other Christians were reportedly martyred, died by driving a dagger into his throat, assisted by his servant Epaphroditus. ❀ Columba died in the early hours of Sunday, June 9, 597. Born in Ireland about 521, Columba and 12 companions established a monastery on the small island of Iona off the coast of Scotland. Here he developed a great missionary training center from which the Scots, among others, were evangelized. ❀ On June 9, 1549, the Church of England adopted The Book of Common Prayer, compiled by Thomas Cranmer. ❀ June 9, 1717, marked the death of Madam Jeanne Marie Guyon, French mystic whose life and writings displayed intense love for Christ. ❀ On the morning of June 9, 1790, Robert Robinson, author of "Come, Thou Fount of Every Blessing," was found dead by friends in the guestroom of their house. As a 17–year-old, Robinson had been convicted of sin while drinking with buddies. He later came to Christ under the preaching of evangelist George Whitefield, and spent his life pastoring churches in Great Britain. "Come, Thou Fount," was written as a concluding poem to one of his sermons. ❀ The father of modern missions, William Carey, died at the crack of dawn, 5:30 a.m., on June 9, 1834. One of his last requests was for the following lines from Isaac Watts to be inscribed on his tombstone: *A wretched, poor, and helpless worm / On Thy kind arms I fall.*

WORSHIP HELPS

Worship Theme:
The essence of Christianity is loving Christ.

Call to Worship:
"Jesus said to him, 'You shall love the LORD your God with all your heart, with all your soul, and with all your mind.' This is the first and great commandment" (Matt. 22:37–38).

Scripture Reading:
Hear, O Israel: The LORD our God, the LORD *is* one! You shall love the LORD your God with all your heart, with all your soul, and with all your strength.... Take careful heed to do the commandment... which Moses... commanded you, to love the LORD your God, to walk in all His ways, to keep His commandments, to hold fast to Him, and to serve Him with all your heart and with all your soul.

You who love the LORD, hate evil! He preserves the souls of His saints; He delivers them out of the hand of the wicked.

Light is sown for the righteous, and gladness for the upright in heart. Rejoice in the LORD, you righteous, and give thanks at the remembrance of His holy name. Love the LORD your God, that you may obey His voice, and that you may cling to Him, for He is your life. Oh, love the LORD, all you His saints! For the LORD preserves the faithful.... Be of good courage, and He shall strengthen your heart, All you who hope in the LORD.

Taken from Deuteronomy 6:4–5; Joshua 22:5; Psalm 97:10–19; Deuteronomy 30:20; and Psalm 31:23–24.

Benediction:
The grace of the Lord Jesus Christ, and the love of God, and the communion of the Holy Spirit be with you all. Amen (2 Cor. 13:14).

STATS, STORIES AND MORE

What Jesus Might Write

Christianity Today once printed a series of letters Jesus might write today to congregations. Imitating the style of Revelation 2–3 the letters dealt with issues confronting the modern church. What do you think Jesus would say to our church this morning?

Comments on Revelation 2

"The head may be right while the heart is going in a wrong direction.... It is right to denounce heresy. We are bound by our covenant with Jesus to resist the devil; in what guise soever he may reveal himself. But beware lest while you hate the deeds of the Nicolaitans your love is decreasing. It is not enough that you are able to put a multitude of heretics to flight; you must watch your love-fires, and continually supply them with the fuel of heaven."

—Joseph Parker (1830–1902)

Organized, But . . .

In his book *Harvest of Humility*, John Seamands told of a wounded German soldier who was ordered to go to the military hospital for treatment. When he arrived at the large and imposing building, he saw two doors, one marked, "For the slightly wounded," and the other, "For the seriously wounded."

He entered through the first door and found himself going down a long hall. At the end of it were two more doors, one marked, "For officers" and the other, "For non-officers." He entered through the latter and found himself going down another long hall. At the end of it were two more doors, one marked, "For party members" and the other, "For non-party members." He took the second door, and when he opened it he found himself out on the street.

When the soldier returned home, his mother asked him, "How did you get along at the hospital?"

"Well, Mother," he replied, "to tell the truth, the people there didn't do anything for me, but you ought to see the tremendous organization they have!"

Many churches have a superb organization. Their people are busy. But unless the love of God is in them and the Spirit of God is free to work through them, the church's ministry will be limited. The church at Ephesus was organized—but dead. Don't let that happen in your church!

Additional Sermons and Lesson Ideas

For Those Who Love Him

Date preached:

SCRIPTURE: 1 Corinthians 2:9

INTRODUCTION: Christianity is not primarily a religion, a routine, or a ritual. It is a relationship. God desires our love, and He has made a handful of His best promises to those who love Him. If we love Christ, what will we do for Him? Obey His Commands (John 14:15, 23; 15:10; 2 John 6). *If we love Christ, what will God do for us?*

1. Remain Faithful to Us (Deut. 7:9; Neh. 1:5).
2. Lavish His Grace on Us (Eph. 6:24).
3. Love Us and Manifest Himself to Us (John 14:21).
4. Love Us and Make His Home with Us (John 14:23).
5. Cause All Things To Work Together for Good (Rom. 8:28).
6. Provide an Unimaginable Future (1 Cor. 2:9).
7. Give Us the Crown of Life (James 1:12).
8. Give Us a Kingdom (James 2:5).

CONCLUSION: As you practice Christianity, has it become more of a ritual, routine, or religion than a personal relationship between you and your Beloved? Come back to your First Love and see how greatly God will bless you.

Why Do the Righteous Suffer?

By Dr. Timothy Beougher

Date preached:

SCRIPTURE: 1 Thessalonians 3:3–4

INTRODUCTION: "In this world," Jesus warned, "you will have tribulation" (John 16:33). Still, we often wonder why the righteous suffer and why problems crowd into our lives. Paul told the Thessalonian Christians not to become shaken or unsettled by them.

1. **The Problem of Suffering**
   A. It doesn't seem fair (Job; Lam. 3:39; 1 Peter 2:19–23).
   B. It is not fun (2 Cor. 11:23–28; Heb. 11:25).
   C. It can cause us to falter (1 Thess. 3:3; John 12:42–43; Job 2:9).
2. **The Perspective of Scripture**
   A. It is part of God's plan (1 Thess. 3:3–4; Phil. 1:29; John 16:33; 1 Peter 4:19).
   B. It is under God's providence (I Cor. 10:13; Gen. 50:20; Rom. 8:28).
   C. It is endurable with God's power (2 Cor. 12:7–10; Phil. 4:13).

CONCLUSION: In the future, we'll fully understand (1 Cor. 13:12; Rom. 8:17–18), but right now we can commit to a life of praise (Matt. 5:11–12; I Peter 1:6–7; 4:12–13; James 1:2–4).

Daily Light

When Anne Graham Lotz faced a sudden crisis with her son's unexpected cancer surgery, she opened a little book called *Daily Light* and found there just the verses she needed: "Many are the afflictions of the righteous, but the Lord delivers him out of them all. . . . We know that all things work together for good. . . . With us is the Lord our God, to help us and to fight our battles. The Lord your God is in your midst, the Mighty One, will save.'

Anne later wrote, "God has spoken to me more often through the verses in *Daily Light* than through any other book, except my Bible."

When CIM missionary Arthur Matthews was trapped in Communist China, uncertain of life or death, he was summoned before authorities who were pressuring him to earn his freedom by agreeing to spy for the Communists. That morning he kissed his wife and little one goodbye, and left for the police station, not knowing if he would ever return. In his pocket, he put a copy of *Daily Light.*

Vance Havner, the quaint North Carolina evangelist and writer, faced the greatest heartbreak of his life when his beloved Sara contracted a fatal disease. He turned to his *Daily Light,* and the reading for the day said: "This sickness is not unto death, but for the glory of God, that the Son of God might be glorified thereby." When Sara died, Havner remembered that Lazarus had died, too. "I felt that God would be glorified in her passing," Havner later wrote, "and He was."

When missionaries Russell and Darlene Deibler were trapped in the South Pacific during the Japanese invasion in 1942, they faced the darkest days of their lives. Russell was shortly hauled away to a concentration camp, never to return. That evening, Darlene found comfort in her *Daily Light.* The reading for the evening of March 13 said: "O my God, my soul is cast down within me. . . . Thou wilt keep him in perfect peace, whose mind is stayed on Thee: because he trusteth in Thee. . . . Cast thy burden upon the Lord."

"For me in my need," she later wrote, "the Lord had directed in the arrangement of the verses."

In the biographies of minister, missionaries, church workers, and individual Christians, it is remarkable how often one comes across references to *Daily Light.*

What is *Daily Light?*

It all began with Samuel Bagster, who was born in England just before the American Revolution. At age 7, he was enrolled in a school taught by the Baptist minister Dr. John Ryland, and at the close of his education he apprenticed to a bookseller. In 1794, at age 21, he opened his own book-shop on the Strand in London, resolving to sell only books of enduring Christian value.

Samuel married Eunice Birch and they had twelve children.

The tenth was named Jonathan. Years later when Jonathan was himself a husband and father, he prepared for family devotions each day by care-fully selecting and compiling verses from throughout the Bible according to various themes. A key verse was always selected first, then Jonathan would search through the Scriptures for similar or related verses, weaving them all together into a tapestry of Scriptures for each morning and evening.

One of Jonathan's sons, Robert, remembered from his childhood how carefully his father compiled the selections: "Few are able to appreciate the heart-searching care with which every text was selected, the days, nay the weeks, of changes, alterations and improvements." Sometimes the day's passage was prayed over for weeks before Samuel was assured it was as full and rich as possible.

It was Robert who, sometime in the mid-1870s, first published this col-lection of 732 Scripture readings—morning and evening portions for 366 days. He was assisted by his daughter, Ann, making *Daily Light* a labor of love spreading over four generations.

Since then, it has become, by all accounts, the most widely read collec-tion of topically-arranged daily Bible readings ever published. Many Chris-tians testify that each reading seems to contain just the truth needed for that day. Even when used year after year, the passages always seem fresh and new.

There are many versions of *DL* available in different formats and trans-lations. For a number of years I used the NIV version of *DL* available through Zondervan, but I've recently switched to the beautiful leather-bound edition in the NKJV, available through J. Countryman.

It's perfect for both personal and family devotions, and I recommend it to newly married couples as a perfect way to enjoy daily devotions together. My wife and I read *Daily Light* every night at bedtime. It is con-venient and compact; and being pure Scripture, it is both timely and time-less.

If you aren't familiar with this old book, find an edition today and shed some light on your daily path. ✿

JUNE 16, 2002

Five Facts for Fine Fathers

Date preached:

Scripture: Proverbs 20:3–7

It is honorable for a man to stop striving,
Since any fool can start a quarrel.

The lazy man will not plow because of winter;
He will beg during harvest and have nothing.

Counsel in the heart of man is like deep water,
But a man of understanding will draw it out.

Most men will proclaim each his own goodness,
But who can find a faithful man?

The righteous man walks in his integrity;
His children are blessed after him.

Introduction: Though our culture is in moral freefall, God has given children someone whose power and prestige is greater than all the influences of society put together. One person, more than any other, can make a difference in a young person's life: his or her father. The importance of a godly dad can't be overstated. But how do we become warm and attentive fathers? How can we improve our parenting skills? In our passage today, we find five facts for fine fathers. A good dad must be:

1. **A Patient Man** (v. 3). A wise father must be patient. Keil and Delitzsch translate this verse: "It is an honor for a man to remain far from strife; but every fool shows his teeth." Have you ever been around an irritable dog that growled and showed its teeth? By the same token, have you ever been around an easily irritated dad who is always growling at his kids? A good dad cultivates a pleasant, patient, positive personality. None of us is totally unflappable, but it often helps to memorize Scripture. When you feel yourself getting angry, instead of cursing or counting to ten, try saying one of these verses to yourself: Ephesians 6:4, Proverbs 15:1, Proverbs 29:11—or Proverbs 20:3. Make up your mind to be patient, and learn to make a strategic exit whenever you find yourself losing control. Ask God to help you control your temper, and learn to smile more at your children.

2. **A Hard Worker** (v. 4). A good father is also a hard-working man, not lazy nor a sluggard. One of the causes of maladjusted, troubled children have been fathers that were too passive, and one of the characteristics of weak, passive fathers is laziness. I'm talking about the man who drags home from work, flops in front of a television, pops open a beer, and stays there all night. That man is setting a sad example for his children. The world is lost, the work of the church is great, the days are short, the opportunities are big. The Bible tells us to redeem the time, because the days are evil. A good dad is a diligent man whose schedule includes time for his wife and children.

3. **A Good Listener** (v. 5). A good dad is also a good listener. For our purposes today, we can paraphrase verse 5 to say: "The thoughts in a child's heart are like deep waters, but an understanding father draws them out." A child's heart is not a spigot, but a well. Good conversation can't be turned on and off at will, you've got to let it bubble up. In other words, parents can't just sit down with their children (especially their teens) and say, "Let's talk." We've got to spend time together in a relaxed setting, giving our children lots of informal opportunities to open up.

4. **A Faithful Friend** (v. 6). A good dad is also a faithful friend. A lot of men say, "I love my wife, and I love my children." But does he take time to be with

>>> *sermon continued on following page*

APPROPRIATE HYMNS AND SONGS

Rise Up, O Men of God, William P. Merrill/William H. Walter; Public Domain.

Rise Up, O Men of God, William P. Merrill/William H. Walter/Bill Batstone/Owens; © 1994 Maranatha Praise, Inc.

As For Me and My House, Tom Brooks/Don Harris/Martin J. Nystrom; © 1994 Integrity's Hosanna Music, Inc.

Family Song, Mary Lang; © 1981 Maranatha Music.

In a Father's Heart, Bob Farrell/Shane Keister/Kathy Trocolli; © 1993 Summerdawn Music (Admin. by Integrated Copyright Group, Inc.)/Jaminall Music. Unaffiliated Catalog (UC)/Steadfast Music (Admin. by Gaither Copyright Management/Careers-BMG Music Publishing, Inc.).

them? Does he meet their emotional needs? Is he their companion? Does he confide to them his thoughts and feelings? Does he fulfill his role as spiritual leader of the household? Is he really faithful before God?

5. **A Righteous Soul** (v. 7). A good dad is a righteous man. He leads a blameless life of high character and caliber. He is committed to Jesus Christ, to His Word, to prayer, and to His church. He is honest, modeling integrity for his children.

Conclusion: The promise at the end of verse 7 says that the children of such a man will be blessed. Happy is the child whose father is a patient man, a hard worker, a good listener, a faithful friend, and a righteous soul. Happy are the children of the dad whose God is the Lord.

FOR THE BULLETIN

❁ Roger Holland was an apprenticed youth in 16th-century England who gave himself to "dancing, fencing, gaming, banqueting, and wanton company." After gambling away his master's money, a young maid named Elizabeth loaned him the outstanding amount and told him of Christ. He received the message, married the messenger, and eventually became a merchant in London. During Queen Mary's reign, Roger was seized and, on June 16, 1558, sent to Newgate Prison because of his Protestant faith. He was later burned at the stake. ❁ Samuel Mills was leader of a group of students at Williams College who met for prayer under a haystack during a rain storm in 1806 and gave themselves to God for overseas service. This haystack meeting is regarded as the beginning of overseas interest among American Christians. Mills later helped found America's first missionary society. While returning from Africa in 1818, he was taken ill with fever and died aboard ship on June 16th. ❁ June 16, 1834, is the birthday of Charles Spurgeon. ❁ On June 16, 1855, William and Catherine Booth of Salvation Army fame were married. ❁ On June 16, 1833, an agitated John Henry Newman was aboard ship on the Mediterranean, angry over conditions both in the church and in his life. The winds were calm, the ship was making no progress. When Newman complained, the captain rebuked him. "One step at a time, young man. We who sail before the wind have learned to wait for the wind." Out of this lesson, Newman wrote his famous hymn, "Lead, Kindly Light."

Worship Theme:
God desires to provide high-caliber husbands and fathers for Christian families.

Call to Worship:
"Rise up, O men of God! Have done with lesser things; Give heart and mind and soul and strength to serve the King of Kings."

Appropriate Scripture Readings:
Ephesians 6:1–4; Deuteronomy 4:4–9; Joshua 24:14–15

Hymn Story:
"Rise Up, O Men of God," was written by a then little-known, 44–year-old Presbyterian minister aboard a steamship on Lake Michigan in 1911. His name was William Pierson Merrill, pastor of Chicago's Sixth Presbyterian Church. Merrill was returning to Chicago from a men's meeting, and to pass the time he picked up an article entitled, "The Church and Strong Men." After reading the article, Dr. Merrill later said, "Suddenly this hymn came up, almost without conscious thought or effort." By the time the steamer docked in Chicago, the poem was complete. Later that year, Dr. Merrill accepted the call to become pastor of New York's Brick Presbyterian Church where he served until his retirement in 1938. He passed away in 1954. He is best remembered for the simple words penned that day aboard ship:

> *Rise up, O men of God!*
> *Have done with lesser things;*
> *Give heart and mind and soul and strength*
> *To serve the King of Kings.*

Service Ideas:
Have preschoolers draw pictures of their dads, scan the pictures, and present on the screen, then ask the congregation to guess who the dad is before flashing up the names of the dad and child. Surprise a dad in your church with a phone call through the public address system from a military son or daughter who can't be home. Ask someone to write and read a tribute to their dad, perhaps an older person who will share memories of a dad now in heaven.

STATS, STORIES AND MORE

The Key to Success

Some time ago, the magazine *Family Circle* commissioned the Gallup organization to study "super-achievers," those adults who have been most successful in accomplishing their goals. The Gallup people interviewed 237 extremely successful people in business, sports, politics, the arts and sciences, trying to find the keys to success. The most important factor: Attention from fathers.

Letter from a dad to his son during World War II (author unknown)

Dear Son, I wish I had the power to write
The thoughts wedged in my heart tonight
As I sit watching that small star
And wondering where and how you are.
You know, Son, it's a fully thing
How close a war can really bring
A father, who for years with pride,
Has kept emotions deep inside.
I'm sorry, Son, when you were small
I let reserve build up that wall;
I told you real men never cried,
And it was Mom who always dried
Your tears and smoothed your hurts away
So that you soon went back to play.
But, Son, deep down within my heart
I longed to have some little part
In drying that small tear-stained face,
But we were men—men don't embrace.
But suddenly I found my son
A full grown man, with childhood done.
Tonight you're far across the sea,
Fighting a war for men like me.
Well, somehow pride and what is right
Have changed places here tonight.
I find my eyes won't stay quite dry
And that men sometimes really cry.
And if we stood here, face to face,
I'm sure, my son, we would embrace.

Additional Sermons and Lesson Ideas

The Hole in the Soul

Date preached:

SCRIPTURE: John 3:1–3

INTRODUCTION: Pascal said, "There is a God-shaped vacuum in the heart which cannot be filled by any created thing, but only by God made known through Jesus Christ." Looking at Nicodemus, you would have noticed:

1. **He was Educated.** Jesus called him, "Israel's teacher" (v. 10).
2. **He was Wealthy.** In John 19, he brought 75 pounds of very expenses spices. He undoubtedly had a fine home with servants.
3. **He Was Powerful.** He belonged to the Jewish Ruling Council. His position was similar to being a United States Senator.
4. **He was Religious.** A Pharisee, one of the most conservative religious leaders in Israel.

CONCLUSION: Yet his heart was empty. Jesus pinpointed his greatest need—to be born again. Some here are educated, wealthy, powerful, and/or religious. But perhaps you need the new birth. Augustine once said, "Thou hast made us for Thyself, and our hearts are restless until they find their rest in Thee."

Reproved, Reassured, and Regulated

Date preached:

SCRIPTURE: 1 Timothy 4:13; 2 Timothy 4:13

INTRODUCTION: Biblical truth reproves, reassures and regulates the Christian. Bishop J. C. Ryle said, "Simple regular reading of our Bibles is the grand secret of establishment in the faith. Ignorance of the Scriptures is the root of all error." Every Christian should have a systematic Bible reading schedule. Why read the Bible?

1. **To Focus on the Savior.** Jesus is the Bible's main character. The Bible deals with redemption.
2. **To Fellowship with the Sovereign.** Bible reading is the primary way the Christian fellowships with the Lord.
3. **To Feed on the Scriptures.** While other books may prove helpful in Christian development, none is more important than the Bible. It is to our souls what green pastures are to sheep.
4. **To Familiarize Yourself with its Subjects.** Everything essential for the Christian is found in the Bible. Reading the Bible regularly and repetitively enables the Christian to discover precepts and principles to live the way God intended.

CONCLUSION: Have you read your Bible today?

JUNE 23, 2002

The Joy of Giving

Date preached:

By Dr. Timothy Beougher

Scripture: Philippians 4:14–23, especially 14–20 Nevertheless you have done well that you shared in my distress. Now you Philippians know also that in the beginning of the gospel, when I departed from Macedonia, no church shared with me concerning giving and receiving but you only. For even in Thessalonica you sent aid once and again for my necessities. Not that I seek the gift, but I seek the fruit that abounds to your account. Indeed I have all and abound. I am full, having received from Epaphroditus the things sent from you, a sweet-smelling aroma, an acceptable sacrifice, well pleasing to God. And my God shall supply all your need according to His riches in glory by Christ Jesus. Now to our God and Father be glory forever and ever. Amen.

Introduction: When we buy something we usually get a receipt showing the date, product, and amount of purchase. Some receipts we discard, but others we keep for various reasons. A receipt is a record of a transaction that has taken place. The book of Philippians is a receipt acknowledging the generous gift the Philippians had sent the Apostle Paul. Epaphroditus had made a six-week journey from Philippi to Rome to deliver this gift, and Paul had sent this letter back, saying in essence, "Received in Full." In doing so, he emphasized that the important thing in giving is not what the gift does for the recipient, but what it does for the giver. This passage describes four things that happen as we give. In giving, we . . .

1. **Become partners with others in ministry** (vv. 14–16). Paul emphasized that He had the ability to live in contentment in any and all circumstances through Christ's empowerment, but he didn't want the Philippians to think he was ungrateful for what they had done. He told them they had done well to share with him. The word "well" means "beautiful," and he later commended them in 2 Corinthians 8:1–5. There he indicated the Philippians had given out of difficult circumstances and extreme poverty, yet with overflowing joy and a desire to share in Paul's ministry. Whenever we support a ministry, we become part of it, partners in it. All over the world, people are hearing the good news of the gospel of Christ because we have given to the Lord's work.

2. **Offer a sacrifice pleasing to God** (vv. 17–18). Everything we do for the Lord counts (1 Cor. 15:58). Here we're told that the Philippians' gift was a fragrant

aroma, an acceptable sacrifice, well-pleasing to God. It isn't so much the amount as the attitude that counts (as in the widow's mite in Luke 7). Paul credited the Philippians with the proper attitude behind their gift—a genuine offering presented to God to promote the spread of the gospel.

3. **Position ourselves for God's giving to us** (v. 19). This promise about God supplying all our needs is given to those who themselves are givers. Some have called this the greatest promise in the Bible, but it is not a universal promise we can claim apart from its context. Verses 14–18 give us the premise to the promise. Notice the parallel passage in 2 Corinthians 9:6–8: If we sow bountifully, God is able to make all grace abound to us, that always having all sufficiency in everything, we may have an abundance for every good deed. There are two extremes in religious circles concerning money: (1) God wants everybody to be a millionaire, the health/wealth gospel; and (2) Having money is evil. According to the Bible, having money is not evil, but making the pursuit of money the all-consuming passion of our lives leads to all kinds of evil. This passage strikes a healthy balance. It does not cover our "greeds" but our "needs."

4. **Help change the world!** (vv. 20–23). Verse 20 is a doxology: "Now to our God and Father be glory forever and ever. Amen." As Paul reflected on God's gracious provisions, he burst into praise. All praise and glory is due the One who cares for us, who meets all our needs. In his closing greetings in verses 21–23, he indicated that the gospel had penetrated the highest strata of the Roman Empire. And—take note—the Philippians, through their giving, had

>>> *sermon continued on following page*

APPROPRIATE HYMNS AND SONGS

God So Loved the World, Jakob Stainer; Public Domain.

For God So Loved the World, Kit Lloyd; © 1979 Maranatha! Music, Inc.

Because I Have Been Given Much, Grace Noll Crowell/Phillip Landgrave; © 1975 Broadman Press (Admin. by Genevox Music Group).

We Give Thee But Thine Own, William W. How/ Lowell Mason/George Webb; Public Domain.

Find Us Faithful, Jon Mohr; © 1987 Jonathan Mark Music/Birdwing Music (Admin. by EMI Christian Music Publishing).

a part in that! They were seemingly a small, insignificant church, yet through their giving they had impacted Caesar's household!

Conclusion: We give not to win His grace but because His grace has won us.

FOR THE BULLETIN

❋ When Emperor Vespasian visited a natural spring for his health, he contracted a bacteria that caused severe diarrhea. On June 23, 79, he reportedly stood to his feet saying, "An emperor ought to die standing," and collapsed into the arms of his attendants. His son, Titus, became emperor that day. Titus is best known for his victory over the Jews and the sacking of Jerusalem. He died two years later at age 42, his last words being, "I have made but one mistake." Nobody knows to what mistake he was referring. ❋ At the Augsburg Conference, being told a position paper was required quickly, Philipp Melanchthon worked into the night of June 23, 1530, writing, rewriting and formulating Protestant doctrines. His paper was read on June 25. Its rejection by the largely-Catholic assembly marked the final break between Protestants and Catholics, but the Augsburg Confession with its definitive expression of Lutheran beliefs, has become the basis of Lutheran theology to this day. ❋ June 23, 1738, is the birthday of Rev. Samuel Medley, hymnist, author of "O Could I Speak the Matchless Worth." ❋ On Friday night, June 23, 1978, twenty black guerrilla slipped into the Emmanuel Christian School in Vumba, Rhodesia (Zimbabwe), soldiers for Robert Mugabe's outlawed Zimbabwe African National Union. They slaughtered thirteen missionaries and school children. One of the little girls had the imprint of a boot on her face. The face of missionary Joyce Lynn was battered beyond recognition. Her left hand was touching the battered head of their week-old infant.

Kids Talk Cut out a round piece of cardboard the size of the bottom of an offering plate. Draw a smiley face with a little smile-like wrinkle on its brow, so that when turned upside it is a frowning face. Tell the children about Mr. Offering Plate. When people are selfish and stingy, it makes him sad, and it also makes the Lord sad. Rotate the plate around to show how happy Mr. Offering Plate is when God's people give. Perhaps share a story about how you learned to begin giving to God's work.

WORSHIP HELPS

Worship Theme:
God meets all the needs in the lives of those who learn the blessings of giving.

Call to Worship:
"For God so loved the world that He gave His only begotten Son, that whoever believes in Him should not perish but have everlasting life. For God did not send His Son into the world to condemn the world, but that the world through Him might be saved" (John 3:16–18).

Appropriate Scripture Reading:
1 Chronicles 29:14–20
2 Corinthians 8:1–7

Pastoral Prayer:
O Lord God, There is no one like You in heaven above or on earth below. You are a God of mercy and a keeper of promises. Not even heaven or the heaven of heavens can contain You. Yet You listen to the cry of Your servants who pray before You day and night. Now please hear in heaven Your dwelling place, and when You hear, forgive; for there is no one who does not sin. Send forth Your mercy toward us. When we experience famine in our life, pestilence or blight or mildew; when the enemy besieges us; whatever plague or sickness there is; teach us to know the plague of our own heart, to spread out our hands toward You, and to seek Your forgiveness. Teach us to fear You all the days we live on the earth. Grant us Your compassion. Teach us the good way in which we should walk and incline our hearts to Yourself, to walk in all Your ways and to keep Your commands and judgments. May Your eyes be open to our supplication, and Your ears open to our cry. (Adapted from Solomon's prayer in 1 Kings 8).

STATS, STORIES AND MORE

Someone Once Said . . .

"I do not believe one can settle how much we ought to give. I am afraid the only safe rule is to give more than we can spare."
—*C. S. Lewis*

"He who gives what he would as readily throw away, gives without generosity; for the essence of generosity is in self-sacrifice."
—*Sir Henry Taylor*

"If you give what you do not need, it isn't giving."
—*Mother Teresa*

Findings from George Barna

- 33 percent of born again Christians say it is impossible for them to get ahead in life because of the financial debt they have incurred (1997).
- 51 percent of Christians and 54 percent of non-Christians believe that no matter how they feel about money, it is still the main symbol of success in life (1997).
- About one-third of all adults — and 16 percent of all born again Christians — gave no money to a church in 1999.
- 8 percent of born again Christians tithed their income to churches in 1999.

Determined Giving

An attitude of determined giving was one of the things that distinguished the survivors from those who perished in the Nazi death camps. If an inmate was near starvation, but he had a crust of bread or a scrap of a potato he could share with his comrade in suffering, he was psychologically and spiritually capable of surviving. One survivor of Treblinka put it this way: "In our group we shared everything; and the moment one of the group ate something without sharing it, we knew it was the beginning of the end for him."

No Pocket

A new employee at a funeral home was surprised to notice that the suits provided by the funeral home for the dead have no pockets. An unknown poet once observed the same thing:

Use your money while you're living,
Do not hoard it to be proud;
You can never take it with you—
There's no pocket in the shroud.

Additional Sermons and Lesson Ideas

How to Get Out of a Bad Mood
Date preached:

SCRIPTURE: Proverbs 15:13, 15, 30 (NIV)

INTRODUCTION: If you want to be well-liked, esteemed, and sought-after—you must learn to be a cheerful person. Not gushing and bubbly and fizzy, but pleasant, upbeat, optimistic, relaxed, and friendly. Three verses in Proverbs 15 give us the secret to acquiring this attitude.

1. **Proverbs 15:13 tells us that a happy heart makes a face cheerful.** When we cultivate our daily devotions and began each day with the Lord, it strengthens our hearts and others will notice it on our faces.

2. **Proverbs 15:15 tells us that a cheerful heart has a continual feast.** One hymnist described the difference Christ makes in our lives with these words: "All things have changed / My eyes once blind now see; / And all of life is not a symphony...." God gives us all things richly to enjoy.

3. **Proverbs 15:30 tell us that a cheerful look brings joy to the heart.** We become carriers of cheer, spreading to others the joy of the Lord in our heart.

CONCLUSION: Martha Washington once said, "I am still determined to be cheerful and happy in whatever situation I may be...." Abraham Lincoln said that a person is about as happy as he makes up his mind to be. Make up your mind to be happy in the Lord.

I Will Fear No Evil
Date preached:

SCRIPTURE: Psalm 71

INTRODUCTION: Walking through life sometimes feels like walking over a swinging bridge with rotten boards. But God has a powerful safety net, as we see in the psalmist's use of the word "afraid."

1. I will not be afraid when surrounded by problems (Psalm 3:5–6).
2. I will not be afraid when the wicked come against me (Psalm 27:1).
3. I will not be afraid of what others can do to me (Psalm 56:11).
4. I will not be afraid of terrors by night or arrows by day (Psalm 91:5).
5. I will not be afraid of evil tidings (Psalm 112:7–8).

CONCLUSION: "Whenever I am afraid, I will trust in you" (Psalm 56:3).

JUNE 30, 2002

The Matchless Christ

Date preached:

Scripture: Mark 4:41 And they feared exceedingly, and said to one another, "Who can this be, that even the wind and the sea obey Him!"

Introduction: People are skeptical about religion today, especially about Christianity. Perhaps there are some skeptical twinges in your mind. How do we know that Jesus was who He claimed to be? One of the evidences for the reality of His claims is found in His uniqueness. A. T. Pierson said, "He stands absolutely alone in history, in teaching, in example, in character, an exception, a marvel, and He is Himself the evidence of Christianity. He authenticates Himself." He is:

1. **Matchless in His Magnetism** (John 12:32). The media today is on a prowl for people with personal magnetism, charisma, and power of personality. Franklin Roosevelt, John F. Kennedy, and Ronald Reagan had it. But only one man has magnetized the world to such an extent that we recognize His centrality in history every time we date a letter or mark a calendar. Only one person has exercised supreme influence over every ensuing generation, touching both peasants and potentates, both rich and poor, both young and old, both men and women.

2. **Matchless in His Teaching** (Matthew 7:28–29). He stepped from the carpentry shop at age 30 with no formal training in either theology or oratory, yet His first public utterance was the greatest sermon the world had ever heard. The multitudes were amazed at His teaching, for He taught with authority. Christ taught the Scripture as if He were its author rather than its commentator. His listeners were astounded at His teaching, and the authorities feared it (Matt. 13:54–46; 11:18). The remarkable thing was the cohesive way that Jesus pulled together all spiritual truth into the reality of the gospel. He taught that He Himself was the centerpiece of Scripture, of history, and of God's plan for redeeming humanity.

. **Matchless in His Claims** (John 4:25–26). Christ claimed to be both God and man, both natures being assimilated perfectly in one personality. The only charge of which they could convict Jesus was His claim to be God. Yet His favorite title for Himself was "Son of Man." He had to be God to forgive and save us (Isa. 43:11), but He had to be human to die for our sins (Heb. 9:22).

4. **Matchless in His Resurrection** (Acts 1:3). No other religious leader ever authenticated his message by rising from death and proving himself alive with "many infallible proofs." Jesus staked His entire reputation on the proposition that He would rise again. He predicted it at the beginning, in the middle, and at the end of His ministry (John 2:19; Matt. 12:40; 17:22–23).

5. **Matchless in His Impact On History.** Someone wrote: "I am far within the mark when I say that all the armies that ever marched, all the navies that ever sailed, all the parliaments that ever sat, all the kings that ever reigned, put together, have not affected the life of man on earth as has that One Solitary Life."

Conclusion: The British scholar C. S. Lewis came to Christ almost against his will, being convinced by the evidence that Christianity was true. He later explained, "A man who was merely a man and said the sort of things Jesus said would not be a great moral teacher. He would either be a lunatic, or else he would be the Devil of Hell. You must make your choice. Either this man was,

>>> *sermon continued on following page*

APPROPRIATE HYMNS AND SONGS

All Hail the Power of Jesus Name, Edward Perronet/Oliver Holden/John Rippon (adapt); Public Domain.

Worthy, You are Worthy, Don Moen; © 1986 Integrity's Hosanna! Music.

Worthy is the Lamb That Was Slain, Don Wyrtzen; 1973 Singspiration Music (Admin. by Brentwood/Benson Music Publishing, Inc.).

Rejoice, the Lord Is King, Charles Wesley/John Darwall; Public Domain.

Jesus, I Am Resting, Resting, Jean Sophia Pigott; Public Domain.

and is, the Son of God, or else a madman or something worse. You can shut Him up for a fool, you can spit at Him and kill him as a demon; or you can fall at His feet and call Him Lord and God. But let us not come with any patronizing nonsense about His being a great human teacher. He has not left that open to us. He did not intend to." Either He was an imposter—in which case you have to explain how He could also have been the greatest spiritual leader and the most selfless, atoning sacrifice the world has ever known; or He was a lunatic— in which case you have to explain how He could have been the wisest teacher the world has ever seen; or He is the God-Man—which is just who He claimed to be. Liar, Lunatic, or Lord. Which is He to you?

FOR THE BULLETIN

❋ Raymond Lull, a sexually indulgent young man, was converted when, while writing erotic poetry, he suddenly envisioned Christ on the cross. He eventually became a missionary to the Muslims of North Africa where he served until old age. On June 30, 1314, he was seized, dragged out of town and stoned. But he advanced Christian missions like no one else in his age and paved the way for everyone since with a burden for the Muslims. ❋ On June 30, 1704, Matthew Henry began writing his great commentary, penning this prayer: "The Lord help me to set about it with great humility." The first volume was finished four years later. By his death at age 52, he had finished his work through the Gospel of John. A group of ministers, using his notes, completed the set. ❋ On June 30, 1780, the first Freewill Baptist church in New England was founded in New Durham, New Hampshire, by Rev. Benjamin Randall. ❋ On Sunday, June 30, 1905, evangelist, Evan Roberts, preached at the parish church of the Church of England in the Welch village of Llandona. Wherever Roberts went, revival occurred, and that day was no exception. Rising to speak, Roberts said: "Our God is a God of happiness and of joy. People may ask why at our meetings we break out into public rejoicings. The answer is simple and sufficient: It is because people there have found God." ❋ On June 30, 1974, Mrs. Alberta King, mother of the late Martin Luther King, was assassinated during a church service.

Worship Theme:
The matchless supremacy of Christ.

Call to Worship:
"Worthy is the Lamb who was slain to receive power and riches and wisdom, and strength and honor and glory and blessing!" (Rev. 5:12).

Hymn Story: "Jesus I Am Resting, Resting, in the Joy of What Thou Art." Roy Orpin, a New Zealander, was deeply moved when he read of the martyrdom of John and Betty Stam in China. Accordingly, he went to Thailand, and there, on April 27, 1961, married an Englishwoman named Gillian, who was also a missionary. The couple moved into a shanty in a Thai village, and spent their first year of marriage amid growing danger. Violence was escalating in Southeast Asia. Gillian became pregnant, and Roy became afraid. "I had no peace," he wrote friends, "until I remembered 2 Corinthians 10:5." Gillian moved to a regional town having a missionary hospital while Roy stayed in the village of Bitter Bamboo to work with a small band of Christians. Suddenly three robbers appeared, demanded his valuables, and shot him. He was taken to a government hospital, and Gillian rushed to his side. He lingered four days. His dying wish was for his wife to join him in singing a favorite hymn. The two lovers raised faltering voices and sang, "Jesus! I am resting, resting / In the joy of what Thou art; / I am finding out the greatness / Of thy loving heart." Then Roy, age 26, passed away. They had been married less than 13 months.

Appropriate Scripture Readings:
Isaiah 53:3–6
Isaiah 61:1–3
Matthew 16:13–17

Benediction:
"Now unto the King eternal, immortal, invisible, the only wise God, be honor and glory for ever and ever. Amen" (1 Tim. 1:17 KJV).

STATS, STORIES AND MORE

Testimony

Perhaps this would be a good sermon in which to share your own testimony or that of a church leader, family member, or close friend.

Someone Once Said . . .

"This Jesus of Nazareth, without money and arms, conquered more millions than Alexander, Caesar, Muhammad, and Napoleon; without science and learning, He shed more light on matters human and divine than all the philosophers and scholars combined; without the eloquence of schools, He spoke such words of life as were never spoken before or since and produced effects which lie beyond the reach of orator or poet; without writing a single line, He set more pens in motion, and furnished themes for more sermons, orations, discussion, learned volumes, works of art, and songs of praise than the whole army of great men of ancient and modern times."

—*Philip Schaff, church historian*

Ben Hur

Lew Wallace was a famous general and literary genius of the nineteenth century who, along with his friend Robert Ingersoll, decided to write a book that would forever destroy what they called "the myth of Christianity." For two years, Wallace studied in the libraries of Europe and America, and then he started writing his book. But while writing the second chapter, he found himself on his knees crying out to Jesus Christ in the words of Thomas, "My Lord and my God." And the book he was writing became the great novel about the times of Christ, *Ben Hur*.

Contrasts in Christ

He began His ministry by being hungry, yet He is the Bread of Life.
Jesus ended His earthly ministry by being thirsty, yet He is the Living Water.
Jesus was weary, yet He is our rest.
Jesus paid tribute, yet He is the King.
Jesus was accused of having a demon, yet He cast out demons.
Jesus wept, yet He wipes away our tears.
Jesus was sold for thirty pieces of silver, yet He redeemed the world.
Jesus was brought as a lamb to the slaughter, yet He is the Good Shepherd.
Jesus died, yet by His death He destroyed the power of death.

—*Gregory of Nazianzus, A.D. 381.*

Additional Sermons and Lesson Ideas

Wrapping Problems in Praise

Date preached:

SCRIPTURE: Psalm 89

INTRODUCTION: Reading Psalm 89 is a roller-coaster experience. The upward progress and emotional momentum suddenly turns downward at verse 38, but such is life. This Psalm teaches us to wrap our problems in praise.

1. **Singing** (vv. 1–37). The first, long section of this Psalm is a song of praising God for His:
   A. **Love and faithfulness** (vv. 1–2).
   B. **Covenant** (vv. 3–4, 19–37).
   C. **Power** (vv. 5–13).
   D. **Righteousness** (vv. 14–18).
2. **Sighing** (vv. 38–51). Here the Psalmist expresses deep disappointment and amazement at the turn his life had taken. There are for all of us trials, disappointments, and deep perplexities.
3. **Shouting** (v. 52). Blessed be the Lord forever! Amen and Amen!

CONCLUSION: Deal with problems in the context of worship. Take the approach of Psalm 89, and surround your problems with praise.

Where There Is No Vision

Date preached:

Dr. Melvin Worthington

SCRIPTURE: Proverbs 29:18

INTRODUCTION: A word from God is essential to the well-being of individuals and nations. One writer translates the verse, "Without a revelation a people become ungovernable..."

1. **The Precepts.** "Where there is no revelation...." God's revelation clearly, concisely and convincingly gives people the proper perspective regarding earthly and eternal things.
2. **The Peril.** "the people cast off restraint...." Without a word we have no message, morals, mission, ministry, methods, ministers—and no miracle of conversion. God's Word confronts, convinces, convicts, corrects, cleanses and changes us.
3. **The Peace.** The last part of Proverbs 29:18 tells us genuine happiness flows from obedience to the Word of God. Those who are ruled by the Bible are happy; not just the hearers of the law, but the doers.

CONCLUSION: If you need vision in your life, turn to God and His Word. Hear it, heed it, and find it your hope.

SPECIAL OCCASION SERMON

A Patriotic Sermon

Date preached:

Scripture Reading: "Righteousness exalts a nation, but sin is a reproach to any people" (Prov. 14:34).

Introduction: As the Ten Commandments are removed from one public building after another, what remains are blank walls, which are too often being pocked with bullet marks or covered with graffiti. If nothing but a blank wall remains in place of a moral code, sooner or later people are going to write on it whatever they want. We are thus living in a nation in which our conduct is being governed, not by the moral laws of God, but by the popular culture of our times. People assume it is possible to have morality without God, but the whole underpinning and basis of morality is the existence of God.

- In his farewell address to the nation, President George Washington said, "Let us with caution indulge the supposition that morality can be maintained without religion. Whatever may be conceded to the influence of refined education on minds of peculiar structure, reason and experience both forbid us to expect that national morality can prevail in exclusion of religious principle."
- Historian Will Durant wrote: "There is no significant example in history, before our time, of a society successfully maintaining moral life without the aid of religion."
- Author Ravi Zacharias put it more bluntly: "There is nothing in history to match the dire ends to which humanity can be led by following a political and social philosophy that consciously and absolutely excludes God."

Without the reality of an eternal God there is no ultimate basis for ethics and there are no moral absolutes. Erwin Lutzer offers a graphic picture of what is happening. Imagine a heavy steel beam, suspended high above a chasm by a single cable attached to the middle of the beam. Two men are on opposite ends, and their weight provides the balance needed to keep the bar horizontal. Now suppose that one of them steadies himself enough to pull out a gun and shoot the other one. The result is that they both fall into the chasm. Those who are trying to destroy belief in God cannot do it without destroying themselves. And if our nation continues to descend into a godless, entertainment-centered moral relativism that holds no fear of God and no reverence for His commands, we will perish as a nation. The blank wall will become a blackboard for the finger of God to write the words of Daniel 5: "Thou art weighted in the balances and found wanting."

What can we do about it?

1. **Keep Our Lives Pure.** We can keep our own lives pure by remaining utterly committed to God and to His commandments in our personal experience. The government can never keep us from exhibiting the Ten Commandments in our daily behavior. The courts can never keep us from living out the gospel. Christian behavior is growing increasingly distinct from that of the world around us. We can live blameless, holy lives, without fault, in the midst of a crooked and perverse generation (Phil. 2:15).

2. **Keep Our Voices Heard.** Christians have civil rights, too. We have freedom of speech and freedom of expression. Students in the public schools have incredible rights when it comes to prayer, Bible study, and equal access for Bible-related events. Not long ago at Northern High School in Silver Spring, Maryland, one of the graduating seniors, a Christian, planned to offer an invocation at the graduation ceremony, but a fellow student objected, saying prayer is inappropriate at a public ceremony. The state attorney general's office informed school officials that graduation prayers violate the constitutional separation of church and state. As a compromise, the Christian student agreed to ask for a 30-second "time for reflection" that did not mention God. The time came for the graduation service, and the student asked for a moment of silence. Suddenly a man in the crowd began to recite the Lord's Prayer aloud, and instantly virtually everyone in the entire 4,000-member audience, including the students, joined in. It was a spontaneous demonstration of our right of free speech as believers in a pluralistic society.

3. **Keep Our Prayers Going.** We can pray for revival. There have been other demoralized times in the history of our nation and in the history of other lands in which judgment was delayed by the winds of revival; and it isn't too

late for our nation to experience an awakening. Psalm 85:6 says, "Will You not revive us again, that Your people may rejoice in You?"

4. **Keep Our Focus International.** Perhaps one of the reasons God allowed the United States of America to come into existence was to help fulfill the Great Commission, to supply the personnel and finances needed for the evangelization of the world. We have been sending missionaries since 1812 when Adoniram Judson went to Burma; and partially as a result of that the world today is experiencing the greatest harvest of souls it has ever seen. Now is no time to stop. United States Christians still have a vital role to play in the evangelization of the world.

Conclusion: More than ever, God wants to use us to transform our society and to evangelize our world. He will do it as we keep our lives pure, our voices heard, our prayers going, and our missionary focus international. The ancient words of 2 Chronicles 7:14 are still faithful and true: "If My people who are called by My name will humble themselves, and pray and seek My face, and turn from their wicked ways, then I will hear from heaven, and will forgive their sin and heal their land."

Protecting the Speaking Voice

Julie Andrews, having damaged her voice through overuse, sought help at New York's Mt. Sinai Hospital. Surgeons were to remove a small, non-cancerous polyp from her vocal cords. She later filed a medical malpractice lawsuit again the hospital and two doctors for ruining her vocal cords and her ability to sing.

"Singing has been a cherished gift," Andrews said, "and my inability to sing has been a devastating blow."

Her husband, Blake Edwards, said, "If you heard [her voice], you'd weep."

Like a vocalist, pastors and preachers must guard their voices as cherished gifts. How can we protect the speaking voice? Here are some tips from a handful of experts.

- Avoid caffeine, which is a diuretic and can dehydrate the voice and dry out the vocal cords.
- Switch to "light" coffee in the mornings, which contains only one-half the caffeine.
- Drink lots of water, along with juices and sports drinks.
- Don't clear your throat. If you have phlegm, swallow or try gently dislodging it. Clearing the throat is very harsh on the vocal cords.
- Avoid yelling or screaming at home, at ball games, or elsewhere. Avoid prolonged conversations in noisy environments.
- Don't preach when your voice is hoarse. When the vocal cords are swollen, they are particularly susceptible to injury, including permanent damage. Whispering does not help. It is vital to rest the voice. Continuing to use a hoarse voice is like running with a sprained ankle.
- Hot showers and facial steamers are good for the voice, for they hydrate the vocal cords.
- Try relaxing your hands, your shoulder, and your neck muscles before speaking. Take several deep breaths. This will relax your voice muscles, allowing them to do their work with less strain.
- Use a public address system whenever possible, even for smaller gatherings.
- Visit a speech therapist to learn proper warm-up exercises and abdominal breathing techniques, especially in the delivery of a speech or sermon.
- Don't smoke.

If hoarseness or voice problems persist for more than a few days, see an ear, nose, and throat specialist. ✸

JULY 7, 2002

SUGGESTED SERMON

The Well-governed Soul

Date preached:

Scripture: Ephesians 3:14–19 For this reason I bow my knees to the Father of our Lord Jesus Christ, from whom the whole family in heaven and earth is named, that He would grant you, according to the riches of His glory, to be strengthened with might through His Spirit in the inner man, that Christ may dwell in your hearts through faith; that you, being rooted and grounded in love, may be able to comprehend with all the saints what is the width and length and depth and height— to know the love of Christ which passes knowledge; that you may be filled with all the fullness of God.

Introduction: This week we celebrated America's 226th birthday, and we're thankful for the liberty and leadership America holds forth to the world. Just as we need a well-managed nation, we also need a well-governed soul. Isaiah 9:6 tells us that governing is among the responsibilities of our Lord: "The government shall be upon His shoulder... and of the increase of His government and peace, there will be no end." The well-governed soul has a...

1. **Commander-in-Chief.** Ephesians 3:14–15 says: "For this reason I bow my knees to the Father of our Lord Jesus Christ, from whom the whole family in heaven and earth is named." In heaven and on earth means those who are alive and those who have departed to be with Jesus. God is not the God of the dead, but of the living (Matt. 22:32). God is the father of His family, the church (the subject of Eph. 3), as it exists both in heaven and on earth. He is head over all, Prime Minister, Potentate, Sovereign, King of Kings, and Ruler of our lives. As such, He makes available to us His resources.

2. **The Treasury Department.** Verse 16 says "that He would grant you, according to the riches of His glory." The book of Ephesians details our wealth in Christ. His resources are infinite, His repositories are overflowing, His vaults are bottomless. The old gospel hymn says: "My Father is rich in houses and lands, / He holdeth the wealth of the world in His hands! / Of rubies and diamonds, of silver and gold, / His coffers are full, He has riches untold."

3. **The Energy Department.** "...to be strengthened with might through His Spirit." Out of His infinite resources, God wants to impart strength to you. When do we need strength? (1) "When the dog bites, when the bee stings." On those occasions when we get a jolt of bad news; (2) "When the roof caves in." During times of disaster and tragedy; (3) "When the days are dreary, the long nights weary." When we endure a period of depression or discouragement, a prolonged trial or tribulation." God has promised strength for His people.

4. **The Interior Department.** "...in the inner man." Old-time Christian mystics talked about the "interior life," the life of the soul. We spend a fortune on our "outer life," on cosmetics, clothes, houses, cars, and externals of life. But most people neglect the cultivation of the inner life. God wants to strengthen us in our interior, to pump His strength into our hearts and souls. He does this by His Holy Spirit who very often uses the Scriptures. How often has a verse of Scripture, previously memorized but long forgotten, flashed to our minds in a moment of need?

5. **The Department of Housing.** "that Christ may dwell in your hearts through faith" (v. 17). The Greek verb means "to settle down and be at home." When our hearts are strong in the Lord, Christ is at home in our hearts. He settles down and serves as host.

>>> *sermon continued on following page*

APPROPRIATE HYMNS AND SONGS

My Faith Looks Up to Thee, Ray Palmer/Lowell Mason; Public Domain.

I Love You Lord, Laurie Kleine; © 1978, 1980 House of Mercy Music (Admin. by Maranatha! Music).

Ah Lord God, Kay Chance; © 1976 Kay Chance.

God of Grace and God of Glory, John Purifoy; © 1985 Purifoy Publishing Company (Admin. by The Lorenze Corporation).

To Him Who Sits On the Throne, Debbye Graafsma; © 1984 Integrity's Hosanna! Music (Admin. by Integrity Music, Inc.).

6. **The Department of Education.** "that you, being rooted and grounded in love, may be able to comprehend with all the saints what is the width and length and depth and height—to know the love of Christ ..." (vv. 17–19). A. T. Pierson observed that Paul "treats the love of God as a cube, having breadth and length, depth and height. The reason is that the cube in the Bible is treated as a perfection of form. Every side of a cube is a perfect square, and from every angle it presents the same appearance. Turn it over, and it is still a cube—just as high, deep, and broad as it was before."

Conclusion: When Christ is Governor of the soul, He imparts strength for the soul every hour and every day.

FOR THE BULLETIN

❋ July 7, 786, marks the death of St. Willibald, disciple of Boniface. His body still lies in the Bavarian cathedral of Eichstätt. ❋ Thomas More was executed on July 7, 1535. Earlier in life, he had wavered between entering politics or the ministry. He opted for politics, becoming a member of Parliament in 1504. During his career, he remained loyal to the Roman Catholic Church. In 1529, Henry VIII made him lord chancellor, but when Thomas refused to obtain the divorce Henry desired from Catherine, he was beheaded. ❋ On July 7, 1637, Samuel Rutherford, exiled Scottish theologian, wrote to fellow-sufferer James Hamilton, saying, "Let no man doubt that the state of our question which we are now forced to stand to by suffering exile and imprisonment is, that Christ should reign over His kirk or not." ❋ On July 7, 1851, Charles Tindley was born into slavery. After the Civil War, he moved to Philadelphia where he was converted and became a church janitor. Later, as a well-known pastor, he wrote such hymns as "Nothing Between," "Take Your Burden to the Lord," and "When the Storms of Life Are Raging." His "I'll Overcome Some Day," became the basis for the Civil Rights song, "We Shall Overcome." ❋ On July 7, 1912, E. M. Bounds preached his last sermon. ❋ On July 7, 1971, the bodies of Paul and Nancy Potter, missionaries to the Dominican Republic, were found by their 10-year-old son. They had been stabbed to death.

WORSHIP HELPS

Worship Theme:
God imparts strength to His people.

Call to Worship:
"The Lord is my strength and song, And He has become my salvation; He is my God, and I will praise Him; My father's God, and I will exalt Him" (Ex. 15:2).

Reader's Theater:

Reader #1: Fear not, for I am with you; Be not dismayed, for I am your God. I will strengthen you, Yes, I will help you, I will uphold you with My righteous right hand.

Reader #2: You in Your mercy have led forth The people whom You have redeemed; You have guided them in Your strength.

Reader #1: For thus says the Lord God, the Holy One of Israel: "In returning and rest you shall be saved; In quietness and confidence shall be your strength."

Reader #2: I will love You, O Lord, my strength. The Lord is my rock and my fortress and my deliverer; My God, my strength, in whom I will trust; My shield and the horn of my salvation, my stronghold. I will call upon the Lord, who is worthy to be praised; So shall I be saved from my enemies.

Both: I can do all things through Christ who strengthens me.

Taken from Isaiah 41:10; Exodus 15:3; Isaiah 30:15; Psalm 18:1–3; Philippians 1:13.

Pastoral Prayer:
O Lord, we are weak and weary and often wicked children, standing in need of Your mercy, which forgives us, and Your grace, which strengthens us. Forgive us now of all our sin, including those secret sins known only to You. May Your rich grace impart strength to our fainting hearts, our zeal inspire. As You have died for us, so may our love for You, pure, warm, and growing be, a living fire. In Jesus' name. Amen.

STATS, STORIES AND MORE

Someone Once Said . . .

"The Lord was pleased to strengthen us, and remove all fear from us, and disposed our hearts to be as useful as possible."

—*Richard Allen (1760 - 1831), African-American Church leader, during a 1793 epidemic*

"May the Lord Jesus strengthen me."

—*Martin Luther, when summoned to Worms*

"Dearest brothers and sisters! You must be strong with the strength that flows from faith! There is no need to be afraid."

—*Newly-elected John Paul II, on his first visit as pope to his native Warsaw, still under Communist control.*

"In the days when the Bible was universally acknowledged in the churches as "God's Word written," it was clearly understood that the promises recorded in Scripture were the proper, God-given basis for all our life of faith, and that the way to strengthen one's faith was to focus it upon particular promises that spoke to one's condition."

—*J. I. Packer, in* Knowing God

A Strong Tower

In 1934, when Adolf Hitler summoned German church leaders to his Berlin office to berate them for insufficiently supporting his programs, he was surprised when Pastor Martin Niemoller stood up to him. That evening his Gestapo raided Niemoller's rectory, and a few days later a bomb exploded in his church. He was later arrested and placed in solitary confinement. Dr. Niemoller's trial began on February 7, 1938. That morning, a green-uniformed guard escorted the minister from his prison cell and through a series of underground passages toward the courtroom. Niemoller was overcome with terror and loneliness. What would become of him? Of his family? His church?

The guard's face was impassive, but as they exited a tunnel to ascend a final flight of stairs, Niemoller heard a whisper. At first he didn't know where it came from, for the voice was soft as a sigh. Then he realized that the officer was breathing into his ear the words of Proverbs 18:10: "The name of the Lord is a strong tower; The righteous run to it and are safe." Niemoller's fear fell away, and the power of that verse sustained him through his trial and his years in Nazi concentration camps.

Additional Sermons and Lesson Ideas

The Burning Book

Date preached:

SCRIPTURE READING: Jeremiah 36

INTRODUCTION: A few years ago, conservative politician Pat Buchanan spoke at Syracuse University. Leftist students disrupted his speech by yelling obscenities, and the demonstrations continued after the speech, culminating with students burning a Bible in front of the chapel. It isn't the first time a Bible has been burned. Here in Jeremiah 36, we have a story of...

1. **Degradation.** See background in 2 Kings 23–24 and 2 Chronicles 36. The reign of Jehoiakim was corrupt and degraded.
2. **Inspiration.** Into this setting, God's inspired word came to and through Jeremiah.
3. **Proclamation.** Jeremiah was underground, but his friends read and preached his words in the temple courts.
4. **Agitation.** The message created quite a storm. In the end, the King cut it up and burned it in his fireplace.
5. **Validation.** The word itself is eternal and settled in the heavens. In the end, the king perished and the word of Jeremiah was fulfilled.

CONCLUSION: God's Word is both indispensable and indestructible, and must be heard and heeded.

A Man Called Jabez

Date preached:

By Drew Wilkerson

SCRIPTURE: 1 Chronicles 4:9–10

INTRODUCTION: Augustine said, "God is more anxious to bestow his blessings on us than we are to receive them." Though Jabez is an obscure biblical character, his unforgettable prayer teaches us....

1. **God is listening.** Jabez believed God would hear and heed prayer.
2. **God wants us to ask for great things.** We approach the throne of grace with boldness.
3. **The greater the blessing the greater the responsibility.** Jabez was an honorable man, dependable, faithful. He asks for God's hand on his life.
4. **Intimacy with God is critical.** Jabez specifically prayed that God would be with him.
5. **The greater the blessing the greater the temptation.** Jabez knew that if God were blessing him, then the enemy would be tempting him. He asked God to keep him from evil.
6. **God's blessing is never in short supply.** God wants the world to be full of Christians willing to pray the Jabez prayer.

CONCLUSION: Write these verses at the front of your prayer notebook or on the flyleaf of your Bible, and learn to pray like Jabez.

Ministering When You Are Ill

An Interview with Dr. Jonathan Thigpen

Past President, Evangelical Training Association

Instead of asking how ALS (Lou Gehrig's disease) has interrupted your ministry, I'd like to ask if it has enhanced your ministry.

Absolutely it has. That's the way to phrase it. In several areas. First, it has created within me a deeper sense of empathy with those who are suffering. I have to confess before I encountered ALS, I would be uncomfortable in certain situations around people in wheelchairs or with certain handicaps. And I was aware of the fact that my discomfort was noticed by those I was trying to help. Since being diagnosed, I have looked at everyone in a wheelchair differently. I clearly see myself in their situation (which is what empathy is). So as I have experienced what small level of suffering I've encountered, it has made me a better minister because I can understand.

Second, my illness has actually focused my attention more sharply on the needs of those who are caregivers. I think one of the areas we most neglect is taking care of caregivers. It's easy to pay attention to the needs of the person with cancer or with heart trouble or with a severe disability. But it's just as easy to forget to minister to the person who is totally healthy but entirely responsible for caring for that loved one. When people ask me how they can pray for me, I immediately tell them to pray for my wife.

Third, when you share your story of what God is doing with your life in spite of serious illness—in my case a terminal illness—the vulnerability you have to display connects at a deep level with others, especially with those who are hurting. It has provided me opportunities to minister that I've never had before. Many people are somewhat intimidated by preachers. But when you can be vulnerable enough to say, "Boy, I'm struggling with this, but God is giving me the strength to face it," they listen. It produces a floodgate of letters, e-mail, or calls from those who have been touched. It has all been a plus to the ministry, rather than a minus.

Have you found that illness adds a note of power to the preached Scriptures?

I think so. When I'm invited to speak now, I first tell people to have a back-up plan, for I might not be able to preach even when I get there. But I also tell them the only way for me to speak is for God to speak through me. That's the way it should always be, but when we're healthy we often fail to rely on the Lord as we should. When I step (or, now, when I'm wheeled) into the pulpit, I am very aware that unless God speaks by His Spirit through my failing voice, nothing of substance will happen. "Not by might, nor by power, but by My Spirit" (Zech. 4:6).

I once asked my seminary professor, Dr. Campbell Wykoff, "What is the role of the Holy Spirit in the teaching process?" He said, "Jonathan, I believe the Holy Spirit is the teacher, and that we are simply teacher's aides." I would say the same thing about preaching. The Holy Spirit is the One who preaches. We are simply there as audio-visual aides to assist the transmission of the message with as little distortion as possible. Oh, every day is a challenge. When our daughter, Jessica, was little, one of the tactics that we would use to encourage her before we started a long trip was to say, "Jessica, this is going to be an exciting adventure!" The same thing is true when you're facing a serious illness. You can dwell on the negatives, but I've tried to consider each day an exciting adventure. If we are convinced, as I am, that God is in control, then every day doesn't have to be a good day, but ministry can happen on good days and bad days. There's the old college definition of flying: "Flying is hours of boredom interspersed with moments of sheer terror." Living with a life-threatening illness is that way. I would not be honest if I didn't say there are times when I've experienced fear and discomfort, but I can tell you that those times are very small compared to those other times when, as a child of God, I have been overwhelmed by a sense of His peace. If it weren't for the down times, I wouldn't have the ability to appreciate the good times.

Do you have any advice for a minister facing illness?

At first, I was very reticent to share about what I was going through. There were a lot of reasons for that. But once I was able to begin sharing what was going on, I was amazed at how my true friends came to the forefront. It is absolutely essential to have two or three or four brothers or sisters in Christ in whom you can share the good, the bad, and the ugly. You know they are standing with you in prayer and willing to listen. I have four or five men who have helped provide the emotional and spiritual support I've needed. There's nothing heroic in trying to go it alone. God is able, but if you are willing to share transparently what's going on in your life, you will discover the reality of God's strength being made perfect in weakness. ✸

JULY 14, 2002

Surviving Deep Waters and Dark Nights

By Dr. Ed Dobson   *Date preached:*

Scripture: Mark 6:46–52   And when He had sent them away, He departed to the mountain to pray. Now when evening came, the boat was in the middle of the sea; and He was alone on the land. Then He saw them straining at rowing, for the wind was against them. Now about the fourth watch of the night He came to them, walking on the sea, and would have passed them by. And when they saw Him walking on the sea, they supposed it was a ghost, and cried out; for they all saw Him and were troubled. But immediately He talked with them and said to them, "Be of good cheer! It is I; do not be afraid." Then He went up into the boat to them, and the wind ceased. And they were greatly amazed in themselves beyond measure, and marveled. For they had not understood about the loaves, because their heart was hardened.

Introduction: Martin Luther said, "The human heart is like a ship on a stormy sea driven about by winds blowing from all four corners of heaven." All of us go through stormy weather, and we sometimes endure dark nights. The Bible gives us a wonderful story for such times, one of Scripture's favorite and most vivid accounts.

Bible Story: Late in the afternoon, having fed 5,000 people, Jesus withdrew to the top of a mountain to pray. From His perch on the mountainside, Jesus saw His disciples straining at the oars of their boat. He could have spoken a word and all their problems would have been resolved, but sometimes Jesus chooses to let us strain at the oars. Often in the struggle we discover great truths about Him. At length, He went to them and pretended to pass them by. The text doesn't tell us why, but my hunch is that Jesus will only get in your boat when you ask Him to. Immediately He spoke to them: "Take courage! It is I. Don't be afraid [stop being afraid]." Instantly, the wind died down, and they were completely amazed. The word means stunned, shocked to speechlessness. The text says they were stunned because their hearts were hard. They had evidently lost their focus, namely, Jesus. When He fed the multitudes, there was great enthusiasm. They got caught up in what had happened, not in the One who made it happen. In good times when bread is multiplied, it's easy to focus on the blessing, not the Blesser. Similarly, in the worst of times, their focus was the storm and on the fear of drowning. They were consumed with the reality of their present circumstances and had lost their focus, namely, Jesus. The main point of this text is Jesus. In good times and bad times, in hunger and in storms, "It is I, be not afraid." This story lends itself to several insights:

1. **When we cannot see Jesus, Jesus sees us.** He is atop of the mountain praying, watching, concerned. He reminds us, "Never will I leave you. Never will I forsake you." When you can't see Jesus through the darkness, be assured He's got his eye on you. "No never alone, no never alone; He promised never to leave me, never to leave me alone."

2. **When you cannot get to Jesus, Jesus eventually gets to you.** He leaves the mountain, walks down to the lake, steps onto the waves, and walks on the water to get to us. He comes to us by praying for us in Heaven (Rom. 8:34) and comforting us on earth by His Holy Spirit (John 14:16–18).

3. **When I don't know what to say to Jesus, He speaks to me.** "Take courage! It is I. Don't be afraid." Sometimes we don't even know what to pray, but Jesus says, "Take heart…. Have courage…. Be brave." How do we develop this kind of courage? By verbalizing His truth. Hebrews 13 says: "He Himself has said, 'I will never leave you nor forsake you.'" So we may boldly say, "The Lord is my Helper; I will not fear."

Conclusion: Get a half dozen 3x5 cards and write the words, "God has said, I will never leave you, I will never forsake you. So we say with confidence, the Lord is my helper, I will not be afraid." Stick them on the bathroom mirror, on the refrigerator, on your dashboard, and under the glass of your desk. Remind yourself frequently that even in deep waters and dark nights, He sees you, He comes to you, and He speaks just the words you need.

APPROPRIATE HYMNS AND SONGS

God Leads Us Along, G.A. Young; Public Domain.

I Will Praise Him Still, Fernando Ortega; © 1997 Dayspring Music Inc./Margee-Days Music (Admin. by Word Music Group, Inc.).

Stand By Me, C.A. Tindley; Public Domain.

Peace In the Midst of the Storm, Stephen R. Adams; © 1978, 1981 Pilot Point Music/Lillenas (Admin. by The Copyright Company).

Turn Your Eyes Upon Jesus, Helen H. Lemmel; Public Domain.

Kids Talk

If you have a set of drums on stage, ask the drummer to simulate a rolling peal of thunder. Otherwise, play a "nature recording" of a rainstorm. Ask the children to describe a particularly bad thunderstorm. How did they feel? Explain that Jesus protects us during storms, and that storms show us how powerful God is.

FOR THE BULLETIN

❀ When four-year-old John Fidanza was critically ill, Francis d'Assisi prayed for him and he recovered, causing his mother to exclaim, "O buon ventura!"—Good Fortune! John Fidanza is therefore known to history as Bonaventura. He was a leading theologian and able administrator of the Franciscans. He passed away on July 14, 1274, during a church festival in Lyons, and his funeral took place in the presence of leaders from all parts of Christendom. ❀ Camillus de Lellis, born in 1550, was addicted to gambling. At age 25, after losing everything including the shirt off his back, he became a Christian. He mobilized volunteers to travel with Italian troops, forming the first "military field ambulance." Camillus organized eight hospitals, pioneered medical hygiene and diet, and successfully opposed the prevailing practice of burying patients alive. On July 14, 1614, after a final tour of his works, Camillus, 64, died. He was declared patron saint of the sick by Pope Leo XIII, and of nurses and nursing by Pope Pius XI. ❀ On July 14, 1785, newly converted William Carey joined the Baptist church. ❀ On July 14, 1789, the Bastille, a grim prison and symbol of the monarchy, was seized by the people at the start of the French Revolution. ❀ The Oxford Movement, which sought to reform and revive the high church adherents of the Church of England, was sparked by a sermon on this day in 1833 by John Keble.

WORSHIP HELPS

Worship Theme:
Jesus comes to us in our difficulties, cares about our calamities, and speaks to us in our storms.

Call to Worship:
He Himself has said, "I will never leave you nor forsake you." So we may boldly say: "The Lord is my helper; I will not fear" *(*Heb. 13:5–6).

Hymn Background:
Charles Albert Tindley was an African-American born to slave parents. He received no education, but had a good mind and taught himself how to read and write, then bettered his education by correspondence courses and night school. He took a job as janitor of a church in Philadelphia, and later, in 1902, became pastor of the same church. The church grew greatly under his ministry, with both blacks and whites flocking to hear his sermons. He has been called America's "Prince of Preachers." He was also the writer of hymns and gospel songs, including this one based on the account of the disciples caught in the storm at sea: "When the storms of life are raging, stand by me...."

Appropriate Scripture Reading:
Job 38:1–3
Psalm 107:23–31

Benediction:
Father, we bow in your presence because You are worthy to be praised. When words escape us, You speak to us with great power, great comfort, great assurance. We will say this week with confidence, "You are our helper." Dismiss us from this place with Your blessing, matchless and mighty and powerful, in the name of Jesus we pray. Amen.

STATS, STORIES AND MORE

Lack of Trust

Martyn Lloyd-Jones, in a sermon on this passage, suggests that Christians should never panic. "I do not care what the circumstances may be," writes Lloyd-Jones, "the Christian should never be agitated, the Christian should never be beside himself like this, the Christian should never be at his wit's end, the Christian should never be in a condition in which he has lost control of himself.... It implies a lack of trust and confidence in Him."

Someone Once Said . . .

"There are some things you learn best in calm, and some in storm."
—*Willa Cather (1876–1947), American novelist*

"Birds sing after storms. Why shouldn't people?"
—*Rose Kennedy*

"God moves in a mysterious way, His wonders to perform. He plants His footsteps in the sea, and rides upon the storm."
—*William Cowper*

Cape of Storms

The southern tip of Africa experiences tremendous storms. At one time, no one knew what lay beyond the cape, for no ship attempting had ever returned to tell the tale. Among the ancients it was know as the "Cape of Storms." But the 16th-century Portuguese explorer, Vasco De Gama, successfully sailed around that point and found beyond the wild raging storms, a great calm sea, and beyond that, the shores of India. The name of that cape was changed from the Cape of Storms to the Cape of Good Hope.

Carey's Storm

William and Dorothy Carey, with four energetic children, sailed aboard the *Kron Princessa Maria* to India in 1793. The journey took five months, and the worst moments came about 1 a.m. on August 26, 1793, when the ship sailed into a terrific storm. Carey was awakened by stools, tables, pots, and glasses flying through the room. Mountainous seas bore down on the ship from every direction, and the ship would rise and plunge almost perpendicularly. The vessel managed to ride out the storm, only to be quickly hit by another one. Carey later wrote: "I hope I have learned the necessity of bearing up in the things of God against wind and tide, when there is occasion, as we have done in our voyage.... In the Christian life, we often have to work against wind and tide; but we must do it if we expect ever to make port."

Additional Sermons and Lesson Ideas

Envisioning the Eternal
Date preached:

By Dr. Melvin Worthington

SCRIPTURE: Isaiah 6:1–13

INTRODUCTION: King Uzziah's death symbolized the passing of a golden age when God flooded the nation with His blessings. Ahaz, the ungodly grandson, was becoming a dominant force in the government. In this setting, Isaiah saw his vision of God. The good King of Israel was dead, but Israel's God still lived.

1. **The Concept of the Sovereign—What Isaiah Saw** (vv. 1–4). Isaiah saw the Lord high and exalted with seraphims ascribing infinite holiness to God, while creation trembled before this majestic sight. A proper concept of the Sovereign means we recognize His *power,* His *position,* and His *purity.*

2. **The Concept of Self—What Isaiah Sensed** (vv. 5–7). In this light, Isaiah saw his own depravity, and that of his people. Comparing ourselves with one another fills us with conceit and complacency, but comparing ourselves with God yields humility and confession.

3. **The Concept of Service—What Isaiah Said** (vv. 8–13). We aren't ready for Christian service until we have seen ourselves in light of the Sovereign. Then we can say, ".... Here am I; send me."

CONCLUSION: Effective Christian service depends on our envisioning the Eternal.

Encouraging Others
Date preached:

By Dr. Timothy Beougher

SCRIPTURE: 1 Thessalonians 3:1–8

INTRODUCTION: Discouragement is the occupational hazard of living today. How easily we become down in the dumps, stuck in the blues, carrying the weight of the world, cast down. The wind goes out of our sails, it rains on our parade, and our bubble bursts.

1. **The Need for Encouragement** (vv. 1–5). We need encouragement because of the *trials* of life, the *temptations* of Satan, and the *turmoil* of emotions.

2. **The Focus of Encouragement** (vv. 3–8). Notice here: *Spiritual truth, spiritual fruit, and spiritual stability.*

3. **The Practice of Encouragement** (Heb. 3:13; 10:25). We encourage others by listening, praying, being transparent, expressing appreciation, challenging others, and sharing God's Word.

CONCLUSION: One of the best ways to overcome discouragement is to focus on others. Who can you encourage this week?

Master Secrets of Prayer

By Cameron V. Thompson

In the early 1970s, three of us students at Columbia Bible College were invited to spend the weekend with Ruth Bell Graham at her rambling log cabin home in Montreat, North Carolina, while her husband, Billy, was away. One of my two companions, Joy Thompson, brought along copies of a booklet her father, Cameron V. Thompson, had written entitled *Master Secrets of Prayer*. Mrs. Graham, deeply concerned at the time for her prodigal children, devoured this little book and ordered a case of them to give to friends. Later I noticed her quoting it in talks she gave and articles she wrote. Her endorsement helped spur sales of the book, and it became one of the most popular publications from Back to the Bible of Lincoln, Nebraska.

I have treasured my copy, too, and its pages are now thumb-smeared, its passages heavily underlined. I've quoted from it a hundred times in sermons and articles.

Now a new expanded edition of *Master Secrets of Prayer* is available from Light for Living Publications of Madison, Georgia. The new edition includes a remarkable spiritual "last will and testament," discovered by Cameron's widow, Dell, about a year after his death.

Cameron Thompson, born in 1912, was raised in Florida, where he studied journalism and spent his time in "selfwill, drunkenness and debauchery." One evening as he walked down a Tampa street, he was startled when a young man darted from a dark alley and said to him, "Say, are you saved?" Then the man disappeared into the night.

"Saved from what?" Cameron pondered as he waited for a traffic light to change. Not long afterward, he became ill and was confined to bed for sixteen months with tuberculosis. The stranger's question haunted him.

One evening Cameron crawled out onto the sloping roof of his home in Tallahassee for some cool night air. In the distance, a tent had been erected for an evangelistic campaign. The evangelist's words sailed through the air and hit Cameron so hard it nearly knocked him off the roof. Speaking of the unsaved person, the evangelist warned: *He too shall drink of the wine of God's indignation and wrath, poured undiluted into a cup of His anger, and he shall be tormented with fire and brimstone in the presence of the holy angels and in the presence of the Lamb.*

Shortly thereafter, ill and possibly dying, Cameron began reading his Bible, and his blood curdled as he read passages about the wrath and judgment of God. He began dwelling on "the awful reality of hell. I thought of little else. . . . Verse by verse I looked, even more intently than a condemned man searching out books of law to escape the electric chair."

Then one day, "I took one last chance, threw myself on the thin hope that Christ might possibly care even for me, begged mercy as a prodigal son, and pleaded with God that He would not send me to that awful place. Oh, wonder of wonders—I found myself safe in the arms of Jesus."

Cameron Thompson enrolled in seminary, then pastored a church in Atlanta, Georgia, before moving to Ecuador to engage in a ministry of Bible distribution. There he founded and directed the Pan American Testament League.

In 1957, four years before he died, Cameron wrote a series of articles about prayer for the *Alliance Weekly*. They were read with interest by Theodore Epp, then director of Back to the Bible, who published them in booklet form in 1959, with these chapter titles:

- The School of Prayer
- The Approach to Prayer
- How to Intercede
- Hindrances to Prayer
- How to Pray
- Some Practical Hints About Prayer

"While I have tried to leave no source unsearched in the vast literature of prayer," wrote Cameron, "most of these principles were discovered in the glorious hours of the early morning as the best of all teachers, the Holy Spirit, suddenly gave me openings in the Word of God.

"No one can in this life pass beyond the kindergarten of prayer. Thank God, there are no Doctors of Prayer, and I am keenly aware that there is yet more land to be possessed. Therefore, these gleanings of a lifetime are sent forth with hope set on the grace of God that He may be pleased to use them for His glory to set the saints everywhere praying."

Well, Cameron Thompson has certainly encouraged me in my own prayer life. I think he will do the same for you. ✿

JULY 21, 2002

Date preached:

Letdowns, Setbacks, Fizzles, and Failures

Scripture: Jeremiah 45 The word that Jeremiah the prophet spoke to Baruch the son of Neriah, when he had written these words in a book at the instruction of Jeremiah, in the fourth year of Jehoiakim the son of Josiah, king of Judah, saying, "Thus says the LORD, the God of Israel, to you, O Baruch: 'You said, "Woe is me now! For the LORD has added grief to my sorrow. I fainted in my sighing, and I find no rest." '

"Thus you shall say to him, 'Thus says the LORD: "Behold, what I have built I will break down, and what I have planted I will pluck up, that is, this whole land. And do you seek great things for yourself? Do not seek them; for behold, I will bring adversity on all flesh," says the LORD. "But I will give your life to you as a prize in all places, wherever you go." ' "

Introduction: In his biography of Winston Churchill, William Manchester tells of a manservant who once decided to stand up to Churchill, who was notoriously hard to work for. The men got into a blazing row, and when it was over, Churchill, his lower lip jutting, said, "You were very rude to me, you know." The servant, still seething, replied, "Yes, but you were rude, too." Churchill grumbled, "Yes, but I am a great man."

The servant later said, "There was no answer to that. He knew, as I and the rest of the world knew, that he was right."

All of us want to be great to some degree. We crave the approval and respect of our peers. We want to reach our goals and achieve our dreams. Even our Lord's disciples asked, "Which of us is greatest?" But life is full of letdowns, setbacks, fizzles, and failures. How do we deal with those? In Jeremiah's writings, there is an odd little chapter from God, addressed personally to Jeremiah's scribe, Baruch. We know that Baruch was a fine young man from a noted family. We later learn that his brother Seraiah was also an important man in Israel (Jer. 32:12; 51:59). Baruch was bright, ambitious, full of promise, known to the political movers and shakers of the day.

I. **His Position** (v. 1). This verse takes us back to Jeremiah 36 where, during the reign of King Jehoiakim, Jeremiah, in hiding, decides to stir things up. Inspired by God, he composes a blistering sermon and asks Baruch to record it by dictation and to read it aloud in the temple. For Baruch, this is political suicide. By remaining true to his spiritual convictions, he is effectively jettisoning his standing and future career. Sometimes we're caught between our principles and our ambitions. Sometimes we have to make hard choices. Will we remain true to God at the cost of forfeiting worldly success? Charles Spurgeon said, "Many through wishing to be great have failed to be good."

2. **His Condition** (vv. 2–3). Baruch made the right decision, but afterward he was angry, frustrated, and downfallen. His emotions are so raw that God used six terms to describe them in verses 2–3: "woe... grief... sorrow... fainted... sighing... no rest."

3. **His Ambition** (vv. 4–5). The problem was inside Baruch's own brain. He needed to change his thinking, to give up his "small ambitions." As it says in the King James Version: "Seekest thou great things for thyself? Seek them not." The Lord didn't forbid him from "seeking great things." The problem was "for thyself." God has a plan for our lives, and in His will there is no failure. Out of His will, there is no success. Paul Robinson, veteran missionary to Uruguay, said, "Don't worry about doing something great. Be great by doing what you can where God has placed you. It will pay off after awhile."

Conclusion: God did give Baruch a long life and a lasting legacy. We know him not only from Scripture, but from archaeology. Excavators have actually found a clay seal bearing his inscription, making him one of the few biblical charac-

>>> *sermon continued on following page*

APPROPRIATE HYMNS AND SONGS

I Would Be True, Howard Walter Arnold/Joseph Yates Peek; Public Domain.

Humble Thyself in the Sight of the Lord, Bob Hudson; © 1978 Maranatha! Music.

Humble My Heart, Michael J. Dwyer; © 1996 Dwyer Tunes (Admin. by Safe Haven Music).

Jesus Is Our King, Sherrell Prebble/Howard Page-Clark; © 1978 Celebration.

Jesus Use Me, Jack Campbell/Billy Campbell; © 1956 Gospel Publishing House (Admin. by Lorenz Corporation).

ters whose existence is proven by the discovery of ancient artifacts. He teaches us that...

A. It's all right to be ambitious, if it is "sanctified ambition"—an eagerness to fulfill God's plan in life and to advance His kingdom.
B. It is dangerous to be driven by selfish ambition. An old Moravian prayer says, "From the desire of being great, good Lord, deliver us!"
C. When letdowns, setbacks, fizzles, and failures occur, we need to recognize the hand and hear the voice of God. Disappointments are often His appointments, for our times are in His hands.

FOR THE BULLETIN

✿ On July 21, 1542, to strengthen the fight against Protestantism, Pope Paul III set up an inquisition. ✿ On July 21, 1773, Pope Clement XIV issues the Papal bull "Dominus ac Redemptor" dissolving the Jesuit Order. It was restored in 1814. ✿ On July 21, 1864, Scottish missionary explorer David Livingstone arrived back in Great Britain for the final time. Returning to Africa the next year, he was lost to the world until discovered by Henry Stanley. In 1873, Livingtone's national workers found him dead on his knees in a posture of prayer. ✿ Wellesley College professor Katherine Lee Bates wrote the original version of her poem "America the Beautiful" on this day in 1893 in Colorado Springs after being inspired by the view from Pike's Peak. ✿ On July 21, 1896, James Stuart Stewart, considered by *Preaching Magazine* the greatest preacher of the 20th century, was born in Dundee, Scotland. His father, who had been converted under D. L. Moody, was a Bible teacher with the YMCA. After pastoring three Church of Scotland congregations, Stewart taught New Testament at the University of Edinburgh and was Chaplain to the Queen of Scotland. His passion was expository preaching, and he was committed to world evangelism. ✿ On July 21, 1925, the "Monkey Trial" ended in Tennessee. The state had banned the teaching of evolution in schools because it challenged the Bible. John Scopes ignored the ban and taught Darwin's theories, for which he was convicted.

WORSHIP HELPS

Worship Theme:
Seek God's will in life, not "great things for thyself."

Call to Worship:
But He gives more grace. Therefore He says: "God resists the proud, But gives grace to the humble." Therefore submit to God. Resist the devil and he will flee from you. Draw near to God and He will draw near to you. Cleanse your hands, you sinners; and purify your hearts, you double-minded. Lament and mourn and weep! Let your laughter be turned to mourning and your joy to gloom. Humble yourselves in the sight of the Lord, and He will lift you up (James 4:6–10).

Responsive Reading:

Men: Likewise you younger people, submit yourselves to *your* elders. Yes, all of *you* be submissive to one another, and be clothed with humility.

Women: For "God resists the proud, but gives grace to the humble."

Men: Therefore humble yourselves under the mighty hand of God, that He may exalt you in due time, casting all your care upon Him, for He cares for you.

Women: Be sober, be vigilant; because your adversary the devil walks about like a roaring lion, seeking whom he may devour.

Men: Resist him, steadfast in the faith, knowing that the same sufferings are experienced by your brotherhood in the world.

Women: But may the God of all grace, who called us to His eternal glory by Christ Jesus, after you have suffered a while, perfect, establish, strengthen, and settle you.

Everyone: To Him be the glory and the dominion forever and ever. Amen.

Taken from 1 Peter 5:5–11.

Offertory Comment:
1 Chronicles 16:29 says, "Give to the Lord the glory due His name; Bring an offering, and come before Him. Oh, worship the Lord in the beauty of holiness!" May the Lord bless us in the giving of our tithes and offerings today.

STATS, STORIES AND MORE

Pursuing His Will

When Charles Haddon Spurgeon, 18, was seeking God's will for his life, his friends and his father advised him to attend college. He applied to Regent's Park College, and an interview was set between the head of the college and young Spurgeon. The meeting was to be in Cambridge at the home of Mr. Macmillan, the publisher. At the appointed time, Spurgeon showed at Macmillan's house. He rang the bell, and a servant showed him into the parlor. There he sat for two hours until at last he called for the servant and was horrified to learn she had forgotten to announce his arrival. Meanwhile the head of the college had sat waiting in an adjoining room until his patience had been exhausted.

Spurgeon's first impulse was to run after the man, to chase him to London, to explain what had happened. But he took a long walk out in the country to calm down, and Jeremiah 45:5 came to his mind so that he almost seemed to hear it audibly.

The Lord seemed to tell him not to worry about the misunderstanding or make extraordinary efforts to clear it up, but to take it as the Lord's will and serve the Lord humbly where he was. As a result, Spurgeon never did make it to college, but it didn't matter. He became the most powerful and successful and fruitful minister in the history of Victorian England, and he later said that he "a thousand times thanked the Lord very heartily for the strange providence which forced his steps into another and far better path."

Awaiting God's Timing

J. Oswald Sanders, missionary statesman, wrote of a time when he wanted a particular position very much. Having friends in positions of influence, he was about ask them to "pull strings" for him. But while walking down the main street in Auckland, New Zealand, turning the matter over in his mind, as he walked past His Majesty's Theatre, Jeremiah 45:5 to his mind with tremendous authority. "I believe that was a real turning point in my service to the Lord," Sanders later wrote. As a result, he did not seek the position, but it later opened to him on its own in God's good timing.

> What may be my future lot,
> High or low concerns me not;
> This doth set my heart at rest:
> What my God appoints is best.

Additional Sermons and Lesson Ideas

What Jesus Cannot Do

Date preached:

By Dr. Ed Dobson

SCRIPTURE: Mark 6:1–6

INTRODUCTION: Thomas Wolfe wrote, *You Can't Go Home Again*. Here, Jesus returned to Nazareth and spoke in the synagogue. The people took offense; He could do few miracles because of their unbelief.

1. **The hardest to reach are family members.** Compare Mark 3:21. The good news is that after Jesus ascended into heaven, His family was in the upper room with the disciples. If you have been sharing with your family, keep praying; it takes time to bring others to Christ.
2. **Jesus does not force Himself on others.** God cannot save a person unless that person asks to be saved. Jesus will not fellowship with us intimately unless we invite Him (Rev. 3:20).
3. **We can limit God by our lack of faith.** The hemorrhaging woman said, "If I can just touch the tassels on His garment, I'll be healed." Faith without obedience isn't faith at all. Lord, increase our faith.

CONCLUSION: God help us to not limit what Christ wants in our lives. May we be delivered from the Nazarene syndrome—to be so close, so conscious, so aware and to leave unchanged.

What The Love of Christ Does To Us

Date preached:

SCRIPTURE: 2 Corinthians 5:14 (KJV)

INTRODUCTION: Some things make a lasting mark. Since there is no greater force than the love of Christ, what impact does it have on us?

1. **The love of Christ explains us.** It turns us into His followers, gives us a new life, and defines who we are. Jesus said that the world would know we are Christians by our love.
2. **It restrains us,** keeps us from sin; Jesus said, "If you love me, keep my commandments."
3. **It sustains us.** Ephesians 3:17 speaks of being rooted and grounded in love. 1 Thessalonians 3:12 speaks of increasing and abounding in love.
4. **It ordains us,** sending us out to the world as His ambassadors.
5. **It constrains us.** We can't keep quiet; we're compelled to share His love with others.

CONCLUSION: Don't just be a recipient of Christ's love; be a conduit. The Lord needs pipelines, not puddles.

JULY 28, 2002

Criteria for Contentment

Date preached:

By Dr. Melvin Worthington

Scripture: Philippians 4:11–13 Not that I speak in regard to need, for I have learned in whatever state I am, to be content: I know how to be abased, and I know how to abound. Everywhere and in all things I have learned both to be full and to be hungry, both to abound and to suffer need. I can do all things through Christ who strengthens me.

Introduction: Let me begin with two old British quotes. The witty Puritan Thomas Watson once said: "Discontent keeps a man from enjoying what he doth possess. A drop or two of vinegar will sour a whole glass of wine." The famous preacher Charles Spurgeon gave us the other side of the picture: "A little sprig of the herb called content put into the poorest soup will make it taste as rich as the Lord Mayor's turtle." It isn't what we have, but what we enjoy that makes for a rich life, and the wise person understands that contentment is not having everything we want, but enjoying everything we have. Contentment is an elusive commodity in today's society, yet it is one of the distinguishing marks of the Christian. What determines contentment? Does it depend on circumstances, church or country? Dissatisfaction, discouragement and division are often symptoms of discontentment in our souls. Contentment must be equated with confidence in the sovereignty of the great I AM over His creation.

1. **The Expectation.** The Scriptures mandate contentment. The Christian should be content with his wages (Luke 3:14), in spite of his circumstances (Phil. 4:11), with food and raiment (1 Tim. 6:8) and with the things which he has (Heb. 13:5). Discontentment is a manifestation of unbelief.

2. **The Essentials.** One of the most serene pictures of a contented soul is found in Psalm 1 where we're given a very picturesque image of trees rising up from the riverbanks, bearing fruit, exhibiting strength. The kind of person described here is:

   A. **Separated from the world.** Unless Christians are rightly related to the world, they will never have contentment in their souls. Biblical separation means rejecting the *counsel* of the ungodly (1:1a), the *company* of sinners (1:1b), and the *contempt* of the scornful (1:1c). Having been saved by the grace of God, the Christian no longer chums with nor follows sinners to do evil. He does not stand in the congregation of sinners.

B. **Saturated by the Word** characterizes the contented Christian (Ps. 1:2). His view of life springs from the Word of God. His delight is in the doctrines of the Bible. He deliberates on its truths day and night, reading and meditating on its words. J. I. Packer says that meditation is the practice of turning each truth we learn *about* God into matter for reflection *before* God, leading to prayer and praise *to* God. "Meditation is the activity of calling to mind, and thinking over, and dwelling on, and applying to oneself, the various things that one knows about the works and ways and purposes and promises of God," Packer writes in his classic *Knowing God.* "It is an activity of holy thought, consciously performed in the presence of God, under the eye of God, by the help of God, as a means of communion with God." Such *saturation with the Scriptures* is the secret to *satisfaction in the soul.*

C. **Situated by the water** (Ps. 1:3). He is like a tree planted by the rivers of water, which is a marvelous picture of the Holy Spirit. God's supply of grace is inexhaustible. Fruitfulness will come in its season.

3. **The End** (1 Timothy 6:6). Personal contentment in one's soul results in proper perspectives, priorities and progress. Godliness with contentment is great gain (1 Tim. 6:6).

>>> *sermon continued on following page*

APPROPRIATE HYMNS AND SONGS

I Am Resolved, Palmer Hartsough/James H. Fillmore; Public Domain.

Center of My Joy, Gloria Gaither/William J. Gaither/Richard Smallmood; © 1987 William J. Gaither, Inc. (Admin. by Copyright Management, Inc.).

Matchless Name, Cary Schmidt; © 1995 Abundant Life Music Company.

I Can Do All Things, Paul C. Smith; © 1998 Integrity's Hosanna! Music.

I Shall Not Be Moved, John T. Benson, Jr.; © 1950 John T. Benson Publishing Company (Admin. by Brentwood-Benson Music Publishing, Inc.).

Conclusion: A pastor in California has a little column that appears every day under the title "Daily Contentment." That's a great description for the Christian life. Perhaps the devil has dropped a few drops of vinegar which the Lord wants to replace with a sprig of the herb contentment. Let's learn to say with St. Paul: "I have learned in whatever state I am, to be content: I know how to be abased, and I know how to abound. Everywhere and in all things I have learned both to be full and to be hungry, both to abound and to suffer need. I can do all things through Christ who strengthens me."

FOR THE BULLETIN

✸ Alcuin died on July 28, 804. He was "Secretary of Education" for Charlemagne, and one of Christianity's great educators, churchmen, writers, and Bible commentators. ✸ On July 28, 1057, Pope Victor II died of fever. He is best remembered for his battle against simony, the "sale" of church offices. ✸ Thomas Cromwell supported the cause of the Reformation in England under the reign of King Henry VIII and was largely responsible for the Reformation Acts between 1532 and 1538. His mistake was urging the King to marry Anne of Cleaves. The King agreed to marry Anne from her picture, but when she showed up at the wedding, he loathed her and began plotting a divorce. The fiasco cost Thomas Cromwell his head. On this day in 1540, he was brought to a scaffold on Tower-hill, where he was executed. ✸ One of the most entertaining, clever, and godly Puritans, Thomas Watson, was buried on July 28, 1686. ✸ Jonathan and Sarah Edwards were married on this day in 1727. ✸ Johann Sebastian Bach, zealous Lutheran composer and organist, passed away on July 28, 1750. He had become blind in his last years, but regained his eyesight a few days before his death. ✸ On July 28, 1858, William Herschel in Jungipur, India, took the print of Rajyadhar Konai on the back of a contract. It was the first use of fingerprints as a means of identification in history.

WORSHIP HELPS

Worship Theme:
Those who are happy in Jesus need little else.

Call to Worship:
As for God, His way is perfect; The word of the Lord is proven; He is a shield to all who trust in Him (Ps. 18:30).

Appropriate Scripture Readings:
Deuteronomy 8:1–5; Proverbs 3:31–35; Romans 12:16–21

Pastoral Prayer:
Almighty and most merciful Father, We have erred and strayed from Your ways like lost sheep. We have followed too much the devices and desires of our own hearts. We have disobeyed Your holy laws. We have left undone those things we ought to have done, and we have done things we should not have done. There is no health in us; but, O Lord, have mercy on us. Move us to confess our faults. Restore those who are penitent; According to Your promises, grant, merciful Father, for Christ's sake, that we may hereafter live godly, righteous, and sober lives, to the glory of Your holy Name. Amen. (Adapted from the *Canadian Book of Common Prayer*)

Kids Talk

Find a catalog from a toy store or the sales pages from a toy store in today's paper. Ask the children what toys they would most like to have. Then wad up the paper, and tell them you have a great secret. Happy people are the ones who know how to enjoy what they have. Unhappy people are the ones who are always wanting what they don't have. Share these three verses (from the Contemporary English Version):

"If you love money and wealth, you will never be satisfied *with what you have.* This doesn't make sense." —*Ecclesiastes 5:10*

"Religion does make your life rich, by making you content *with what you have.*" —*1 Timothy 6:6*

"Don't fall in love with money. Be satisfied with what you have. The Lord has promised that he will not leave us or desert us." —*Hebrews 13:5*

STATS, STORIES AND MORE

Contentment

"A contented mind is the greatest blessing a man can enjoy in this world."
—*Joseph Addison (1672–1719), English poet*

"The discontented man finds no easy chair."—Benjamin Franklin
"It is great wealth to a soul to live frugally with a contented mind."
—*Lucretius (99 B.C.–5 B.C.), Roman poet*

"Contentment is something that depends a little on position and a lot on disposition."
—*Anonymous*

Meditation

"Holding the Word of God in your heart until it has affected every phase of your life....This is meditation."
—*Andrew Murray*

"Meditation is the skeleton key that unlocks the greatest storeroom in the house of God's provisions for the Christian."
—*from* A Primer on Meditation

"Meditation is simply thought prolonged and directed to a single object. Your mystic chambers where thoughts abide are the secret worship of an unseen Sculptor chiseling living forms for a deathless future. Personality and influence are modeled here."
—*A. T. Pierson*

Be Content

Years ago, Bill Gothard sent out this message in birthday cards to his students: "Contentment is realizing that God has already provided everything we need for our present happiness." The 17th century preacher Thomas Fuller wrote, "Contentment consisteth not in adding more fuel, but in taking away some fire; not in multiplying wealth, but in subtracting men's desires."

A Line on Happiness

There's an old story about a rich businessman who was disturbed to find a fisherman sitting lazily beside his boat. He told him he should be out fishing, and when the man asked "Why?" the industrialist said, "You could earn more money and buy a better boat so you could go out further, catch more fish, and buy more boats and make even more money. Soon you'd be rich like me, and then you could sit down and enjoy life."

"What do you think I'm doing now?" asked the fisherman.

Additional Sermons and Lesson Ideas

Follow the Leader

Date preached:

By Drew Wilkerson

SCRIPTURE: Hebrews 13:17

INTRODUCTION: Much is written today about leadership, but little is said about follower-ship. There is biblical counsel given concerning the responsibilities of a leader... but here are also guidelines given for those who follow. Hebrews 13:17 instructs Christians how to follow their leaders.

1. **Do not be afraid to follow.** Christians are not to be suspicious of their leaders. Many church attendees have been burned before, but the past cannot be allowed to dictate the present. Just as leaders are called to lead, followers must faithfully submit to the leaders God has appointed over them.
2. **Leaders are responsible to God.** Sheep need not be reluctant to follow their shepherds. Leaders are accountable to God, and God will take care of safe-guarding his sheep.
3. **Obedience leads to joy.** Nothing is more satisfying than knowing that God is pleased with us. If we do what we are called to do we can trust God to take care of us. Obedience always leads to joy, joy in our lives and joy for those who lead.

CONCLUSION: The fastest way to be a good leader is to follow one with humility and faithfulness.

Woe is Me

Date preached:

SCRIPTURE: Various

Introduction: If you've felt sorry for yourself recently, you're in good company. Eight times (in the NKJV), biblical characters uttered those three pathetic words: "Woe is me."

1. **Psalm 120:5.** The Psalmist is praying, for his soul is disturbed by the militant, warlike tones of those around him.
2. **Jeremiah 4:31.** Israel is depressed about the violence that has overtaken the land.
3. **Jeremiah 10:12 and 15:10.** Jeremiah, the melancholy prophet, is feeling sorry for himself because he has been called upon to minister in a very tragic age.
4. **Jeremiah 45:3.** Baruch is struggling with his fading ambitions.
5. **Micah 7:1.** The Prophet Micah feels very alone.
6. **Isaiah 6:5.** Isaiah feels undone in the presence of a holy God.
7. **1 Corinthians 9:16.** St. Paul imagines how terrible it would be for him if he didn't go about doing God's will

CONCLUSION: We're all tempted to feel sorry for ourselves, but the key to joy is learning to replace "Woe is me!" with "Praise the Lord!"

Seventeen Reasons to Keep Your Morale Up When Numbers Are Down

One of my biggest emotional struggles in ministry through the years has involved numbers. If our attendance averages year-to-date were higher than the previous year's, I felt encouraged. But if they slipped below the previous year's levels, a little bit of panic crept into my heart. Even today, I find it much more exhilarating to preach to a full house than to a half-empty room.

"Those empty benches are a serious trial," one preacher said, "and if the place be large and the congregation small the influence is seriously depressing." That particular preacher seldom saw an empty seat, yet the empathetic Spurgeon instinctually understood the great pastoral temptation of letting one's morale rise and fall with statistics.

Success in our world is usually defined digitally. Poll figures. Batting averages. Income levels. Large crowds, big bucks, and high yields. The result? Many pastors feel unsuccessful and disappointed, for we're likely serving double-digit congregations, not mega-ones. Furthermore, we labor alongside lay workers who often face "low turn-outs." Just last week I saw a volunteer standing in the foyer looking glum. He told me he had expected 100 people to register for a particular activity, and only 30 signed up. He was as discouraged as Elijah in the wilderness.

The famous missionary Mary Moffat expressed the feelings of many when she wrote, "Could we but see the smallest fruit, we could rejoice midst the privations and toils which we bear; but as it is, our hands do often hang down."

Well, of course, numbers *are* important for they represent souls. The reason we count numbers, someone said, is because numbers count. Sometimes lean statistics denote laziness, carelessness, personal failure, or spiritual powerlessness. Furthermore, envy has no place in our hearts. We thank God for today's super-sized congregations, even if someone else leads them.

But church history, common sense, and the Scriptures also present another set of truths for those of us who seldom preach to sellout crowds.

1. The servant is not above his Master.
As he pressed the demands of discipleship, Jesus saw His own crowds dwindle. "From that time many of His disciples went back and walked

with Him no more. Then Jesus said to the twelve, 'Do you also want to go away?'" (John 6:66–67). We shouldn't be too surprised, therefore, to find that biblical preaching doesn't always attract multitudes. Warren Wiersbe wrote, "We dare not measure the quality of our sermons by the quantity of the statistics. If we do, we might become either too elated or too depressed, and both pride and discouragement are sins. One day our Lord gave a sermon on the Bread of Life and lost His whole congregation, and yet false prophets always seem to have a crowd."

2. God sovereignly assigns tasks as He will.

"And they came to John and said to him, 'Rabbi, He who was with you beyond the Jordan, to whom you have testified—behold, He is baptizing, and all are coming to Him!' John answered and said, 'A man can receive nothing unless it has been given to him from heaven. . . . He must increase, but I must decrease.'" (John 3:26–27, 30).

Paul wrote in Romans 12:6: "Having then gifts differing according to the grace that is given to us, let us use them."

John Oxenham wrote:

> *Is your place a small place?*
> *Tend it with care!—*
> *He set you there.*

> *Is your place a large place?*
> *Guard it with care!—*
> *He set you there.*

> *Whate'er your place, it is*
> *Not yours alone, but His*
> *Who set you there!*

3. Success and statistics are not synonyms.

In their book, *Liberating Ministry from the Success Syndrome*, Kent and Barbara Hughes describe their anguish when, early in ministry, they were given a promising church-planting effort in Southern California. When the work foundered, Kent grew depressed. *If church attendance was up, I was up; if it was down, so was I. And the numbers had been going down for a long time.* But gradually the Lord led the Hughes to ponder these questions: *Can a man be a success in the ministry and pastor a small church? What is failure in ministry? What is success in ministry?* From the experience, Kent learned that God defines success in ministry as being faithful, serving others, loving and trusting Him, praying, pursuing holiness, and developing a positive attitude. This liberating discovery enabled Hughes to plunge back into his work, despite its paucity, with joy and enthusiasm. *We saw how success was equally possible for those in the most difficult of situations . . . as well as those having vast ministries.*

According to A. P. Fitt, D. L. Moody never counted converts. "He depreciated the boastful use of statistics. People used to ask him what were the most notable conversions he had achieved, and the greatest meetings he ever conducted. They could not draw him out on such matters."

Senator Mark Hatfield, while touring Mother Teresa's work in Calcutta, asked her how she could bear her load without being crushed by it. "My dear Senator," she replied, "I am not called to be successful, but faithful."

4. Small is not bad.

We can often do more with less, and sometimes the scope of our impact is in reverse proportion to the size of our audience. Jesus had more success with one Samaritan woman than with all Jerusalem, and Gideon found 300 committed men preferable to 32,000 vacillators. God called Philip from a city-wide revival to a congregation of one in the desert.

Carl S. Dudley wrote, "In a big world, the small church has remained intimate. In a fast world, the small church has been steady. In an expensive world, the small church has remained plain. In a complex world, the small church has remained simple. In a rational world, the small church has kept feelings. In a mobile world, the small church has been an anchor. In an anonymous world, the small church calls us by name."

Matthew 18:20 is a divine promise, not a lame consolation: "For where two or three are gathered together in My name, I am there in the midst of them."

5. Oaks start from acorns.

After the Civil War, John Broadus, burdened for more preachers to heal the nation's wounds, prepared a seminary course on homiletics. To his dismay only one student, a blind man, enrolled in the class. "I shall give him my best and I shall pursue my lectures as planned," said Broadus. Day after day, Broadus gave his lectures conversationally to his solitary, sightless student—lectures so powerful they later became the classic *The Preparation and Delivery of Sermons.*

Remember the old gospel song that says:

> *Little is much when God is in it;*
> *Labor not for wealth or fame.*

There's a crown and you can win it,
If you'll go in Jesus' name.

6. You can often light a fire in the rain.

Mrs. William Butler and Mrs. E. W. Parker of India envisioned a woman's missionary society for the denomination, the Methodist Episcopal Church. But on the day of its organizing, a pelting rain kept the women at home. Only six showed up. Mrs. Butler and Mrs. Parker, however, "spoke as eloquently as if to hundreds." Out of that meeting came the Women's Foreign Missionary Society of the Methodist Episcopal Church.

7. God anticipated our feelings of failure.

The messages of Haggai and Zechariah were specifically given to encourage those whose work seemed small and futile in their own eyes. The remnant of Jews who had returned to restore their nation had worked very hard, clearing away debris, recovering stone, restoring the foundations of buildings. While working on the temple, a wave of depression swept over them. So much work, and yet it seemed so pitifully small and bare compared with the grandeur that had once been the Solomonic temple. They gave up.

"Thus the work of the house of God which is at Jerusalem ceased, and it was discontinued until the second year of the reign of Darius king of Persia. Then the prophet Haggai and Zechariah the son of Iddo, prophets, prophesied to the Jews who were in Judah and Jerusalem, in the name of the God of Israel, who was over them. So Zerubbabel the son of Shealtiel and Jeshua the son of Jozadak rose up and began to build the house of God which is in Jerusalem; and the prophets of God were with them, helping them" (Ezra 4:24—5:2).

God sent Haggai and Zechariah to remind the remnant that the glory of the latter temple would be greater than that of the former one, for in the temple they were seeking to rebuild, the Desire of all Nations—the Messiah Himself—would minister (Hag. 3:7)

"How does (your work for the Lord) look to you now? Does it not seem to you like nothing? But now be strong . . . and work. For I am with you . . . I will fill this house with glory," said Haggai (Hag. 2:3–4, 7).

"Who despises the day of small things?" echoed Zechariah (Zech. 4:10).

Many times when I've grown discouraged, I've turned to these two prophets and reminded myself that God anticipated discouragement among His workers; thus He set aside two books of the Bible just for them.

8. There are no small churches.

"I do not believe there are any small churches," Joseph Parker once said. "I am more and more convinced that we should be very careful what epithets we attach to the term 'church.'"

9. Who knows the impact even a poor sermon might have on all subsequent church history!

January 6, 1850, was bitterly cold in Colchester, England, a hard-biting blizzard keeping most worshipers at home. At the Primitive Methodist Chapel on Artillery Street only about a dozen showed up. When it became apparent not even the pastor would arrive, an unlettered man rose and spoke haltingly from Isaiah 45:22, then the crowd dispersed, thinking the day's service a loss—not realizing that a 15–year-old-boy had wandered into the room, heard the sermon, and given his life to Christ.

Years later that boy, Charles Spurgeon, wrote: "Don't hold back because you cannot preach in St. Paul's; be content to talk to one or two in a cottage. You may cook in small pots as well as in big ones. Little pigeons can carry great messages. Even a little dog can bark at a thief, wake up the master, and save the house. . . . Do what you do right thoroughly, pray over it heartily, and leave the result to God."

10. Your congregation is bigger than you think.

In one of his inimitable lectures, F. W. Boreham said, "Has not every preacher an invisible congregation? At every service, there is a dim, unseen, listening throng."

Who are they? Christ is present, the angels gather, and don't forget those outside the church who will be touched by your sermon through its impact on your listeners. And there is yet another audience, said Boreham, a vast one who will be affected more than we can ever know: "There are generations yet unborn. Posterity is simply the invisible congregation, sitting a little further down the aisle."

Here's an example. James Taylor so detested itinerant preachers that he often pelted them with rotten eggs. One day a Wesleyan circuit rider entered town, and James went to disrupt the meeting. But the preacher's text—"As for me and my household, we will serve the Lord"—struck Taylor like an arrow, for he had recently proposed to a young lady. On the morning of his wedding, James retired to the fields, knelt in the grass, and earnestly asked Christ to be his Savior. He prayed so long he was late for his wedding. Rushing to the chapel, he shocked his bride by announcing he had been saved.

Eight generations have since passed, each filled with Christian workers who have served the Lord around the world—among them, James Taylor's great-grandson, Hudson Taylor, founder of the China Inland Mission.

If the Wesleyan preacher had only known. . . .

11. God even can work in bad weather and sparse crowds.

The aforementioned Hudson Taylor was once advised to cancel an appointment on a stormy night in Birmingham, England. "I must go," he replied, "even if there is no one but the doorkeeper." Only a dozen people showed up that night, but the meeting hummed with unusual spiritual power. Half of those present later became missionaries or gave their children as missionaries, and the rest became faithful supporters of China Inland Mission for years to come.

In *The Life of Edward Payson* it is recorded that, on a stormy Sunday, the famous preacher had but one hearer. Mr. Payson preached his sermon, however, as carefully and as earnestly as though the great building had been thronged with eager listeners. Several months later his solitary listener called on him.

"I was led to the Savior through that service," he said. "For whenever you talked about sin and salvation, I glanced around to see to whom you referred, but since there was no one there but me, I had no alternative but to lay every word to my own heart and conscience!"

12. Statistics, while often diagnostically helpful, can be dangerous to your spiritual health.

Few can observe another's success without feelings of envy; and when our vital statistics are sized up beside another's, it tends to produce feelings of inferiority in some and superiority in others. "Each one should test his own actions," says Galatians 6:4. "Then he can take pride in himself without comparing himself to someone else."

Or, as Paul put it in 2 Corinthians 10:12: "For we dare not class ourselves or compare ourselves with those who commend themselves. But they, measuring themselves by themselves, and comparing themselves among themselves, are not wise."

Some ministers even lie to preserve their bragging rights. A friend told me of going to a meeting in which the host pastor, looking over the crowd, crowed, "What a great number we have tonight! I suppose there are 600 present." My friend, sitting in the back, decided to do an actual count—coming up with half that.

Don't forget that while the Lord led Moses to "number" the children of

Israel for practical reasons, the devil tempted David to number them for evil ones.

Vance Havner said, "Watch for souls and not for statistics. God keeps the books. Matthew Henry lamented over the poor response to his ministry and felt that his labors were done, since so many had left and few had been added. But he still feeds us with messages not too well appreciated in his own time. One of the many delusions from which the ministry needs to be delivered today is the notion that a preacher may be judged by the size of his crowd. The man who thinks he is too big for a little place is too little for a big place."

13. Apples are only "in season" in October.

My father owned an orchard in the Carolina mountains. I'd watch him work eleven months a year mowing, spraying, pruning, repairing, fertilizing, all without seeing a single mature apple. He labored with the confidence that, barring a late freeze, the harvest was coming. Similarly, we're told to preach the Word "in season and out of season" (2 Tim. 4:2). Seed takes time to germinate, and fruit takes time to ripen. "I planted, Apollos watered, but God gave the increase" (1 Cor. 3:6). I once heard of a man who was converted at age 116 by recalling a text of a sermon he had heard 100 years before. "And let us not become weary while doing good," says Galatians 6:9, "for in due season we shall reap if we do not lose heart."

14. God's promises cannot fail.

We not only walk by faith, we work by faith. Remember Isaiah 55:10–11? God's Word, like rain and snow from heaven, will not return to Him void. Peter Cartwright once planned an evangelistic crusade in which, on the first night, only one person showed up. Cartwright nonetheless preached his best for 45 minutes to a one-eyed Presbyterian elder. "It was the greatest sermon I ever heard," said the elder, spreading the news all over town. The next night, the hillside was covered with horses and wagons, the hall overflowed, and revival came.

"He who continually goes forth weeping, bearing seed for sowing, shall doubtless come again with rejoicing, bringing his sheaves with him" (Ps. 126:6).

15. If we are faithful in little, God will sooner or later entrust us with much.

George Matheson grew discouraged over his small crowd one winter's evening in Innellan, Scotland. He had worked hard on his sermon, but the sparse numbers and empty chairs nearly defeated him. He nevertheless did his best, not knowing that in the congregation was a visitor from the large St. Bernard's Church in Edinburgh, which was seeking a pastor. "Make every occasion a great occasion," said Matheson, who was to spend the rest of his career at St. Bernard's. "You can never tell when somebody may be taking your measure for a larger place."

16. Our reward in heaven is not based on the size of our audience on earth.

Remember the Lord's chosen adjectives: "Well done, *good* and *faithful* servant" (Matt. 25:21).

17. Our significance rests in Christ, not in crowds.

It's our walk with Christ, not our work for Him, that is most important. I've read that Washington Gladden, well-known Massachusetts pastor of an earlier era, grew discouraged during a season of little success. One day he climbed up to the belfry to think, and he wondered if, had he been unconverted, he might have jumped from the height. Instead he had a long talk with the Lord, and from that experience wrote out a prayer which I sometimes pray before going into the pulpit:

> *O Master, let me walk with Thee*
> *In lowly paths of service free;*
> *Tell me Thy secret; help me bear*
> *The strain of toil, the fret of care.*

All of us want to leave a mark, and we passionately fear a fruitless ministry. But the Bible assures us that our work, properly committed to him and faithfully executed, is never wasted. We are doing more good than we know, and the extent of our fruitfulness will be known only in heaven. Our self-worth doesn't rest in fame but in faithfulness.

We have to work on keeping our attitude upbeat and positive, even when numbers are down, and it helps if we don't take ourselves too seriously. Once, just as an oratorio of his was about to begin, several of George Frideric Handel's friends gathered to console him about the extremely sparse audience attracted to the performance. "Never mind," Handel said, "the music will sound better" due to the improved acoustics of a very empty hall.

That isn't an easy lesson, but once learned it prevents a lot of stomach spasms, migraines, and Monday morning blues.

"Therefore, my beloved brethren, be steadfast, immovable, always abounding in the work of the Lord, knowing that your labor is not in vain in the Lord" (1 Cor. 15:58). ❁

AUGUST 4, 2002

SUGGESTED SERMON

Fitting into Our Loincloths

Date preached:

Scripture: John 13:1–17, especially verses 1–5 *Now before the Feast of the Passover, when Jesus knew that His hour had come that He should depart from this world to the Father, having loved His own who were in the world, He loved them to the end. And supper being ended, the devil having already put it into the heart of Judas Iscariot, Simon's son, to betray Him, Jesus, knowing that the Father had given all things into His hands, and that He had come from God and was going to God, rose from supper and laid aside His garments, took a towel and girded Himself. After that, He poured water into a basin and began to wash the disciples' feet, and to wipe them with the towel with which He was girded.*

Introduction: A recent study of student morality by the Josephson Institute found 71 percent of high schoolers cheated on a test and 92 percent lied to parents in the past year. Professor James Davison Hunter of the University of Virginia, after a ten year study, determined that a "death of character" is occurring in the United States. He suggests that people are more concerned today about feeling good than about being good, and a fellow researcher has determined that our culture today is suffering from "self-esteemia."

So many of these problems would dissolve in a good basin of water if we would just learn the art of washing feet. Alexander Maclaren called John 13–17, "the Holy of Holies of the New Testament". Nowhere else have we the heart of God so unveiled to us. This section of Scripture begins in John 13 with the washing of the disciples' feet. Ordinarily the cleansing of feet was done before the meal by the lowest-ranking servant in the household. When none of the disciples were willing, Jesus Himself rose during the meal to do it. It was one of the most usual and unnatural acts of His life and ministry. What was its purpose?

1. **To Demonstrate His Love** (v. 1). Love is here established as a theme in the Upper Room Discourse, occurring 31 times in chapters 13—17 (whereas it had been previously found only 6 times in chapters 1—12). Jesus genuinely felt affection for these twelve men (even Judas, whose feet He subsequently washed). And He has affection for you and me. There was never a truer song than, "Jesus loves me, this I know; for the Bible tells me so."

2. **To Model Humility.** Since the transfiguration, the disciples had been squabbling among themselves, jockeying for position. Luke tells us that this discussion continued even in the Upper Room on the eve of the Lord's crucifixion (see Luke 22:24–30), which undoubtedly prompted Jesus to do as He did. It is a remarkable picture: Jesus removed His garments (plural), presenting Himself as an Oriental slave, wearing nothing but a loin-cloth (Phil. 2:7). The flowing outer garment and the tunic (as well as the belt) had been laid aside. It wasn't necessary to disrobe so completely to wash feet, but Jesus was making a point, girding Himself with humility (1 Pet. 5:5). How easily the world's competitive spirit filters into the hearts of Christians and Christian workers who become envious of one another's success. How seldom we think of ourselves as servants for Christ's sake.

3. **To Represent His Entire Mission.** According to the old commentator Matthew Henry, many interpreters consider Christ's washing his disciples' feet as a representation of *his whole undertaking*. He knew that He was equal with God, and all things were His; yet He rose from His table in glory, laid aside His robes of light, girded Himself with our nature, took upon Himself the form of a servant, "came not to be ministered to, but to minister," poured out His blood in death, and thereby prepared a laver to wash us from our sins (Rev. 1:5). Having provided cleansing, He rose up, clothed Himself anew with glory, and resumed His seat in heaven. On the eve of His

>>> *sermon continued on following page*

APPROPRIATE HYMNS AND SONGS

Jesu, Jesu, Tom Colvin; © 1969, 1989 Hope Publishing Company.

An Upper Room Did Our Lord Prepare, Fred Pratt Green/John Weaver; © 1974. 1990 Hope Publishing Company.

Broken and Spilled Out, Bill George/Gloria Gaither; © 1984 William J. Gaither Inc./Yellow House Music (Admin. by Brentwood-Benson Music Publishing, Inc.).

Community of Christ, Shirley Erena Murray; © 1992 Hope Publishing Company.

Jesus' Hands Were Kind Hands, Margaret Cropper; © 1979 Stainer & Bell, Ltd. (Admin. by Hope Publishing Company).

crucifixion, Jesus pre-enacted the entire event! We come to Him for complete salvation (as a bath), then we also come day-by-day for daily renewal, to keep our feet clean on the highway of life.

Conclusion: Have you been bathed in the blood of the Lamb? Then you're to be like Him, clothed in the same attitude, taking the form of a servant. If you've been struggling with dishonesty, character issues, pride, and "self-esteemia," take up the basin and the towel. "If you know these things," said Jesus in verse 17, "blessed are you if you do them."

FOR THE BULLETIN

❋ On August 4, 1521, Pope Urban VII born as Giambattista Castagna. He was elected Pope in September 1590, but died of malaria before his coronation. ❋ Jean-baptiste Vianney, born into a peasant family of farmers in France in 1786, was ordained a priest at age 29, having struggled with poor grades and the upheavals caused by the French Revolution. He was sent as curate to an obscure village where, to everyone's surprise, he became a brilliant preacher and sought-after counselor. He seemed to possess extraordinary psychological insight and would often tell people, "You're spiritual problems do not lie in the matters you have mentioned, but in another area entirely." Some suggested he was a mind-reader. He sometimes spent 18 hours a day counseling, and people came for hundreds of miles to hear him preach. He died on this day in 1859 at age 73. ❋ "Sunshine" Harris spent most of his life on Chicago's streets, living on stale wine and cigarette butts. One day at the Old Pacific Garden Mission, someone gave him a New Testament. On this day in 1899, he was saved at age 71, and he spent the rest of his life, working at the Mission, telling everyone who would listen how Christ had changed his life. ❋ After two years hiding in an Amsterdam back room, Anne Frank, her sister, her parents, and four other Jews were discovered by the Gestapo in August 4, 1944. The diary she kept was found after the war and has been published in over 30 languages. ❋ Evangelist Gipsy Smith died on August 4, 1947.

WORSHIP HELPS

Worship Theme:
God's love is expressed to us through Christ, resulting in our becoming people of compassion and humility.

Call to Worship:
But God demonstrates His own love toward us, in that while we were still sinners, Christ died for us (Rom. 5:8).

Reader's Theater

Reader 1: By this we know love...

Reader 2: ...because He laid down His life for us.

Reader 1: And we also ought to lay down our lives for the brethren.

Reader 3: But whoever has this world's goods, and sees his brother in need, and shuts up his heart from him, how does the love of God abide in him?

Reader 2: My little children...

Reader 1: ...let us not love in word or in tongue, but in deed and in truth.

Reader 3: And by this we know that we are of the truth, and shall assure our hearts before Him. For if our heart condemns us, God is greater than our heart, and knows all things.

All: Beloved, if our heart does not condemn us, we have confidence toward God.

Rdrs. 1/2: And whatever we ask we receive from Him, because we keep His commandments and do those things that are pleasing in His sight.

Reader 3: And this is His commandment: that we should believe on the name of His Son Jesus Christ...

All: ...and love one another...

Reader 1: ...as He gave us commandment.

Taken from 1 John 3:16–23.

STATS, STORIES AND MORE

Someone Once Said . . .

"Envy is rebellion against God's leading in the lives of his children. It's saying that God has no right to bless someone else more than you."
—*Erwin Lutzer*

"[Envy is] one of the most cancerous and soul-destroying vices there is.... It is terribly potent, for it feeds and is fed by pride, the taproot of our fallen nature."
—*J. I. Packer*

"Envy can ruin reputations, split churches, and cause murders. Envy can shrink our circle of friends, ruin our business, and dwarf our souls.... I have seen hundreds cursed by it."
—*Billy Graham*

"The envious man feels other's fortunes are his misfortunes; their profit, his loss; their blessing, his bane; their health, his illness; their promotion, his demotion; their success, his failure."
—*Leslie Flynn*

"Love is the glue that cements friendships, but jealousy is the slime that keeps it from sticking."
—*John Dryden as quoted by Pat Riley in* The Winner Within

Stage Love

Gordon MacDonald, in *Restoring Your Spiritual Passion,* citing a passage from Henri Nouwen, describes an actor who noticed the hypocrisy of his fellow actors during a particular play. While rehearsing the most moving scenes of love, tenderness, and intimacy, the actors were so jealous of each other and so apprehensive about their chances of "making it" that the back stage scene was one of hatred, harshness, and mutual suspicion. Those who kissed each other on the stage were tempted to hit each other behind it, and those who displayed such love before an audience felt nothing but hostile rivalry as soon as the footlights were dimmed.

Enemies

When Narvaez, the Spanish patriot, lay dying, his father-confessor asked him whether he had forgiven all his enemies. Narvaez looked astonished and said, "Father, I have no enemies, I have shot them all."

Additional Sermons and Lesson Ideas

The Imagination of God

Date preached:

By Drew Wilkerson

SCRIPTURE: Jeremiah 33:3

INTRODUCTION: God's resources are never restricted. His creativity knows no boundaries. Often we may feel stifled in this life, but we need not be. D. L. Moody said, "If God is your partner, make your plans big." The solution to a new beginning can be found in Jeremiah 33:3.

1. **Call Out to God.** We can never be afraid to ask God for help. God has all that we need to do what He is calling us to do. All we have to do is begin by humbling ourselves and ask.
2. **Listen for God's Answer.** God will respond to our prayers. He is ready to reveal Himself if we will listen with an open mind. Then, when the time is right, we will hear from God.
3. **Believe in Surprises.** God promises to tell us great and unsearchable things we do not know. This is because the imagination of God is limitless. All we have to do is rekindle our child-like faith and believe that God will surprise us with something fresh and new.

CONCLUSION: This verse and its New Testament twin (Eph. 3:20–21) are there for you today. Find a quiet place and claim them.

Three Ways to Lengthen Your Life

Date preached:

SCRIPTURE: Psalm 90:10–12

INTRODUCTION: Everything around us has a limited lifespan. A pencil with hard lead will write 30,000 words or draw a line 30 miles long, then it's used up. An average 100–watt light bulb will last about 750 hours then it is burned up. A one-dollar bill lasts approximately 18 months in circulation before it becomes worn out. But what about people? We may lengthen our days if we:

1. **Fear God and Cultivate a Heart of Wisdom.** (Ps. 34:11; Prov. 9:11; 10:27).
2. **Live Obediently.** (Deut. 4:40; 5:32; 6:1; 25:15; 30:19; 1 Kings 3:14; Prov. 3:1, 13–18; 4:10; 1 Pet. 3:8).
3. **Honor Our Parents.** (Ex. 20:12; Deut. 5:16; Eph. 6:1–3).

CONCLUSION: Everything into which Satan seeks to lure us is self-destructive. God wants you to live a long live, even unto eternity (John 3:16).

AUGUST 11, 2002

SUGGESTED SERMON

Ridicule, Revenge, and Retaliation: Handling Criticism

Date preached:

By Kevin Riggs

Scripture: Nehemiah 4:1–23 and 6:1–14; especially 4:1 But it so happened, when Sanballat heard that we were rebuilding the wall, that he was furious and very indignant, and mocked the Jews.

Introduction: In a Charlie Brown comic, Linus is seated with a troubled look on his face, his security blanket over his shoulder, his thumb in his mouth. Turning to Lucy, he asks, "Why are you always so anxious to criticize me?" Her response: "I just think I have a knack for seeing other people's faults."

"What about your own faults?" Linus asks. Without hesitation, Lucy replied, "I have a knack of overlooking them." Do you have a "Lucy" in your life? Are you a "Lucy" in someone's life?

Context: Nehemiah teaches us that motion always causes friction. In other words, the only sure way to escape criticism is to do nothing. Nehemiah had five critics:

- Sabballat (4:1) — Governor of Samaria, Nehemiah's chief political opponent.
- Tobiah (4:3) — Governor of the Transjordan under Persia.
- Geshem (2:19) — An Arab politician.
- The Ammonites (4:7) — Descendants of Lot, long time enemies of the Jews.
- The "men of Ashdod" (4:1) — Western neighbors of Jerusalem.

Nehemiah was opposed from all sides: Sanballat to the North; Tobiah to the East; the Arabs to the South; men of Ammon and Ashdod" to the West. Have you gone through a time of opposition? Nehemiah has words of counsel about such times. His experience teaches us the characteristics of a destructive critic and how to handle such people.

1. **Characteristics of a Destructive Critic**
   A. **Their attacks are personal** (2:19; 6:2). Nehemiah's enemies were cruel and angry. A person who has your best interest at heart will correct you, but you will know they are doing it out of love.

B. **They question your motives** (2:19; 6:6). Thirteen years before Nehemiah's efforts, the king had squashed plans to rebuild the wall. If word got back to him that Nehemiah was disloyal, hopes of rebuilding the wall would end. When you try to do something good, people may question your motives. The harder you try to keep your motives pure, the more others will call them into question.

C. **They spread rumors** (6:6–8). When you're trying to make a difference, don't be surprised when others spread rumors. You may be the last one to hear the rumor (1 Pet. 3:15–16).

D. **They run with other critics** (4:1–2). An honest critic will love you enough to speak to you in private and try to resolve the problem.

E. **They resist change.** Sanballat and Tobiah both held important positions and stood to lose their standing if the wall was rebuilt.

F. **They have a human perspective** (4:2 and 4:4). What Nehemiah was undertaking was humanly impossible. But Nehemiah's perspective convinced him that he had better things to do then fight with Sanballet.

G. **They are sarcastic** (4:3). Nehemiah's wall was over 9 feet wide, too big for a fox to destroy. Sarcasm is a ploy to belittle you and what you are doing.

H. **They use intimidation** (6:9, 10–13). People use intimidation to get you to compromise what you believe. Remember this: God is bigger than your critics.

I. **They try to discourage those around you** (4:10, 12, 16–23). Destructive critics will try to turn your friends against you. To keep everyone encouraged, Nehemiah provided for their safety and kept them focused on the big picture.

>>> *sermon continued on following page*

APPROPRIATE HYMNS AND SONGS

To God Be the Glory, Fanny J. Crosby/William H. Doane; Public Domain.

Begin My Tongue Some Heavenly Theme, Isaac Watts; Public Domain.

Hope Set High, Amy Grant; © 1991 Age to Age Music, Inc. (Admin. by The Loving Company).

Jesus, My Jesus, Carol Cymbala; © 1991 Word Music, Inc./Carol Joy Music (Admin. by Integrated Copyright Group, Inc.).

May You Run and Not Be Weary, Handt Hanson/Paul Murakami; © 1991 Changing Church Forum, Inc.

2. How to Handle Destructive Critics and Criticisms

A. **Prayer.** Prayer is a major theme throughout Nehemiah. When criticized, ask God if the criticism is just. Pray for courage to change. Pray for those who are doing the criticizing. Pray for humility and the ability not to take things personal. Pray for wisdom, strength, and discernment to keep doing what you know is right.

B. **Perspective.** Nehemiah knew his critics' problems were not problems with him, but with God. When you remind yourself God is in control, you recognize criticism for what it is and don't allow it to dissuade you.

C. **Persistence.** The best way to prove a critic wrong is to outlast him, doing what you know God has called you to do. Many times the race doesn't go to the swift, but to the one who perseveres.

Conclusion: Are you going through a time when it seems everything you try is being met with opposition? Do you feel like your critics are being destructive instead of constructive? Recognize that when you step out on faith, follow God, and try to make a difference, you will be criticized. Expect it and deal with it through prayer, keeping the proper perspective, and being persistent.

FOR THE BULLETIN

❀ On August 11, 117, Hadrian was proclaimed emperor of Rome. He was by and large a peace-loving man, but he suppressed a revolt of the Jews that broke out in Palestine following the planting of a Roman colony in Jerusalem and did not protect Christians who were convicted by legal means. ❀ Susanna was chosen by Emperor Diocletian to be the bride for his son. She refused because of her intense Christian faith, and consequently she was beheaded on this day in 290. ❀ Clare, founder of the order of Poor Clares and devoted friend and colleague of St. Francis, died on this day in 1253. ❀ On August 11, 1588, the theologian Jacob Arminius was called to the pastorate of the city church in Amsterdam. The minutes state: "The deacons being invited to the meeting of the elders, Arminius was in the presence of all presented with the call of this city. Whereupon it was impressed upon him that he should help carry the burden of the city just as did the other ministers, in visiting the sick as well as in other things." ❀ On August 11, 1778, Augustustus Toplady, 38, died. He is best remembered as the author of the hymn "Rock of Ages." ❀ Today is the birthday of Charles Fowler, Methodist statesman, who was born in 1837, and of Wilfrid Barbrooke Grubb, Scottish missionary, who was born in 1865. He was called "the Livingstone of South America."

WORSHIP HELPS

Worship Theme:
Critics come and go, but what we are before God is all-important.

Call to Worship:
You shall fear the LORD your God; you shall serve Him, and to Him you shall hold fast.... He is your praise, and He is your God, who has done... great and awesome things (Deut. 10:20).

Appropriate Scripture Reading:
Proverbs 15:1–5; Mark 14:3–9; James 4:11–12

Pastoral Prayer:
Our Father in Heaven, we thank You for the beauty of the earth and for the glory of the skies. We praise You, for this is the day that You have made. We exalt You, for morning by morning new mercies we see. And Lord, we desire that Your name will be exalted from the rising of the sun to the place where it sets. We desire that Your Spirit will fill our hearts this day. Give us the ability to shut out yesterday's stress and tomorrow's uncertainties. Give us this day our daily bread, our needed manna, for we do not live by bread alone, but by every word from Your mouth. In Jesus name, Amen.

Benediction:
"Let the words of my mouth, and the meditation of my heart, be acceptable in thy sight, O LORD, my strength, and my redeemer" (Ps. 19:14 KJV).

Kids Talk

Have a large "paper doll" that you've cut from a poster board. Pass the doll around and ask each child to make a tiny tear in it. When you take the doll back, try to mend it with tape, but show the children how damaged the doll is. Explain to them that when they insult others, calling them names or saying cruel things, it hurts that person and is hard to fix.

STATS, STORIES AND MORE

Many Forms

Criticism can come in many forms. Chris Loftis has written a children's picture book entitled "The Words Hurt," based on the premise that physical abuse is not the only thing that scars a child. Words hurt too, and children often have no way of handling the harsh criticism of parents. Psychologist Charles Schaefer wrote, "Words can wound our children deeper than a blow. Many of the seemingly harmless things that so easily pop out of our mouths—like 'Why can't you be more like your brother?'—can cause emotional injury and chip away at a child's self-esteem. The words parents use form the basis of a child's sense of self."

Verbal Bullets

"Verbal Bullets"—Types of verbally abusive behavior that can occur at home, school, or in the workplace.

- Put downs
- Yelled at
- Nagged at
- Ridiculed
- Use of words like "stupid"
- Called names
- Trivialized
- Threatened
- Insulted

Nine to One

In his book *The Youth Builder,* Jim Burns talks about the importance of building up young people with affirmation and trust. What he says about criticism applies to every age group: "For every critical comment we receive, it takes nine affirming comments to even out the negative effect in our life. Most young people receive more critical comments a day than encouraging ones. You can have a very positive, life-transforming effect when you develop a ministry of affirmation."

Good Advice

A minister named Bob Cook once came to Harry Ironside, asking the famous Bible teacher how he should respond to criticisms leveled against him. Ironside's advice: "Bob, if the criticism about you is true, mend your ways. If it isn't, forget about it!"

The same point was put this way by another man: "Never fear criticism when you're right; never ignore criticism when you're wrong."

Put yet another way: "Don't mind criticism. If it's untrue, disregard it; if it's unfair, keep from irritation; if it's ignorant, smile; if it's justified, learn from it."

Additional Sermons and Lesson Ideas

How to Wake Up in the Morning

Date preached:

SCRIPTURE: Psalm 118:24

INTRODUCTION: This may come as a surprise to some of us, but there is a fine biblical art to waking up in the morning. God is a God of glory and grace who gives us a fresh start every 24 hours. In the Psalms, we discover three habits for greeting each new day.

1. **A Habitual Set of Devotions** (Pss. 5:3; 55:16; 88:13; 143:8). Jesus followed this example in Mark 1:35.
2. **A Happy Set of Dispositions** (Ps. 90:14). Moses asks the Lord to satisfy him early with mercy so that he can rejoice all day. Also see Psalms 119:24; 57:8; 59:16; 92:2; 108:2.
3. **A Holy Sense of Duty** (Pss. 104:22–23; 139:16; 101:8).

CONCLUSION: "Awake, my soul, and with the sun thy daily stage of duty run! / Shake off dull sloth, and joyfully rise to pay thy morning sacrifice."

Consider Christ

Date preached:

Dr. Melvin Worthington

SCRIPTURE: 1 Thessalonians 1:1–3

INTRODUCTION: Christ is pictured in the Old Testament sacrifices and presented in the New Testament Scriptures. We call Him "our Lord Jesus Christ," the name with which He is identified in 1 Thessalonians 1:1–3.

1. **Christ Our Master.** The term "Lord" identifies Him as our Master. We owe Him allegiance, affection and adoration. Obedience to His commandments evidences our love for Him.
2. **Christ Our Mediator.** The term "Jesus" identifies Him as our mediator. 1 Timothy 1:5–6 explains, "For there is one God, and one mediator between God and men, the man Christ Jesus; who gave Himself a ransom for all."
3. **Christ Our Messiah.** The term "Christ" identifies Him as our Messiah. From the early pages of the Bible, the coming of the *Christos*, the Messiah, was foretold. John begins his Gospel by stating, "In the beginning was the Word and the Word was with God and the Word was God."

CONCLUSION: Is He your Master? Your Mediator? Your Messiah? Is He your *Lord Jesus Christ?*

AUGUST 18, 2002

Can't Hold It In

Date preached:

Scripture: 2 Kings 7:9 Then they said to one another, "We are not doing right. This day is a day of good news, and we remain silent."

Introduction: All successful football teams have a 12th player—the crowd. The volume and enthusiasm of the home-field audience can make the difference between a win and a loss. In the frenzy of a game, it's hard to sit still and keep quiet. The same is true whenever we have good news. We can't hold it in. We want to share. In Scripture, we see the same principle at work about sharing spiritual truth.

1. **Good News Is for Sharing** (2 Kings 6:24—7:9). The city of Samaria was under siege; within was famine and starvation. Outside the walls were four lepers who decided to defect to the enemy in hopes of staying alive. Approaching the opposing camp, they found it deserted and began helping themselves to food and provisions. Suddenly, coming to their senses, they said, "This isn't right. This is wonderful news, and we aren't sharing it with anyone!" (TLB). It isn't right when we discover the wonderful news of Christ, but don't pass it on.

2. **Wineskins about to Burst** (Job 32:15–21). Young Elihu described himself as "pent up and full of words... .the spirit within me urges me on. I am like a wine cask without a vent. My words are ready to burst out! I must speak to find relief..." (NLT). How descriptive of Christians who are filled with the Spirit.

3. **Volcano about to Erupt** (Ps. 39:1–3). David decides to keep his mouth shut, but, "My heart was hot within me; while I was musing, the fire burned." We need a fire in our belly, spilling over into the lava of a loving witness.

4. **A Fire in the Bones** (Jer. 20:1–9). Jeremiah had been beaten and humiliated in the stocks for his preaching. In reaction, he tells the Lord he is quitting the ministry. But the fire in his bones would not be quenched. Vance Havner

said that Jeremiah did not merely have something to say; he had to say something. In one of his messages, Havner asked why we don't have a similar "bone fire." Turning to Acts 19:19, he read about the Ephesians who, coming to Christ, burned their sinful paraphernalia in a bonfire. Havner suggested we can't have *bone fire* until we have a *bonfire*.

5. **Can't Stop Preaching** (Acts 4:18–20). The apostles had "bone fire," telling the Sanhedren they could not stop telling what they had seen and heard. Once, when Indian evangelist Sundar Singh was in the forbidden land of Nepal preaching the gospel, he was arrested and thrown into prison. He preached to the other prisoners with great effect. When the jailer ordered silence, Sundar replied, "I must obey my Master and preach His gospel regardless of threats or sufferings." The authorities put him in solitary confinement in a foul-smelling cattle shed. They tied his hands and feet to a post, and removed his clothing. They threw leeches on him, which fastened to his body and sucked his blood. Sundar simply raised his voice to heaven in prayer and song. Concluding him mad, the jailers released him, and he went on his way—preaching.

6. **Woe Is Me if I Preach Not the Gospel** (1 Cor. 9:16). Paul's words were echoed centuries later when John Hus told the archbishop of Prague, "Shall I keep silent? God forbid! Woe is me, if I keep silent. It is better for me to die than not to oppose such wickedness, which would make me a participant in their guilt and hell."

>>> *sermon continued on following page*

APPROPRIATE HYMNS AND SONGS

A Charge to Keep I Have, Charles Wesley/Lowell Mason; Public Domain.

Blessed to Be a Blessing, Scott Wesley Brown/Dwight Liles/ Niles Borop/Claire Cloninger; © 1988 BMG Songs, Inc./Pamela Kay Music/Niles Borop Music/Arisoe Music/Word Music, Inc. (Admin. by Word Music Group, Inc.).

Break Out O Church of God, Wesley L. Forbis/Aaron Williams; © 1990 Broadman Press (Admin. by Genevox Music Group).

Community of Christ, Shirley Erena Murray; © 1992 Hope Publishing Company.

Freely, Freely, Carol Owens; © 1972 Bud John Songs, Inc. (Admin. by EMI Christian Music Publishing).

7. **Compelled By Love** (2 Cor. 5:14). The love of Christ constrained Paul to share Christ. John Geddie, pioneer Canadian missionary to the New Hebrides Islands, was shocked by the butchery, brutality, and sensual evil of those he came to win. But he wrote in his diary, "The love of Christ sustains us and constrains us. My heart pants to tell this miserable people the wonders of redeeming love." John Wesley wrote: "The love of Christ doth me constrain / To seek the wandering souls of men, / With cries, entreaties, tears, to save, / To snatch them from the gaping grave." George Whitefield simply said, "I'll preach Christ till I do to pieces fall."

Conclusion: Vance Havner lamented that many of us are like arctic rivers—frozen at the mouth. Ask the Lord for a thaw, for a fire in your bones, for a Spirit-compulsion to share Christ. May He kindle afresh the fire within until we can't hold it in any longer.

FOR THE BULLETIN

❂ August 18, 328, marks the death of Helena, mother of Constantine. At age 80, she toured the Holy Land, locating and excavating traditional sites associated with Christ. ❂ Walahfrid (called Strabo because he squinted) was a gifted young scholar, a Christian, and a diplomat. He began writing poetry as a boy, and was described as amiable, genial, and witty. He died on a peace mission while crossing the Loire on August 18, 849. ❂ On August 18, 1276, Pope Hadrian V died, about fifty days after becoming pope. ❂ August 18, 1503 also marks the death of Pope Alexander VI and the collapse of Borgia power. He was one of history's most corrupt popes, but he was also a generous patron of the arts who subsidized Michaelangelo's "Pieta." ❂ Anne Hutchison, mother of 14 children, left England on August 18, 1634, sailing to the New World for religious liberty. She became a noted and controversial Christian leader. In 1643, she and her family were murdered by Indians in New York. ❂ On August 18, 1732, in an emotion-packed service, Leonard Dober and David Nitschmann were commissioned for missionary service at Herrnhut, beginning the great Moravian missionary advance. That night 100 hymns were reportedly sung as the congregation bid them good-bye and Godspeed. ❂ On August 18, 1808, American frontier evangelist Peter Cartwright married Frances Gaines on her 19th birthday. ❂ On August 18, 1917, missionary Cameron Townsend departed Los Angeles for Central America. He would later found Wycliffe Bible Translators.

Worship Theme:
The love of Christ compels us to share the message of Christ.

Call to Worship:
For the Love of Christ compels us, because we judge thus: that if One died for all, than all died; and He died for all, that those who live should live no longer for themselves, but for Him who died for them and rose again (2 Cor. 5:14–15).

Scripture Reading:
"You are My witnesses," says the Lord, "And My servant whom I have chosen, that you may know and believe me, And understand that I am He..." "It is not for you to know the times of seasons which the Father has put in His own authority. But you shall receive power when the Holy Spirit has come upon you; and you shall be witnesses to Me in Jerusalem, and in all Judea and Samaria, and to the end of the earth. . . ." Now then, we are ambassadors for Christ, as though God were pleading through us: we implore you on Christ's behalf, be reconciled to God. For He made Him who knew no sin to be sin for us, that we might become the righteousness of God in Him. . . . Do not fear, nor be afraid; Have I not told you from that time, and declared it? You are My witnesses. Is there a God besides Me? Indeed there is no other Rock; I know not one.

Taken from Isaiah 43:10; Acts 1:7–8; 2 Corinthians 5:20–21; Isaiah 44:8.

Pastoral Prayer:
Almighty God, we ask You this: that You might make us to be not only Your worshippers but Your witnesses. Kindle the fire in our bones. Loosen our reluctant lips. Fan into flames the gift within each of us. Fill us with your Spirit, and make us Your witnesses. In this very church, Lord, may there be, one year from today, men and women, boys and girls, who at this moment are far from You, unconcerned, lost. Help us to reach them, O Lord, with Your message of hope through Jesus Christ. In the words of the old song, Lord, lay some souls upon our hearts and love those souls through us. We ask in Jesus' name. Amen.

STATS, STORIES AND MORE

Someone Once Said:
"In the Great Commission the Lord has called us to be—like Peter—fishers of men. We've turned the commission around so that we have become merely keepers of the aquarium. Occasionally I take some fish out of your fishbowl and put them into mine, and you do the same with my bowl. But we're all tending the same fish." —Sam Shoemaker, Episcopalian bishop

Findings by George Barna:
- 7 out of 10 Americans have no clue what "John 3:16" means (1994).

- 58 percent of born again Christians claimed they have shared their faith with a non-Christian during the past year (1999).

- Only about half (53 percent) of born again Christians feel a sense of responsibility to tell others about their faith (1999).

Take It to the World
Fritz Kreisler (1875–1962), the world-famous violinist, earned a fortune with his concerts and compositions, but he generously gave most of it away. So, when he discovered an exquisite violin on one of his trips, he wasn't able to buy it. Later, having raised enough money to meet the asking price, he returned to the seller, hoping to purchase that beautiful instrument. But to his great dismay it had been sold to a collector. Kreisler made his way to the new owner's home and offered to buy the violin. The collector said it had become his prized possession and he would not sell it. Keenly disappointed, Kreisler was about to leave when he had an idea. "Could I play the instrument once more before it is consigned to silence?" he asked. Permission was granted, and the great virtuoso filled the room with such heart-moving music that the collector's emotions were deeply stirred. "I have no right to keep that to myself," he exclaimed. "It's yours, Mr. Kreisler. Take it into the world, and let people hear it." —from *Our Daily Bread*, February 4, 1994

Additional Sermons and Lesson Ideas

A Longing to Get Along

Date preached:

By Dr. Timothy Beougher

SCRIPTURE: Philippians 2:1–4

INTRODUCTION: A father heard a commotion in his yard and saw his daughter and her friends fighting like cats and dogs. Running out, he asked what was wrong. "Nothing, daddy," came the reply. "We're just playing church!" In today's text, we see that even a strong, thriving church has to work on maintaining unity. At the end of chapter 1, Paul challenges them to be unified externally against a hostile world. In chapter 2, his appeal for unity is more internally focused.

1. **The Why of Unity** (v. 1)—So we can experience...
   A. Encouragement in Christ.
   B. Consolation of Love.
   C. Fellowship of the Spirit.
   C. Affection and Mercy.
2. **The What of Unity** (v. 2)—Unity is being...
   A. Like-minded.
   B. In the same love.
   C. Of one accord and one mind.
3. **The How of Unity** (vv. 3–4).
   A. Do nothing from selfishness or conceit.
   B. Humbly regard the importance of others.

CONCLUSION: If we are to live this way, we must look to Christ as our example. Lord, give us the mind of Christ (verse 5).

The Trust Test

Date preached:

By Drew Wilkerson

SCRIPTURE: Malachi 3:6–10

INTRODUCTION: Believing in God and trusting God are not necessarily the same thing. Many believe in God, but trusting God is much harder, especially when it comes to money. In Malachi 3:6–10 God instructs us to "Be" obedient to Him in three areas.

1. **Be Honest.**
2. **Be Faithful.**
3. **Be Expectant.**

CONCLUSION: Trusting God always has an impact on our check stubs.

The Pastor and His Kids

Perhaps my wife and I did fairly well as parents, but on reflection, we could have done things better. It seems a pity that by the time we figured that out, the kids were grown.

Looking back, I'm thankful God gave us the wisdom to love our children, to read to them each night and vacation with them each year, to involve them in our church work, and to teach them God's Word. I'm thankful for the advice garnered from older and wiser Christians about child-rearing, and I appreciate the shelf of parenting "how-to" books that gave us guidance. But I sometimes suffer pangs of guilt over missed opportunities and misguided reactions, and if I could do it over again, I would do several things differently.

"Singing I Go . . ."

During the early years I felt we couldn't afford a stereo system, so, except for a succession of portable cassette players, we had little Christian music in our house. Yet Ephesians 5:19 tells us to "sing and make music to the Lord" in our hearts—and homes.

In his autobiography, *Then Sings My Soul*, George Beverly Shea, long-time soloist for the Billy Graham crusades, tells of growing up in a pastor's home in Canada. Every morning of his childhood, Bev's mother, a gifted musician, would sit down at the piano, hit the chords, and begin singing in a sweet soprano voice the old gospel song:

> *Singing I go along life's road,*
> *Praising the Lord, praising the Lord,*
> *Singing I go along life's road,*
> *For Jesus has lifted my load.*

No wonder George Beverly Shea came to be called "America's beloved gospel singer." The way we are awakened in the morning has a big impact on our attitude all day long. I could have filled our rooms with much more Christian music, especially when the children were pre-teens. There are several Christian radio stations in my area, and a wealth of compact disks feature the rich hymnody of the church as well as the best in contemporary Christian music. If I could do it over, I'd have a home filled with more "hymns, psalms, and spiritual songs."

One Hundred Verses

I'd also have my children memorize more of the Bible. We were not total failures here, for we helped them learn the better-known Scriptures, and in Sunday school they were always memorizing snippets of verses. But I wish we'd taken it more seriously.

When I was growing up in the Tennessee mountains in the 1950s, we learned scores of verses in the public schools. Each week a gentleman came to our classroom, told a flannel-graph Bible story, listened as we recited our verses, and rewarded those who had memorized the required passages. In the first grade, I got a wall plaque for memorizing John 3:16. In the second grade, a beautiful little Gospel of John for learning the Twenty-third Psalm. In the third grade, we earned lovely New Testaments for reciting 25 more verses. In the fourth grade, complete Bibles for 50 verses. And in the upper grades, those who learned 100 verses received free weeks at summer camp.

Those verses have circulated through my mind ever since, offering me comfort during distress, strength during temptation, and giving me the right words in counseling others.

Since America's public schools no longer condone such practices, the job must be done at home and church, and I didn't do a good enough job at our house. I had good intentions, and even once made a list of the top 100 verses I wanted my children to memorize. But it just never happened.

If I had it to do over, I'd diligently help my girls hide God's Word in their hearts. Ruth Bell Graham tells of growing up as a "missionary kid" in China and coming under the godly influence of Miss Lucy Fletcher, who offered her students a whopping five dollars for memorizing the Sermon on the Mount. Ruth spent hours and hours going over Matthew 5, 6, and 7. "When the time came to recite it," she recalls, "I made one mistake, so I got only $4.50. But I wouldn't take one thousand times that amount in place of having memorized it."

Chores

Children need chores. Studies have shown that children who grow up with assigned tasks develop self-discipline more quickly, plus a healthier respect for work and personal responsibility. We weren't overly successful in this, and it showed up later during the teen years when my kids seemed content to let my wife and I bear the load while they hung out with friends and kept the phone lines occupied.

This doesn't mean they're destined for a lifetime of laziness. I seldom had chores growing up, and I'm a workaholic now. But in the short run, I think it makes it harder on their self-respect when they don't carry their own weight.

"You Worry Too Much"

Recently I asked my 19-year-old how I could be a better parent. Without even pausing to think, she said, "You're too anxious, Dad. You worry too much about us. I wish you could trust God with us."

She doesn't fully realize there are good reasons for parents *to worry*—but I haven't yet learned that there are better reasons *not to worry*. By worrying, I've often frustrated my children—not to mention my Heavenly Father, who keeps giving me verses on the subject.

- Do not fret—it only causes harm (Ps. 37:8 NKJV).
- Don't worry about anything; instead, pray about everything (Phil. 4:6 TLB).
- Casting the whole of your care—all your anxieties, all your worries, all your concerns, once and for all—on Him; for He cares for you (1 Pet. 5:7 AB).
- Therefore do not worry (Matt. 6:34).

Recently while studying the books of Exodus and Numbers, the Lord seemed to tell me that anxiety is more or less the same transgression that kept the Israelites out of Canaan for 40 years: fear that He can't take care of the giants we're facing. Worry denies God's power, disavows His promises, and discounts His presence. This is a message that keeps reappearing in my Bible studies. Just the other evening, baffled by my two turbulent teens and unable to sleep, I found these five words in Exodus 18:19 (NKJV): *Bring the difficulties to God.* I was reminded of the old song that says, "Bring your burdens to the Lord, and leave them there." I'm late in learning this truth.

Hook, Line, and Sinker

When I was a boy, my Uncle Walter tried to turn me into a fisherman, and it was a disaster. Arriving at his house, I'd spend the first hour sweating in his garden with shovel and pick, trying to break up the ground and search for earthworms. I hardly ever found enough to fill the can.

Then we'd pile into his car (dogs in the trunk) for the drive to the lake. There I'd have to impale the worm on the hook. I recoiled at the task, but Uncle Walter would laugh at me, assuring me that worms felt no pain. Looking at the poor worm writhing on the barb, I wasn't convinced.

Then there was the matter of casting the hook into the water. Nine times out of ten, it ended up in the tree limbs over our heads, requiring a half-hour or so to extricate. Sometimes, it would even fly around and lodge in my backside, which was acutely embarrassing to a chubby, ten-year-old boy like me.

It was a great relief when the hook and sinkers finally plopped into the water, but there was nothing to do then but sit in the heat and wait . . . and wait. I hardly ever got a bite. But when I did, I felt badly for the fish. How would I feel, I wondered, being dragged through the lake by a hook in my lip?

Once ashore, the fish would flop and flounder on the dock, desperate for water, dying painfully of reverse suffocation. Then came the gutting and cleaning and boning and cooking . . . and I didn't even like fish.

It wasn't that I was a sissy, for I engaged in other pursuits that required strength and stamina. It's just that I never got hooked on fishing. So when my middle child developed an interest in this hobby, I kept putting her off. "Well, it's pretty hot to go fishing. Why don't we play putt-putt? How about an ice cream? What about a bicycle ride? Let's go to the mall instead." Occasionally, I'd arrange for an uncle or a friend to take her to the lake or river.

Looking back, I realize that I was missing invaluable, irreplaceable time with a child who needed greater bonding with her dad on her terms and on her turf.

If I could do it over again, I would take her fishing.

None of us gets out of parenting without some regrets—sometimes a lot of them. If Joseph could tell his brothers not to be distressed or angry with themselves over their past sins (Gen. 45:5), I know our Lord Jesus can forgive all my faults and heal my failures. So despite it all, I'm glad for the opportunity of being a dad, and I'm proud of my children whose strengths and qualities I credit to God's over-ruling, under-girding grace.

And in His sly, infinite wisdom, He is giving me another chance to put into practice the lessons learned late.

As a Grandpa. ✹

AUGUST 25, 2002

Exceedingly Abundantly Above All

Date preached:

9 |24| 11

Scripture: Ephesians 3:20–21 *Now to Him who is able to do exceedingly abundantly above all that we ask or think, according to the power that works in us, to Him be glory in the church by Christ Jesus to all generations, forever and ever. Amen.*

Introduction: When word of the Nazi invasion of Poland reached China, the church there was stunned. The world was at war, and China was, at that very moment, under assault from Japan. On that Sunday, Watchman Nee called his church to prayer, telling them that prayer was a weapon for which there was no defense. Then he added these powerful words: "Prayer can do anything God can do." That is the very point Paul is making here in Ephesians 3:20–21.

Background: These two verses conclude the first half of Ephesians. Chapters 1–3 concern doctrine, telling us of our wealth in Christ. Ephesians 4–6 concern duty, and tell us about our walk in Christ. At the end of Ephesians 3, Paul offers a prayer for his readers, then ends with this great doxology in which we learn three things:

1. **God Overwhelms Our Minds.** "Now to Him who is able to do exceedingly abundantly above all that we ask or think...." Genesis 41:40 says that when Joseph became Prime Minister of Egypt, the seven years of plenty yielded grain, "as the sand of the sea, until he stopped counting for it was immeasurable." The Queen of Sheba found Solomon's Empire beyond anything she could have imagined (1 Kings 10:7). "The half has never been told," she said. Paul said about heaven that eye has not seen, nor ear heard what God has in store for us (1 Cor. 2:9). Paul has already talked about the "immeasurable riches" of God's grace (Eph. 2:7 NRSV). Here in Ephesians 3:20–21, we discover that God's answers to prayer are beyond our ability to measure, to comprehend, or even to fully claim (see also Jer. 33:3). God not only does what we can ask or imagine; He does *all* that we can ask or imagine. Not only that, He does *above all* we can ask. He does *abundantly above all* we can ask. He does *exceedingly abundantly above all* we can ask or imagine. No wonder John Newton wrote: "Thou art coming to a King; / Large petitions

with thee bring; / For His grace and power are such / None can ever ask too much."

2. **God Overcomes Our Weaknesses.** "according to the power that works in us...." His power works in us by and through our prayers. In many European cities, you can still see trams and trolleys with long poles reaching up to overhead wires and drawing down power to the engines. Imagine how useless it would be for the people in that trolley to sing and shout and preach and hold a great meeting, but without a pole connecting with the overhead power. Getting out the trolley, they would still be at the same place. When we bow our knees to the Father of our Lord Jesus Christ (v. 14), we are connecting with the power that overcomes our weakness and works mightily within us (see Rom. 8:26).

3. **God Overhears our Praise.** "...to Him be glory in the church by Christ Jesus to all generations, forever and ever. Amen." Our prayers and praises are as interwoven as God's hearing and His answering. In the seventeenth century, John Trapp wrote: "He lets out His mercies to us for the rent of our praise, and is content that we may have the benefit of them so He may have the glory."

>>> *sermon continued on following page*

APPROPRIATE HYMNS AND SONGS

May the Mind of Christ My Savior, Kate B. Wilkinson/A. Cyril Barham/Gould; Public Domain.

A Heart for God, Dave Hall; © 1991 Dave Hall (Admin. by Worship to the Nations Music).

As We Come to Thee in Prayer, Ralph Carmichael; © 1970 Bud John Songs, Inc. (Admin. by EMI Christian Music Publishing).

Break My Hear, O God, Dennis Jernigan; © 1990 Shepherd's Heart Music (Admin. by Word Music Group, Inc.).

Clear My Mind, Dan Marks; © 1981 Maranatha! Music.

Conclusion: Do you have a place of prayer? It is hard to have a regular habit of prayer without a regular location to which to resort. Jesus called it a "closet" (Matt. 6:6). John Wesley had a small, little prayer room built just off his bedroom, and this became the "powerhouse of Methodism." Baptist missionary Matthew Yates, when he was in seminary, used a hollow tree in the nearby woods. D. L. Moody, at one point in his life, found an abandoned coal pit, and there he went each day. Find a place, and begin calling upon the Lord who is able to do great and mighty things, exceedingly abundantly above all that we ask or think. He overwhelms our minds, overcomes our weaknesses, and overhears our praise. To Him be glory in the church by Christ Jesus to all generations, forever and ever. Amen.

FOR THE BULLETIN

✸ While Emperor Diocletian was attending a play in Rome ridiculing Christians, a actor named Genesius, suddenly under conviction, cried out, "I want to receive the grace of Christ, that I may be born again." Diocletian immediately ordered Genesius tortured, but the actor remained true to his newfound faith and was beheaded August 25, 303. ✸ The famous Council of Nicaea ended on this day in 325 with the adoption of the Nicene Creed and its critical definition of the person and work of Jesus. ✸ The first Christian worship service in North America was celebrated in Florida on this day in 1563. It was the feast of St. Augustine. The city of St. Augustine, founded two years later, remains the oldest continuing town in the United States. ✸ As they left for Copenhagen to find a ship for St. Thomas, the first two Moravian missionaries, Leonard Dober and David Nitschmann, received final blessings from Count von Zinzendorf, who accompanied them part way, on August 25, 1732. ✸ August 25, 1832, marks the death of Adam Clarke, British clergyman and author of a popular commentary on the Scriptures which he wrote over a period of 45 years. Though receiving little formal schooling, Clarke taught himself Hebrew and other languages and became a profound student of Scripture. Wesley appointed him an itinerant preacher, and he became among Methodism's most effective evangelists. In addition to his eight-volume commentary, he wrote several other books including a six-volume biographical dictionary and a two-volume memoir of the Wesley family.

Worship Theme:
The greatness of the God who hears and answers our prayers is immeasurable.

Call To Worship:
Call to me and I will answer you, and will tell you great and hidden things that you have not known (Jer. 33:3).

Scripture Medley:
Have all the workers of iniquity no knowledge, Who eat up my people as they eat bread, and do not call on the LORD! You call on the name of your gods, and I will call on the name of the LORD; and the God who answers by fire, He is God." If we ask anything according to His will, He hears us. And if we know that He hears us, whatever we ask, we know that we have the petitions that we have asked of Him. Ask, and it will be given to you; seek, and you will find; knock, and it will be opened to you. For everyone who asks receives, and he who seeks finds, and to him who knocks it will be opened. Or what man is there among you who, if his son asks for bread, will give him a stone? Or if he asks for a fish, will he give him a serpent? If you then, being evil, know how to give good gifts to your children, how much more will your Father who is in heaven give good things to those who ask Him! Arise, call on your God.

Taken from Psalm 14:4; 1 Kings 18:24; 1 John 5:14; Matthew 7:7–11; Jonah 1:6.

Benediction:
May the great God of Heaven and Jesus Christ our Lord overwhelm our minds, overcome our weaknesses, and overhear our praise throughout this day and week, to His glory. Amen.

Gifts in Abundance

Evangelist John R. Rice once imagined being given a guided tour of
heaven by the angel Gabriel. By and by, they came to a large building.
Inside was floor after floor of beautiful gifts, all wrapped and ready to be
sent. "'Gabriel, what are all these?' asked Rice. Gabriel replied that they
were answers to prayer. "We wrapped these things," he said, "but people
never called for them.'"

A Real Appeal

Darlene Deibler Rose, missionary to New Guinea, was imprisoned in a
Japanese concentration camp during World War II. The food she was
given was scant and loathsome. One day, looking out her cell window, she
saw a distant bunch of bananas. Instantly she craved the bite of banana.
Everything inside her wanted one. She could smell and taste them. Drop-
ping to her knees, she prayed, "Lord I'm not asking you for a whole
bunch.... I just want one banana. Lord, just one banana."

Then she began to rationalize. How could God get a banana through
prison walls? "There was more of a chance of the moon falling out of the
sky than of one of [the guards] bringing me a banana," she realized. Bowing
again, she prayed, "Lord, there's no one here who could get a banana to
me. There's no way for You to do it. Please don't think I'm not thankful for
the rice porridge. It's just that—well, those bananas looked so delicious!"

The next morning, she heard the guard coming down the concrete walkway. It was the warden of the POW camp who had taken kindly to her. He
looked at her emaciated body and, without saying a word, turned and left,
locking the door behind him. Sometime later, another set of footsteps
echoed down the walkway. The key turned and the door opened. The guard
threw a huge yellow bundle into the cell, saying, "They're yours!" She
counted them. It was a bundle of 92 bananas!

As she began peeling her bananas, Ephesians 3:20 came to her mind,
and she never afterward read that verse without thinking of bananas.

Additional Sermons and Lesson Ideas

The Four Sides of God's Love

Date preached:

SCRIPTURE: Ephesians 3:17–18

INTRODUCTION: A. T. Pierson observed that Paul "treats the love of God as a cube, having breadth and length, depth and height... a perfection of form. Every side of a cube is a perfect square, and from every angle it presents the same appearance." The Holy of Holies was cube-shaped, so is the New Jerusalem, and so is the love of God.

1. **The Width of His Love.** His outstreached arms can encompass all humanity (John 3:16). His love removes our sins "as far as the east from the west" (Ps. 103:12).
2. **The Length of His Love.** Eternal, providing His children with everlasting life.
3. **The Depth of His Love.** Reaching down to the most horrid and hopeless sinner.
4. **The Height of His Love.** "As the heavens are high above the earth, so great is His mercy toward us" (Ps. 103:11).

CONCLUSION: Elisabeth Barrett Browning wrote, "How do I love thee? Let me count the ways. I love thee to the depth and breadth and height My soul can reach...." But only God loves us with infinite dimensions. He loves you to an endless degree.

The ABCs of Body Building

Date preached:

By Drew Wilkerson

SCRIPTURE: Selected verses from Psalm 119

INTRODUCTION: It is worthwhile to exercise and build up our bodies physically, but spiritual bodybuilding yields eternal as well as earthly results. To become "buff" spiritually all we need to know are our ABCs.

1. **A = Attitude** (Ps. 119:1–2, 105). Attitude is crucial in every aspect of life. To become spiritually fit we need the right attitude, which comes from obeying God's Word. His Word will light our path if we will allow it to.
2. **B = Balance** (Ps. 119:9–16). Maintaining balance is essential if we want to grow spiritually. God is looking for people who will seek Him with their whole hearts and not neglect His Word.
3. **C = Consistency** (Ps. 119:147). If we want to become spiritually fit we must be disciplined. We must be consistent and seek God. Every day is a new day to place our hope in Him.

CONCLUSION: If we will take the time to be in God's Word we will become spiritually fit. It's as simple as ABC.

SEPTEMBER 1, 2002

SUGGESTED SERMON

Why Prudence Isn't a Bad Word   *Date preached:*

Scripture: Proverbs 1:4

Introduction: In our microwave, drive-through, 60-second society, we want things quickly. Some churches are now even offering "express services" for busy weekenders—worship services guaranteed not to exceed 40 minutes. Well, there is one book of the Bible, believe it or not, that provides wisdom in quick, bite-sized chunks. Drive-through wisdom. Microwave wisdom, in quick, fast chunks. It is the book of Proverbs. A "proverb" has been described as a heavenly rule for earthly living. It is when the *wit* of one becomes the *wisdom* of many. The ability to distill and condense great truths in simple, quotable statements makes for unique literature, and everyone from Benjamin Franklin ("Poor Richard") to Yogi Berra has tried his hand at it. In Proverbs 1:4, we're told that one of the results of studying the book of Proverbs will be the acquisition of "prudence." In recent years, "prudence" has conjured images of prim and proper old ladies, or doddery, prunish old men. The related words, "prude" and "prudish," have even worse connotations. But the dictionary defines "prudence" as "the ability to govern and discipline oneself by the use of reason; shrewdness in the management of affairs; good judgement in the use of resources." Since this is a quality most of us badly need, I would like to tell you that this word occurs 31 times in the Bible (NKJV), half of them (15 times) in the Book of Proverbs, where we learn:

1. **Prudent people are like cats—they know that some things are best covered up.** "But a prudent man covers shame" (Prov. 12:16). The NRSV says "ignore an insult." Matthew Henry said, "It is kindness to ourselves to make light of injuries and affronts, instead of making the worst of them." Most of us are too sensitive, too touchy, and too easily offended. It's often better to laugh off a criticism and complaint, to have a "duck's back" attitude about the rudeness of other people. Prudent people don't take themselves too seriously.

2. **Prudent people give cautious answers** (Prov. 12:23). The NCV says "they don't tell everything they know." Jesus often withheld information, giving only partial or concealed answers. He wasn't being dishonest, but prudent. We

don't have to say everything we know. Very often the wisest people give the shortest and quietest answers.

3. **Prudent people think ahead** (Prov. 14:8 NLV). "[The prudent] look ahead to see what is coming." Most of us make spot decisions, without thinking through the implications. We make an impulse purchase, then suffer financial stress later when the bill comes in. We join a team or club without considering how much of our time will be demanded. One of the earmarks of prudence is to "look before we leap."

4. **Prudent people have a healthy skepticism.** They don't believe everything they hear (Prov. 14:15). Most of us have learned through sad experience not to put too much stock in the promises of politicians during the election season. We need to practice the same cautious listening when it comes to what we're being told by the media and in the colleges and universities. Sometimes the experts and professors are still seeking for wisdom when the janitors and cooks have found it long ago.

5. **Prudent people handle correction well** (Prov. 15:5). When was the last time you felt defensive and offended? Perhaps your husband or wife made a suggestion about your behavior or appearance? Perhaps a co-worker or supervisor offered some unsolicited advice. Wise people listen to criticism, discarding what is invalid and heeding the rest.

>>> *sermon continued on following page*

APPROPRIATE HYMNS AND SONGS

Immortal, Invisible, God Only Wise, Walter Chalmers Smith/John Robert; Public Domain.

Be Thou My Vision, Eleanor Hull/Mary E. Byrne; Public Domain.

Unto the King, Joey Holder; © 1984 Far Lane Music Publishing.

Everlasting, Rick Founds; © 1990 Maranatha Praise, Inc. (Admin. by The Copyright Company).

Only in the Cross, Mark Altrogge; © 1991 PDI Praise/Dayspring Music, Inc. (Admin. by Word Music Group, Inc.).

6. **Prudent people study** (Prov. 18:15) "The heart of the prudent acquires knowledge." Prudent people turn off the television, and open the bookcase. They take classes and courses. They become personal students of the Scriptures.

7. **Prudent people take precautions.** (Prov. 22:3 and 27:12). They don't live in fear, but they fasten their seatbelt, establish an emergency fund, monitor their investments, do maintenance on their homes and cars, and guard against "the evil day."

Conclusions: According to Proverbs 1:1–4, we develop prudence by studying the Proverbs. Since there are 31 chapters, it almost seems that God intended for us to read one chapter a day. Since today is the first day of the month, why not ask the Lord to develop within you a more prudent mind and heart. Begin today with Proverbs 1, and read a chapter from this book each day, reading carefully, perhaps comparing one translation with another, and underlining the verses that most impress you. Memorize and meditate on the Proverbs of Solomon. And by the time October rolls around, you'll be a wiser and more prudent person.

FOR THE BULLETIN

❀ Adrian IV, the only English pope, died on this day in 1159. ❀ On September 1, 1181, aged, feeble Lucius III began his papacy. His pontificate laid the foundation for the Inquisition. ❀ In the 1490s, Rome seethed with gossip that Lucrezia Borgia was sleeping with her father, Pope Alexander VI. When Lucrezia became pregnant, the Vatican sought to hide her condition, but word filtered out. The child was named Giovanni. On September 1, 1501, the pope issued two extraordinary edicts. The first, which was made public, identified Giovanni as another man's child. But the second, a top secret document in church vaults, identified Giovanni as the pope's own son, making Pope Alexander both the child's father and his grandfather. ❀ On September 1, 1553, Bishop John Hooper was arrested. While studying at Oxford, he had discovered the book of Romans which "seriously affected the salvation of my soul." His Reformation beliefs put him at risk, and when "Bloody" Queen Mary ascended the throne and unleashed a storm against Protestants, he was arrested and thrown into Fleet prison where his clammy bed of rotten straw lay beside the city sewer. He was later executed. ❀ On September 1, 1784, John Wesley ordained Thomas Coke and Frances Asbury to serve in America. ❀ American frontier evangelist Peter Cartwright was born on September 1, 1785. ❀ On September 1, 1957, evangelist Billy Graham concluded his successful New York City Crusade with a massive rally in Times Square.

Worship Theme:
God is all-wise, and He imparts wisdom to those who fear Him.

Call to Worship:
The fear of the LORD is the beginning of wisdom, and the knowledge of the Holy One is understanding (Prov. 9:10).

Pastoral Prayer:
Lord, You are the "Rabbi of Israel," the teacher of the soul, and we are your students, gathered here, as it were, for instruction. Teach us Your ways, O Lord, and show us Your paths. Grant us wisdom. Teach us to number our days that we may gain a heart of wisdom. Teach us to count our blessings, that we might have a thankful spirit. Teach us to add to our faith virtue, self-control, perseverance, and godliness. Give us, O Lord, multiplied wisdom, the wisdom from above, pure, peaceable, gentle, and full of mercy and good fruits. And teach us to reckon ourselves dead to sin, but alive to God through faith in Jesus Christ. In Jesus' name, Amen.

Responsive Reading:

Leader: God is wise in heart and mighty in strength. Who has hardened himself against Him and prospered?

People: He removes the mountains, and they do not know when He overturns them in His anger;

Leader: He shakes the earth out of its place, and its pillars tremble;

People: He commands the sun, and it does not rise; He seals off the stars; He alone spreads out the heavens, And treads on the waves of the sea;

Leader: He made the Bear, Orion, and the Pleiades, And the chambers of the south;

All: He does great things past finding out, Yes, wonders without number.

Taken from Job 9:4–10.

STATS, STORIES AND MORE

Thinking Ahead

For which of you, intending to build a tower, does not sit down first and count the cost, whether he has enough to finish it— lest, after he has laid the foundation, and is not able to finish, all who see it begin to mock him, saying, 'This man began to build and was not able to finish.' Or what king, going to make war against another king, does not sit down first and consider whether he is able with ten thousand to meet him who comes against him with twenty thousand? Or else, while the other is still a great way off, he sends a delegation and asks conditions of peace. So likewise, whoever of you does not forsake all that he has cannot be My disciple.

—Jesus, in Luke 14:28–33.

Three Sieves

In her book, *Edges of His Ways,* missionary Amy Carmichael shared three "sieves" through which she tried to filter every word she spoke: Is it true? Is it kind? Is it necessary?

Proverbs: Distilled Wisdom

The ability to reduce profound ideas to simple statements requires great wisdom. The Unitarian clergyman Robert Fulghum became famous because of his essay, "Everything I Really Need to Know I Learned in Kindergarten." He suggests that the simple rules learned in kindergarten will do for life. Rules like: Share everything. Play fair. Don't hit people. Put things back where you found them. Clean up your own mess. Flush. Remember that warm cookies and cold milk are good for you.

When Ernest Hemingway graduated from high school his parents wanted him to go to college, but he left home instead to take a job with the *Kansas City Star* as a cub reporter. His editor told him to use short sentences, avoid slang, speak plainly, and shy away from adjectives. Hemingway later said that those were "the best rules I ever learnt for the business of writing." Using them, he became one of the best writers of the twentieth century.

The ability to distill profound subjects into a handful of simple, easy-to-remember rules is a mark of profound wisdom. Consider, then, how profoundly wise is Almighty God—for He reduced all our obligations and responsibilities in life to ten simple rules called the Ten Commandments. The book of Proverbs offers 31 chapters of pithy, personal, poignant wisdom for the taking.

Additional Sermons and Lesson Ideas

Relationships in a Model Church

Date preached:

By Dr. Timothy Beougher

SCRIPTURE: 1 Thessalonians 5:12–15

INTRODUCTION: Most of our problems in life involve other people, human relationships, getting along with those in our family, our church, our school, our work environment, our city, our world. We've had trouble getting along since the days of Cain and Abel. Much of Paul's writing dealt with relationships. Here in 1 Thessalonians 5, he speaks of...

1. **Relating to Leaders in the Church** (vv. 12–13). The responsibility of leaders is: hard work, leadership, and giving admonitions. Our response to leaders should be to respect them, esteem them, and live in peace with them.

2. **Relating to Others in the Church** (vv. 14–15). Our actions: 1) warn those who are idle; 2) encourage the timid; and 3) help the weak. Our attitudes: 1) patience; 2) forgiveness; 3) kindness.

CONCLUSION: The best way of getting along with others is with simplicity. Simply take these rules at face value and put them into practice.

Jesus' Second Family

Date preached:

SCRIPTURE: Mark 3:31, 32

INTRODUCTION: The family unit in our society is in trouble today and needs TLC, but in this passage, Jesus' own family was becoming a problem. He used the occasion to tell us about His "second" family, which is made up of those who do the will of His heavenly Father.

1. **This Family Has a Loving Heavenly Father** (Rom. 8:15–16). The term "Abba" is akin to our "Daddy," a term of affection for the father in the family.

2. **This Family Has Many Earthly Fathers and Mothers** (1 Cor. 4:15 and 1 Thess. 2:7, 11). These are the men and women who share in the joy of leading others to Christ.

3. **This Family Has Unlikely Brothers and Sisters** (Philemon 15). One day these two men were master and slave. The next, they were brothers.

4. **This Family Has a Constant Stream of New Children** (Heb. 2:13). The spiritual maternity wards of God's worldwide church are experiencing record numbers of conversions around the world as more and more people are being "born again."

CONCLUSION: Aren't you glad you're "a part of the family of God?"

A Light to the Gentiles

John Barrage expected to follow his father into livestock, but he could never learn the ropes. His frustrated dad finally said, "John, I find you cannot form any idea of the price of cattle, and I shall have to send you to college to be a light to the Gentiles." Thus John went to Cambridge, then entered church work, but without personally experiencing the gospel.

His preaching was striking, his life upright, his energy boundless, his ministry worthless. His message, devoid of the death and resurrection of Christ, was like a solar system without the sun. For years he thrashed around brilliantly, but fruitlessly.

In 1755 he became vicar in out-of-the-way Everyone, and there at age 42 he finally agonized about his own soul. "Lord," he began crying, "if I am right, keep me so; if I am not right, make me so, and lead me to the knowledge of the truth in Jesus." One morning sitting before an open Bible these words flashed to mind: "Cease from thine own works; only believe." He immediately started preaching salvation by grace through faith alone. Soon one of his parishioners visited him. "Why, Sarah," he said, "what is the matter?"

"I don't know," said the woman. "Those new sermons! I find we are all lost now. I can neither eat, drink, nor sleep. I don't know what will become of me." Others echoed the same cry. Barrage's church soon swelled with villagers giving their lives to Christ. People flocked from all parts, and the buildings proved too small. On May 14, 1759, Barrage began preaching outdoors. "On Monday," he wrote, "we called at a farmhouse. After dinner I went into the yard, and seeing nearly 150 people, I called for a table and preached for the first time in the open air. We then went to Melded, where I preached in a field to about 4,000 people."

His remaining 30 years found him preaching the gospel in season and out, indoors and out. He never married, always resided alone, and remained in rural parishes until his death at age 77 in 1793. He was the Whitefield of the English countryside. ✾

Quotes for the Pastor's Wall

❝ He was mighty in the Scriptures and his greatest power in preaching was the way in which he used the Sword of the Spirit upon men's consciences and hearts. . . . Sometimes one might have thought, in listening to his solemn appeals, that one was hearing a new chapter in the Bible when first spoken by a living prophet. **❞**

**—Hudson Taylor, about his mentor
and fellow missionary, William Burns**

SEPTEMBER 8, 2002

SUGGESTED SERMON

The Grandest People of All
Date preached:

Scripture: Proverbs 17:6a Grandchildren are the crowning glory of the aged (NLT).

Introduction: The Bible exalts the role of grandparents, and our society is slowly catching up to the Bible's ancient wisdom. Today is National Grandparents Day, and increasing numbers of psychologists are touting the importance of the grandparent-grandchild relationship. "The bond between a child and a grandparent is the purest, least psychologically complicated form of human love," says Dr. Arthur Kornhaber. He claims that grandparents can offer an emotional safety net when parents falter. They pass on traditions in the form of stories, songs, games, skills, and crafts. And they have another magical ingredient that parents often lack—time. Kornhaber has found that children who are close to at least one grandparent are more emotionally secure than other children; and they have more positive feelings about older people and about the process of aging.

Bible Background: F. W. Boreham wrote, "Grandfatherism gives every man a second chance. If his parents fail him, his grandparents may yet prove his salvation." Perhaps history's most dramatic illustration of that truth is the story of King Manasseh in 2 Chronicles 33. Manasseh has been called the most wicked man who ever lived, but in his old age he repented and turned to God. The son who succeeded him was evil, but Manasseh's grandson, Josiah, became one of the best and most beloved kings in Jewish history (2 Chron. 34). By studying the chronology, we learn that the last six years of Manasseh and the first six years of Josiah overlap; and the last six years of Manasseh were his repentant years, his godly years, his years of reform and contrition. It was too late for him to influence his own son, Amon. But it wasn't too late for Josiah, and we can easily picture the old king spending long hours with his small grandson, telling him, "Now, one day you're going to be king. Don't make the mistakes I did. From the beginning, serve the Lord." This grandfather who had been the most violent and wicked man in his nation's history, gave himself to God with just enough time to spare to implant his newly-found faith in the tender heart of his little grandson. Paul said to Timothy, "I have been reminded of your sincere faith, which first lived in your grandmother Lois..." How can grandparents use their grand positions to the best advantage? Proverbs 17:6 says that grandchildren are a crown to the aged. Today, I'd like to give you four tools for polishing the crown.

1. **Prudence.** Grandparents sometimes feel inclined to give more advice or direction than the parents want at the very time new parents are insecure in their new role. It takes a little time for grandparents to find the right balance, learning to be involved without interfering. Grandparents have a lifetime of wisdom stored up, and often know the best times to speak up, and the best times to remain quiet.

2. **Presence.** It's vital for grandparents to be as accessible as possible. Do all you can to spend time with your grandkids. Make open your home. Make open your schedule. Make your house user-friendly for youngsters. Talk to them, tell them stories and read them Scripture. In our mobile society, many people don't live near their grandchildren. But use e-mail. Many grandparents send a little e-note each day to their technology-savvy grandkids. And a week here or there, a vacation, and regular phone calls help fill in the gap.

3. **Provision.** Grandparents can provide materially for their grandchildren. Just a little bit here and there. Clothing. Books. Toys. Tools for a hobby. A little seed money for college. People over 50 are, on average, a more affluent segment of our population, holding 50 percent of the country's disposable

>>> *sermon continued on following page*

APPROPRIATE HYMNS AND SONGS

When Love is Found, Brian Wren; © 1983 Hope Publishing Company.

Would You Bless Our Homes and Families, William Farquharson, Ron Klusmeier; © 1974 Worship Arts (Admin. by Ron Klusmeier).

We Are a Family, David Holsinger; © 1989 Master Song Music.

They'll Know We Are Christians By Our Love, Peter Scholtes; © 1966 F.E.L. Publications (Admin. by The Lorenze Corporation).

The Joy of Your Way, Jack Hayford; © 1978 Rocksmith Music (Admin. by Mandina/Rocksmith Music).

A Christian Home, Barbara Hart/Jean Sibelius; © 1965, 1986 Singspiration Music (Admin. by Brentwood-Benson Music Publishing, Inc.).

income and more than 75 percent of its financial assets. But advertisers have a hard time reaching these people because senior adults have learned through the years to be cautious with their money. Businesses are learning, however, to appeal to their role as grandparents.

4. **Prayer.** Samuel said to the Israelites, "God forbid that I should sin against heaven by failing to pray for you." And often, grandparents often have more time for prayer and Bible reading than anyone else.

Conclusion: What tools are necessary for effective grandparenting? Prudence, presence, provision, prayer—and maybe just a dash of patience. Powerful tools for crown-polishing. For children's children are a crown to the aged—and those who realize that are the grandest people of all.

FOR THE BULLETIN

❋ On September 8, 1227, just as Holy Roman Emperor Frederick II was embarking on a new crusade to the Holy Land, his army was stricken with an epidemic fever. Pope Gregory IX, angry that the crusade was hampered, excommunicated him, starting a feud between Frederick and the papacy that was to last for years. When the crusade resumed the following year, Frederick obtained Jerusalem after complex negotiations with Sultan al-Kamil of Egypt and had himself crowned king of Jerusalem in the Church of the Holy Sepulchre. Eschatological prophecies about his rule were made, and the Emperor considered himself to be a messiah. His entry into Jerusalem was compared with that of Christ on Palm Sunday. When he died unexpectedly in 1250, Europe was shaken and doubts arose that he was really dead. False Fredericks appeared everywhere, and a legend arose that he had been encapsulated in a volcano in Sicily and would return as the latter-day emperor to punish the church and reestablish the Holy Roman Empire. But within 22 years after his death, all his descendants were dead, victims of the battle with the papacy that Frederick had begun. ❋ On September 8, 1565, Spaniard Don Pedro Menendez de Aviles founded the first Catholic settlement in America at St. Augustine, Florida. ❋ On this day in 1847, the early Southern Baptist missionary Matthew Yates reached the coast of Shanghai. In his diary that day he wrote, "Oh, that we may begin and carry on our work of teaching the Chinese in the fullness of the spirit of the gospel of Christ! The obstacles are many; the instruments are weak; but God is omnipotent."

WORSHIP HELPS

Worship Theme:
God created grandparents for a special ministry to children.

Call to Worship:
"Take heed to yourself, and diligently keep yourself, lest you forget the things your eyes have seen, and lest they depart from your heart all the days of your life. And teach them to your children and your grandchildren..." (Deut. 4:7–9).

Responsive Reading:

Leader: In You, O LORD, I put my trust; Let me never be put to shame...

People: Do not cast me off in the time of old age; Do not forsake me when my strength fails.

Leader: The righteous shall flourish like a palm tree, He shall grow like a cedar in Lebanon.

People: Those who are planted in the house of the LORD shall flourish in the courts of our God.

Leader: They shall still bear fruit in old age; They shall be fresh and flourishing, To declare that the LORD is upright;

All: He is my rock, and there is no unrighteousness in Him.

Taken from Psalms 71 and 92.

Background on "Grandparents Day"
"I couldn't believe it!" was the response of Mrs. Marian McQuade, a housewife in West Virginia, when the White House called with a message from President Jimmy Carter telling her that her campaign to establish a National Grandparents Day had been successful. A grandmother and great-grandmother herself, she had been working toward this for years, inspired by memories of her own grandmother. "After working all day on the farm," Marian recalled, "Grandma would walk off to visit elderly people of the community. Often I would tag along, and I never forgot talking to those delightful people. That's where my love and respect for oldsters started." Her campaign proved successful, and in 1979, President Carter established the first Sunday following Labor Day as National Grandparents Day each year.

STATS, STORIES AND MORE

Stats

- Grandparents aren't necessarily old. The average age in America at which a woman becomes a grandmother is 46; and many in America become grandparents at 29 or 30.
- There are 60 million grandparents in America today, and the number is accelerating rapidly because baby boomers are entering the grandparenting years.
- Grandparenting is more complicated than it used to be. Responsibilities now often include step-grandparenting; and increasing numbers of grandparents are going to court for the right to visit their grandchildren. Twelve states now allow grandparents to petition for visitation rights without prerequisites. Support groups exist to give grandparents advice on legal actions.
- The mobility of society means that many grandparents are no longer just around the corner or the curve from their grandchildren; so they have to learn the techniques of long-distance grandparenting. More and more grandparents find themselves providing regular childcare, and approximately 3.2 million American children live full-time with their grandparents. In 867,000 American homes, grandparents are raising their grandchildren in the place of parents.

Grand...

Grandparents are *grand* parents. In the dictionary the word *grand* means: "having more importance than others; foremost; having higher rank; large and striking in size, scope, extent, or conception; lavish, marked by regal form and dignity; intended to impress; very good; wonderful."

What is a Grandmother?

An 8-year-old wrote, "A grandmother is a lady who has no children of her own, so she likes other people's boys and girls. Grandmas don't have anything to do except be there. If they take us for walks, they slow down past pretty leaves and caterpillars. They never say 'Hurry up.' Usually they are fat but not too fat to tie shoes. They wear glasses, and sometimes they can take their teeth out. They can answer questions like why dogs hate cats and why God isn't married. They don't talk like visitors do which is hard to understand. When they read to us, they don't skip words or mind if it is the same story again. Everybody should try to have a grandma, especially if you don't have television, because grandmas are the only grownups who always have time."

Additional Sermons and Lesson Ideas

A Tonic For Tension
Date preached:

SCRIPTURE: Psalm 3

INTRODUCTION: Tension headaches, nervous stomachs, and spastic colons are signs of the times. In Psalm 3, King David had reason for all three, having been driven from his palace by rebel forces commanded by his son, Absalom (2 Sam. 15–18), yet he found a tonic for tension.

1. **Storms Blow In** (vv. 1–2). David's critics claimed not even God could help him. Sometimes everything goes wrong in our lives.
2. **Faith Looks Up** (vv. 3–4). Our response: "But you are a shield around me, Lord."
3. **We Lie Down** (vv. 5–6). Faith enables us to rest, both physically and mentally.
4. **God Goes Forth** (vv. 7–8). As we lie down to rest, the Lord gets up ("Arise, O Lord! Deliver me."

CONCLUSION: Learn the reality of singing with your heart: "Jesus, I am resting, resting, in the joy of what Thou art!"

The Journey Home
Date preached:

By Drew Wilkerson

SCRIPTURE: Joel 2:12

INTRODUCTION: Here the prophet Joel explains how a lost soul can return to God. The journey back may seem long, but it starts with only three steps of faith.

1. **Fasting.** To return to God with all of our hearts, it helps to embrace the discipline of fasting. To fast means to go without something, usually food, for a period of time. Fasting from food helps us focus intently on God and expresses the seriousness of our desires.
2. **Weeping.** When we weep we allow God to cleanse us from the inside out. Remorse for sins is vital; when we realize we have sinned against God, weeping is an appropriate response. Initially, crying is exhausting physically and emotionally. Yet when we have no tears left to cry, it's amazing how much lighter our burdens feel.
3. **Mourning.** We must become genuinely sorrowful for our sins if we want God to forgive us and restore us. Only when we regret or mourn the sins we have committed against God can God set us free.

CONCLUSION: Joel goes on to tell us that God has abounding love waiting for those who rend their hearts and return to Him. The journey home may not be an easy road, but God has an unbelievable welcome waiting for us.

SEPTEMBER 15, 2002

Fashioned in the Fire

Date preached:

By Dr. Melvin Worthington

Scripture: Daniel 3:1–30, especially verses 16–18 Shadrach, Meshach, and Abed-Nego answered and said to the king, "O Nebuchadnezzar, we have no need to answer you in this matter. If that is the case, our God whom we serve is able to deliver us from the burning fiery furnace, and He will deliver us from your hand, O king. But if not, let it be known to you, O king, that we do not serve your gods, nor will we worship the gold image which you have set up."

Introduction: Television actress Heather Graham recently told *Talk* magazine that she resents the "church" because of her upbringing. "Organized religion, in my experience" she said, "has been destructive. Why do I have to do what all these men are saying? Why is a woman's sexuality supposed to be so evil?" While the church isn't perfect, much of today's criticism and rejection of Christianity is driven by a desire to cast off moral restraints. We want to be our own gods, to make our own decisions, and to bow to the image of pleasure, power, possessions, or personal opinion. Situations often arise requiring us to take a stand on the principles of God's Word regardless of the consequences. Obedience to Scripture is an obligation, not an option, for Christians. Loyal obedience brings abundant blessing. Daniel 3 tells of three young men—Shadrach, Meshach and Abednego—who faced this dilemma 2,500 years ago.

1. **The Occasion** (vv. 1–7). *The Dedication of the Image* (vv. 1–3): Nebuchadnezzar, erecting a great image of himself in the plain of Dura, invited assorted dignitaries to its dedication. These princes, governors, captains, judges, treasurers, counselors, sheriffs and rulers assembled and stood before the image, awaiting instruction. *The Directive to the Individuals* (vv. 4–7): When the multitude heard the music, they were to fall down and worship the image. Those who disobeyed would be cast into a fiery furnace.

2. **The Offenders** (vv. 8–18). All bowed and worshiped the image except Shadrach, Meshach and Abednego. *The Accusation* (vv. 8–12): Certain Chaldeans informed the king of the disobedience of the Hebrews and

reminded him of the penalty for disobeying his instructions. *The Anger* (vv. 13–15): Nebuchadnezzar was furious and summoned the young men. He offered them another chance to submit. *The Allegiance* (vv. 16–18): "We have no need to answer you in this matter," was the reply. "If...our God whom we serve is able to deliver us from the burning fiery furnace, and He will deliver *us* from your hand, O king. But if not, let it be known to you, O king, that we do not serve your gods, nor will we worship the gold image."

3. **The Outcome** (vv. 19–30). Their refusal enraged the king, and they were cast into the fire, but a fourth man joined them in the flames, and they were delivered unharmed.

4. **The Observations.** *(1) They Would Not Bow.* In spite of the king's rage and threats, they refused to serve his gods or worship the golden image. There are a host of false gods today, all demanding worship. Popularity. Pleasure. The Good Life. The Acquisition of "Things". We must have nothing in our lives more important to us than our Lord Jesus Christ. *(2) They Would Not Bend.* After taking their stand, Shadrach, Meshach and Abednego refused to reconsider their action. Crowds, confrontations and convenience must not cause us to waver in obedience. The instant availability of temptation and sin on the internet, in movies, and on television, must be resisted. Disobedience is always dishonoring. *(3) They Would Not Burn.* In a rage Nebuchadnezzar

>>> *sermon continued on following page*

APPROPRIATE HYMNS AND SONGS

How Firm a Foundation, John Rippon; Public Domain.

Trust and Obey, James H. Sammis/Daniel B. Towner; Public Domain.

I've Been Changed, Mosie Lister; © 1958. Renewed 1986 Lillenas Publishing Company (Admin. by The Copyright Company).

I'll Obey, Jim Custer/Tim Hosman; © 1983 C.A. Music (Admin. by Music Services).

This is a Good Day, Donald Bedford; © 1992 Maranatha! Music.

commanded the Hebrews be thrown into an inferno. The fire was so hot it incinerated the guards. When the king peered into the furnace, he saw four men walking in the fire and the fourth was like the Son of God. He called for the release of the men and found to his amazement that the fire had no effect on them.

Conclusion: When one obeys God, the fiery trials are a means of trying, testing and tempering. During periods of great affliction the Lord often gives the greatest victories. Rather than losing, by obeying the Word of God these lads were promoted in the province of Babylon and their God acknowledged as the true and living God. Servants of God are revealed, refined, reaffirmed and reassured in the fiery furnace of trials and tribulation. They are fashioned in the fire.

FOR THE BULLETIN

❋ On September 15, 1732, the first two Moravian missionaries arrived in Copenhagen, seeking a ship to the Danish West Indies. They found nothing but opposition and discouragement. Even if they found a ship to take them to St. Thomas, they were told, they would never be allowed to preach to the slaves there. Leonard Dober and David Nitschmann replied they would be willing to become slaves themselves if necessary. Their resolve paved the way for the Protestant era of world missions. ❋ David Livingstone's passion for missionary exploration sometimes came at the expense of his family. In August of 1851, he started out on an arduous jungle trek with his wife Mary, great with child. On September 15th, she delivered her fifth baby on the Zouga River. Livingstone devoted only a line to the birth in his journal, devoting more space to the crocodile eggs he had found. ❋ Antoinette Brown created a stir when she enrolled at Oberlin College for graduate studies in theology and considered entering the ministry. When she was offered a preaching ministry at a large New York City church, she felt too inexperienced for a large pulpit, accepting a call instead to a small Congregational church, having "neither steeple or bell," in South Butler, New York. There on September 15, 1853, Antoinette Brown became the first regularly ordained woman minister in America. ❋ On September 15, 1877, the old Pacific Garden Mission opened in Chicago. ❋ On this day in 1963, at 9:22 in the morning, a bomb exploded under the Sixteenth Street Baptist Church in Birmingham, Alabama, as 400 African-American Christians worshiped. The rafters collapsed, pews and windows were destroyed, and the head of Christ was blown off the stained glass window. Four little girls were killed, and 17 others were injured.

WORSHIP HELPS

Worship Theme:
The Lord is God Almighty who alone is to be worshipped and obeyed.

Call to Worship:
And God spoke all these words, saying: "I am the LORD your God, who brought you out of the land of Egypt, out of the house of bondage. You shall have no other gods before Me" (Ex. 20:1–3).

Scripture Reading and Hymn Stanza:
"Beloved, do not think it strange concerning the fiery trial which is to try you, as though some strange thing happened to you; but rejoice to the extent that you partake of Christ's sufferings, that when His glory is revealed, you may also be glad with exceeding joy. If you are reproached for the name of Christ, blessed are you, for the Spirit of glory and of God rests upon you." Put differently,

> *When through fiery trials thy pathway shall lie,*
> *My grace, all sufficient, shall be thy supply:*
> *The flame shall not hurt thee; I only design*
> *Thy dross to consume, and thy gold to refine.*

Taken from 1 Peter 4:12–14 and "How Firm a Foundation."

Offertory Comments:
In her famous "Golden Speech," her last speech to Parliament, given in 1601, Queen Elizabeth I sought to reassure her people that she was neither selfish nor greedy. In one memorable line, she said, "What you bestow on me, I will not hoard it up, but receive it to bestow on you again." Whether Elizabeth was sincere or not is open to question, but that should certainly be our attitude as Christians. What God bestows on us, we are not to hoard up or hold in tight-fisted selfishness. We receive it to bestow back for His purposes, like the old hymn that says, "We give Thee but Thine own, what'er that gift may be." May the Lord bless our open hands and our faithful gifts this day.

Benediction:
The grace of the Lord Jesus Christ, and the love of God, and the communion of the Holy Spirit be with you all. Amen.

STATS, STORIES AND MORE

From Matthew Henry

Shadrach, Meshach, and Abednego did not hesitate whether they should comply or not. Life or death were not to be considered. Those that would avoid sin, must not parley with temptation when that to which we are allured or affrighted is manifestly evil. Stand not to pause about it, but say, as Christ did, Get thee behind me, Satan. They did not contrive an evasive answer, when a direct answer was expected.

A Modern Example

Charles Turner, in his book *Chosen Vessels: Portraits of Ten Outstanding Christian Men,* tells the story of missionary Stanley Soltau. While serving in Korea in the 1920s, Soltau met Chinsoo Kim, a student whom he embraced as a son. Chinsoo went on to seminary, and was ordained a minister. The two men became inseparable.

In 1936, the occupying Japanese government ordered all Korean schools to bow before the goddess Amaterasu-Omi-Kami, patron saint of the Japanese army. Mission schools were not exempt, and Christian students and teachers suddenly faced the same challenge encountered by the Hebrew children. Intense persecution raged against the Christians, with over 60,000 arrests.

As Stanley left Korea, Chinsoo met him at the station. "Father," Chinsoo said as the train prepared to depart, "I fear hard times ahead for us. . . . The stand we are taking against shrine worship—tell me again that we are doing the right thing."

"There is no question about it," answered Stanley. As he boarded the train, Chinsoo pressed a paper into his hand. Taking his seat, Stanley read it: "Of one thing I am certain, you will never feel ashamed of your son. Whatever comes, I am looking to the Lord for his enabling power..."

Years later Stanley learned of Chinsoo's fate. Soon after their parting, Chinsoo had been arrested by the Japanese police because of his refusal to bow before the Shinto shrine. He was imprisoned and brutally tortured. One winter day, a friend passing the jail saw a pile of corpses, frozen, stacked like firewood. Among them was Chinsoo. From the day Stanley heard it until he passed away in 1972, he carried Chinsoo's death around with him just as he carried the death of Christ in his heart.

Additional Sermons and Lesson Ideas

Complete Christians

Date preached:

Dr. Melvin Worthington

SCRIPTURE: Ephesians 4:11–16

INTRODUCTION: God has given everything necessary for the edification, establishment and equipping of His church.

1. **The Established Offices** (v. 11). God "gifts" those individuals who serve in the offices, and He establishes offices that are divine, distinct, designated, designed, directed and distributed for the well-being of the Church.
2. **The Explained Objective** (vv. 12–15).
    A. God's Purpose — "...to prepare God's people for works of service..."
    B. God's Perfecting — "so that the body of Christ may be built up..."
    C. God's Product — "...until we all reach unity...and become mature."
3. **The Expected Outcome** (Eph. 4:16). The Church is an organism which is *ordered*, an organization which is *outfitted*. Pastors and teachers have the task of perfecting and bringing to completeness the saints in order that they might effectively, earnestly and enthusiastically do the work of the ministry.

CONCLUSION: There's a place for you at this church!

Individual Repentance

Date preached:

By Charles H. Spurgeon

SCRIPTURE: Jeremiah 18:11

INTRODUCTION: This is the voice of mercy, anxious about each individual. It is Jehovah's words.

1. **What? Return!** This includes Stopping. Turning around. Hastening back.
2. **When? Now!** Every step away makes it more difficult to return, and there's no promise for future opportunities.
3. **Who? Every one!** We're more apt to notice our neighbor's sin than our own, but each of us must give an account for ourselves.
4. **From What? His evil way!** There is none good, not one.
5. **To What? Ways and doings that are good!** Negative religion is not enough, there must be positive goodness.

CONCLUSION: Personal repentance is of utmost importance, and practical repentance is an absolute necessity.

E. M. Bounds

If God were blessing your church in direct proportion to your prayer life, how would it be doing? If the breadth of your preaching matched the depths of your praying, how powerful would your pulpit ministry be? Or how weak?

Edward M. Bounds, whose writings on prayer are classics, makes us face those questions every time we pick up his books. Bounds was born into a strong Christian family in Shelbyville, Missouri, on August 15, 1835. His father, a businessman and political leader, ran the local hotel and mill. But when the elder Bounds died from tuberculosis at age 44 in 1849, his family seemed emotionally lost. Young Edward, 14, along with his older brother Charles, soon joined a wagon train for the California Gold Rush of '49. The next four years tested Edward's Christian roots as he faced hardship with little to show for it amid the drunkenness, gambling, prostitution, and unrestrained atmosphere of the Wild West.

Disillusioned, Edward returned to Missouri, where he studied law in Hannibal and was licensed as the state's youngest attorney. But his heart was restless. In the late 1850s, hearing reports of revivals spreading across the nation, Edward attended a brush arbor meeting on the banks of the Mississippi River in LaGrange, Missouri, and was so moved that he resigned the law and moved to the village of Palmyra, Missouri, to attend Bible school. Two years later, on February 21, 1860, he preached before the local quarterly meeting and was appointed a Methodist circuit-rider for a rural district in Missouri. For the next year, Edward rode his horse from town to town and from farm to farm, doing pastoral work, preaching, teaching, leading Bible studies, and praying with his extended flock.

On April 12, 1861, shots were fired at Fort Sumter, sparking the War Between the States. Residents of Missouri were divided on whether to support the North or the South, and Edward became caught up in events when he was asked to preach the funeral of a 17-year-old who had been seized by Union forces and held under the frozen Grand River until he drowned.

On November 14, 1862, Edward's name appeared on a list of men to be arrested, and he was taken into custody and eventually imprisoned in Lynch's Slave Pit, amid unspeakable filth in a cold cell so crowded it was impossible to sit down. By the end of the year, he was banished from the North, and, on February 20, 1863, was given a pass through lines of war to secure a safe passage to the southern states. He walked over 200 miles before purchasing a mule in Arkansas and continuing southeast.

At age 28, Bounds joined the Confederate army as a chaplain, which put him in the middle of the most tragic battles of the war. He was wounded by a Union saber at the Battle of Franklin; and, when Confederate forces were routed at the Battle of Nashville, he stayed behind to care for the wounded and dying. On December 17, 1864, he was classified as captured, though not imprisoned, and was allowed to minister to wounded soldiers and to townspeople, holding Bible studies and prayer meetings. He also promoted plans for a Civil War cemetery in Franklin, which today is the only cemetery in America wholly filled with fallen Confederate soldiers.

B. F. Haynes, who was saved under Bound's ministry and who later became president of Asbury College, recalled his impressions of E. M. Bounds during this time: "His preaching profoundly impressed me, his prayers linger until today as one of the holiest and sweetest memories of my life. His reading of hymns was simply inimitable. . . . I never hear these hymns today or think of them that the scene is not reenacted of the little hazel-eyed, black-haired pastor with a voice of divine love standing in

---

We have emphasized sermon-preparation

until we have lost sight of the important thing

to be prepared—the heart.

—E. M. BOUNDS

---

the pulpit of the old Methodist church, reading one of these matchless hymns in a spirit, tone, and manner that simply poured life, hope, peace, and holy longings to my boyish heart."

When the war ended, Bounds continued preaching and pastoring in Middle Tennessee until late 1871, when, at age 36, he moved to Alabama to pastor a church, and there he began his writing ministry by contributing a column to the local paper, the *Eufaula Times*. It was also in Eufaula, while conducting a funeral, that he met Emma Elizabeth Barnette, with whom he almost instantly fell in love. When he returned to Missouri to pastor a Methodist Episcopal church in St. Louis, he kept up correspondence with Emma, and, on September 19, 1876, they were married. He was 41. The couple set up housekeeping in St. Louis, and their first child, a little girl, was born about a year later. Residents of St. Louis often saw Bounds reading and studying his Bible while riding horseback through the streets, visiting the sick and making soul-winning calls.

In 1883, Bounds was asked to become associate editor of the *St. Louis Christian Advocate,* and his writing ministry took a more serious turn. At the same time Emma's health began to fail, and, fearing the worst, Bounds gathered up his family and returned to Alabama, where her father, a medical doctor, attended her. As her condition worsened, Bounds stayed by her bedside, reading Scripture and praying. She passed away on February 18, 1886, at age 30.

Bound's friend, Dr. Luther Smith, was concerned about him during this time, and a couple of months after Emma's death, he invited Edward to preach at Southern University in Greensboro, Alabama. A spirit of revival swept over the campus and more than 100 were saved. At the same time, Bounds was awarded an Honorary Doctorate of Divinity Degree. This was much against his will, for it hurt his modesty. When one lady addressed him as "Doctor," he replied with a pained expression, "Sister Hill, if you love me, call me Brother Bounds."

On her deathbed, Emma, concerned for her husband and children, had expressed a wish for Edward to marry her cousin, Harriet A. Barnett. On October 25, 1887, Emma's father performed the ceremony. From the first, Harriet called him, "Doctor," and taught the children to do the same.

The next year, Bounds resigned his position in St. Louis to move back to Nashville to become associate editor of the *Nashville Christian Advocate,* the official paper of the Methodist Episcopal Church South. He was now in his mid-fifties, preaching, writing, editing a magazine, and still fathering children. (In all, he had nine children, three from his first marriage and six from his second).

Bounds' ministry with the *Nashville Christian Advocate* was marred by controversies in his denomination, but Bounds was chiefly concerned about the absence of power in the pulpit. He noticed that although pastors were better trained than ever and had more resources, they evidenced little spiritual unction. He addressed the issue in an article containing the following succinct words that foreshadow his later writings on prayer:

> The power of the preacher lies in his power of prayer, in his ability to pray so as to reach God, and bring great results. The power of prayer is rarely tested, its possibilities seldom understood, never exhausted. The pulpit fixed and fired with holy desires on God, with a tireless faith, will be the pulpit of power. . . . To pray over our sermons like we say grace over our meals does no good. Every step of the sermon should be born of the throes of prayer, its beginning and end should be vocal with the plea and song of prayer. Its delivery should be

impassioned and driven by the power of prayer. . . . Prayer that carries heaven by storm, that moves God by a relentless advocacy, these make the pulpit a throne, its deliverances like the decrees of destiny.

Bounds' articles became widely read, bringing him many speaking invitations and much respect. Still, unhealthy winds were blowing through his denomination, and it was with a foreboding spirit that he boarded a train on May 6, 1893, at Nashville's Union Station, bound for Memphis for the annual meeting of his denomination. He checked into the Peabody Hotel and started mingling with the 2,500 delegates. It proved a divisive time, and Bounds returned to Nashville troubled.

In 1894, at age 59, worn out by denominational politics, he resigned his position and moved his family into the home of his father-in-law in Washington, Georgia. Edward had no source of income, and for a time his family was dependent on his in-laws, which caused tongues to wag. Bounds hoped to return to an itinerant ministry, but he was ostracized by his denomination and few people reached out to him.

One man, however, remained faithful. Rev. C. L. Shelton, who was conducting meetings in Bound's old stomping grounds of Franklin, Tennessee, sent for him. Soon others asked him to speak here and there, and his ministry began to flourish again. Calls started coming from across the nation.

All the while, E. M. Bounds was growing in his personal prayer habits. Each morning he would rise at 4 A.M. and pray until breakfast at seven. Every afternoon when home he would go on a "prayer walk," in which he prayed for the people in the houses he passed. Often the mid-morning hours would find him in the little prayer chamber he established on the second floor of his home, and here in the atmosphere of prayer he would scratch out on little scraps of paper his thoughts about prayer. An idea for a book burned in his heart and he began putting down his thoughts under the simple title, *Preacher and Prayer.*

In the spring of 1905, while speaking at an annual Bible conference in Atlanta, Bounds met a local Atlanta pastor named Homer Hodge, who later wrote: "When I met this great saint in May 1905 he was seventy years old. He was then writing his *Preacher and Prayer.* . . . He coaxed us to rise with him at 4:00 a.m. and wrestle for a lost world and for money to publish his books."

In 1907, at the urging of Dr. G. Campbell Morgan, Bounds traveled to London to present his manuscript to the editors of Marshall Brothers, who agreed to publish it.

For several years, E. M. Bounds enjoyed his work, praying, preaching, and setting forth his thoughts about prayer. In late 1912 and early 1913, Bounds continued meeting with Dr. Hodge about his books, and Hodge became the primary force behind getting his manuscripts into printed form. Bounds himself was growing weaker. When he died on August 24, 1913, at age 78 in his home in Washington, Georgia, he was not particu-

What the Church needs today is not more machinery

or better, not new organizations or more and novel methods,

but men whom the Holy Ghost can use—men of prayer,

men mighty in prayer.

—E.M. BOUNDS

larly well-known or outwardly successful. But he had left behind in manuscript form and on miscellaneous scraps of paper some of history's richest ideas about the life of prayer.

Dr. Homer Hodge assumed responsibility for crafting these writings into books. Hodge once said, "I have been among many ministers and slept in the same room with them for several years. They prayed, but I was never impressed with any special praying among them until one day a small man with gray hair and an eye like an eagle came along. We had a ten-day convention. We had some fine preachers around the home, and one of them was assigned to my room. I was surprised early next morning to see a man bathing himself before day and then see him get down and begin to pray. I said to myself, 'He will not disturb us, but will soon finish,' and he kept on softly for hours, interceding and weeping softly, for me and my indifference, and for all the ministers of God. He spoke the next day on prayer. I became interested for I was young in the ministry, and had often desired to meet with a man of God that prayed like the saints of the Apostolic age. Next morning he was up praying again, and for ten days he was up early praying for hours. I became intensely interested and thanked God for sending him. 'At last,' I said, 'I have found a man that really prays. I shall never let him go.' He drew me to him with hooks of steel."

Largely due to Homer Hodge, E. M. Bounds is now remembered as one of Christianity's most prolific and eloquent writers on the subject of prayer. His books became classics long after his body was deposited in the old Methodist graveyard in Washington, Georgia.

His initial book, *Preacher and Prayer,* was later retitled *Power Through Prayer,* but it is still addressed primarily to those in ministry. I have an old copy under the original title which I keep on the bookshelf over my desk with a bookmark at the place where I left off at the last reading. I frequently pick it up and read a few paragraphs or a page or two, carefully underlining the best sentences in pencil. Apart from the Bible, it provides more motivation for a solid, daily prayer life than anything else. Here is how it begins:

> We are constantly on a stretch, if not on a strain, to devise new methods, new plans, new organizations to advance the Church and secure enlargement and efficiency for the gospel. This trend of the day has a tendency to lose sight of the man or sink the man in the plan or organization. God's plan is to make much of the man, far more of him than of anything else. Men are God's method. The Church is looking for better methods; God is looking for better men. "There was a man sent from God whose name was John." The dispensation that heralded and prepared the way for Christ was bound up in that man John. "Unto us a child is born, unto us a son is given." The world's salvation comes out of that cradled Son. When Paul appeals to the personal character of the men who rooted the gospel in the world, he solves the mystery of their success. The glory and efficiency of the gospel is staked on the men who proclaim it. When God declares that "the eyes of the Lord run to and fro throughout the whole earth, to show himself strong in the behalf of them whose heart is perfect toward him," he declares the necessity of men and his dependence on them as a channel through which to exert his power upon the world. This vital, urgent truth is one that this age of machinery is apt to forget. The forgetting of it is as baneful on the work of God as would be the striking of the sun from his sphere. Darkness, confusion, and death would ensue.
>
> What the Church needs today is not more machinery or better, not new organizations or more and novel methods, but men whom the Holy Ghost can use—men of prayer, men mighty in prayer. The Holy Ghost does not flow through methods, but through men. He does not come on machinery, but on men. He does not anoint plans, but men—men of prayer. ✸

SEPTEMBER 22, 2002

SUGGESTED SERMON

The Power of a Proper Perspective

Dr. Timothy Beougher   *Date preached:*

Scripture: Philippians 1:12–26, especially verses 19–26 For I know that this will turn out for my deliverance through your prayer and the supply of the Spirit of Jesus Christ, according to my earnest expectation and hope that in nothing I shall be ashamed, but with all boldness, as always, so now also Christ will be magnified in my body, whether by life or by death. For to me, to live is Christ, and to die *is* gain. But if I live on in the flesh, this will mean fruit from my labor; yet what I shall choose I cannot tell. For I am hard-pressed between the two, having a desire to depart and be with Christ, which is far better. Nevertheless to remain in the flesh is more needful for you. And being confident of this, I know that I shall remain and continue with you all for your progress and joy of faith, that your rejoicing for me may be more abundant in Jesus Christ by my coming to you again.

Introduction: A shoe salesman was sent to a remote part of the country. When he arrived, he was dismayed because everyone was barefooted. He wired his company, "No prospect for sales. People don't wear shoes here." Later another salesman went to the same territory. He too immediately sent word to the home office, but his telegram read, "Great potential! People don't wear shoes here!" Everything depends on our perspective.

1. **A Proper Perspective Transforms Circumstances** (vv. 12–13). Here was an apostle who wanted to travel far and wide to share the gospel, but he is imprisoned. The world was waiting to be conquered by his message, but this message appeared conquered by his chains. He wanted to go to Rome as a preacher; instead he went as a prisoner. Yet note how Paul's perspective transformed his circumstances. We might have wondered why God was not working things out like we planned them, but instead of complaining, take advantage of the situation. He said, "I want you to know, brethren, that the things which happened to me have actually turned out for the furtherance of the gospel...." Paul was confined, yet this physical confinement was providing Paul with the opportunity to communicate the Good News in places where normally he would have had no access. A proper perspective does not complain about what God does not do but looks ahead at what God is going to do.

2. **A Proper Perspective Transforms Relationships** (vv. 14–18). Paul was able to rejoice, not in the motives of his critics, but in the fact that Christ was being preached! Regardless of their motivation, their message was orthodox. They preached Christ! He could not rejoice over their faulty motivation, but he could rejoice that Christ was preached, and that sinners were being saved. A proper perspective will allow you to even view your critics in a different light. It puts a positive spin on every circumstance—not an unrealistic one, but one that accounts for God's providence, presence, promises, and power.

3. **A Proper Perspective Transforms Uncertainties** (vv. 19–26). "I know that this will turn out for my deliverance through your prayer and the supply of the Spirit of Jesus Christ," he said. Paul's assurance that his problems would work for good was not simply a matter of positive thinking. It was Christ's strength, not his own, that empowered him. He said, "I will be delivered" (v. 19); "I will not be ashamed" (v. 20); "I will have sufficient courage" (v. 20); "I will exalt Christ" (v. 20). Then he gives the key verse that summarizes and explains his whole perspective on life: "For to me to live is Christ and to die is gain" (v. 21).

Conclusion: How would you fill in the blanks at the end of those statements: For to me to live is _____? Possessions? Prestige? Pleasure? Paul was eager for death, but willing to live for the furtherance of the gospel. How

>>> sermon continued on following page

APPROPRIATE HYMNS AND SONGS

Breathe on Me, Edwin Hatch/B.B. McKinney; Public Domain.

We Are a New Creation, Henry Smart/Jane Parker Huber; © 1981 Jane Parker Huber (Admin. by Westminster John Knox Press).

For Me to Live is Christ, Gary Mathena/Ed Kee; © 1982 New Spring Publishing (Admin. by Brentwood-Benson Music Publishing Co.).

He is Lord, Traditional; Public Domain.

For the Lord, He is Great, Billy Funk; © 1989 Integrity's Praise! Music.

would you end the last statement? To die is _____? Most people live as though they would say: "For me to live is money and to die is to leave it all behind.... To live is fame and to die is to be forgotten.... To live is power and to die is oblivion.... To live is pleasure and to die is tragedy." Paul filled in both blanks with Christ. How about you? How's your perspective?

FOR THE BULLETIN

❀ In 286 A.D., the 6,666 soldiers of the Theban legion were ordered by Maximian to destroy Christianity in Gaul. This was a Christian legion, and they refused to carry out the order. On September 15, 286, Maximian ordered the massacre of the entire legion. ❀ Shoemaker John Noyes of Laxfield, Suffolk, was led to the stake on the morning of September 22, 1557, where he knelt, prayed, and recited Psalm 50. When the chain enveloped him, he said, "Fear not them that kill the body, but fear him that can kill both body and soul and cast it into everlasting fire." The ashes of his body were buried in a pit, and with them one of his feet, whole to the ankle, with the stocking on. ❀ On September 22, 1776, Nathan Hale was executed as a spy by the British, saying, "I only regret that I have but one life to lose for my country." He was a Christian. ❀ On September 22, 1862, U.S. President Abraham Lincoln issued the preliminary Emancipation Proclamation, declaring all slaves in rebel states free as of January 1, 1863. ❀ C. S. Lewis came to Christ on this day in 1931 while riding to a zoo in his brother's motorcycle sidecar. "When we set out I did not believe that Jesus is the Son of God and when we reached the zoo I did," he later recalled. ❀ On September 22, 1966, Wheaton College Chancellor V. Raymond Edman rose to address the students in chapel. As he spoke of entering the presence of a king, he slumped over, succumbing to a heart attack.

Worship Theme:
Viewing life from God's perspective transforms our attitudes in every area and comprises the essence of wisdom.

Call to Worship:
Let this mind be in you which was also in Christ Jesus, who, being in the form of God, did not consider it robbery to be equal with God, but made Himself of no reputation, taking the form of a bondservant, and coming in the likeness of men. And being found in appearance as a man, He humbled Himself and became obedient to the point of death, even the death of the cross. Therefore God also has highly exalted Him and given Him the name which is above every name, that at the name of Jesus every knee should bow, of those in heaven, and of those on earth, and of those under the earth, and that every tongue should confess that Jesus Christ is Lord, to the glory of God the Father (Phil. 2:5–11).

Appropriate Scripture Readings:
Proverbs 2:1–8
Matthew 5:1–12
James 3:13–18

Pastoral Prayer:
O Lord, You are the high and lofty One who inhabits eternity, whose name is Holy. Your ways are not our ways, nor Your thoughts our thoughts. Yet You condescend to dwell with those whose hearts are humble and lowly. You impart wisdom. You allow us to look at life through the bifocals of faith, and You rejoice the heart of Your servants. Lord, find in us a home for Yourself and dwell among us today. Teach us to love each other and to bear one another's burdens. Grant us today the undergirding of Your promises, and the uplift of Your Holy Spirit. In Jesus' name, Amen.

STATS, STORIES AND MORE

Perspective on Place

Sir Alexander Fleming made his discovery of penicillin while working in a dusty old laboratory. A mold spore, blown in through a window, landed on a culture plate he was about to examine. Some years later, he was taken on a tour of an up-to-date research lab, a gleaming, air-conditioned, dust-free, super-sterile setting. "What a pity you did not have a place like this to work in," his guide said. "What you could have discovered in such surroundings!"

"Not penicillin," Fleming replied.

Not Done To, But Doing

In his book, *Basic Christian Discipleship*, Billy Beacham tells of a woman who complained to her pastor about her situation at work. Pastor to woman: "Where do you put lights?" Those five words totally changed her perspective and her attitude. Instead of viewing herself as a victim, she became a victor and began reaching out to others in love.

Living Above the Circumstances

Missionary physician Bill Wallace remained in China during the Communist takeover, performing medical duties with a hero's valor. He was called the best surgeon in China. Finally, during the pre-dawn of December 19, 1950, Communist solders came to arrest him on trumped-up espionage charges. He was placed in a small cell where he preached to passersby from a tiny window. Brutal interrogations followed, but Wallace endured by posting verses of Scripture on the walls of his cell. When he died from the ordeal, the Communists tried to say he had hanged himself; but his body showed no signs of suicide. He was buried in a cheap wooden coffin in a bamboo-shaded cemetery. The inscription on his grave simply said: For to Me To Live Is Christ.

Six Brief Words

British pastor George Duncan was once invited to preach live from Keswick, England, on the BBC. He choose this text, saying it summed up the "full-orbed and balanced experience" of the Christian in "six unforgettable words, which in English at least are words of one syllable each, and should therefore not be beyond the understanding of the youngest or simplest of us." Victorious Christianity, Duncan said, is something personal—*for me.* . . . It is something practical—*to live.* . . . And it is something possible—*is Christ!*

Additional Sermons and Lesson Ideas

What To Do With Difficult People
Date preached:

SCRIPTURE: Psalm 5

INTRODUCTION: Many of our problems in life come from difficult people. We need God's wisdom, for sometimes we should ignore them (Prov. 26:4); rebuke them (Prov. 24:25), forbear them (Eph. 4:2), or endure them (Heb. 12:3). One thing we must always do is to lay the situation before God in prayer. In Psalm 5, David talks with God about some who had been boastful (v. 5) and deceitful (v. 6).

1. **We Relay Our Prayers To Our Hearing God** (vv. 1–3). David's prayers were:
   A. **Earnest.** "my words...my meditation...the voice of my cry."
   B. **Early.** "In the morning..."
   C. **Expectant.** "And I will look up."
2. **We Refer Our Problems To Our Holy God** (vv. 4–10). God is not pleased with difficult, boastful people, but we can worship Him in fear and commit our cause to Him.
3. **We Render Our Praises To Our Helping God.** "Let all those rejoice who put their trust in You...because You defend them."

CONCLUSION: We need case-by-case wisdom in knowing how to deal with problem people. But in every case, we can direct our prayers to God and look up.

Early in the Morning
Date preached:

SCRIPTURE: Mark 16:1–2

INTRODUCTION: It took effort for the women in Mark 16 to rise in the chilly, early morning darkness, but it was worth it. The Bible speaks frequently of the blessings of the morning hours.

1. **It is a Time for Devotion** (Mark 1:35; Luke 21:38; Ps. 5:3; 88:13; Isa. 26:9).
2. **It is a Time for Singing** (Ps. 59:16).
3. **It is a Time for Executing God's Commands** (Gen. 22:3; Josh. 3:1).
4. **It is a Time for Going About Our Daily Duties** (Prov. 31:15).

CONCLUSION: Proverbs 6:9–11 warns about wasting the morning hours. Start every day on the right foot. Begin every morning saying, "This is the day that the Lord has made!"

SEPTEMBER 29, 2002

SUGGESTED SERMON

The Temptation of Jesus

Date preached:

By Dr. Ed Dobson

Scripture: Mark 1:12–13 Immediately the Spirit drove Him into the wilderness. And He was there in the wilderness forty days, tempted by Satan, and was with the wild beasts; and the angels ministered to Him.

Introduction: Even before Internet pornography, rampant materialism, and on-line gambling, there was temptation. Even Jesus faced it, and in studying His example, we can learn a lot about being victors. In Matthew 4, we have a much longer account of the temptation of Christ, but Mark, known for his brevity, gives us three phrases that will suffice for today's study.

1. **Christ Was Led by the Spirit.** The word *led* or *sent* does not convey the idea of gentle guidance. It is a very forceful verb that literally meant *to drive someone out*. This word was later used for Jesus driving out demons. When Satan came to Adam and Eve, he took the initiative, resulting in sin entering the human race; but in this story, Jesus deliberately, under the power of the Spirit, went forth to confront Satan, resulting in victory being made available to the human race. What does this teach us? (1) Living a life that pleases God does not exempt us from temptation. No sooner had God said, "You are My beloved Son, in whom I am well pleased," than we read, "Immediately the Spirit drove Him into the wilderness." (2) Being led by the Spirit doesn't exempt us from temptation. None of us are exempt. As long as we're in this body of flesh, we're going to struggle. The good news is that if we allow the Spirit to lead us, He will empower us to overcome temptation (Gal. 5:16).

2. **He Was Tempted by Satan.** The word *tempted* has two ideas: An attraction toward sin, and a test or trial. In this case, it was temptation toward sin. Suppose you were given the assignment to expose someone to the temptations of Satan in their most potent form. Where would you take that person? Las Vegas? Hollywood? In the ancient world, the place would have been the city of Corinth, a pagan place full of sensuality and materialism. But the devil

took Christ to the desert—no people, no buildings, no activity. Why? To remind us that temptation is not so much outward "stuff," but first and foremost an inward struggle (Mark 7:21; James 1:13). My problem with temptation is not the attractive stuff around me; it is a heart problem. My problem is my own evil desire.

3. **Christ Was Strengthened by the Angels.** Jesus was led by the Spirit and tempted by Satan, but He was not abandoned by God. Perhaps the angels did for Jesus what they had done for Elijah, bringing him bread and water. Somehow they took care of Him. We may wonder if God really cares about our struggles. Yes, He cares and He provides all the assistance we need to be victors over temptation, trials, and troubles.

Conclusion: Jesus was in all points tempted just like us, though without sin. He responded to Satan three times, saying: *It is written, It is written, It is written.* He had committed God's Word to memory, and in the face of temptation He responded with Scripture. We need to be filled with the Scripture and with the Spirit day by day, moment by moment. The Bible is our offensive weapon against Satan, the sword of the Spirit. Even in our modern age of technology, we'll never face any temptation that isn't addressed in the Bible. There are verses for every challenge we'll ever face, and we need to find and memorize the verses we're apt to need along the way. In this way, God provides the resources we need

>>> *sermon continued on following page*

APPROPRIATE HYMNS AND SONGS

We Are More Than Conquerors, Steve Fry; © 1986 Birdwing Music (Admin. by EMI Christian Music Publishing).

Victory in Jesus, Eugene M. Bartlette; © 1939 Mrs. E.M. Bartlette. Renewed 1967. Assigned Albert E. Brumley and Sons (Admin. by Integrated Copyright Group, Inc.).

At the Name of Jesus, Pamela Hall; © 1993 Welcome Home Press (Admin. by Integrated Copyright Group, Inc.).

Christian Do You Struggle, Bert Polman/John Mason Neale/John B. Dykes; © 1987 CRC Publications.

Faith Is the Victory, John H. Yates/Ira D. Sankey; Public Domain.

to counter temptation. He doesn't abandon us. He always provides a divinely-planned exit (1 Cor. 10:13). And if God provides a way of escape, we don't have to give in to sin. Strengthened by His Word and filled with His Spirit, we have the ability to remain self-controlled, and to say "No," to the devil's allurement (Titus 2:11–14). Think about the area of temptation with which you are struggling. Talk to God about it, and yield that area to the control of the Spirit. Ask Him to help you, through His Spirit, to take the way of escape.

FOR THE BULLETIN

❋ Pope Leo I, known in history as Leo the Great, was consecrated on September 29, 440. His pontificate of 21 years is second only to that of Gregory I in its impact on the early history of the Catholic church, and in many ways he made the papacy into the power it came to be. He was an uncompromising foe of heresy and he emphasized the human/divine nature of Christ. ❋ William the Conqueror invaded England to claim English throne on September 29, 1066. ❋ On Saturday, September 29, 1770, an aging, feeble George Whitefield rode to Exeter, New Hampshire, where a crowd assembled and he stood precariously atop a barrel. Gaining strength, Whitefield kept his audience spellbound for two hours. Then he suddenly cried, "I go! I have outlived many on earth but they cannot outlive me in heaven. My body fails, my spirit expands." It was his last sermon. He died in his bed that night. ❋ On September 29, 1866, the *Lammermiur* limped into Shanghai, having barely survived a typhoon in the South China Sea. The crew became so paralyzed with fear, they gave up their efforts to save the ship. One passenger, however, remained unafraid—missionary Hudson Taylor. Gathering the crew together, he told them he believed God would bring them through, but that everything depended upon the greatest care in navigating the ship. Reassured by his demeanor, the men went back to work and the ship stayed afloat. ❋ Newly elected Pope John Paul I died on September 29, 1978. Several investigative articles and books have suggested he was secretly assassinated.

WORSHIP HELPS

Worship Theme:
We are more than conquerors through Christ Jesus our Lord.

Call to Worship:
Yet in all these things we are more than conquerors through Him who loved us (Rom. 8:37).

Readers' Theater:

Reader 1: How can a young man cleanse his way? By taking heed according to Your word.

Reader 2: With my whole heart I have sought You; Oh, let me not wander from Your commandments!

Reader 3: Your word I have hidden in my heart, That I might not sin against You. Revive me according to Your word.

Reader 2: Strengthen me according to Your word.

Reader 1: Be merciful to me according to Your word.

All: Deliver me according to Your word.

Rdrs. 1/2: Your word is a lamp to my feet.

Reader 3: And a light to my path.

Reader 1: Uphold me according to Your word, that I may live; and do not let me be ashamed of my hope.

Reader 3: Hold me up, and I shall be safe, and I shall observe Your statutes continually.

Reader 1: Direct my steps by Your word, and let no iniquity have dominion over me.

Reader 2: The entirety of Your word is truth, and every one of Your righteous judgments endures forever.

Taken from Psalm 119:9–11, 25, 28, 58, 170, 105, 116–117, 133, 160.

Benediction:
Bless us all, O Lord, men and women, boys and girls, dads and moms, sons and daughters, brothers and sisters, friends and family, young and old. Grant Thy blessings as we depart this place, that we might be more than conquerors through Jesus Christ our Lord. Amen.

STATS, STORIES AND MORE

Maybe One Day . . .

"I remember talking to a dear brother in his nineties, a committed believer. He said, 'You know, I used to think when I turned sixty that I would get to the point where I really wouldn't be tempted. Then I turned sixty. I thought well, maybe when I turn seventy, then I'll be exempted.' And he said, 'I turned seventy and nothing changed. So then I thought, well maybe when I turn eighty. Then I thought, well, surely when I turn ninety it will be better.' Now he is in his mid-90s and convinced that until we see Jesus all of us on a regular basis will struggle with temptation. Pleasing God, being led by the Spirit, living a long life, growing in our faith, all of these are important, but none of them exempt us from temptation."

—*Pastor Ed Dobson*

Eye of the Beholder

Malcolm Muggeridge, the famous British philosopher and journalist who converted to Christianity late in life, once told of working as a journalist in India as a young man. One evening he walked down to the river for a swim. As he entered the water, he saw an Indian woman from the nearby village who had come for her evening bath. Muggeridge immediately felt the allurement of the moment, and he was besieged by temptation. He had lived with this kind of temptation all his adult life, but until this moment he had fought it off out of respect for his wife Kitty. But tonight, he was weak and vulnerable. He hesitated just a moment, then swam furiously across the river toward the woman, literally trying to outdistance his conscience. But when he was just a few feet away from her, he emerged from the water and what he saw took his breath away. She wasn't a beautiful, young maiden, but old and hideous, with wrinkled skin, and worst of all, she was a leper. He said later, "The creature grinned at me, showing a toothless mask." Muggeridge muttered, "What a dirty, lecherous woman!" But as he swam away from her, a sudden shock gripped him: "It wasn't just the woman who was dirty and lecherous," he said. "It was my own heart."

Additional Sermons and Lesson Ideas

Winning Over Worry
Date preached:

By Drew Wilkerson

SCRIPTURE: Matthew 6:25–34

INTRODUCTION: Someone said, "Worry is like a rocking chair: It gives you something to do, but it doesn't get you anywhere." Here, Jesus gives us three truths for overcoming worry.

1. **Place the right value on life.** If God is able to care for the birds, how much more will He take care of His children? Our English word *worry* comes from the German word, "wurgen," meaning, "to strangle." Worry can choke us, but God wants us to live life to the fullest.
2. **Possess the right attitude in life.** No one can add an hour or an inch to life by worrying. In fact, worry does the opposite, reducing our life span and robbing us of joy. We must remember that our attitude is our choice.
3. **Pursue the right focus for life.** Seek first the Kingdom of God. Hebrews 12 tells us to fix our eyes on Jesus. When Christ is our focus, the things of this world are put into the proper perspective.

CONCLUSION: Bring your burdens to the Lord, and take away His values, His attitude, and His focus. It will take the air out of the balloon of anxiety.

Church Check-Up: A Brief Survey of 1 Timothy
Date preached:

SCRIPTURE: 1 Timothy 3:14–15

BACKGROUND: Paul, released from prison shortly after the end of book of Acts, made a "victory lap" around the empire, visiting previous churches. He was alarmed to discover that his strongest church, the one in Ephesus, was displaying unhealthy symptoms. He left Timothy behind to deal with the problems, and shortly afterward sent him these instructions.

Book Outline: Paul tells us how to deal with six different aspects of church life:

-   Chapter 1: Dealing with false teachers in the church
-   Chapter 2: The role of prayer and of women
-   Chapter 3: Leadership issues: Elders and Deacons
-   Chapter 4: The Pulpit Ministry
-   Chapter 5–6a: Dealing with various cliques and groups in the church
-   Chapter 6b: Money issues

CONCLUSION: 1 Timothy shows us how to create and maintain healthy Christians and healthy churches. Study it to be wise. Heed it to be strong.

OCTOBER 6, 2002

SUGGESTED SERMON

Turning Clay Into Rock

Date preached:

By Kevin Riggs

Scripture: Luke 5:1–11, especially 3–8 Then He got into one of the boats, which was Simon's, and asked him to put out a little from the land. And He sat down and taught the multitudes from the boat. When He had stopped speaking, He said to Simon, "Launch out into the deep and let down your nets for a catch."
But Simon answered and said to Him, "Master, we have toiled all night and caught nothing; nevertheless at Your word I will let down the net." And when they had done this, they caught a great number of fish, and their net was breaking. So they signaled to their partners in the other boat to come and help them. And they came and filled both the boats, so that they began to sink. When Simon Peter saw it, he fell down at Jesus' knees, saying, "Depart from me, for I am a sinful man, O Lord!"

Introduction: Public opinion surveys continually show that *education* is among the issues of most concern to Americans. We want well-educated children in quality learning environments. Jesus, the "Master Teacher," wants to develop us to our full potential, and He masterfully uses whatever learning environment is available at any given time. With Peter, Jesus turned the Sea of Galilee into a classroom, and an old boat into a student's desk. Peter no doubt looked every part the fisherman. He was rough and rugged with the jaws of a fighter and tough leather skin. However, through several encounters recorded in the Gospels, he became a big-hearted individual—a rock with a soft heart. Peter was a son of the sea, and from his encounters with the sea Jesus taught him great lessons, turning him from clay to rock.

1. **Luke 5:1–11.** In this passage, Jesus boarded Peter's boat and taught the crowds. Then he told Peter to drop his nets into the water. Peter explained they had been fishing all night without catching a single fish, but when Peter dropped the nets again, he caught more fish than he could haul in. *From this encounter Peter saw Jesus as Master and himself as a sinner.* God can do little with us until we realize that, left to ourselves, we are sin-riddled and iniquity-filled.

2. **Matthew 17:24–27.** A tax collector asked Peter if he had paid his taxes. Jesus told Peter to go to the Sea of Galilee and fish. The first fish Peter caught had

the tax money in its mouth. *From this encounter Peter saw Jesus as Provider and himself as needy.* Have you had similar occasions in life? Perhaps your mailbox became a classroom as you opened the mail to find a provision at the moment of need.

3. **Matthew 8:23–27.** In this story, Peter's boat was caught in a severe storm. In their terror the disciples awoke Jesus, who scolded them for their weak faith, spoke a few words, and the storm ceased. *From this encounter Peter saw Jesus as Protector and himself as fearful.* How often does God use a severe storm to teach us the same?

4. **Matthew 14:22–33.** Jesus sent His disciples across the Sea of Galilee ahead of Him. At about 4 a.m., Jesus approached the boat walking on water. Peter got out of the boat and walked toward Jesus, but the moment he took his eyes off Jesus he started to drown. *From this encounter Peter saw Jesus as his Confidence and himself as a doubter.* The Lord has trouble using timid, fearful, anxious, and cowardly people. He uses daily life situations to establish Himself as our Confidence.

5. **John 21:1–17.** After Jesus' resurrection, Peter decided to go fishing. After fishing all night without catching anything he saw Jesus standing on the shore. Jesus told him to throw his nets on the other side of the boat, and when he did, he caught more than he could handle. Back on shore, Jesus ate

>>> *sermon continued on following page*

APPROPRIATE HYMNS AND SONGS

Channels Only, Mary E. Maxwell/Ada Rose Gibbs; ©Public Domain.

A Man With a Perfect Heart, Jack Hayford; © 1995 Annamarie Music (Admin. by Maranatha! Music).

Jesus At Your Holy Table, Tom Allen/ James H. Wood; © 1958 Broadman Press (Admin. by Genevox Music Group).

Like a Glass Here Is My Heart, Dennis Jernigan; © 1995 Shepherd's Heart Music Inc. (Admin. by Word Music Group, Inc.).

Sanctify My Heart, John Chism/Gary Sandler; © 1994 Integrity's Hosanna! Music (Admin. by Integrity Music, Inc.).

with Peter and re-commissioned him as His apostle. *From this encounter Peter saw Jesus as his very Purpose for living and himself as a servant.* This was Peter's final lesson. He was now no longer clay, but rock.

Conclusion: In some of the martial arts, combatants learn to use whatever is at hand as a weapon, whether it's a tree limb, a broom handle, or the stapler off the desk. In a similar way, Jesus uses whatever is at hand as a teaching tool to develop and disciple us. All of life becomes a classroom, and class is in session every day. What is God teaching you today? Is your heart open? Or are you missing the lessons? He wants to turn you and me from clay into living stones, strong and established, for His kingdom.

FOR THE BULLETIN

❀ John de Trocznow lost an eye while at war and became known to history by his nickname, Zisca, meaning "One-eyed." He was a disciple of John Hus and after Hus's martyrdom, Zisca led a war of independence against the Pope and the Emperor. A random arrow struck his remaining eye, and when extracted the barb pulled out his eyeball, leaving him totally blind. He nevertheless led his army to victory. When grateful countrymen offered him the crown of Bohemia, he refused, telling them to "trust yourselves no longer in the hands of kings, but to form yourselves into a republic." Zisca died of the plague on October 6, 1424, being the national hero of Czechoslovakia and a hero to Reformers and to blind people everywhere. ❀ On October 6, 1536, William Tyndale was executed. ❀ On October 6, 1829, missionary Alexander Duff sailed from Portsmouth, England, aboard the *Lady Holland,* bound for India. Late at night the following February, still at sea, the ship struck a reef and sank. Passengers managed to escape to a small island where Duff's Bible washed ashore. The rest of his library of 800 volumes was lost.

❀ On October 6, 1934, Bishop Theophil Wurm of Wurttemburg was arrested by the Nazis, marking the beginning of the seizure of church leaders by the Third Reich. ❀ October 6, 1945, marks the death of George Coles Stebbins, 99, who composed the music to 1,400 hymns, including "Saved by Grace," "Have Thine Own Way," Jesus, I Come," and "Take Time to be Holy."

Worship Theme:
Jesus, the Master Teacher, uses all of life for our sanctification.

Call to Worship:
"Praise Him for His grace and favor to our fathers in distress; Praise Him, still the same as ever, slow to chide, and swift to bless."

Appropriate Scripture Readings:
Psalm 90:1–12; Psalm 143:10–12; Isaiah 4:1–4; 1 Timothy 4:12–16

Pastoral Prayer:
Teach us Your ways, O Lord, and show us Your paths. For Your ways are good ways, and all Your paths are wise. Teach us common sense, Lord, as You define it. Give us Your wisdom for raising our children, for solving our problems, for investing our time and money, and for establishing our priorities. Help us see life in the light of eternity, and see You in the light of Your Word, that we might become as solid as rocks, as wise as serpents, as harmless as doves, and as useful vessels in Your hands. In Jesus' Name, Amen.

Offertory Thought: 1 Chronicles 29:14
- "For all things come from You, and of Your own we have given You" (NKJV).
- "Everything we have has come from you, and we give you only what you have already given us!" (NLT).
- "We have only given back what is already yours" (CEV).
- "But who am I, and who are my people, that we should be able to give as generously as this? Everything comes from you, and we have given you only what comes from your hand" (NIV).
- "We give Thee but Thine own / Whate'er the gift may be: / All that we have is Thine alone, / A trust, O Lord, from Thee" —William W. How

Benediction:
May the words of our mouths and the meditations of our hearts be acceptable unto You, O Lord, our Rock and our Redeemer.

STATS, STORIES AND MORE

"Learn of Me"
- The Greek text of the Gospels calls Jesus "teacher" 45 times.
- That which Jesus did is called "teaching" 45 times.
- Those who followed Him were called disciples (learners) 215 times.
- Jesus' Sermon on the Mount (Matt. 5–7) is described as a time when Jesus opened His mouth and taught the people.

God's Provision in a Fish
In a prayer letter to his supporters, evangelist Billy Graham told of a mother in an African nation who came to Christ and grew strong in her commitment to the Lord. As sometimes happens, however, this alienated her from her husband, and over the years he grew to despise her devotion to Christ. His bitterness reached a climax when he decided to kill his wife, their two children and himself, unable to live in such self-inflicted misery. But he needed a motive. He decided that he would accuse her of stealing his precious keys—keys to the bank, the house, and the car. Early one afternoon he left his bank and headed for the tavern. He paused at the Nile and dropped the keys into the river. He spent all afternoon drinking and carousing.

Later that afternoon, his wife went to the fish market to buy the evening meal. She purchased a large Nile perch. As she was gutting the fish, to her astonishment, in its belly were her husband's keys. How had they gotten there? She didn't know; but she cleaned them up and hung them on the hook.

Sufficiently drunk, the young banker came home that night and pounded open the front door shouting, "Woman, where are my keys?" She picked them off the hook in the bedroom, and handed them to her husband. When he saw the keys, by his own testimony he immediately became sober and was instantly converted. He fell on his knees sobbing, asked for forgiveness, and confessed Jesus Christ as his Lord and Savior.

Additional Sermons and Lesson Ideas

Overcoming Hopelessness

Date preached:

SCRIPTURE: Psalm 6

INTRODUCTION: Pessimistic people are lurking around every corner. Sometimes they are as close as our own thoughts, for all of us go through bouts of the blues. David struggled with these feelings in Psalm 6.

1. **Our Troubled Soul** (vv. 1–3). David is fearful of displeasing God, yet troubled in his bones, asking God how long these feelings will last: "My soul also is greatly troubled....O Lord—how long?"
2. **Our Only Hope.** He feels he might die, describing himself as weary, wasting away, and weeping. But by pleading to God, he appeals to the One who is his only hope: "Return, O Lord, deliver me! Oh, save...!"
3. **Our Renewed Strength.** Through a season of honest, earnest prayer, David drew close and received God's imparted strength. A distinct change of tone occurs in verse 8, as he takes command of his feelings. "The Lord has heard my supplication! The Lord will receive my prayer."

CONCLUSION: Honest, earnest prayer is our greatest secret in chasing away the blues and restoring our souls.

Spiritual Fitness

Date preached:

By Kevin Riggs

SCRIPTURE: 1 Timothy 4:6–10

INTRODUCTION: We live in a fitness-crazed society. And while we do need to take care of our physical bodies, more important is to keep our spiritual lives in shape. In this passage of Scripture, Paul gives us some principles for maintaining spiritual strength.

1. **Eat well (v. 6).** The phrase "brought up" could be translated "nourished up." We should be constantly feeding on the words of God.
2. **Exercise regularly (vv. 7–8).** From the word "train" we get our word "gymnasium." Just as physical strength requires constant physical exercise, so spiritual strength requires constant spiritual exercise.
3. **Exert yourself (v. 10).** Both the words "labor" and "strive" are athletic terms. Just as athletes exert energy to win a competition, so we are to give all we have in service to God.

CONCLUSION: As physical strength takes effort to build and maintain, so does spiritual strength. Spiritually speaking, we need to eat well, exercise regularly, and exert ourselves. Let's not become out-of-shape Christians.

The Way of Escape

Every pastor needs to cultivate the fine art of self-intervention. There are times when sin's pull and Satan's pressures are focused on those in ministry, and falling into a spiritual, emotional, or physical sin is as easy as doing nothing. Spiritual maturity consists of recognizing those times and, when no one else is around to intervene, learning to effect a self-intervention.

Sooner rather than later.

My friend, Lance Woodard, learned this lesson, but only in the nick of time.*

Lance and Joy Woodard, seminary sweethearts, had been married 20 years. Lance was good-looking, out-going, an effective minister, and a red-blooded male. Joy was attractive, bright, and effective in her career as an educator. Their marriage was solid, still sparking with romance. Most of their ministry had been invested in the rural South, but an opportunity in the Northeast proved irresistible. A large church in Philadelphia recruited Lance as minister of stewardship, offering him a large salary boost and a job description that ideally fitted his gifts. Lance and Joy packed their belongings, shipped them to a storage area, and moved temporarily into a sparsely furnished suburban apartment outside Philadelphia.

Two days later, Joy's elderly parents were critically injured in a car wreck near their home in Arkansas. Joy, an only child, flew to their side at once. Their recovery was slow and uncertain, and, with Lance's blessing, she stayed near them six months, leaving Lance to adjust by himself to a bare apartment, a new job, and a large city.

Despite his personable demeanor, Lance found it difficult to develop friendships in the church. Until now, he'd always been out and about with his people, visiting and counseling and being in their homes. But his new ministry kept him in his office most of the time. And he frequently flew to Arkansas on weekends to be with Joy, thus depriving himself of Sundays in his new church.

He also found little companionship with other staff members beyond office hours. Everyone was working themselves to exhaustion due to the church's aggressive stance toward growth. What little time remained beyond the 50 and 60–hour work week was jealously guarded by the church staff for their own families and pursuits. Lance, on the other hand, had fewer responsibilities, more time on his hands, and no family nearby.

It all began to take its toll. Lance found he had underestimated the pressures of being a thousand miles from his wife. Though he didn't immediately realize it, he had overestimated his own personal discipline and maturity. His new surroundings provided temptations that exceeded his expectations, and sometimes his resistance.

The anonymity of metropolitan life disoriented him. The cable television offered an alluring assortment of late night diversions. Even worse, a pornographic filmmaking studio started production in his own mind. And Amber, a young, attractive secretary at church, frequently starred in the title role.

Lance's evening fantasies became office-hour daydreams, and the struggle for his mind seemed a losing battle. Bible study helped, of course, and so did prayer. But sometimes his spiritual disciplines seemed unable to withstand the invasion of the barbarians sacking his mind. As the weeks away from his wife lengthened, Lance grew exhausted. The constant, inner battle for pure thoughts left him sleepless, frazzled, and distracted.

It was with considerable relief that Lance packed his bags for the annual staff get-away in Cape May on the New Jersey coast, his first retreat since coming with the church. He expected it to be spiritually refreshing, a time of renewal in which he could shore up his spiritual life and begin to bond with some of the other church staffers. Lance, who had always loved traveling, learned that Cape May was the first beachside resort in America, and that it still retained its Victorian charm despite having become a popular center for executive retreats and business conferences. He packed his bags and prayed for revival.

"And so we went on the infamous retreat," Lance later said. "There were about 30 of us, primarily the ministerial staff and secretaries. It was a beautiful spot and the weather was perfect. Sunny, but lots of breezes during the day. The facility was like a giant park, with lots of walking trails. It was secluded and quiet, with cabanas, tennis courts, swimming pools." Best of all, it was within walking distance to the quaint village of Cape May itself, and the main street was filled with shops and little restaurants.

The church staff gathered during the mornings and early afternoons for prayer, Bible studies, brainstorming, and hard-nosed planning. But from mid-afternoon, the group was on their own, free to relax.

One evening after supper, Lance decided to walk into the village for ice cream. Several others joined him, but later the party scattered. Lance found himself alone with Amber, and when he mentioned he wanted to walk some more, she said, "Me too."

No alarm bells sounded. "Oh, I might have said to myself, 'What would people think?'" Lance later admitted. "But there weren't any people around, and it was really quite innocent. I wasn't thinking anything about it at that point. I was almost old enough to be Amber's father."

Amber was, in fact, twenty-five, about fifteen years younger than Lance. She was about five-foot-eight, with rust-colored hair, oval eyes, and pleasing form. She had an easy way about her, conveying her warm personality and obvious intelligence with grace. And she was single.

"I had been wondering why Amber had never married," Lance told me. "As we walked along that evening, she begin to open up and tell me her story. She told me about the death of her father, how much she missed him, how lonely she was. She told me of her failed romance. While a student at Penn State, she had become involved with a young man who had later ditched her. She told me how deeply she had hurt, and of how she still hurt. All the time, as we walked, I was feeling rather fatherly, rather pastoral. I tried to gently counsel and encourage her."

The next day staff members crowded into vans for the return trip. Lance and Amber ended up in the back of a van on a seat containing some luggage. They found themselves pressed together.

Back in the apartment that evening, he struggled with rip-roaring thoughts. Until the retreat, it hadn't yet dawned on Lance that Amber might harbor romantic thoughts toward him. Now he wondered. He wanted to call her.

He chose to avoid the phone that night. But the next day, as Lance prepared to leave town to rejoin his wife in Arkansas for the weekend, he stopped in Amber's office to say goodbye. It was late afternoon. The church offices were empty now, the day spent. The two of them were alone. Amber rose from her desk and embraced him mid-room. Lance started to pull away, and eventually did; but a sense of horror came over him. During the flight to Little Rock, Lance thought of all he had to lose: his reputation, his ministry, his job. And most of all his Joy.

Would it be worth it? Of course not. And yet . . .

When Lance returned to Pennsylvania Monday morning, he appeared jovial as ever, his easy personality and quick smile intact. But he felt as vulnerable as a city with breached walls. He needed someone to take him by the shoulders and shake him. He needed someone to stop him, but no one had observed the problem. He needed an intervention, but no one knew the danger.

Summoning all his willpower, Lance Woodard staged his own intervention. He took himself by his own shoulders, shook himself, and, falling on the grace of God, sought a way of escape.

On the first day back from Arkansas, Lance arrived at the church offices early, knowing the senior pastor, Tom Wiseman, arrived at dawn. Lance had known and respected Pastor Tom for years, and though they had never become intimate friends, Lance had confidence in Tom's discretion and wisdom.

Lance knocked on his pastor's door and Tom accepted the interruption graciously. After some small talk, Lance said, "Tom, you once mentioned the value of accountability groups. I think I'd like to do start one with you, if you're willing."

Tom looked at Lance through perceptive eyes. Then he smiled. "You know, Lance, I've been thinking the same thing myself. How about you and me and . . . let's see, why don't we include Deon?" Deon was about ten years younger than Lance, but he'd been at the church far longer. Lance thought about it a moment, then agreed. Almost immediately, the three men began meeting once or twice a week before breakfast.

"We worked on the assumption that confessing our faults to one another was both healthy and biblical," Lance said. "And we had two ground rules: total confidentiality and total honesty. We agreed to face direct questions about our thoughts, our spiritual perceptions, and the scriptural lessons the Lord was teaching us."

For the first two or three weeks, Lance participated in a general way, sharing nothing very specific. Soon however Lance's confidence grew enough to allow him to share with gradually increasing honesty, and it quickly became apparent to the other men that Lance's problems were specific rather than general.

During the middle of a session shortly thereafter, Deon looked at Lance and asked him bluntly, "What's her name?"

Lance hesitated, his face flushed, his heart racing. He didn't want to say, and for a moment there was nothing between the men but silence. Then Pastor Tom asked gently, "Is it Amber?"

Lanced nodded. "It's Amber," he said.

Tom and Deon agreed that Amber was attractive, intelligent, and interesting. They acknowledged that they, too, like most men, faced similar struggles. "You're not the first person to fight this battle," they assured him.

At each meeting thereafter, Tom and Deon always asked Lance specifically if he was having continuing daydreams about Amber. At the office, they discretely made certain that Lance and Amber were together less frequently and never by themselves. The two men often dropped by unexpectedly at Lance's apartment. They'd always have some item of business, some excuse; but while Lance saw through their smokescreen, he never resented it. He was glad, in fact, for their involvement.

Whether right or wrong, Amber was never approached. "After all," Lance later said, "I still don't know if she was trying to initiate anything or not. She might have been totally innocent. The battle zone was within me."

Lance, Tom, and Deon maintained their intense accountability for about four months, then their schedules became more hectic. Tom, taking a sabbatical, left for a series of overseas missions trips. Deon and Lance met less frequently in their morning sessions, but they undertook building a house together in the inner city. Much of their spare time and many of their Saturdays were spent working side-by-side with saws, hammers, and nails. The physical exertion was good for Lance, and the project distracted him from less healthy activities.

Just as the building project ended, Joy's parents recovered sufficiently for her to rejoin her husband. Feeling like newlyweds, Lance and Joy found a house, vacated their apartment, reclaimed their furniture, and settled down again to establish their normal and comfortable homelife.

Today their marriage is a model for others. While Lance regrets not fending off temptation earlier, he's equally thankful to God for his narrow escape. In counseling now with other ministers, he ceaselessly advocates self-restraint, self-discipline, and, when necessary, self-intervention. "Keep your armor on and your guard up. Defeat is not inevitable," he says, "and temptation is not irresistible. We have the power of Calvary and the means of grace. We may not be perfect, but God expects us to maintain consistent victory over all known sin. We can be 'more than conquerors through Him who loved us.'"

Therefore let him who thinks he stands take heed lest he fall. No temptation has overtaken you except such as is common to man; but God is faithful, who will not allow you to be tempted beyond what you are able, but with the temptation will also make the way of escape, that you may be able to bear it (1 Cor. 1:12–13). ✱

*This story is true. The names and some of the details
have been altered to protect identities.

Quotes for the Pastor's Wall

" Our prayers should be insistent. There comes a time, in spite of our soft, modern ways, when we must be desperate in prayer, when we must wrestle, when we must be outspoken, shameless and importunate. . . . It is not that we overcome the reluctance of God, but rather that we take hold of His willingness, plowing through principalities and powers, inviting His almighty power into our desperate needs. "

—Cameron V. Thompson

OCTOBER 13, 2002

SUGGESTED SERMON

How Can I Find God's Will For Me

By Dr. Melvin Worthington   *Date preached:*

Scripture: Proverbs 3:5–6: Trust in the LORD with all your heart, And lean not on your own understanding; In all your ways acknowledge Him, And He shall direct your paths.

Introduction: When Eskimos travel through northern Alaska, they are often in danger, for there are no natural landmarks and few permanent roads. In a snowstorm, even familiar trails are hard to follow, and the possibility of freezing to death is a constant threat. So the trails are marked with tripods, each bearing reflective tape. By following the tripods, the travelers can find their way. As we read the Bible, we continually come across the truth that God erects tripods for His children. This is not only assumed but illustrated over and over. We need divine guidance. Human schemes are wretched substitutes for divine guidance. Life is made up of choices, and very often we have no idea what choice to make. But wise Christians learn to spot God's tripods.

1. **The Prerequisites for Divine Guidance.** The first prerequisite is confidence in the Sovereign: "Trust in the Lord with all your heart." The second prerequisite is caution regarding one's self: "And lean not on your own understanding." The third prerequisite is consideration: "In all your ways acknowledge Him." Our actions must be examined in light of God's will for our lives, consulting Him, recognizing that His plan for us is best (Jer. 29:11).

2. **The Promise of Divine Guidance.** "And He shall direct your ways." Proverbs 3:6b assures us that God guides His children in their daily lives. The Christian should never wonder or worry if God will guide. His guidance is *personal.* He wants to direct us—strait and plain—safely to our journey's end. God's guidance is *practical.* The Lord is vitally interested in directing us in every area, under all circumstances. God's guidance is *perfect*—infallible, reliable, and trustworthy. Divine guidance is *patient.* He leads His children step by step (Ps. 23:2).

3. **The Principles for Divine Guidance.** *Submission to the Sovereign* is a key principle in guidance (Rom. 12:1; Jonah 1:1–2). The Lord is not looking for better methods or bigger men or women. He is looking for surrendered hearts. Another principle of divine guidance is *searching the Scriptures* (Ps. 119:105). God speaks to His children through His Word. *Supplication in the Spirit* (James 1:5) is necessary to obtain divine guidance. Daily, disciplined, diligent prayer is never a waste of time, and very often the Lord gives us insights while we are in the very act of praying. We also need *suggestions from our soulmates*—the advice of our close friends and family members (Prov. 15:22). A final principle is *satisfaction in the soul* (Isa. 26:3), an inner conviction or "gut instinct," a sense of peace from God about a possible course of action. In his booklet, *Getting to Know the Will of God,* Dr. Alan Redpath tells about trying to decide whether he should enter the ministry or stay in his present profession as a chartered accountant of the staff of Imperial Chemical Industries, Ltd. He made a list on paper of all the reasons for staying in business, and each morning during his devotions, he asked the Lord to show him particular Bible verses that would counter or affirm the reasons listed. "Lord," he prayed, "I am not here to evade you. I am here because I want to know your will." What happened? "Day by day I turned to my Bible. Almost every day a verse seemed to speak to me and I began to write that verse against one of the arguments. At the end of a year, every argument in favor of staying in business had been wiped out. It took over a year, but I was not in a hurry. I

>>> *sermon continued on following page*

APPROPRIATE HYMNS AND SONGS

I Surrender All, Judson Vandeventer/ Winfield S. Weeden; Public Domain.

'Tis So Sweet To Trust In Jesus, Louisa Stead/William J. Kirkpatrick; Public Domain.

Trust in the Lord With All Your Heart, Rick Powell/Sylvia Powell; © 1977 Matterhorn Music, Inc.

All of My Life, Troy Shaw; © 1990 Integrity's Hosanna! Music (Admin. by Integrity Music Group, Inc.).

God's Gonna Do It Again, David Baroni/Niles Barop; © 1994 Niles Barop Music/Integrity's Praise! Music (Admin. by Integrity Music Group, Inc.).

was willing to wait; I wanted it to be in God's time. Too much was at stake to dash into the thing. I wanted to intelligently find the will of God. And I found it as I sought the Lord through my daily reading and meditation."

Conclusion: The great question is not "Will God guide me?"—but "Am I willing to be led?" Are you willing to do whatever He asks? Whenever? Wherever? His plans are perfect, His paths are pleasant, and His presence is promised for every step of the way. George Truett once said, "To know the will of God is the greatest knowledge. To do the will of God is the greatest achievement."

> *If thou but suffer God to guide thee*
> *and hope in him through all thy ways,*
> *he'll give thee strength, whate'er betide thee,*
> *and bear thee through the evil days.*

FOR THE BULLETIN

❋ On October 13, 54, Emperor Claudius died after eating poisonous mushrooms and was replaced by Nero. ❋ Crusaders returning from Palestine and Constantinople brought with them a treasure trove of "relics"—sacred objects from the Holy Land. All Europe was astir, bishop vying with bishop, church competing with church, to acquire and display various holy items. It isn't surprising, then, that England was beside itself on October 13, 1247, when some of "Christ's blood" arrived in London. King Henry III fasted and prayed through the night of October 12; then as morning broke he marched through London's streets, accompanying the priests in full regalia. He held aloft the vase containing the holy liquid. ❋ The "Knights of Christ and of the Temple of Solomon," organized to protect European Christian pilgrims traveling to the Holy Land, became very wealthy. Philip the Fair of France, eyeing their wealth, used a disgruntled knight to bring charges against the Order. On the night of October 13, 1307, the "most accursed day in history," all the Templars in France were rounded up and arrested. Philip used torture to obtain confessions, and many of the knights died in indescribable agony. Pope Clement was persuaded to disband the Templars and expand the persecution across Europe. ❋ October 13, 1605, marks the death of Calvinist Theodore Beza. ❋ Knowles Shaw, author of "Bringing in the Sheaves" was born on October 13, 1834. ❋ The funeral service for Catherine Booth, co-founder with her husband of the Salvation Army, was conducted on October 13, 1890. Prior to her burial, 27,000 people viewed her body.

WORSHIP HELPS

Worship Theme:
If we trust in the Lord with all our heart and acknowledge Him in all our ways, God will direct our steps.

Call to Worship:
Who is like You, O Lord, among the gods? Who is like You, glorious in holiness, fearful in praises, doing wonders? You in Your mercy have led forth the people whom You have redeemed; You have guided them in Your strength... (Ex. 15:11–13).

Medley of Scripture Reading:
The Lord is my shepherd; I shall not want. He makes me to lie down in green pastures; He leads me beside the still waters. He restores my soul; He leads me.... Lead me, O Lord, in Your righteousness. Lead me in Your truth and teach me. Teach me Your way, O Lord, and lead me in a smooth path. For You are my rock and my fortress; Therefore, for Your name's sake, lead me and guide me. I will instruct you and teach you in the way you should go; I will guide you with My eye. Search me, O God, and know my heart; try me, and know my anxieties; and see if there is any wicked way in me, and lead me in the way everlasting.

Taken from Psalm 23:1–2; 5:8; 25:5; 27:11; 31:1; 32:8; 139:23–24.

Kids Talk

Have a toy bird, a picture of a bird, or even a live bird in the cage. Do a little research about migratory patterns and help the children grasp the wonder of God's creative genius in implanting an "advanced guidance system" in the tiny brains of migratory birds. Remind them that God is even more concerned about us than about the sparrows of the air. Share with the Proverbs 3:5–6, assuring them that God has a wonderful plan for their lives.

STATS, STORIES AND MORE

Someone Once Said . . .

"To go as I am led, to go when I am led, to go where I am led... it is that which has been for twenty years the one prayer of my life."
—A. T. Pierson

"God generally guides me by presenting reasons to my mind for acting in a certain way."
—John Wesley

"God generally guides [us] by the exercise of [our] sanctified judgment."
—J. Oswald Sanders

"The man or woman who is wholly and joyously surrendered to Christ can't make a wrong choice—any choice will be the right one."
—A. W. Tozer

"Has it ever struck you that the vast majority of the will of God for your life has already been revealed in the Bible? That is a crucial thing to grasp."
—Paul Little in Affirming the Will of God

"Belief that divine guidance is real rests upon two foundation-facts: first, the reality of God's plan for us; second, the ability of God to communicate with us. On both these facts the Bible has much to say."
—J. I. Packer

"Never doubt in the darkness what God has shown you in the light."
"The will of God—nothing more, nothing less."

Navigational Systems

Billions of dollars are spent on modern guidance and navigational systems. During the arms race of the Cold War, missiles became capable of hitting targets thousands of miles away with reasonable accuracy. The Cruise Missile represented a breakthrough in its ability to consistently land within meters of its intended target. This stunning accuracy was a direct result of the guidance system called TERCOM, which stands for TERrain COntour Matching. The technology behind the TERCOM guidance system has been around for a long time, the first test of an aircraft with a TERCOM guidance system occurring in 1961. But the technology didn't appear promising at the time and was largely forgotten until the advent of small, powerful computers in the 1970s. God's guidance system has been around a long time, and is programmed according to the instructions of Proverbs 3:5–6.

Additional Sermons and Lesson Ideas

The Best Christians Are Dead Christians

Date preached:

SCRIPTURE: Colossians 3:1–4

INTRODUCTION: As missionary James Calvert approached the Fiji Islands, the captain of the ship tried to discourage him from setting ashore on a cannibal island. "You will lose your life and the lives of those with you if you go among such savages," he said. Calvert only replied, "We died before we came here." This passage says, "For you died, and your life is hidden with Christ in God."

1. **Dead People Have a New Master.** This passage tells us that Christ is: (1) Risen; (2) Reigning; and (3) Returning.
2. **Dead People Have New Values.** Seek (set your hearts on) things above.
3. **Dead People Have a New Perspective.** We're not enchanted with the things of earth, but hidden with Christ in God.
4. **Dead People Have a New Future.** "When Christ appears...."

CONCLUSION: Can you sing, "Dying with Jesus, by death reckoned mine; Living with Jesus, a new life divine; Looking to Jesus till glory doth shine, Moment by moment, O Lord, I am Thine"?

Right Where You Are

Date preached:

By Kevin Riggs

SCRIPTURE: Various Scriptures.

INTRODUCTION: Posted throughout most amusement parks are maps, and on each map there is usually some type of icon indicating, "You are here." One thing the Bible teaches is that wherever we are, that is where God will meet us. A quick survey of eight individuals in the Bible underline this truth.

1. **Moses** (Ex. 3:1–4). God met Moses while Moses was on the job.
2. **Elijah** (1 Kings 19:3–9). God met Elijah while Elijah was depressed.
3. **Jonah** (Jonah 2:1). God met Jonah while Jonah was running from Him.
4. **The Demon-Possessed Man** (Mark 5:15). God met the demon-possessed man in the middle of all his problems.
5. **A Centurion** (Mark 9:24). God met the Centurion in the middle of his doubts.
6. **Zacchaeus** (Luke 19:3). God met Zacchaeus while Zacchaeus was only mildly curious in Jesus.
7. **The Criminal** (Luke 23:43). God met the criminal while he was dying.
8. **Saul** (Acts 9:24). God met Saul in the middle of Saul's religion.

CONCLUSION: Wherever you are, Jesus will meet you there.

OCTOBER 20, 2002

SUGGESTED SERMON

Green Leaf in Drought Time

Date preached:

By Drew Wilkerson

Scripture: Jeremiah 17:7–8 "Blessed is the man who trusts in the LORD, And whose hope is the LORD. For he shall be like a tree planted by the waters, Which spreads out its roots by the river, And will not fear when heat comes; But its leaf will be green, And will not be anxious in the year of drought, Nor will cease from yielding fruit.

Introduction: The prefix *un* can mean "to reverse action." In a nutshell, this is the meaning of God's intervention in our lives. He wants to reverse the negative actions and decisions we make. George Eliot said, "It is never too late to be what we might have become." The good news is that God is in the business of transformation! He wants to help us become our best. But just how do we change? Often we know what we need to do differently, but we lack either the desire or the ability to put the change into effect. In the two verses of today's text, the prophet Jeremiah helps us out.

1. **Trust Unconditionally.** We don't have the strength to change ourselves, but God does; and change comes about as we trust Him to work His grace through our lives. In verse 9 Jeremiah acknowledges the root problem concerning trust when he says, "The heart is deceitful above all things and beyond cure." Trust is an essential need in our world today, but it is in short supply... *except in God's economy.* Notice what Jeremiah tells us, "Blessed is the man who trusts in the Lord, whose confidence is in him." We don't need to worry or fret. God is able to handle all of the concerns we bring Him. In fact, when we decide we want to partner with God to change, we are promised blessings. As St. Augustine put it, "God is more anxious to bestow His blessings on us than we are to receive them." We must believe that God can think pure thoughts through us, love unlovely people through us, do blessed deeds through us, that He can, in short, live His Christ-life through us by His Spirit. Major Ian Thomas once said, "All there is of God is available to the man who is available to all there is of God."

2. **Grow Uninhibitedly.** Richard Foster said, "Superficiality is the curse of our age. The doctrine of instant satisfaction is a primary spiritual problem. The desperate need today is not for a greater number of intelligent people, or gifted people, but for deep people." Jeremiah describes for us the picture of a healthy Christian who is changing and growing in his or her walk with God. The growing child of God will be like a tree planted by the water. The roots are deep, spreading out, bringing nourishment and maturity. It is no secret that every person needs to grow. It is not natural or easy, but it is possible. The key is to embrace the life God has given us with enthusiasm. Then can we become intimate with God. We will grow without limit, and our roots will go deep.

3. **Live Unforgettably.** Jeremiah reminds his readers that those who are intimate with God will not fear change, but embrace it, becoming a little more like Christ every day. Someone once said, "Don't wait for your ship to come in, swim out to it." The Christian who is deeply rooted in God does not have to worry or fear. When life becomes intense and someone turns up the heat, it is okay. Our roots are refreshed by living water. Our leaves, our attitudes toward others, are always green. Even in times of drought, our lives produce fruit. Christians who are always changing and growing leave a lasting impact on all they touch. They are unforgettable! Such a man was Arthur Matthews, the last CIM missionary to get out of China. He endured months

>>> *sermon continued on following page*

APPROPRIATE HYMNS AND SONGS

My Faith Looks Up to Thee, Ray Palmer/Lowell Mason; Public Domain.

A New Creature, L.O. Sanderson/Thomas O. Chisholm; © 1935. Renewed 1963 L.O. Sanderson (Admin. by Leon B. Sanderson).

Lord, Be Glorified, Bob Kilpatrick; © 1978 Bob Kilpatrick Music (Admin. by The Lorenz Corporation).

The Path of the Righteous, Michael Massa; © 1987 Integrity's Hosanna! Music (Admin. by Integrity Music Group, Inc.).

Your Grace, Andy Park; © 1998 Mercy/Vineyard Publishing.

of terror and uncertainty, but he later said that by leaning on Jeremiah 17:7–9, he remained victorious in his spirit. His biography by Isabel Kuhn is entitled, *Green Leaf in Drought Time.*

Conclusion: Are your leaves green in drought time? People can be very shallow in this day of "instant life." But, only through the daily process of change can we grow into the people God has ordained us to be. Robert Browning said, "My business is not to remain myself, but to make the absolute best of what God made." Jeremiah tells us the secret of change. It is locked up in two little letters, "un." It is time to reverse the negative actions and habits that are keeping us from becoming intimate with God. It is time to change, and with God's help we can. With God's help we will.

FOR THE BULLETIN

❋ In 858, Emperor Michael III deposed Ignatius, Patriarch of Constantinople, and replaced him with a scholar and diplomat, Photius. When Ignatius refused to abdicate, the Eastern church was left with the problem of having two leaders. When Emperor Michael was assassinated, Photius was condemned to prison. On October 20, 869, he appeared before the Council of St. Sophia, but on being questioned he either kept silent or answered in the words of Christ before Pilate. Not until Ignatius's death in 877 did Photius resume his office. ❋ Peter Damian, a Benedictine monk, advocated self-flagellation as a means of subduing worldly pleasures. Monks began lashing themselves while reciting the Psalms. This practice remained localized and limited to monasteries for 200 years, but in the thirteenth century, it enflamed the masses. Great parades of thousands from all classes and of all ages marched through the streets singing hymns and scourging themselves. On this day, October 20, 1349, self-flagellation was condemned by a papal bull. ❋ On October 20, 1894, missionary Julia K. MacKenzie sailed for China. ❋ October 20, 1913, marks the death of Mary Lathbury, author of "Break Thou The Bread of Life." She was an artist whose illustrations appeared in magazines and children's books. But, plagued with poor eyesight, she closed her shop and retreated to Lake Chautauqua in New York. She later wrote her hymn while sitting on a hillside overlooking the lake and reading the story of Christ feeding the multitudes. ❋ October 20, 1632, is the birthday of Sir Christopher Wren, architect.

WORSHIP HELPS

Worship Theme:
God changes those who trust Him, giving them a flourishing and fruitful life

Call to Worship:
Praise the LORD from the earth, You great sea creatures and all the depths; Fire and hail, snow and clouds; Stormy wind, fulfilling His word; Mountains and all hills; Fruitful trees and all cedars... Let them praise the name of the LORD (Ps. 148:7–9, 13).

Hymn Story: My Faith Looks Up To Thee
"My Faith Looks Up To Thee" was written by school teacher Ray Palmer, 22, in New York City. One evening Palmer sat at his desk and wrote this poem as a personal prayer to the Heavenly Father, weeping over the words as he wrote them. He penned this in his diary, "I wrote tonight a simple poem. I wrote just what I felt with little effort. I recollect that I penned the last words with tender emotion." He copied the words into the little leather journal he carried with him. Two years passed, and one day he chanced to meet Dr. Lowell Mason, "the father of American hymnology," who asked if he had any words for a new hymn. The two men ducked into a store and Palmer copied the words of "My Faith Looks Up To Thee," which Mason put into his pocket. That afternoon, as the musician read the words at home the music came easily. Two days later, the men bumped into each other again. "Mr. Palmer," said Mason, "you may live many years and do many good things, but I think you will be best known to posterity as the author of 'My Faith Looks Up to Thee.'"

Benediction:
O God, grant to us now glimpses of Your beauty, and make us worthy at length to behold it unveiled for evermore; through Jesus Christ our Lord. Amen.

STATS, STORIES AND MORE

Someone Once Said . . .

"Be willing to give up all that you now are to be all that you can become."
"We cannot become what we need to be by remaining what we are."
"It's not the mountain we conquer, but ourselves."
—*Edmund Hillary, first to climb Mt. Everest*

"When you're through changing, you're through."
—*Bruce Barton*

Hoping in the Lord

Charles Price Jones, born in Georgia in 1865, was an African-American holiness preacher in the Deep South who endured much persecution and abuse. In 1900 in McComb, Mississippi, Jones was holding revival services when a white bootlegger fired five shots into the meeting. Though no one was killed, Jones was greatly disturbed. He turned in his Bible to Jeremiah 17:7. Inspired by that verse, he wrote the hymn "Happy with Jesus Alone."

John Gill's Comments on Jeremiah 17:8

Not as a "heath or shrub," but as a "tree," a green olive tree, a palm tree, a cedar in Lebanon, a fruitful flourishing tree; and he is one that really is a tree of righteousness, that is filled with the fruits of righteousness; and not like one of the trees of the wood, that grows wild, or as a wild olive tree, but as one "planted" in a garden, vineyard, or field; and is one that is planted in Christ, in the likeness of His death and resurrection, and in the house of the Lord; and that not only by means of the engrafted word, and of gospel ministers, who plant and water instrumentally; but by the Lord himself, as the efficient cause; and therefore called "the planting of the Lord"; and such plants as shall never be plucked up (Isa. 60:21)... such an one is rooted in Christ, and in the love of God, which is as a river; with which being watered, he casts out his roots as Lebanon, as the cedars there; and is both firm and fruitful (Hos. 14:5).

Additional Sermons and Lesson Ideas

A Portrait of Peace

Date preached:

SCRIPTURE: Psalm 131

INTRODUCTION: God gave each of us an outsized capacity for imagination. Many sports teams employ psychologists to help their players visualize winning games. In Psalm 131, the writer uses his powers of imagination to visualize himself as calmed and quieted.

1. **A Statement of Humility** (v. 1). Be careful about your motives and ambitions. We put ourselves under dysfunctional pressure when we strive for things simply to feed our pride. David warns here about over-reaching.
2. **A Picture of Tranquility** (v. 2). As a small child feels secure sleeping in the arms of a parent, so we should feel secure in our Heavenly Father's arms.
3. **An Attitude of Stability** (v. 3). We are called to *hope* in the Lord from this time forth and forever. Hope is steady, stable trust in a guaranteed outcome, regardless of the shifting sands of ups and downs.

CONCLUSION: The next time you are tired, tense, and troubled, try a little sanctified visualization.

Truths for Today

Date preached:

By Dr. Melvin Worthington

SCRIPTURE: 2 Timothy 3:1–17

INTRODUCTION: We're alarmed about the disintegration of society, but a casual reading of the Bible reminds us that the world has always been a dangerous place for God's people. Human history is filled with wars, death, pestilence, persecution and pain. Paul describes our era as "perilous times." What instructions are we given for living through evil days?

1. **The Perilous Times** (vv. 1–9). World conditions will get progressively worse. Trials, persecutions and afflictions will intensify from Pentecost unto the second coming of the Lord.
2. **The Personal Testimony** (vv. 11–13). In the midst of this darkness, Paul didn't wring his hands and give up ministering to such a perverted and profane society. He simply appealed to his own life, labor and legacy. One of the greatest influences we can have in society is to demonstrate Christianity by our lives.
3. **The Prescribed Truth** (vv. 14–17). Timothy had known the Scriptures since his early years. Now he was to continue in them. The Bible is a living, lasting and life-giving book, perfect, powerful, profitable and productive. It is sufficient for doctrine, reproof, correction and instruction.

CONCLUSION: In perilous times, we must persevere with the Bible in our hands and the witness of the Spirit in our hearts.

John Livingstone

Among the Scottish Presbyterians—the "Covenanters"—was John Livingstone, born at Kilsyth, Scotland, in 1603, the son of a minister. John attended college intending to become a doctor, but he grew troubled about his life's calling and resolved to set aside a day for prayer. *Accordingly, on the day appointed, he retired to Cleghorn wood, where, after much confusion in the state of his soul, he at last thought it was made out to him that he must preach Jesus Christ.*

On January 2, 1625, he preached his first sermon in his father's pulpit. He was soon preaching regularly. For a while, Livingstone wrote out all his sermons, reading to the people from a manuscript. But one day when he rose to preach, he spotted some friends who had already heard the sermon he planned to give. He quickly chose a new text and scribbled some notes. He discovered *more assistance and more emotion in his own heart than ever he had found before; which made him never afterwards write any more of his sermons, except such short notes for the help of his memory.*

His greatest sermon was delivered on Monday, June 21, 1630. The night before, he and his companions had devoted the entire evening to prayer. Now Livingstone felt weak and frightened as he stepped into the pulpit, but, mustering his strength, he read his text, Ezekiel 36:25–26.

Here he was led out in such a melting strain, that, by the downpouring of the Spirit from on high, a most discernible change was wrought upon above 500 of the hearers, who either dated their conversion, or some remarkable confirmation, from that day forward.

It was the highlight of his ministry, but it wasn't the end of it. He continued preaching in Scotland until driven to Holland, where he served the Lord in exile until his death at age 78. ✴

Quotes for the Pastor's Wall

❝ But such a preacher I have never heard, and hope I never shall again. It was beyond description. I cannot say he preached false doctrine, or true, or any doctrine at all, but pure unmixed nonsense. Not one sentence did he utter that could do the least good to any one soul. Now and then a text of Scripture or a verse quotation was dragged in by head and shoulders. I could scarce refrain from stopping him. ❞

**—Charles Wesley in 1751,
on hearing a sermon by Methodist lay preacher
Michael Fenwick**

OCTOBER 27, 2002

The Fine Art of Forgiveness

Date preached:

Scripture: Matthew 18:21–35, especially verses 21–22 Then Peter came to Him and said, "Lord, how often shall my brother sin against me, and I forgive him? Up to seven times?" Jesus said to him, "I do not say to you, up to seven times, but up to seventy times seven."

Introduction: If you've ever gotten to a concert early, you've probably heard the musicians tuning their instruments. It isn't a particularly pleasant sound, but we know it is necessary for the harmony to come later. Instruments slip out of tune so easily. So do relationships. Many times harmony is missing from our relationships because our hearts are out of tune. In his book, *Untwisting Twisted Relationships,* William Backus wrote, "Though we expect from our relationships the sweetest moments life can offer, the brutal fact is that what parents, spouses, sweethearts, friends, and neighbors say and do can cause a large share of life's miseries." One of our greatest challenges is to learn the fine art of forgiveness. In today's passage, Jesus had been talking about harmony, telling the disciples how to work through interpersonal difficulties. While He was speaking, a question formed in Peter's mind. "Lord," he asked, "how often shall I forgive my brother?" In response, Jesus said, in effect, "There is no limit to mercy. You are to go right on forgiving, even if you must do so seventy times seven." To illustrate this, Jesus went on to tell them the parable of the unforgiving debtor. He had been forgiven of, say, $20 million, but he was unwilling to forgive his brother of a $20 debt. How, then, do we learn to forgive? There is no easy formula, but here are five suggestions that will help:

1. **Make Certain You've Received and Experienced God's Forgiveness Yourself.** When we receive Christ as Savior, we receive His forgiveness, and our sins are cast as far from us as east from west (Ps. 103:12). It isn't enough just to receive this forgiveness; we must experience it. That is, we must realize how fully we've been freed from guilt, shaking off our shame and leaving it behind us. A young minister was excessively harsh with his wife and congregation, often irritable and on edge. At the urging of friends, he sought counseling, and the root cause of his bitter attitude was unmasked. While in the armed forces in Korea, he had spent two weeks of R and R in Japan.

Walking the streets of Tokyo, lonely and homesick, he had fallen into temptation and visited a prostitute. He had confessed his sin to the Lord a thousand times, and in his head he knew he was forgiven. But the memory and the guilt plagued him, and he hated himself. His embittered attitude was poisoning his other relationships. When he finally visualized the extent of God's infinite forgiveness, he was set free and his whole attitude changed.

2. **Write Out Your Feelings of Resentment and Bitterness.** We can deal with spiritual problems better when we write them in a journal. This compresses angry-red, envious-green, and depression-blue emotions into black-and-white words that can be identified and dealt with. Offer your list to God in prayer, asking Him to flush these feelings from your system by the living waters of His Holy Spirit.

3. **Choose to forgive the person who wronged you.** Forgiveness isn't a feeling you float into, it is a choice you make.

4. **Keep on forgiving.** Forgiveness means never bringing up the issue again. When you forgive someone you're saying, "By the grace of God, this matter is gone. I will never bring it up again." Some people bury the hatchet, but keep the map showing where it lies. When Jesus told us to forgive our brother seventy times seven, He wasn't necessarily implying that the person

>>> *sermon continued on following page*

APPROPRIATE HYMNS AND SONGS

Whiter Than Snow, James Nicholson/William G. Fischer; Public Domain.

White As Snow, Leon Olguin; © 1990 Maranatha Praise, Inc./Sound Truth Publishing (Admin. by Maranatha! Music).

Wonderful, Merciful Savior, Dawn Rogers/Eric Wyse; © 1989 Word Music, Inc./Dayspring Music, Inc. (Admin. by Word Music Group, Inc.).

Forgive One Another, Lenny LeBlanc/Kelly Willard/Rita Balouche/Bill Batstone; © 1990 Maranatha! Music/Doulos Publishing (Admin. by Maranatha! Music).

Chose to Forgive, Rick Riso/Mark Levang; © 1994 Integrity's Hosanna! Music/Integrity's Praise! Music/Mom's Fudge Music (Admin. by Integrity Music, Inc.).

had sinned against us 490 times. Perhaps they have only sinned against us once, but we have to get on our knees 490 times, because the old resentments keep popping into our hearts.

5. **Continue growing in Christ.** It takes a lot of maturity to learn the fine art of forgiveness. It can't be accomplished apart from an increasingly mature Christianity. The older we grow in age, the deeper we should grow in Christ, and the higher we should grow in Calvary.

Conclusion: Perhaps you need the forgiveness of God today. Perhaps you need a forgiving spirit. Christ wants to forgive you of a debt of $20 million toward Him, and He wants you to forgive the $20 debts against you. Ephesians 4:31–32 says, "Get rid of all bitterness, rage, anger, harsh words, and slander, as well as all types of malicious behavior. Instead, be kind to each other, tenderhearted, forgiving one another, just as God through Christ has forgiven you."

FOR THE BULLETIN

❋ Constantine, battling for control of the Roman Empire, reached within five miles of Rome on October 27, 312. That night he had a dream that convinced him that his own destiny lay with Christianity. The next day, he entered Rome. ❋ On October 27, 623, Pope Honorius began his papacy. ❋ On October 27, 1516, Luther began lecturing from the book of Galatians. ❋ Michael Servetus was a physician whose study of theology led him to abandon the doctrine of the Trinity. He corresponded with John Calvin on the subject, nevertheless continued in his heresy, denying also the true divinity of Christ. In Geneva, Calvin had him arrested. On this day in 1553, Servetus was burned at the stake. ❋ On October 27, 1670, Vavasour Powell died in London's Fleet prison. He was one of the most celebrated and popular preachers of his day, and throngs of people went to hear him at fairs, markets, in the fields, and on the mountains of Wales. He is buried in Bunhill Fields. ❋ Francis Asbury, Methodist pioneer, arrived in America on October 27, 1771. He wrote, "This day we landed in Philadelphia where we were directed to the house of Mr. Francis Harris who kindly entertained us and brought us to a large church where we met with a considerable congregation. The people looked on us with pleasure, receiving us as angels of God. When I came near the American shore, my very heart melted within me." ❋ On October 27, 1978, the complete New International Version of the Bible was first published.

WORSHIP HELPS

Worship Theme:
We best experience God's forgiveness when, with it, we forgive both ourselves and those who have sinned against us.

Call to Worship:
Oh, give thanks to the LORD, for He is good! For His mercy endures forever (1 Chron. 16:34).

Appropriate Scripture Readings:
Numbers 14:17–19; 1 Kings 8:33–36; 1 John 1:1–9

Offertory Comments:
Though churchgoers are giving more dollars than they did 30 years ago, the portion of their disposable income it represents is less, according to a study of 30 mainline Protestant and evangelical denominations by Empty Tomb Inc., an Illinois research group. For 10 denominations and the Southern Baptist Convention, whose finances were studied more closely, the picture was even grimmer. Their percentage of giving was lower than it had even been in 1933, at the height of the Depression. The denominations received more than $17 billion in contributions three years ago, compared with $2.7 billion in 1968. But that growth did not keep track with increases in income. On average, churchgoers were giving just 2.5 percent of their after-tax income to churches in 1998, contrasted with 3.1 percent in 1968.

Pastoral Prayer:
Father of Mercy, we are attracted to and attached to our sins as with superglue, and unless You lessen their hold on our hearts, we are without hope. O Lord, convict us. Lord, give us repentant hearts and teach us how to repent, how to change our ways, how to break free from old patterns, how to put off the "old man." Help us to put on the new man, making no provision for the flesh to fulfill the lusts thereof. And, Lord, teach us to forgive those who have sinned against us. Melt every bitter thought in the bubbling oil of Your compassion. Sweep away every resentment with the broom of Your love. Help each of us to forgive with our hearts that one person against whom we still hold a grudge. In Jesus' name, Amen.

STATS, STORIES AND MORE

Someone Once Said . . .

"Every one says forgiveness is a lovely idea, until they have something to forgive."

—*C. S. Lewis*

"The West remembers enough about Christianity to feel guilty for its sins, but not enough to recall where forgiveness comes from."

—*Dave Breese*

Clara Barton

Clara Barton, founder of the American Red Cross, was reminded one day of a vicious deed that someone had done to her years before. But she acted as if she had never even heard of the incident. "Don't you remember it?" her friend asked. "No," came Barton's reply, "I distinctly remember forgetting it."

Corrie Ten Boom

It wasn't easy for Corrie Ten Boom to forgive her Nazi captors who had tormented her at Ravensbrück and had caused the death of her sister Betsy. Ten years after her release, Corrie ran into a lady who wouldn't look her in the eyes. Asking about her, Corrie was told the woman had been a nurse at a concentration camp. Suddenly the memories flashed back. Corrie recalled taking Betsy to the infirmary to see this woman. Betsy's feet were paralyzed and she was dying. The nurse had been cruel and sharp-tongued.

Corrie's hatred returned with vengeance. Her rage so boiled that she knew of but one thing to do. "Forgive me," she cried out, "Forgive my hatred, O Lord. Teach me to love my enemies."

The blood of Jesus Christ seemed to suddenly cool her embittered heart, and Corrie felt the rage being displaced with a divine love she couldn't explain. She began praying for the woman, and one day shortly afterward she called the hospital where the nurse worked and invited the woman to a meeting at which she was speaking. "What!" replied the nurse. "Do you want *me* to come?"

"Yes; that is why I called you."

"Then I'll come."

That evening the nurse listened carefully to Corrie's talk, and afterward Corrie sat down with her, opened her Bible, and explained 1 John 4:9. The woman seemed to thirst for Corrie's quiet, confident words about God's love for us, his enemies. That night, a former captive led her former captor to "a decision that made the angels sing."

Additional Sermons and Lesson Ideas

A Heart for God's Word

Date preached:

By Ed Dobson

SCRIPTURE: Mark 4: 13–20

INTRODUCTION: The seed in this story represents God's Word. The purpose of the seed is to take root, grow, and produce fruit. The various soils represent our hearts. Some people have:

1. **Resistant hearts**, like hardened soil. Satan, like a bird, seeks to separate us from God's Word.
2. **Impulsive hearts.** Initially these people embrace the Word with enthusiasm, but just as quickly they fall away. They had no depth, no serious commitment, just an impulsive, emotional response to God.
3. **Some have divided hearts.** Our obsession with temporal things can choke the Word of God in our lives.
4. **Some have good soil.** Notice the verbs in verse 20: "Hear... Accept... Bear fruit...." The good soil represents someone who continually listens to God's Word, continually accepts it, and who is continually producing good fruit.

CONCLUSION: God's Word embraced in our heart will sustain us until we see Jesus. Deep in the recesses of our souls, God's Word embraced and welcomed and hidden and loved and practiced sustains us through all of life until we see Christ.

My God, My God, Why?

Date preached:

SCRIPTURE: Matthew 27:45–46

INTRODUCTION: The biggest little word in the dictionary is "Why?" We are tempted a thousand times to ask "Why?" when heartache and disaster strike. But just as the seven lean cattle in Pharaoh's dream swallowed up the seven fat cows, so the "Why?" of the Lord Jesus Christ on the cross swallows up all our other whys.

1. **The Curtain of Darkness** (v. 45). It was a real darkness, but it also represented sin, judgment, sadness, and hell.
2. **The Cry of Distress** (v. 46). Martin Luther once set himself to study this profound saying of Jesus. For a long time, he continued in deepest meditation, then finally exclaimed in amazement, "God forsaken of God! Who can understand it!"

CONCLUSION: All our whys are going to be answered in heaven. Until then, we live by promises, not by explanations; but one day our question marks will be straightened into exclamation points, and our "alas" will turn into "Hallelujah!"

How To Enjoy a Long Pastorate

An Interview with Rev. L. H. Hardwick, Jr.

Senior Pastor of Christ Church, Nashville, for 50 years

Is there a single, master-secret to a long pastorate?

I don't think so. There are a number of secrets. Recently I listed ten things I've learned about ministry after 50 years in the same church:

- I've learned we must be absolutely sure of God's call.
- I've learned the value of humility.
- I've learned the importance and value of love, understanding, and fair play.
- I've learned the value and power of faith—faith in God, in God's Word, in myself, and in the gifts that God has given me.
- I've learned the value of patience and perseverance. My old district superintendent used to tell us, "Boys, keep your reverse gear in working order." In other words, there are times we have to back up and wait on the Lord.
- I've learned to be an encourager, a healer. I try to preach to heal, inspire, motivate, and encourage.
- I've learned the value of peace and harmony and good fellowship. I'm better as a lover than as a fighter.
- I've learned to be a strong visionary leader. I tell ministers to be cautious until God gives you a clear vision for you and your church, but once you have the vision be willing to take the risks necessary to accomplish it.
- I've learned that people respond to excellence. We must do all that we do with excellence.
- And I have learned the value and importance of celebratory worship and praise.

Do you think some people leave the ministry because they're insecure of their call?

Yes. And because their ambitions are not godly ambitions. We must be absolutely sure of God's call. It comes in different ways to different persons. Abraham and Paul are examples of dramatic calls. Jeremiah was called at birth. In my own life, I've known since I was five years old that I was supposed to be a pastor.

Would you be happy in a smaller church?

My happiness is not based on the size of the church as much as on feeling that I'm doing what I need to be doing to bring people to God, to help them grow up in the faith, and to learn the value of worship in their daily lives.

How do you begin to develop excellence in a church's ministries?

I don't know exactly; I just know that it's necessary. People respond to excellence. In your preaching, you may not have the gifts to be a great orator, but you can study and prepare and preach as good as you can do. It's also true in our sacramental duties— baptisms, weddings, baby dedications. These things need to be done with good taste and class. To be sloppy with the things of God is insulting and inexcusable. I come from a poor background in West Tennessee. We were not "dirt poor," but we were poor. We attended a Pentecostal church, and it was the lowest on the rungs in the church ladder as far as status was concerned. But I learned there that things can still be done with excellence.

Do you ever repeat sermons?

Yes, definitely. I always date my sermons. For instance, last night . . . We're getting ready to move in some new directions, and last night I preached on the subject of change. It was a sermon I had preached in the late 80s. I used basically the same outline, but different illustrations. Yes, I'll go back to messages I preached in the past. You can always use the sermon outline as a framework to hang the message you want to give to your people.

Over the years, has Christ Church had consistent growth, or have there been ups and down in the church's statistics?

We have had about five different growth periods in these 50 years, three plateaus, and a couple of periods of decline. When we were thinking of moving from Woodbine into a new area of town we faced a decline. I could see that the old Woodbine area was going down and becoming industrial, and I knew that our future lay further out. Still we had people coming from all over town; and particularly some of the older people didn't want to move. I try to be a consensus builder. I tried to build a consensus and was pretty well able to do it to buy property in 1972, but in the process we dropped from a high average of 366 to a low of about 181 over about four years. The interesting thing is that during that period, our finances didn't drop. We lost some people by moving out here, but ultimately we gained more than we lost. Finally, even most of the people we lost came back.

What is your average attendance today?

About 3,600.

Do you have any advice for a minister who is about to leave his church or his ministry due to discouragement?

I understand it in one way; but in another way I'm a little frustrated about it. As I mentioned, I've learned to wait and persevere patiently. Let patience have her perfect work. Peter said that if we do well and suffer for it patiently, this is acceptable to God. Discouragement is present in any profession. If you're a businessman you go through highs and lows. I have businessmen here in the church that have gone through bankruptcy. Those people who are resilient when they get knocked down will get up again, and they will succeed. My old pastor used to say, "It doesn't matter how many times life knocks you down. What really matters is how many times you get up." We have all kinds of problems in the ministry. The church is a volunteer-led institution, in many ways the most difficult institution there is. In the military, people obey orders, or else. In business, people work or lose their jobs. In the church we have absolutely nothing we can hold over people's heads to make them work or volunteer or sing in the choir or usher. But God has made it that way because He wants us to learn to live together, endure together, and work together. The church is a mutual toleration society. A lot of preachers give up and quit when they could press on and succeed.

Do you have any plans to retire?

No! I've only been here 50 years. Why should I retire at this young age in my life? ✱

Bill Borden

A layer of sweat lathered his body and drenched his bed in the drab turn-of-the-century Cairo hospital. Looking at him, you wouldn't have recognized him as a millionaire . . . a brilliant scholar . . . or even as a young, well-built athlete.

He was all those things . . . and more!

Bill Borden grew up on Chicago's Gold Coast. His family's fortune had come from real estate and from Borden's Condensed Milk. But when Bill was seven, his mother discovered the sincere milk of the Word, becoming a Christian and joining Moody Church. Bill began attending too, and was soon led to Christ by Pastor R. A. Torrey.

Bill attended an elite boarding high school and excelled in both academics and athletics. He graduated fourth in his class, and as a reward, his father gave him a year-long trip around the world. Bill left California aboard a ship that carried several missionaries bound for Asia.

From Japan he wrote his mother: "Your request that I pray for God's very best for my life is not hard to do, for I've been praying that for a long time. Although I've never thought seriously about being a missionary until lately, I was somewhat interested in that line. I think this trip is going to show me things in a new light. I met such pleasant young people on the steamer who were going out as missionaries and meeting them influenced me. . . . I don't know what you will think of this."

From Japan, Bill and his guide crossed Asia to Europe. In Rome, Bill received a reply to his letter. His mother rejoiced at his growing interest in missions; his father wanted him to wait until he was 21 before making a vocational decision.

In England, Bill encountered Pastor Torrey, who was preaching in London. Borden attended one of the services, and Torrey challenged his listeners to surrender their lives totally to Christ. Bill was deeply moved as he stood with others and sang the hymn, "I Surrender All." Back in America, Borden entered Yale University. A friend later wrote: "Bill came to college far ahead, spiritually, of any of us. He had already given his heart in full surrender to Christ. He had formed his purpose to become a missionary, and all through college and seminary that purpose never wavered. We, his classmates, learned to lean on him and find in him strength as solid as a rock."

Bill joined 4,000 others from across the nation at a student convention that year in Nashville, Tennessee. Missionaries from 26 countries spoke of their fields, and one of them, Samuel Zwemer, made a moving appeal for Muslim evangelization: "Of course it will cost life. It is not an expedition of ease nor a picnic excursion to which we are called. It is going to cost many a life, and not lives only, but prayers and tears and blood."

Borden returned to Yale committed to reaching the Chinese Muslims. But his eyes saw present needs, not just future challenges. Concerned that New Haven had no rescue mission, he purchased a downtown building, started a work, and hired a director. Then Bill Borden—a handsome, athletic, brilliant college sophomore worth 40 to 50 million dollars by today's standards—spent his evenings witnessing to broken men. He also led Bible studies on campus. He was chairman of the Student Missionary Union. He played football and baseball for Yale, and he was on the wrestling team. He was near the top of his class and was elected president of Phi Beta Kappa. Atop all that, he oversaw an incredible financial portfolio, devouring the *Wall Street Journal* daily and making frequent business trips to Chicago.

Following graduation, Bill attended Princeton Seminary and served on the boards of Moody Bible Institute, China Inland Mission, and the National Bible Institute. He graduated from Princeton in 1912 and, after summering in Switzerland, he returned to tour American colleges on behalf of China Inland Mission. At Andover he expressed his burden for missions this way: "If ten men are carrying a log, nine of them on the little end and one at the heavy end, and you want to help, which end will you lift?"

When a friend asked him about getting married he replied that he thought it cruel for a man to ask a girl to go with him to one of the most difficult mission fields; he said he had no intention of marrying. He felt it would be wrong to the girl and would hinder his highest efficiency in the field he had in view.

Another friend observed, "No one would have known from Borden's life and talk that he was a millionaire; but no one could have helped knowing that he was a Christian and alive for missions."

When Bill was ordained into the ministry at Moody Church the newspapers made much of it, and the nation followed him on December 17, 1912, as he boarded the S. S. Mauritania bound for language study in Egypt. On the night before his departure, his frail mother fell asleep asking herself again and again, "Is it, after all, worth while?" In the morning she awoke, a quiet voice in her heart answering, "God so loved the world that He gave His only begotten Son."

"It was strength for the day," she said, "and for all the days to come."

Arriving in Cairo in 1913 at age 25, Bill immediately plunged into Arabic and Chinese studies. But within weeks, he developed a headache and fever. On Easter Sunday, the small missionary community in Cairo was shocked to hear that Bill had cerebral meningitis. Serum was injected into his spinal cord. Over the next several days, his friends watched with growing anxiety.

Mrs. Borden had left America to join Bill for a vacation in Lebanon, but being informed of his illness, she diverted toward Egypt. His sister in London also set out for Cairo. In America, prayer circles were activated from coast to coast. Strong men wept at the thought of losing him.

Bill's sister arrived at his bedside. Finally, his aged mother reached the Egyptian border and started by train for Cairo, arriving there at 1 p.m.

Bill had passed away four hours earlier.

A wave of sorrow arose around the world. Practically every American newspaper told Borden's life story. Biographies of him were translated into Chinese and shipped across the nation he had dreamed of reaching.

R. A. Torrey wrote Mrs. Borden, "I know of no young man in this country or in England from whose life I expected greater things. But God has His own way of carrying out His purposes. He has some larger plan of usefulness through your son's departure than could have been realized by his remaining here."

Indeed, hundreds of young people, stirred by his example, offered themselves for overseas service. When his will was opened, it was discovered that Bill had left almost his entire fortune to Christian and missionary causes. Even today, his example has moved a new generation to consider global missions.

How can we explain such a life? A final message from Bill Borden—a paper stuffed under his hospital pillow—told the secret. On it he had scribbled a message that summarized his life: "No Reserve! No Retreat! No Regrets!"

"Of course it will cost life," Zwemer had said. "It is not an expedition of ease nor a picnic excursion to which we are called. It is going to cost many a life."

It did. And it does! ✿

NOVEMBER 3, 2002

Principles for Prosperity

Date preached:

By Melvin Worthington

Scripture: Daniel 6:1–30, especially verses 1–4, 28 It pleased Darius to set over the kingdom one hundred and twenty satraps, to be over the whole kingdom; and over these, three governors, of whom Daniel was one, that the satraps might give account to them, so that the king would suffer no loss. Then this Daniel distinguished himself above the governors and satraps, because an excellent spirit was in him; and the king gave thought to setting him over the whole realm. So the governors and satraps sought to find some charge against Daniel concerning the kingdom; but they could find no charge or fault, because he was faithful; nor was there any error or fault found in him.... So this Daniel prospered in the reign of Darius and in the reign of Cyrus the Persian.

Introduction: *Successful, prosperous* and *great* are words we'd like to see used about ourselves. At the opening of Daniel 6, the prophet is described as "distinguished." At the end of the chapter he is described as "prosperous." Daniel was declared prosperous and successful from a Divine standpoint, and we would be wise to learn the principles which contributed to his remarkable life.

1. **Discernment of the Will of God** (chapters 1–6). The first principle was Daniel's discernment of the will of God for his life. He recognized he lived in Babylon by the will of God, not by chance. God had orchestrated the circumstances, causing all things to work together for Daniel's good. His ministry in the Babylonian court glowed with the conviction of being where God wanted him to be. This was the secret to his steadfastness and stability. Every Christian has the obligation of finding, following and finishing the will of God, of resting in God's sovereign leadership.

2. **Disposition in the Work of God** (v. 3). Daniel's disposition in the work of God magnified his ministry for a prolonged period in Babylon. He was preferred above other court leaders because of his excellent spirit. Daniel possessed divine genius, and when he spoke or acted it was with wisdom. He outshone all others. The spirit that characterized Daniel was genial, tender, sympathetic, seeing something good in the worst of men. An excellent spirit raises

us to supremacy. We should do and say things with excellence, knowing we represent the King.

3. **Discreet in our Walk with God** (vv. 4–5). Another pillar in Daniel's life was discreetness in his walk with God. Those who would enjoy permanent prosperity must walk so as to be above reproach. Daniel's purpose and policy were tested at every point, yet no character blemish could be found because he was faithful. He made up his mind to remain unspotted from the world. Can you say the same?

4. **Disciplined in our Worship of God** (v. 10). Daniel was disciplined in his worship of God, praying regularly with his windows open toward Jerusalem. Learning that his enemies were plotting his death, he went home, knelt, and prayed three times a day as he had been doing. His response to the king's decree was prayer. This is what our response should be. Rather than fussing and feuding we should give ourselves to prayer, praising God for His goodness and petitioning Him for our needs.

5. **Dependence on the Word of God** (v. 23). Dependence on the Word of God contributed to Daniel's prosperity. In the story of the lion's den, Daniel chose to obey God's Word instead of that of Darius. He chose to depend on God's promises rather than yield to society's pressures. Consequently, the king

>>> *sermon continued on following page*

APPROPRIATE HYMNS AND SONGS

I Will Celebrate, Rita Balouche; © 1990 Maranatha Praise, Inc. (Admin. by The Copyright Company).

I Will Praise Him, Margaret Jenkins Harris; Public Domain.

Come We That Know the Lord, Isaac Watts/Aaron Williams; Public Domain.

God Is Able, Chris Machen/Robert Sterling; © 1988 Word Music, Inc./Desert North Music/Two Fine Boys Music (Admin. by Word Music Group, Inc.).

God With Us, Graham Kendrick; © 1988 Make Way Music (Admin. by Music Services).

realized that Daniel had been protected by his God. The Word of God is our authority and anchor in all circumstances. Reliance upon the Word of God results in prosperity.

6. **Display the Wisdom of God** (vv. 1–30). In all his actions, Daniel displayed the wisdom of God. Those who lack wisdom are admonished to ask for it (James 1:5). Daniel's entire life pivoted on divine wisdom. Being a Christian does not give one the right to act foolishly.

Conclusion: Incorporating these six principles in our lives will bring abundant and abounding blessings. Character does not hinder one's career. Daniel had served in Babylon for about 80 years at this point. He had a much bigger influence on Babylon than Babylon did on him. When we walk with the Lord, the world takes notice.

FOR THE BULLETIN

❋ In the fall of 1414, Pope John XXIII convened an ecumenical council in Constance aimed at eradicating "heresy" from the Western Church. Against the advice of friends, the Bohemian Reformer, John Hus, departed for Constance, arriving there by horseback on November 3, 1414. He was seized, thrown into a miserable cell near the latrines with their overpowering stench, and eventually condemned and burned at the stake. ❋ On November 3, 1534, England's Parliament passed the Act of Supremacy making King Henry VIII head of the English church, a role formerly held by the Pope. ❋ November 3, 1723 is the birth date of Samuel Davies, early American Presbyterian minister whose eloquent sermons electrified and inspired Patrick Henry. Davies was among the founders and presidents of Princeton University. He died at age 38. ❋ Alexander Cruden was born in Scotland on May 31, 1699. His father, a strict Puritan, forbade games on the Lord's Day, so Alexander entertained himself by tracing words through the Bible. He eventually moved to London and began working on his *Concordance*, which, when published in 1737, became an immediate success. On November 3, 1737, Alexander Cruden presented his concordance to Queen Caroline. It is still one of the most widely-used Bible study tools available. ❋ November 3, 1783, Robert Raikes published a notice in his newspaper about the success of his Sunday school, sparking the worldwide Sunday school movement. ❋ November 3, 1850, is the birth date of John Watson, Scottish Presbyterian clergyman and writer. ❋ This is also the birthday of Edith Schaeffer, born this day in 1914.

WORSHIP HELPS

Worship Theme:
God prospers those who exhibit an excellent spirit before Him.

Call to Worship:
Therefore by Him let us continually offer the sacrifice of praise to God, that is, the fruit of our lips, giving thanks to His name (Heb. 13:15).

Responsive Reading:

Leader: But as for you, speak the things which are proper for sound doctrine: that the older men be sober, reverent, temperate, sound in faith, in love, in patience....

People: The older women likewise, that they be reverent in behavior, not slanderers, not given to much wine, teachers of good things...

Leader: ...that they admonish the young women to love their husbands, to love their children, to be discreet, chaste, homemakers, good, obedient to their own husbands, that the word of God may not be blasphemed.

People: Likewise, exhort the young men to be sober-minded, in all things showing yourself to be a pattern of good works...

Leader: ...in doctrine showing integrity, reverence, incorruptibility, sound speech that cannot be condemned, that one who is an opponent may be ashamed, having nothing evil to say of you.

Taken from Titus 2:1–9.

Benediction:
"The LORD bless you and keep you; The LORD make His face shine upon you, And be gracious to you; The LORD lift up His countenance upon you, And give you peace" (Num. 6:24–26).

STATS, STORIES AND MORE

From Vance Havner

God "millennialized" the lions. Spurgeon said, "How could lions eat him when most of him was grit and backbone!" It was not Daniel who had insomnia; it was Darius who needed a sedative.... We may not admit it, but this troubled generation secretly wonders whether the God we preach about is able to deliver us. It sounds fine in a Sunday sermon, but will it work in a lion's den? When trouble comes; when sickness lays us low; when we bury our dearests in lonely graves; when fondest dreams have faded; when enemies rise up like a flood; when evil days come and the years draw nigh when we say we have no pleasure in them—is our God able when we reach the lion's den?

C. I. Scofield

After the Civil War, President Ulysses S. Grant appointed C. I. Scofield, a brilliant lawyer, as United States Attorney for Kansas. But Scofield's career was marred by alcoholism until his conversion to Christ at age 36. Scofield then became a great Bible student, a pastor and evangelist, founder of the Central American Mission, and editor of his famous reference Bible. He once said:

"Shortly after I was saved, I passed the window of a store in St. Louis where I saw a painting of Daniel in the lions' den. That great man of faith, with his hands behind his back and those beasts circling him, was looking up and answering the king, who was anxious to know if God had protected him.

"As I stood there, great hope flooded my heart. Only a few days had passed since I, a drunken lawyer, had been converted; and no one had yet told me anything about the keeping power of Jesus Christ. I thought to myself, there are lions all about me too, such as my old habits and sins. But the One who shut the lions' mouths for Daniel can also shut them for me! I knew that I could not win the battle in my own strength. The painting made me realize that while I was weak and helpless, my God was strong and able. He had saved me, and now He would also be able to deliver me from the wild beasts in my life. O what a rest of spirit that truth brought me."

Additional Sermons and Lesson Ideas

Song of the Crucified

Date preached:

SCRIPTURE: Psalm 22

INTRODUCTION: Though it was written hundreds of years before Christ, Psalm 22 takes us to the foot of the cross and shows us the fourfold sequence of events that comprises Christianity:

1.   **Crucifixion** (vv. 1–21a). The Psalmist gives us a gripping, visual account of crucifixion, even though that method of death by execution had yet to be invented.
2.   **Resurrection** (v. 21b). "You have answered me!"
3.   **Adoration** (vv. 22–26). "You who fear the Lord, Praise Him!"
4.   **Proclamation** (vv. 27–31). "All the ends of the earth shall...turn to the Lord!"

CONCLUSION: The cross is the centerpiece of history, and Christ was appointed unto death from before the foundation of the world, for our sins, for our salvation.

Hidden Help

Date preached:

By Melvin Worthington

SCRIPTURE: Psalm 119:11

INTRODUCTION: Let me share two quick principles with you: (1) Christians whose lives are characterized by dedication, discipline and dependability have the Word of God hidden in their hearts. (2) Christians who are hounded by doubts, dissatisfaction, disobedience and disbelief have neglected to hide the Word of God in their hearts. Psalm 119 is the longest chapter in the Bible. It deals almost exclusively with the Word of God and its place in the believer's life.

BACKGROUND: Psalm 119 has a threefold theme. (1) *The Revelation of the Sovereign*, (2) *The Responsibility of the Saint* and (3) *The Reliability of the Scriptures*. Read the Psalm with this theme in mind.

1.   The Precepts: "Your Word..."
2.   The Process: "...have I hid..."
3.   The Place: "...in my heart..."
4.   The Purpose: "...that I might not sin against You."

CONCLUSION: We must not treat the Word as a protective charm to be worn, but hide it in our hearts as a rule of life. Time spent thoughtfully treasuring up the Word of God is as essential to the Christian as is refueling in mid-flight to the nation's long-range bomber strike force.

The Peculiar Preacher

The Lord gives each of us a unique personality, and His choicest servants have sometimes been, well, peculiar. "Uncle" Bob Sheffey was among them.

Sheffey was born on Independence Day, 1820. When his mother died, an aunt in Abingdon, Virginia, took him in. There, over Greenway's Store, he was converted on January 9, 1839. Feeling the call to preach, he dropped out of college and started through the Virginia hills as a Methodist circuit rider, preaching the gospel.

He did it oddly. For example, one day he was called to a cabin on Wolfe Creek. He had previously tried to win this family to Christ, but without success. As he rode up this time, things were different. A member had been bitten by a rattlesnake. There seemed little hope. Entering the house, Sheffey sank to his knees and prayed, "O Lord, we do thank thee for rattlesnakes. If it had not been for a rattlesnake they would not have called on You. Send a rattlesnake to bite Bill, one to bite John, and send a great big one to bite the old man!"

He is well-remembered for prayers like that. An acquaintance said, "Brother Sheffey was the most powerful man in prayer I ever heard, but he couldn't preach a lick." Once, encountering moonshiners in the mountains, he dismounted, knelt, and offered a long prayer for God to "smash the still into smithereens." He rose, smoothed his trousers, and continued his journey. A heavy tree fell on the still, wrecking it. The owner rebuilt it, and Sheffey prayed again. This time a flash flood did the job.

His prayers were honest, down-to-earth, and plain-spoken—even routine prayers like grace at meals. Once, being entertained in a neighborhood home, he was asked to offer thanks. Sheffey, who loved chicken-and-dumplings, said, "Lord, we thank Thee for this good woman; we thank Thee for this good dinner—but it would have been better if the chicken had dumplings in it. Amen."

Robert Sheffey's unorthodox prayers and sermons ushered many mountaineers into the kingdom and earned him the title the *Peculiar Preacher.* ✿

Quotes for the Pastor's Wall

66 When one for the first time mounts the pulpit, no

one would believe how very afraid one is! One sees

so many heads down there! Even now when I am in

the pulpit I look at no one but tell myself they are

merely blocks of wood which stand there before

me, and I speak the word of my God to them. 99

—Martin Luther

NOVEMBER 10, 2002

The Romans Road

Date preached:

Scripture: Romans 6:23 For the wages of sin is death, but the gift of God is eternal life in Christ Jesus our Lord.

 Introduction: When people want to realign their lives spiritually, to come to the cross, to meet the Savior, what do they do? How does it happen? How are we actually "born again," to use our Lord's phrase? Today I'd like to take you down an old road, often called "The Roman's Road." For some of you this is elementary and repetitive, but I'd like to stir up your memories. For others, let me be your tour guide for the next few minutes. We're going to look at four brief passages from the book of Romans, and you may want to jot these verses in the front of your Bibles. You can use them to lead others to faith in Jesus Christ.

1. **Romans 3:23—All Have Sinned.** We seldom have objections to this point, even among agnostics, atheists, existentialists, mystics, post-moderns, and cultists. Few claim to be perfect or sinless. The Russian novelist Aleksandr Solzhenitsyn noted it would be different if there were "evil people somewhere insidiously committing evil deeds, and it were necessary only to separate them from the rest of us and destroy them. But the line dividing good and evil cuts through the heart of every human being." Psychologist Carl Jung wrote, "All the old primitive sins are not dead but just crouching in the dark corners of our modern hearts—still there, and still as ghastly as ever." Someone once sat down beside Will Rogers at a dinner and in the course of the conversation asked the comedian this question: "What's wrong with the world, anyway?" Rogers drawled in reply, "Well, I dunno, I guess it's people." And I guess it is, for there is no such thing as evil in the abstract.

2. **Romans 6:23—The Wages of Sin is Death.** This is the Bible in a nutshell. The verse begins by telling us the result of our sinfulness. God is life and light, pure and perfect. His presence cannot abide sin. We're thus separated from Him by our sins; and as a result we die, just like the limb of a tree when sawed from the main trunk. The word *death* is used in the Bible in the

sense of *separation*. Physical death occurs when the soul is separated from the body (James 2:26; Matt. 27:50). But there is a second death, and that, too, is separation (Rev. 20:14). It occurs when the spirit and body are separated from God eternally—and this is the condition the Bible calls "hell." C. S. Lewis once went to hear a young parson deliver a sermon. Very much in earnest, the young man ended his message like this: "And now, my friends, if you do not believe these truths, there may be for you grave eschatological consequences." Lewis later visited the young minister and asked him, "Did you mean that they would be in danger of hell?" "Why, yes," said the parson. "Then why in the world didn't you say so?" Lewis replied.

3. **Romans 5:8—God Demonstrates His Love.** The word "demonstrates" is a solid, active verb. Most of us have feelings of love toward someone else—it may be a husband or wife or child or parent. But those feelings don't mean a great deal until we manifest or demonstrate our love, until we find a need in that person's life and proceed to meet that need without thought for anything in return. Many people long for a friend or family member to do this. That's what God was doing at the cross. God demonstrated His own love for us in this—that while we were yet sinners, Christ died for us. This is the meaning of Calvary (Isa. 53:5).

4. **Romans 10:9–10, 13—We Can Be Saved.** There is a truth we believe and a person we receive. We commit ourselves to Christ by faith, asking Him to

>>> *sermon continued on following page*

APPROPRIATE HYMNS AND SONGS

Born Again, Andrew Culverwell; © 1974 Manna Music, Inc.

Can You Believe, Alvin Miranda; © 1996 Integrity's Hosanna! Music/Bargain Basement Music (Admin. by Integrated Copyright Group, Inc.).

Christ Receiveth Sinful Men, Erdmann Neumeister/James MacGranahan; Public Domain.

Enter In, Neil Bush/Michael Cowan; © 1997 HPP Publishing Company.

Without Him, Mylon Lefevre; © 1963 Angel Band Music (Admin. by Gaither Copyright Management).

forgive our sins and to take control of our lives. "Just as I am without one plea,/ But that thy blood was shed for me, / And that Thou bidd'st me come to Thee, / O Lamb of God, I come!"

Conclusion: It's never too late—and never too soon—to come to Jesus Christ, just as you are.

FOR THE BULLETIN

❀ Pope Leo I (Leo the Great) died on November 10, 461, after a pontificate of 21 years. He was the strongest man in the West (exercising authority over Rome, Spain, and North Africa), and the molder of the modern papacy. ❀ November 10, 1483 is the birthday of Martin Luther. ❀ Lott Carey, born into slavery around 1780 on a plantation in Virginia, was able to purchase his own freedom in 1813. He became a preacher and missionary, arriving in Africa in March, 1821. His work was primarily in Monrovia, Liberia. He died November 10, 1828, from injuries sustained when someone knocked a candle into a mixture of gunpowder. ❀ After missionary explorer David Livingstone had not been heard from in years, the *New York Herald* sent reporter Henry M. Stanley to find him. He finally found him in Ujiji, near Lake Tanganyika, on November 10, 1871. Dismounting from his horse, he really did utter the famous phrase, "Dr. Livingstone, I presume." ❀ On November 10, 1942, buoyant after the desert victory at El Alamein, British Prime Minister Winston Churchill said: "This is not the end. It is not even the beginning of the end. But it is, perhaps, the end of the beginning." ❀ New Tribes missionaries Cecil Dye, Bob Dye, Dave Bacon, George Hosbach, and Eldon Hunter ventured into the forests of Bolivia without guns on November 10, 1944, in an effort to reach the savage Ayore Indian tribe. They were not heard from again, and search parties later found fragments of their belongings.

WORSHIP HELPS

Worship Theme:
Jesus Christ came to earth to seek and to save those who are lost.

Call to Worship:
For the message of the cross is foolishness to those who are perishing, but to us who are being saved it is the power of God (1 Cor. 1:18).

Responsive Reading:

Leader: For consider Him who endured such hostility from sinners against Himself...

People: He is despised and rejected by men, a Man of sorrows and acquainted with grief.

Leader: And we hid, as it were, our faces from Him.

People: He was despised, and we did not esteem Him. Surely He has borne our griefs and carried our sorrows....

Leader: But He was wounded for our transgressions,

People: He was bruised for our iniquities.

Leader: For Jews request a sign, and Greeks seek after wisdom; but we preach Christ crucified, to the Jews a stumbling block and to the Greeks foolishness,

Everyone: But to those who are called, both Jews and Greeks, Christ the power of God and the wisdom of God.

Taken from Hebrews 12:3; Isaiah 53:3–5; 1 Corinthians 1:22–24.

Pastoral Prayer:
Heavenly Father, When we survey the wondrous cross on which the Prince of Glory died, our richest gain we count but loss, and pour contempt on all our pride. Remind us anew that it is His blood, freely shed, that has the power to cleanse us of all envy, dishonesty, pride, sexual sin, racial prejudice, self-destructive addiction, and evil imagination. Lord, remind us anew that if we confess our sins, You are faithful and just to forgive our sins and to cleanse us from all unrighteousness. Father, cleanse us. Restore us. Give us a new morning, a new day, for beneath that cross of Jesus we fain would take our stand, the shadow of a mighty Rock within a weary land. We pray this in His wondrous name. Amen.

STATS, STORIES AND MORE

I Am

In response to an article in *The Times* of London entitled, "What's Wrong with the World?" Chesterton replied, "I am. Yours truly. G. K. Chesterton."

Hell

When evangelist Vance Havner was beginning his ministry, he pastored a country church where a farmer didn't like the sermons he preached on hell. The man said, "Preach about the meek and lowly Jesus." "That's where I got my information about hell," Havner replied.

His Greatest Discovery

Dr. Henry "Fritz" Schaefer earned his Ph.D. in chemical physics from Stanford University. For 18 years, he served as professor of chemistry at the University of California, Berkeley. Since 1987, Dr. Schaefer has been Graham Perdue Professor of Chemistry and Director of the Center for Computational Quantum Chemistry at the University of Georgia. He is the author of more than 800 scientific publications and has presented plenary lectures at more than 135 national and international scientific conferences. During the comprehensive period of 1981–1997, he was the sixth-most highly cited chemist in the world out of a total of 628,000 chemists whose research was cited. In a recent lecture, after listing some of his discoveries, Dr. Schaefer said this: "However, the most important discovery of my life was my discovery of Jesus Christ. In 1973, I discovered the Jesus Christ of history, the Jesus whose life is described on the pages of the New Testament."

From *Pilgrim's Progress*

Now I saw in my dream, that the highway up which Christian was to go, was fenced on either side with a wall, and that wall was called Salvation. Up this way, therefore, did burdened Christian run, but not without great difficulty, because of the load on his back.

He ran thus till he came at a place somewhat ascending, and upon that place stood a cross, and a little below, in the bottom, a sepulchre. So I saw in my dream, that just as Christian came up with the cross, his burden loosed from off his shoulders, and fell from off his back, and began to tumble, and so continued to do, till it came to the mouth of the sepulchre, where it fell in, and I saw it no more.

Additional Sermons and Lesson Ideas

God Is Not Dead Nor Doth He Sleep

Date preached:

SCRIPTURE: Psalm 10

INTRODUCTION: Our "Why?" questions are painful, for they express a tinge of doubt about God's goodness and power. Yet the greatest characters of Scripture sometimes asked them. For example, consider Psalm 10, which divides into four sections:

1. **A Question** (v. 1). The writer begins, "Why do you stand afar off? Why do you hide?"
2. **A Perception** (vv. 2–11). The Psalmist is perplexed, for it seems to him the wrong side is winning, that the wicked are prevailing, that the righteous are suffering at their hands.
3. **A Realization** (vv. 12–15). Further reflection shows the perception to be faulty. God *does* see, and He *is* concerned.
4. **A Proclamation** (vv. 16–18). "The Lord is King forever and ever...."

CONCLUSION: We may begin our prayers by asking "Why?" but we shouldn't end there. There are better answers, like the old Christmas carol, written during the Civil War, that says: "Yet pealed the bells more loud and deep: 'God is not dead nor doth He sleep; The wrong shall fail, the right prevail, With peace on earth, good will to men.'"

Wisdom in the Night

Date preached:

By Dr. Melvin Worthington

SCRIPTURE: John 3:1–21

INTRODUCTION: When Jesus met under cloak of darkness with Nicodemus, He stressed four simple truths regarding the new birth:

1. **The Must** (vv. 1–7). The new birth is not optional. The Bible teaches that all men are dead in trespasses and sins without the new birth.
2. **The Mystery** (vv. 8–13). When Nicodemus expressed astonishment, Jesus used the wind to explain the new birth. Much about the wind is mysterious and inexplicable. We know neither where it originates nor its destination, yet we do not deny its presence. So with the actions of the Spirit in performing the new birth.
3. **The Means** (vv. 14–18). God loved the world so much He sent His son, not to condemn the world, but that through Him the world might be saved.
4. **The Marks** (vv. 19–21). Coming to Christ, we begin living in the light.

CONCLUSION: Can the born-again birthmarks be seen in us? One may reach heaven without education, money or rank, but no one enters heaven without the new birth.

NOVEMBER 17, 2002

SUGGESTED SERMON   *Date preached:*

Lifestyle of the Righteous and Faithful

Scripture: Ephesians 4:17–32, especially verse 17 This I say, therefore, and testify in the Lord, that you should no longer walk as the rest of the Gentiles walk...

Introduction: Few words are subject to more adjectives than the popular term *lifestyle*. Almost every day we hear something about a healthy lifestyle, an expensive lifestyle, a gay lifestyle, a Hollywood lifestyle. A popular television program of a few years ago touted the lifestyles of the "rich and famous." Today, we're looking at a passage that describes a distinctively Christian lifestyle.

1. **The World Around Us** (vv. 17–19). The apostle Paul is speaking insistently. He is very much in earnest. He is most emphatic. He is "saying and testifying" that we no longer walk (behave, live, lead a lifestyle) like the world around us. In verses 18 and 19, he gives us a very vivid description of a culture that disregards God and His Word. It is futile, dark, alienated from God, ignorant, and blind. In verse 19, it is described as being "past feeling," The Greek word means to lose the ability to feel shame or embarrassment. Our culture has given itself over to lewdness (behavior completely lacking in moral restraint, usually with the implication of sexual licentiousness) "to work all uncleanness with greediness." This description is played out for us each night when we turn on our televisions. The actress Heather Graham recently gave an interview in which she was very bitter toward the church because, she said, it stifled her sexuality. Her exact quote was, "Why do I have to do what all these men are saying? Why is a woman's sexuality supposed to be so evil?" Well, sexuality in itself isn't evil; it was created by God. But the Bible warns that God intends for us to be responsible moral and spiritual people, but we are living in a world that no longer tolerates moral restraint or biblical values.

2. **The Change Within Us** (vv. 20–24). But we have not so learned Christ, wrote the apostle. In other words, when we become Christians, something different happens within us, something that separates us from the world and gives us a distinctive lifestyle. Paul goes on to describe the change in

terms of wardrobe. At Calvary, we take off the old, sin-splattered rags of self-righteousness, we are bathed in the blood of Christ, and we put on a new wardrobe of holy living.

3. **The Demands Upon Us (vv. 25–32).** Verse 25 begins with the word, "There-fore," indicating that in light of the world around us and the change within us, there are now some demands upon us. God expects a certain lifestyle from His people. In the remainder of the chapter, five areas are dealt with.

    A. **Our Morality** (vs.25). We are to be people of integrity.

    B. **Our Mood** (vv. 26–27). We're all bound to become angry from time to time, but we must be careful about how we express that anger and how long we stay angry, otherwise we'll give the devil a foothold in our lives.

    C. **Our Money** (v. 28). We must never come by one cent in a deceptive or dishonest way. Christians are to be hard-working people, earning money with the express purpose of sharing some of it with others.

    D. **Our Mouths** (vv. 29–30). The word "grieve" is a strong and emotional word. Paul could have said, "Do not displease or disappoint the Holy Spirit." But the word "grieve" conveys emotional suffering and deep sor-row. When we engage in unwholesome talk, it causes emotional suffer-ing and deep sorrow to the Holy Spirit who lives within our hearts.

    E. **Our Magnanimity** (vv. 31–32). Is there someone you haven't forgiven? God has forgiven you of all your sins in Christ; should you not also reflect His compassion and forgive your enemy?

>>> *sermon continued on following page*

APPROPRIATE HYMNS AND SONGS

Change My Heart, O God, Ed Kerr; © 1992 Integrity's Hosanna! Music (Admin. by Integrity Music Inc.).

Alas and Did My Savior Bleed, Isaac Watts/Wilson Hugh; Public Domain.

Christ In Me, Michael O'Brien; © 1998 Designer Music (Admin. by Brentwood/Benson Music Publishing, Inc.).

Fill My Cup, Lord, Richard Blanchard; © 1959 Richard Blanchard; Assigned 1964 Word Music, Inc. (Admin. by Word Music Group, Inc.).

Give Me A New Heart, John Wyrosdick; © 1992 Mercy/Vineyard Publishing.

Conclusion: In view of the world around us and the change within us, these are the demands upon us in terms of our morality, our moods, our money, our mouths, and our manner, our magnanimous hearts. As it is put elsewhere in Scripture: "I beseech you therefore, brethren, by the mercies of God, that you present your bodies a living sacrifice, holy, acceptable to God, which is your reasonable service. And do not be conformed to this world, but be transformed by the renewing of your mind, that you may prove what is that good and acceptable and perfect will of God" (Rom. 12:1–2).

Kids Talk

Tell the children the story of the Titanic, perhaps using a toy boat in a pail of water. Ships are meant to be in the ocean, but tragedy occurs when the ocean gets into the ship. God has placed us in the world, but we must be careful not to let the world get into us. End with a practical application.

FOR THE BULLETIN

❀ St. Gregory, Bishop of Tours, died November 17, 594. He is best remembered for his 10–volume history of the Franks. ❀ On November 17, 1417, the Council of Constance chose Cardinal Oddone Colonna as Pope Martin V, ending the 39–year chaos of the Great Schism in which three rivals claimed the papacy. ❀ Mary Tudor, daughter of Henry VIII and Catherine of Aragon, was a zealous Roman Catholic under whose reign Cramner, Latimer, Ridley, and nearly 300 other Protestant leaders were burned at the stake, giving her the name "Bloody Mary." She died from the plague immediately after hearing early mass before dawn on November 17, 1558. ❀ November 17, 1668, marks the death of Joseph Alleine, English Puritan and author of the classic *Alleine's Alarm*. He was ousted from his church as a dissenter in 1662, and imprisoned in 1663 for singing psalms and preaching to his family in his own home. He died from overwork and exhaustion at age 34. ❀ Rodney (Gipsy) Smith, one of England's most colorful evangelists, was converted on November 17, 1874, at age 16. While attending a Primitive Methodist Chapel on Fitzroy Street in Cambridge, he heard George Warner, the preacher, give the invitation and went forward. Someone nearby whispered, "Oh, it's only a Gypsy boy." But during his lifetime he led thousands to Christ. ❀ November 17, 1961, marks the death of C. H. Mason, founder of the Church of God in Christ.

Worship Theme:

The Christian is to maintain a lifestyle in sharp contrast to those in the world around us.

Call to Worship:

I beseech you therefore, brethren, by the mercies of God, that you present your bodies a living sacrifice, holy, acceptable to God, which is your reasonable service. And do not be conformed to this world, but be transformed by the renewing of your mind, that you may prove what is that good and acceptable and perfect will of God (Rom. 12:1–2).

Pastoral Prayer:

For today's prayer, adapt this prayer from Martin Luther which uses the Lord's Prayer coupled with an appropriate preamble: O heavenly Father, dear God, I am a poor unworthy sinner. I do not deserve to raise my eyes or hands toward You or to pray. But because You have commanded us all to pray and have promised to hear us and through Your Son Jesus Christ have taught us both how and what to pray, I come to You in obedience to Your word, trusting in Your gracious promise. I pray in the name of my Lord Jesus Christ together with all Your saints and Christians on earth as He has taught us:

> Our Father, who art in heaven, hallowed be thy name, thy kingdom come, thy will be done on earth as it is in heaven. Give us this day our daily bread; and forgive us our trespasses, as we forgive those who trespass against us; and lead us not into temptation, but deliver us from evil. For Thine is the kingdom, the power, and the glory forever. Amen.

STATS, STORIES AND MORE

Quotes on Anger

"He that would be angry and not sin, must be angry at nothing but sin."
—*Rev. William Secker, 17th Century British minister*

"Anyone can become angry. That is easy. But to be angry with the right person, to the right degree, at the right time, for the right purpose, and in the right way—that is not easy."
—*Aristotle*

"The size of a man can be measured by the size of the thing that makes him angry."
—*J. K. Morley*

Forgiveness

In her book, *Climbing*, missionary Rosalind Goforth tells of the rage she harbored against someone who had harmed her and her husband. For more than a year, she would not talk to that person who lived near them on their missionary station in China; and four years passed and the matter remained unresolved and, to an extent, forgotten.

One day the Goforths were traveling to a meeting elsewhere in China. For months, Rosaland had felt a lack of power in her Christian life, and in her room she cried to God to be filled with the Holy Spirit.

An inner voice said, "Write to [that one] and ask forgiveness for the way you have treated him." My whole soul cried out "Never!" Again I prayed as before, and again the Inner Voice spoke clearly as before. Again I cried out in my heart, "Never; I will never forgive him!" When for the third time this was repeated, I jumped to my feet and said to myself, "I'll never, never forgive!"

Shortly afterward Rosalind was reading in *Pilgrim's Progress* about the man in the cage moaning, "I have grieved the Spirit, and He is gone: I have provoked God to anger, and He has left me." A terrible conviction came upon her. Finally, talking with a fellow missionary, she burst into sobs and told him the whole story. "But Mrs. Goforth," he said, "are you willing to write the letter?"

At length Rosalind replied, "Yes." She jumped up, ran into the house, and wrote a few lines of humble apology for her actions, without any reference to the other part. The joy and peace of her Christian life returned. "From that time," Rosalind wrote, "I have never dared *not to forgive*."

Additional Sermons and Lesson Ideas

Good Things

Date preached:

SCRIPTURE: 2 Timothy 1:14

INTRODUCTION: A wonderfully simple phrase in the Bible describes the practical daily gifts of God's grace. He fills our lives with "good things."

1. We should rejoice in every good thing God has given us (Deut. 26:11).
2. Not a word has failed of any good thing the LORD has spoken to us (Josh. 21:45).
3. Those who seek the LORD lack no good thing (Ps. 34:10).
4. No good thing does God withhold from those who walk uprightly (Ps. 84:11).
5. He who finds a wife finds a good thing (Prov. 18:22).
6. We should be zealous in every good thing (Gal. 4:18).
7. God desires to teach us about the good things He gives (Philemon 6).

CONCLUSION: Count your "good things," name them one by one; and it will surprise you what the Lord has done.

What a Difference a Week Makes

Date preached:

By Kevin Riggs

SCRIPTURE: John 12:12–19

INTRODUCTION: The people of Jerusalem hailed Jesus as the King of the Jews, but a week later they shouted, "Crucify Him." What happened?

1. **Their attitude changed because their faith was shallow.** When things were going well they shouted, "Hosanna," but when things turned bad they yelled, "Crucify Him." A shallow faith one day praises God and the next day curses Him.
2. **Their attitude changed because their faith was self-seeking.** The people expected the Messiah to deliver them from the Roman government and make all their problems go away. A self-seeking faith believes in Jesus for what he/she can get out of it.
3. **Their attitude changed because their faith was short-sighted.** On Palm Sunday, all the people could see was the immediate. But when the present wasn't what they wanted it to be, they gave up. A shortsighted faith focuses on the present and forgets the promises of the future.

CONCLUSION: Do you praise God one day and curse Him the next? Are you following God for what you can get out of it? Do you focus on the present? The way to keep our faith from being shallow is to grow in the knowledge of Christ. The way to keep our faith from being self-seeking is to give more than we receive. The way to keep it from being shortsighted is by not forgetting the grace God has bestowed.

John Ploughman's Talks

"Whenever a new book comes out," wrote John Ruskin, "I read an old one." Ruskin knew that shallow minds devour books-of-the-moment, but wiser readers digest authors of the past who still speak volumes. With that it mind, I'd like to recommend your spending a quiet evening with John Ploughman.

Ploughman was the creation of British pastor Charles Haddon Spurgeon (1834–1892). Spurgeon is called "The Prince of Preachers," but he could well be dubbed "The King of Classics." He is arguably Christian history's best-selling author, with more words in print than anyone else, living or dead. In all, he wrote 135 books and edited another twenty-eight. If we include pamphlets, the total number of Spurgeon's volumes rises to 200. His collected sermons stand as the largest set of books by a single author in the history of Christianity.

Not bad for a country boy who never attended college, who suffered debilitating bouts of gout and depression, who cared for an invalid wife, and who died at age 57.

But Spurgeon enjoyed a phenomenal mind and exceptional gifts. He read six books a week, preached as many as ten times Sunday-to-Sunday, and once said he counted eight sets of thoughts passing through his mind at the same time while preaching. He was seldom heard by fewer than 6,000, and on one occasion his audience numbered nearly 24,000—all this before the days of microphones and mega-churches.

In 1865, Spurgeon launched a magazine called *The Sword and The Trowel* in which he regularly included maxims under the penname of John Ploughman. The character was actually based on an old farmer, Will Richardson, in Spurgeon's hometown of Stambourne. As a boy, Spurgeon had spent many an hour in the furrows behind Richardson's plow, listening to the man's homespun quips, quotes, comments, and common sense. Years later, in his garden house where *The Sword and the Trowel* was edited, Spurgeon's mind wandered back to those scenes as he composed Ploughman's proverbs.

John Ploughman quickly became for Spurgeon what Poor Richard had been for Benjamin Franklin—his most popular character. When the proverbs were collected and issued as *John Ploughman's Talks*, it became his best-selling book, leading to a sequel, *John Ploughman's Pictures*.

In his *Talks*, John Ploughman covers topics like: Grumblers . . . Debt . . .

Things Not Worth Trying . . . Patience . . . Men Who Are Down . . . Very Ignorant People . . . Fault . . . Hope . . . Home . . . and the Preacher's Appearance.

Modern readers will find the language and farming allusions dated, and the ideas Victorian; but the wisdom is enduring. Listen, for example, to Ploughman's thoughts about thinking: "Some will say they cannot help having bad thoughts; that may be, but the question is, do they hate them

---

It is not how much we have, but how much we enjoy

that makes happiness. It is not the quantity of our goods, but the

blessing of God on what we have that makes us truly rich.

—JOHN PLOUGHMAN

---

or not? Vain thoughts will knock at the door, but we must not open to them. Though sinful thoughts rise, they must not reign. He who turns a morsel over and over in his mouth, does so because he likes the flavor; and he who meditates upon evil, loves it, and is ripe to commit it. Snails leave their slime behind them, and so do vain thoughts.

"Good thoughts are blessed guests, and should be heartily welcomed, well fed, and much sought after. Like rose leaves, they give out a sweet smell if laid up in the jar of memory. They cannot be too much cultivated; they are a crop which enriches the soil."

Someone once defined a proverb as a "Heavenly Rule for Earthly Living." It is when the *wit* of one becomes the *wisdom* of many. The ability to distill and condense great truths in simple, quotable statements makes for unique literature, and everyone from King Solomon to Yogi Berra has tried his hand at it.

Spurgeon's fertile mind produced pithy adages and precepts like amber waves of grain, and we can still reap the harvest. Just set aside your modern best-seller awhile, put your hand to the Ploughman, and don't look back. ✸

NOVEMBER 24, 2002

SUGGESTED SERMON

Conceptualizing The Church

Date preached:

By Melvin Worthington

Scripture: Matthew 16:13–20, especially verses 15–18 He said to them, "But who do you say that I am?" Simon Peter answered and said, "You are the Christ, the Son of the living God." Jesus answered and said to him, "Blessed are you, Simon Bar-Jonah, for flesh and blood has not revealed this to you, but My Father who is in heaven. And I also say to you that you are Peter, and on this rock I will build My church, and the gates of Hades shall not prevail against it.

Introduction: The church is out of favor today. There is a widespread feeling that spirituality is great, but the church isn't. But someone once said, "The world at its worst needs the church at its best." Today's message is not an attempt to exegete the scripture text, but to use the text as a basis for a comprehensive view of Christ's church as revealed in the Bible. Too often the model for the church is based on an educational, military, or corporate model. The biblical model emphasizes a family, a fellowship, a flock, a building, a bride, and a body.

1. **The Meaning Which Defines the Church.** The word *church* is used at least two ways in the New Testament. First, it designates the invisible body of believers of all the ages and all around the world. Second, it describes a local church as it exists in specific geographical locations.

2. **The Metaphors Which Describe the Church.** Paul used the term *body* to describe the church (1 Cor. 12), emphasizing the unity, unselfishness, uniqueness and understanding of the body. He used the term *building* to describe the church (Eph. 2), and both he and John used the term *bride* to describe the church (Eph. 5; Rev. 19), emphasizing our intimate and eternal union with our Savior.

3. **The Ministries Which Denote the Church.** What is the church to do? The Great Commission calls for *evangelism* and *missions* (Matt. 28). It also calls for *education,* teaching Christians to obey all Christ has told us. *Edification* remains a key component of our ministry (Eph. 4). Pastor-teachers have a

unique responsibility to build up believers so they can effectively do the work of the ministry. *Establishment* should be given a significant place in the ministry of the church (Acts 11). Believers need to be taught what they are to believe, why they believe it, and how to defend it. *Encouragement* is so critical that two of Paul's missionary journeys were largely devoted to encouraging previously planted churches (Acts 14; 17; 20).

4. **The Ministers Who Direct the Church.** God has given the church pastor-teachers to tend and train the flock (Eph. 4). Pastor-teachers are to be called, consecrated, compassionate, courageous, consistent, compelled and commissioned. They must teach the scriptures, try the spirits, and tend the saints.

5. **The Message Which Distinguishes the Church.** The church has a unique message of salvation, sanctification, separation, stewardship and service.

6. **The Motivation Which Drives the Church.** The church is driven by two major motivating factors—love and loyalty. The greatest commandment is to love the Lord. Closely akin to love is loyalty. Throughout the Bible, great emphasis is given to loyalty and love as motivation for faithful service.

7. **The Membership Which Delineates the Church.** The church is made up of those who have been redeemed. Church membership is serious matter and

>>> *sermon continued on following page*

APPROPRIATE HYMNS AND SONGS

A Glorious Church, Ralph E. Hudson; Public Domain.

Except the Lord Build the House, Dan Marks; © 1983 Maranatha! Music.

I Will Build My Church, Graham Kendrick; © 1988 Make Way Music (Admin. by Music Services).

People of God, Wayne Watson; © 1982 Singspiration Music (Admin. by Brentwood/Benson Music Publishing, Inc.).

Blest Be the Tie That Binds, John Fawcett/Johann G. Nageli; Public Domain.

should not be taken lightly. Before uniting with a church, Christians should make sure they are in agreement with the doctrinal beliefs of the church and are willing to make a total commitment to the church and its ministries.

Conclusion: One evening during Vacation Bible School, a new student was brought into the room. The little boy had one arm missing, and the teacher was nervous that one of the other children would say something insensitive to him. At the end of the evening, she asked the children to join her in their usual closing ceremony. "Let's make our churches," she said, putting her hands together to form the "church."

"Here's the church and here's the steeple, open the doors and..." Suddenly the awful truth struck her. The very thing she had feared that the children would do, she had done. As she stood there speechless, the little girl sitting next to the boy reached over with her left hand and placed it up to his right hand and said, "Josh, let's make the church together."

FOR THE BULLETIN

❂ About noon on November 24, 1572, the dying Scottish Protestant reformer John Knox asked his wife to read him the fifteenth chapter of 1 Corinthians. About 5 p.m., he asked her to "Go read where I first cast my anchor," which was John 17. From that time, he sank rapidly until evening prayers, about 11 p.m., during which he passed away. ❂ On November 24, 1703, German-born pastor and hymn writer, Justus Falckner, was ordained as the first Lutheran pastor in America. ❂ November 24, 1713, marks the birth of Father Junipero Serra, Spanish missionary to western America. From 1769, he established 9 of the first 21 Franciscan missions founded along the Pacific coast, and baptized some 6,000 Indians before his death in 1784. ❂ On November 24, 1802, Robert Morrison, 20, wrote to a Bible School in London, seeking admission. He was accepted at once and, against the will of his father, set sail from Newcastle to London. He later became the founder of Protestant missions in China. ❂ On November 24, 1836, Robert Murray McCheyne was ordained into the ministry. ❂ Charles Darwin's "Origin of Species" was published on November 24, 1859. ❂ On November 24, 1876, Philip Bliss introduced and sang the hymn "It is Well with My Soul," at a D. L. Moody Campaign. One month later, he died in a terrible train wreck. ❂ November 24, 1964, medical missionary Dr. Paul Carlson was slain in the Congo.

WORSHIP HELPS

Worship Theme:
Christ is building His church, and the gates of hell shall not prevail against it.

Call to Worship:
This is the message which we have heard from Him and declare to you, that God is light and in Him is no darkness at all (1 John 1:5).

Hymn Story:
John Fawcett was ordained on July 31, 1765, and began pastoring a poor church in Wainsgate. One day, he was invited to London's famous Carter's Lane Church. The following Sunday he broke the news to his church, and when the day of departure came, church members assembled sadly. "John," his wife said, "do you think we're doing the right thing? Will we ever find a congregation to love us and help us with the Lord's work like this group here?" John was silent a moment, then amid joyous tears, they unloaded their wagon. Fawcett stayed at Wainsgate the rest of his life. Out of this experience, he wrote the world-famous hymn, "Blest Be the Tie that Binds."

Scripture Medley:
Now you are the body of Christ, and members individually. You are God's field, you are God's building. You are a chosen generation, a royal priesthood, a holy nation, His own special people, that you may proclaim the praises of Him who called you out of darkness into His marvelous light; who once were not a people but are now the people of God, who had not obtained mercy but now have obtained mercy. Do you not know that you are the temple of God and that the Spirit of God dwells in you? Therefore let no one boast in men. For all things are yours: whether Paul or Apollos or Cephas, or the world or life or death, or things present or things to come—all are yours. And you are Christ's, and Christ is God's.

Taken from 1 Corinthians 12:27; 1 Corinthians 3:9; 1 Peter 2:9–10; 1 Corinthians 3:16; 1 Corinthians 3:21–23.

STATS, STORIES AND MORE

Where Two or Three

When Louis XIV, the Sun King, was ruling in France, he arrived at his chapel one Sunday to find no one else present except Archbishop Fenelon, the court preacher. Surprised at all the vacant seats, the King inquired, "Where is everybody? Why isn't anyone else present this morning?" Fenelon answered "I announced that Your Majesty would not be here today, because I wanted you to see who came to the service just to flatter you and who came to worship God."

God in Attendance

During the presidency of Franklin Roosevelt, a parishioner called his church one Christmas Eve. "Tell me, Reverend," he inquired, "are you holding a Christmas Eve service tonight, and do you expect President Roosevelt to attend?"

"I'm not sure about the President's plans for this evening," replied the pastor, "but I can say that we fully expect God to be in our church tonight, and we feel secure in the knowledge that His attendance will attract a reasonably large congregation."

From a Sermon by Charles Spurgeon

"The Holy Spirit being with us, He can move the whole church to exercise its varied ministries. This is one of the things we want very much—that every member of the church should recognize that he is ordained to service. Everyone in Christ, man or woman, hath some testimony to bear, some warning to give, some deed to do in the name of the holy child Jesus; and if the Spirit of God be poured out upon our young men and our maidens, each one will be aroused to energetic service. Both small and great will be in earnest, and the result upon the slumbering masses of our population will surprise us all."

The Way Some Churches Work

A certain congregation was about to erect a new church building. The building committee, in consecutive meetings, passed the following resolutions:

1. We shall build a new church.
2. The new building is to be located on the site of the old one.
3. The material in the old building is to be used in the new one.
4. We shall continue to use the old building until the new one is completed.

Additional Sermons and Lesson Ideas

The Bible's Foundational Text for Parents

Date preached:

SCRIPTURE: Deuteronomy 6:4–9

INTRODUCTION: These are difficult days for parents to raise children, but Christian parents are not without resources, nor are we without biblical advice. Deuteronomy 6 is Golden Rule for parents, pointing out three simple habits that can make the difference in our families.

1. **Love the Lord** (v. 5). The most important thing we can do as parents is to love the Lord with all our heart, soul, and strength.
2. **Keep God's Commands in Your Hearts** (v. 6). Our children need to see us reading, loving, and studying the Scriptures.
3. **Teach Your Children Diligently.** The best way is the most natural. We are to talk about the Word of God when we sit at home and when we walk along the road, when we lie down and when we get up. Post the Scriptures on the walls of your house (and on the doors of your refrigerator).

CONCLUSION: Begin today making these habits a part of your home. They work!

Our Dwelling Place

Date preached:

SCRIPTURE: Psalm 90

INTRODUCTION: When we fly over a range of mountains, our perspective is vastly different than when we're driving through them. When we're struggling through a mountain of problems, it helps to rise to a higher plane. Psalm 90 is our boarding pass.

1. **Our God from Everlasting to Everlasting** (vv. 1–2). Moses, the writer of Psalm 90, reminds us that our Dwelling Place is from everlasting to everlasting.
2. **Our Lot from Year to Year** (vv. 2–12). Mincing no words, the Psalmist speaks of the brevity of life and the importance of spending our few years here in wisdom.
3. **Our Needs from Day to Day** (vv. 13–17). Our Eternal God has compassion on us, He satisfies us early and makes us glad, healing all our hearts, meeting all our needs.

CONCLUSION: Learn to add the conclusion of this Psalm into your prayers: Let the beauty of the Lord be upon me, and establish the work of my hands.

SPECIAL OCCASION SERMON

A Thanksgiving Day Sermon

Date preached:

Scripture Reading: Romans 8:28 and Ephesians 5:20

Introduction: If we had time to take a roving microphone from pew to pew and from person to person today, asking for your favorite verse of Scripture, many of you would give John 3:16, Psalm 23:1, or Proverbs 3:5–6. But some of you would cite Romans 8:28, a verse that has provided more comfort for God's people in times of disappointment and distress than perhaps any other. This is a promise we can never exhaust or wear out. Because of the truth of this verse, we can be thankful every day regardless of circumstances.

Context: As wonderful as Romans 8:28 is, it's even more wonderful when you see its context. Romans 8 tells us about the Holy Spirit, who takes the work of Christ and applies it to our lives. According to verse 26, the Holy Spirit helps us in our weakness. What kind of weakness? We are weak in many ways, but in this passage the apostle Paul is specific about the particular weakness he is addressing—our prayer lives. We are weak when it comes to prayer. In what way? Well, we are weak in many ways, but here again Paul has something specific in mind. We are weak in our ability to know what we should ask. Many times we really don't know what we should specifically pray for. We are not omniscient. We don't know everything, nor can we see into the future. So we don't know whether the things we're asking for will turn out good or bad for us.

An old story illustrates: A Chinese gentleman lived on the border of China and Mongolia. In those days, there was constant conflict and strife along the perimeter. The man had a beautiful horse. One day, she leaped over the corral, raced down the road, crossed the border, and was captured by the Mongolians. His friends came to comfort him. "That's bad news," they said sadly. "What makes you think it's bad news?" asked the Chinese gentleman. "Maybe it's good news." A few days later the mare came bolting into his corral, bringing with it a massive stallion. His friends crowded around. "That's good news!" they cried. "What makes you think it's good news?" he asked. "Maybe it is bad news." Later, his son, while riding the stallion and trying to break it, was thrown off and broke his leg. "That's bad news," cried the friends. "What makes you think it is bad news?" asked the Chinese gentleman. "Maybe it's good news." One week later, war broke out with Mongolia, and a Chinese general came through, drafting all the young men. All later perished, except for the young man who couldn't go because his leg was broken. The man said to his friends, "You see, the things you thought were bad turned out good; and the things you thought were good turned out bad."

And thus it is with us. We don't know if the things we want will really be good for us, or bad. We can't see the future. That's why James tells to us to pray, saying, "If it be thy will. . . ." But God *does* know the future. He is Alpha and Omega, the First and the Last. He knows the end from the beginning, and He knows how all things will turn out. Verse 26 says that the Holy Spirit prays for us according to the will of God with intensity, with groanings that words cannot express. And God answers the Holy Spirit's pleas on our behalf. The result is Romans 8:28! As the Holy Spirit prays for us, God answers His prayers, therefore all the things turn out for our good in the unfolding providence of the Lord. Hudson Taylor once said:

> *Ill that God blesses is our good*
> *And unblest good is ill.*
> *And all is right that seems most wrong*
> *If it be his sweet will.*

Example #1: For several years, Frank Fortunato, staff member with Operation Mobilization, directed the ministries of the *Logos* Gospel Ship as it sailed into various ports around the world to present the gospel. While Frank was finishing a furlough in the States, the *Logos* was in the Mediterranean wanting to dock in Istanbul, but OM leaders didn't expect to be able to stay there long. Turkey is closed to the Gospel, and the *Logos* crew expected the government to order them away as soon as it realized that *Logos* was a Christian endeavor. The workers aboard the *Logos* prayed that they might be able to stay at least 48 hours. As the ship entered the harbor, the pilot momentarily lost his bearings and collided with a barge. Nothing like that had ever happened before. The *Logos* wasn't hurt, but the barge sustained damage and several people were thrown into the ocean. They were rescued, but the Turkish police impounded the *Logos* until the authorities sorted out what had happened. Meanwhile the missionaries were free to roam the city. They offered to organize a city-wide concert, and government officials permitted it. Meanwhile, Frank flew into Istanbul to rejoin the

Logos. As he was being driven from the airport he was astounded to see his name blaring from huge banners. He couldn't read the Turkish writing, but he could recognize his name. "What do those banners say?" he asked. His driver replied, "It says that a Mr. Frank Fortunato is going to lead a citywide concert here the day after tomorrow." Frank was flabbergasted, but he went to work. He deliberately selected a series of Christian songs and hymns that would take the audience through the gospel a step at a time. Each song explained some aspect of the gospel in logical sequence, and a large crowd was exposed to the words. To make a long story short, because of a dangerous collision at sea, the gospel of Christ was spread to one of the most closed nations on earth. Instead of being in Istanbul for two days as they had prayed, the missionary ship and its crew were there for two months, using every possible means to plant the gospel.

Example #2: When Ken Hansen was the president and CEO of Service Master International, he would sometimes visit friends and employees who were hospitalized. When recovery appeared to be long and difficult, Ken would take the patient's hand and say something like this: "You know, I have had a number of serious operations. I know something of the pain and troubling thoughts you are having. There are two verses I want to give you—Genesis 42:36 and Romans 8:28. We have the option of these two attitudes. We need the perspective of the latter." Then he would read the two verses. In Genesis 42:36, the patriarch Jacob, upset over his children, said, "All these things are against me." In Romans 8:28 Paul said that all these things work together for good. Every day we have to choose which of these verses we're going to live by.

Conclusion: As this process unfolds, Romans 8:29 tells us that God is fashioning us into the likeness of His Son. A sculptor once carved a magnificent lion out of a solid block of stone. When asked how he had accomplished such a marvelous masterpiece, he had a simple answer. "That's easy," he said. "All I did was to chip away everything that didn't look like a lion." Through the pressures of life, the Lord chips away those things in our lives that don't look like Jesus Christ. Romans 8:28 thus really serves as the basis for biblical thanksgiving. Many people espouse the importance of positive thinking or possibility thinking. Much research has been done on the power of optimism. But positive thinking and optimism are empty clouds unless you have an Almighty God who controls the universe in His sovereignty and who is willing to make such a promise to His people. We do have such a God, and we do have such a promise. It provides a solid theological foundation for genuine, biblical, positive thinking.

I don't know what pressures or problems you may be going through today, but none of them is beyond the reach of Romans 8:28. It is because of Romans 8:28 that we can have peace that passes all understanding. It is because of Romans 8:28 that we can cast our burdens on the Lord. It is because of the "all things" of Romans 8:28 that we can obey the "all things" of Ephesians 5:20: ". . . giving thanks always for all things to God the Father in the name of our Lord Jesus Christ."

THOUGHTS FOR THE PASTOR'S SOUL

God Calls Us to Be Faithful, Not Famous

- William Carey, the "Father of Modern Missions," labored for seven years in India before baptizing his first convert. Mary Drewery, in her biography of Carey, said, "The number of actual conversions directly attributable to him is pathetically small; the number indirectly attributable to him must be legion."

- America's first missionary, Adoniram Judson, labored for seven years in Burma before seeing his first convert.

- On May 16, 1819, Pomare II was baptized—the first convert on the island of Tahiti after 22 years of tears and toil by missionaries Mr. and Mrs. Henry Nott.

- Missionary Allen Gardiner traveled repeatedly to South America, trying to evangelize the islands of Patagonia and Tierra del Fuego. He eventually died of starvation without seeing a single soul saved, but the South American Missionary Society he founded has been sending missionaries and saving souls for over 150 years.

- Jimmy Aldridge and his colleagues with Free Will Baptist Foreign Missions worked for nine years in Bondoukou in the Ivory Coast of West Africa before seeing their first converts in the villages.

- In 1939 the first Sudan Interior Mission workers went to Doro in southern Sudan to share the gospel with the Mabaan people, who had never heard of Christ. Years passed, and three SIM workers were buried at Doro and more than 50 worked there diligently from 1939 to 1964, when they had to leave because of Civil War. When they left there were only a handful of baptized believers in good standing. But when they were able later to return to the Sudan, they were amazed to find large groups of witnessing believers, with nearly 300 waiting to be baptized. ✿

DECEMBER 1, 2002

First Sunday of Advent

The Advent of Grace   *Date preached:*

By Drew Wilkerson

Scripture: John 1:14–18 "And the Word became flesh and dwelt among us, and we beheld His glory, the glory as of the only begotten of the Father, full of grace and truth. John bore witness of Him and cried out, saying, This was He of whom I said, He who comes after me is preferred before me, for He was before me. And of His fullness we have all received, and grace for grace. For the law was given through Moses, but grace and truth came through Jesus Christ. No one has seen God at any time. The only begotten Son, who is in the bosom of the Father, He has declared Him."

Introduction: Grace is a five-letter word that can also be spelled J-E-S-U-S. On this first day of December and first Sunday of Advent, it sets the tone for our coming celebrations. The Word—God Himself—became flesh and dwelt among us. That's not a popular message in a day when nativity scenes are being ousted from parks and Christmas carols from schools. But it's the theme of our lives, and nothing is stopping you and me from keeping Christ central to our celebration, even as we pray for others to find Him too. Thomas Brooks wrote, "Saving grace makes a man willing to leave his lusts as a slave is willing to leave his galley, or a prisoner his dungeon, or a thief his bolts, or a beggar his rags." Grace is the key, and while it appears in human form in Bethlehem, it is explained theologically in the epistles. This morning, I would like to show you the facets of grace Paul outlines in the book of 2 Corinthians.

1. **Facet #1—God's Grace Is Our Grace** (2 Cor. 6:1–2). The church in Corinth was in trouble, morally and doctrinally confused, and divided. Writing to them, Paul pleaded with them not to waste God's grace. Christ came to earth that grace be given to us. This is not our grace. It is a gift from God to be treasured and experienced every day.

2. **Facet #2—God's Grace Is Relational Grace** (2 Cor. 8:8–9). Paul realized the church in Corinth was on the verge of becoming selfish with the grace God had given them. But, just as God had freely given grace to the Corinthians, they were to freely express the grace of God to others. The sincerity of our grace will be tested time and time again in the way we lavish God's grace on

others. It makes us reach out to others in tangible ways that meet their needs. We become not just recipients but conduits of God's grace.

3. **Facet #3—God's Grace Results in Abounding Grace** (2 Cor. 9:6–11). God's grace should motivate each Christian to be a gracious giver. Just as the grace of God caused Him to give us His own Son at Christmas, it motivates us to give of ourselves, as well. Giving should be the result of an inward resolve resulting in an outward expression. Therefore, when we give we do so cheerfully, knowing that we are giving as an extension of God's grace to us. The supply of God's riches will never run dry. It is always abounding. Perhaps this Christmas season, there is a special need you can meet in someone's life. Perhaps God will lead you to take on a special project, to find a family or individual to care for.

4. **Facet #4—God's Grace is a Conquering Grace** (2 Cor. 10:3–5). If we want to be full of God's grace we cannot be full of self. Grace is not to be used as an excuse for sin. Instead grace is to be used as a divine weapon to tear down strongholds and set us free! We fight spiritual battles constantly, and by exercising God's grace we can be more than conquerors.

5. **Facet #5—God's Grace is Enough Grace** (2 Cor. 12:7–10). The word sufficient in this setting means "more than enough." God told Paul that His power was

>>> *sermon continued on following page*

APPROPRIATE HYMNS AND SONGS

Amazed At His Amazing Grace, C.S. Grogan; © 1985 Tennessee Music and Printing Company (Admin. by SpiritSound Music Group).

Shine On Us, Michael W. Smith/Deborah D. Smith; © 1996 Milene Music, Inc./Deer Valley Music (Admin. by Acuff-Rose Music Publishing, Inc.).

Advent Canticle, Mark Hayes; © 1983 Sound III, Inc./Universal-MCA Music (Admin. by Universal-MCA Music Publishing).

Enter Now, Dennis Allen/Nan Allen; © 1994 Van Ness Press (Admin. by Genevox Music Group).

Come, Thou Long Expected Jesus, Charles Wesley/Rowland H. Pritchard; Public Domain.

made perfect in weakness. The more a Christian acknowledges his or her weaknesses the more evident the power of God's grace becomes. The grace of God is enough. It is all we need.

Conclusion: Karl Barth said, "Grace must find expression in life, otherwise it is not grace." God wants to fill us full of His grace—full of Jesus. And He wants us to be free from self and free to give in every facet of our lives. This is all possible through the gift of grace found in Jesus Christ.

FOR THE BULLETIN

❈ On December 1, 1170, Thomas à Becket returned from exile in France, electrifying England. King Henry II shouted, "By the eyes of God, is there none of my cowardly courtiers who will deliver me from this turbulent priest?" Four knights took the challenge, and on December 29, fell on Becket at the high altar during evening vespers. "In the name of Christ and for the defense of His church, I am ready to die," Becket uttered as the blows fell. ❈ On November 31, 1521, Pope Leo X, whose excesses had provoked Luther's Protest, held an all-night party at the Vatican featuring alcohol, gambling, music, acrobats, fireworks, and theatricals. At dawn on December 1, he felt ill, and at nightfall he died. ❈ On December 1, 1789, Doctor Joseph Ignace Guillotine introduced his invention for executing people by decapitation. ❈ December 1, 1798, marks the birth of Albert Barnes, American Presbyterian clergyman and Bible commentator. ❈ On December 1, 1909, ground was broken for Bob Jones College in Panama City, Florida. The university later moved to Greenville, South Carolina. ❈ On December 1, 1917, Father Flanagan founded "Boy's Town." ❈ On December 1, 1929, bingo was invented. ❈ On December 1, 1970, the mother of Soviet Christian dissident Georgi Vins, Lydia Vins, was arrested while in the house with her grandchildren. When placed on trial in Kiev, she gave a spirited defense. As she was being led away to the labor camps, believers in the streets surrounded the police car singing hymns.

Worship Theme:
The grace of God is supremely seen in Jesus Christ, and, when applied to our lives, makes us not just recipients but conduits of His love.

Call to Worship:
Grace, mercy, and peace from God the Father and Christ Jesus our Lord (2 Tim. 1:2).

Scripture Reading:
But Noah found grace in the eyes of the LORD.... and I have found grace in Your sight.... Now therefore, I pray, if I have found grace in Your sight, show me now Your way.... teach me Your paths. Lead me in Your truth and teach me, for You are the God of my salvation.... For the law was given through Moses, but grace and truth came through Jesus Christ. Through Him we have received grace.... For by grace you have been saved through faith, and that not of yourselves; it is the gift of God, not of works, lest anyone should boast. Grow in the grace and knowledge of our Lord and Savior Jesus Christ. To Him be the glory both now and forever. Amen.

Taken from Genesis 6:8; Exodus 33:16; Exodus 33:16; Psalm 25:4–5; John 1:16–17; Romans 1:5–6; Ephesians 2:5–6; 1 Peter 3:18.

Pastoral Prayer:
Heavenly Father, as we approach this Christmas season, we pray not just for ourselves, but for all the world, that Christ would be welcomed here. May His name be magnified in Asia, from the Middle East to the Far East. May His name be praised in Africa, from Algiers to Cape Town. May His name be honored across Europe and America. May He be glorified in Central and South America, in the South Pacific, from pole to pole, from the rising of the sun to the place where it sets. Let every kindred, every tribe on this terrestrial ball, to Him all majesty ascribe, and crown Him Lord of all. And may He be praised in our midst this day. In Jesus' name, Amen.

STATS, STORIES AND MORE

Someone Once Said

"Ponder the achievement of God. He doesn't condone our sin, nor does He compromise His standard. He doesn't ignore our rebellion, nor does He relax his demands. Rather than dismiss sin, He assumes our sin and, incredibly sentences Himself. God's holiness is honored. Our sin is punished... and we are redeemed. God does what we cannot do so we can be what we dare not dream: perfect before God."
—*Max Lucado,* In The Grip of Grace

"Those who would avoid the despair of sinfulness by staying far from God find they have also missed the forgiving grace of God."
—*Charles E. Wolfe*

"There is nothing little about God. He forgives great sins to great sinners after great lengths of time; gives great favors and great privileges and raises us up to great enjoyments in the great Heaven of the Great God."
—*Charles Spurgeon*

"Today, many Christians have a sound biblical doctrine of grace to which they give full mental assent. It is a truth they believe about God, but it is not their gut-level basis of living with God, themselves and others. It is doctrinal but not relational; it is believed but not lived out."
—*David A. Seamands in* Healing Grace

Recognizing the Reality

J. Oswald Sanders tells about a time when the Keswick teacher and popular preacher Prebendary Webb-Peploe was a young man. One of his dear children died suddenly while the family was vacationing at the seaside. Returning from the funeral, the stricken father knelt in his study, pleading with God to make His grace sufficient in this hour of sorrow. But his heart seemed unresponsive in prayer or to a word of Scripture. All seemed dark and numb. Finally he looked at the text that had long hung over the mantelpiece in the room, and for the first time he noticed that one word was in all capital letters: My grace IS sufficient for thee." Rev. Webb-Peploe cried, "Lord, forgive me. I have been asking Thee to make Thy grace sufficient for me, and all the time Thou hast been saying to me, 'My grace IS sufficient.' I thank Thee for sufficient grace, and I appropriate it now.

Additional Sermons and Lesson Ideas

Things to Consider

Date preached:

SCRIPTURE:

INTRODUCTION: In Isaiah 1:3, the Lord lamented, "The ox knows its owner And the donkey its master's crib, but...My people do not consider." The word "consider" occurs 84 times in the Bible (NKJV), meaning to ponder and think about. Here are some things God wants us to consider:

1. **The Wonders of God's Creation** (Ps. 8:3). "When I consider Your heavens, the work of your fingers" (also Job 37:14).
2. **What God Has Done for Us** (1 Sam. 12:24). "Consider what great things He has done for you."
3. **Ants** (Prov. 6:6). "Consider her ways and be wise."
4. **Ravens and Lilies** (Luke 12:24–27). "Consider the ravens...Consider the lilies" (also Matt. 6:28).
5. **Our Latter End** (Deut. 32:29). "Oh... they would consider their latter end!"
6. **Jesus** (Heb. 3:1). "Therefore, holy brethren, partakers of the heavenly calling, consider the Apostle and High Priest of our confession, Christ Jesus."

CONCLUSION: It's impossible to be wise without taking time to think, to ponder, to reflect, and to consider. As Paul told Timothy, "Consider what I say, and may the Lord give you understanding in all things" (2 Tim. 2:7).

A Humble Holiday

Date preached:

SCRIPTURE: Luke 1:39–54

INTRODUCTION: You wouldn't think it by taking a shopping trip to our affluent malls, but Christmas began as a very humble event, an event that exhibited the greatest humility the world has ever seen—the God of glory being laid in a cattle trough. We see:

1. **Humility Exhibited in Mary's Situation.** Everything about Mary was humble—her hometown, her poverty, her hardships, her displacement in Bethlehem, her setting.
2. **Humility Expressed in Mary's Song.** In her Magnificat, she spoke of how God resists the proud but exalts the lowly.
3. **Humility Exemplified in Mary's Son.** Jesus came: "Out of the Ivory Palaces, into a world of woe."

CONCLUSION: We take pride in birth and rank, but He was a carpenter's son. We take pride in possessions, but He had no where to lay His head. Is there any way in which we can observe Christmas with the personal humility that reflects our Savior? God exalts the proud, but gives grace to the humble.

The Practice of the Presence of God

After 23 years in the pastorate, I'm seldom shocked. But I was a little surprised recently with Joey, a typical teen. Mixed up. Battling hormones. Confused. Experimenting. The other day he sauntered into my office, slouched in the chair, and told me he'd found a book that had really gotten hold of him. Pulling a tattered paperback from his coat pocket, he handed it to me.

It was over 300 years old—*The Practice of the Presence of God*—written in the seventeenth century by a Parisian cook named Nicholas Herman (pronounced är-män'), otherwise known as Brother Lawrence.

Who is this outdated mystic who can still reach teenage boys?

Nicholas was born in Lorraine, France, in 1605, but little is known of his early life. He reached his own teen years at the onset of the Thirty Years' War, during which he fought for the French army, was seriously wounded, and was lame for the rest of his life. Converted at age 18, he went to work as a footman for a local official in the treasury.

Years passed, and at age fifty Nicholas joined a Carmelite monastery in Paris, where he was dubbed Brother Lawrence and assigned to the kitchen, a task that struck him as insulting and humbling. For the next several years, he went about his chores, miserable but dutifully, until gradually recognizing his unhealthy attitude.

He began reminding himself frequently that God's presence continually hovered about him, and his disposition changed. Even the most menial tasks, Lawrence realized, if undertaken for God's glory, are holy; and wherever the Christian stands—even in a hot, thankless kitchen—is holy ground, for the Lord is there, too.

Many more years passed, and Brother Lawrence's countenance and demeanor gradually changed until others began asking him a reason for his radiance. He was sought out and his advice valued. Christian leaders listened to him, and one man was particularly impressed—the Abbot of Beaufort.

The two met four times and exchanged fifteen letters to discuss Brother Lawrence's walk with the Lord. The Abbot made notes of the conversations and preserved the letters, compiling them into the book known today as *The Practice of the Presence of God*. It was published in the mid-1600s, shortly after Lawrence's death.

One of the best things about this book is its brevity. My edition is only 35 pages, making it inexpensive, and it can be re-read frequently and absorbed. It begins in a simple, pedestrian manner: "The first time I saw Brother Lawrence was upon the third day of August, 1666. He told me that God had done him a singular favor in his conversion at age eighteen."

The Abbot went on to quote Brother Lawrence as saying, "We should establish ourselves in a sense of God's presence by continually conversing with Him." Lawrence admitted that practicing the presence of God requires applying ourselves to it with some diligence at first, but in due time "His love inwardly excites us to it without any difficulty." The Christian life is "a continual conversation with Him. . . . We need only to recognize God intimately present with us."

The Abbot wrote, "It was observed that in the great hurry of business in the kitchen he still preserved his recollection and heavenly-mindedness.

The presence of God (is) a subject which, in my opinion,

contains the whole spiritual life; and it seems to me that

whoever duly practices it will soon become spiritual.

—BROTHER LAWRENCE

He was never hasty nor loitering, but did each thing in its season, with an even, uninterrupted composure and tranquility of spirit."

"The time of business," said the Brother, "does not with me differ from the time of prayer, and in the noise and clatter of my kitchen, while several persons are at the same time calling for different things, I possess God in as great tranquility as if I were upon my knees at the blessed sacrament."

I'd like to recommend taking a little trip to Paris, to the Carmelite monastery, to visit Brother Lawrence. Sit down with him amid the clutter and clatter of his kitchen, listen to his conversations, read his letters, ponder his advice, and let him help you cultivate the practice of the presence of God. ✻

DECEMBER 8, 2002

Second Sunday of Advent

The Most Unusual Message in History

Date preached:

Scripture: Luke 1:26–38, especially verses 30–34 Then the angel said to her, "Do not be afraid, Mary, for you have found favor with God. And behold, you will conceive in your womb and bring forth a Son, and shall call His name JESUS. He will be great, and will be called the Son of the Highest; and the Lord God will give Him the throne of His father David. And He will reign over the house of Jacob forever, and of His kingdom there will be no end."

Introduction: A little girl once opened a big box under the Christmas tree to find a giant doll that, when set upright, towered over her. Her parents noticed a few minutes later that the doll had fallen to the side, but the little girl was having a ball playing in the oversized box. We're apt to do the same at Christmas, discarding the baby but having a great time with the wrappings. At the outset of the season, I'd like to turn us toward that Baby. Here in Gabriel 's announcement, we learn four things about Him:

1. **His Name** (verse 31). "Jesus" is the Greek form of the Hebrew "Joshua," meaning "Jehovah Saves," or "Salvation of Yahweh." Woven into the syllables of that name, we see the suffering He would endure, the salvation He would bestow, and the splendor He would display. Throughout the Gospels, we find that name over and over—172 times in Matthew alone: "Jesus was born in Bethlehem....Jesus was led up by the Spirit....Jesus began to preach....Jesus went about all Galilee, teaching...." The greatest songs in history have been about this sweet name: "Jesus, the name that charms our fears, that bids our sorrows cease.... Jesus loves me this I know, for the Bible tells me so....Jesus is the sweetest name I know, and He's just the same as His lovely name." The name *Jesus* contains and conveys His mission—to seek and to save those who are lost.

2. **His Nature.** In Gabriel's brief announcement, four different "sonships" are given to Jesus. He is: (1) Son of Mary (v. 31); (2) Son of the Highest (v. 32); (3) Son of David (v. 32); and (4) Son of God (v. 35). Two of these references imply

His human nature (son of Mary; son of David), and the other two refer to His divine nature (Son of the Highest; Son of God). He is both God and Man. Only Christianity presents a God who, out of love, became a human being through the womb of a virgin to provide atonement for sin.

3. **His Nobility** (vv. 32–33). He will be given to throne of David and will reign over the house of Jacob forever. His kingdom will never end. His is a *powerful* kingdom. If the skies could part as they did for Stephen in Acts 7, we would see Jesus on His throne, worshipped by angels, feared by demons. His is a *permanent* kingdom. He rules over the stars and planets, over all time and space. His is a *providential* kingdom. Behind the scenes of history is His all-controlling hand. His will be a *political* kingdom, for one day the earth will be full of the knowledge of the Lord as the waters cover the sea (Hab. 2:14). His is a *personal* kingdom—He wants to be king of our hearts.

4. **His Nativity** (vv. 34–35). Here we enter one of Christianity's deepest and holiest mysteries. Jesus was born without human interaction, of divine conception, of a virgin who had never known a man. Gabriel explained it using two phrases: "The Holy Spirit will come upon you", and "the power of the Highest will overshadow you." Similar language in the Old Testament describes the clouds of glory resting on the tabernacle in the wilderness. In some mys-

>>> *sermon continued on following page*

APPROPRIATE HYMNS AND SONGS

Emmanuel, Bob McGee; © 1976 C.A. Music (A div. of Christian Artists Corporation) (Admin. by Music Services).

His Name Be Glorified, Carol Cymbala; © 1992 Word Music, Inc./Carol Joy Music (Admin. by Integrated Copyright Group, Inc.).

I Sing Praises, Terry MacAlmon; © 1989 Integrity's Hosanna! Music (Admin. by Integrity Music, Inc.).

Jesus is the Sweetest Name I Know, Lela Long; Public Domain.

Comfort, Comfort Now My People, Johannes Olearius/Louise Bourgeois/Catherine Winkworth; Public Domain.

terious way, the creative power of God was to rest on Mary as the clouds of glory had rested upon the ancient tabernacle. As a result, the child Mary bore would be called the Son of God.

Conclusion: Mary's response to this message was simple and sincere: "Behold, the maidservant of the Lord! Let it be to me according to your word." When we come face-to-face with God's wondrous plan for us—a plan that is always centered around Jesus Christ—there is no response better than: "Behold, I am your servant. Let it be to me according to Your word."

FOR THE BULLETIN

❋ A drastic dip in the temperature on December 8, 1607, made it hard for the translators of the King James Bible. The ice on the Thames was thick enough for coaches to drive over. London was ill-equipped for near-zero weather, and the translators at Westminster could hardly hold their books, pens, and papers unless hovering near the fireplaces. ❋ On December 8, 1630, Roger Williams sailed secretly for America to escape religious persecution. He eventually founded Providence, later the capital of Rhode Island. ❋ The great Puritan Richard Baxter died at four o'clock in the morning on this day in 1691. His last words concerned "the shortness of time, the importance of eternity, the worth of souls, the greatness of God, and the grace of Christ." ❋ On December 8, 1807, Dorothy Carey died in India after years of mental illness. Her husband William noted in his journal, "This evening Mrs. Carey died of the fever under which she has languished some time. Her death was a very easy one, but there was no appearance of returning to reason." ❋ On December 8, 1854, Pope Pius IX described the virgin Mary as sinless, proclaiming the dogma of the Immaculate Conception. ❋ On December 8, 1936, missionaries John and Betty Stam were beheaded in China. ❋ On December 8, 1940, a landmine blasted the roof off All Soul's Church in London, spreading debris throughout the building and forcing the congregation to temporarily meet elsewhere.

WORSHIP HELPS

Worship Theme:
Jesus Christ is both God and Man, His life brings salvation to the world, and His kingdom has no end.

Call to Worship:
But we see Jesus, who was made a little lower than the angels, for the suffering of death crowned with glory and honor, that He, by the grace of God, might taste death for everyone (Heb. 2:9).

Readers' Theater:

Reader 1: Behold, you will conceive in your womb and bring forth a Son, and shall call His name JESUS. He will be great, and will be called the Son of the Highest; and the Lord God will give Him the throne of His father David.

Reader 2: And He took bread, gave thanks and broke it, and gave it to them, saying, "This is My body which is given for you; do this in remembrance of Me."

Reader 1: The Holy Spirit will come upon you, and the power of the Highest will overshadow you; therefore, also, that Holy One who is to be born will be called the Son of God.

Reader 2: Likewise He also took the cup after supper, saying, "This cup is the new covenant in My blood, which is shed for you.

Reader 1: Behold, I bring you good tidings of great joy which will be to all people. For there is born to you this day in the city of David a Savior, who is Christ the Lord.

Reader 2: Father, if it is Your will, take this cup away from Me; nevertheless not My will, but Yours, be done.

Both: And Jesus said to him, "Today salvation has come to this house... for the Son of Man has come to seek and to save that which was lost."

Taken from Luke 1:31–32; 22:19; 1:35; 22:20; 2:10–11; 22:42; 19:9–10.

STATS, STORIES AND MORE

A Confined Space

The missionary Sundar Singh worked among the Hindus who were pantheists and were fond of saying that God is everywhere and in everything. One day Sundar came to a river he had to cross. No boat was available, but a man gave him a large, deflated water skin to use as a flotation device. Sundar inflated it with air and crossed the river safely. Turning to the Pantheistic Hindu crowd watching, he said something along these lines: "Now see here, there was plenty of air all around me, but it was incapable of getting me across the river until it was confined in the narrow space of this float."

He continued, "It is true that God is all around us. He is omni-present. But in order to save us, He had to come down to be confined to the small space of a human being. He became a man who died and rose again. And thus He can get us across the river to the other shore safely."

If Christ Appeared

One day a number of prominent authors and publishers had gathered in a London club room, and the conversation veered to a discussion of some of the illustrious figures of the past. One of the men said, "What would happen if Milton were to enter this room?"

"We would give him an ovation as might compensate for the tardy recognition accorded him by the men of his own day," suggested someone.

"What if Shakespeare entered?"

"We would arise and crown him master of song," said another.

"And if Jesus Christ were to enter?"

"I think," said Charles Lamb in the ensuing silence, "we would all fall on our faces."

Matthew Henry on Gabriel's Message

JESUS! the name that refreshes the fainting spirits of humbled sinners; sweet to speak and sweet to hear, Jesus, a Savior! We know not His riches and our own poverty, therefore we run not to Him; we perceive not that we are lost and perishing, therefore a Savior is a word of little relish....Mary's reply to the angel was the language of faith and humble admiration, and she asked no sign for the confirming her faith. Without controversy, great was the mystery!

Additional Sermons and Lesson Ideas

Messages from the Manger

Date preached:

By Dr. Timothy Beougher

SCRIPTURE: Selected verses in Matthew 2 and Luke 2

INTRODUCTION: We commemorate famous people's birthdays not because of anything outstanding about their birth, but because their accomplishments in life were noteworthy. But when we consider Jesus Christ, we see that not only was His life significant, His birth was also.

1. **His Birth Reveals His Person.** His humanity; His deity; His humility.
2. **His Birth Reveals His Mission.** He came to save His people from their sins. The gifts of gold (for a king); frankincense (for a priest), and myrrh (for those who die) give us a summery of His purpose in coming to earth.
3. **His Birth Reveals the Character of God.** In the events at Bethlehem, we see the glimpses of God's Sovereignty, His glory, and His love

CONCLUSION: "Oh, come, let us adore Him!"

Shattered

Date preached:

SCRIPTURE: Jer. 19:10; Mark 14:3

INTRODUCTION: Have you ever dropped an expensive vase or glass to have it shatter at your feet? Sometimes we feel shattered ourselves, by the blows of life. Two people in the Bible shattered bottles, and both teach us a lesson.

1. **Jeremiah's Shattered Bottle.** In the middle of a dramatic sermon, Jeremiah took a bottle and shattered it on the rocks. He was warning of coming judgment, telling us how sin and evil can shatter our hearts and homes and nation.
2. **Mary's Shattered Bottle.** Mary's alabaster box speaks of Christ, who was shattered, and whose fragrance speaks of God's mercy and forgiveness. Jesus said that she was preaching a sermon about His coming death and resurrection. He Himself is the answer to judgment, sin, death, and hell.

CONCLUSION: While Jeremiah's bottle reminds us of God's judgement, Mary's bottle reminds us of God's mercy. Both are vivid pictures. Consider our Lord Jesus Christ, broken and shattered for us that in Him we might be whole.

DECEMBER 15, 2002

SUGGESTED SERMON *Third Sunday of Advent*

Looking Forward By Looking Backward

By Dr. Timothy Beougher *Date preached:*

Scripture: Matthew 1:1–17, especially verse 17 So all the generations from Abraham to David are fourteen generations, from David until the captivity in Babylon are fourteen generations, and from the captivity in Babylon until the Christ are fourteen generations.

Introduction: With every passing year, stores prepare for the Christmas season earlier. They used to wait until December, then they began at Thanksgiving, then at Halloween, and now they begin in mid-summer! Merchants look forward to Christmas with great anticipation. How much more should we who worship Him? Just as the genealogy of Jesus Christ helps us anticipate His life on earth, the study of it can help us celebrate His birth. We can look forward by looking backward at the lessons we can learn from His family tree. Both Matthew and Luke present a detailed ancestry of Jesus Christ. Matthew gives us 42 generations of Jesus' ancestors, and Luke gives us 77 generations. As a Hebrew writing for Hebrews, Matthew begins his genealogy with Abraham and follows the line through David to Jesus via Joseph's family, giving us the legal lineage. Luke gives us the biological lineage. As a Gentile writing to Gentiles, he traces Christ's lineage from Adam through David via Mary's line. In it we see:

1. **God's Grace Displayed in the Lives of Individuals.** The story of Christ is the story of grace (John 1:16). In studying Jesus' genealogy, we see some names that surprise us: *Tamar* (v. 3), a Gentile of questionable character; *Rahab* (v. 5), a Gentile and a converted prostitute; *Manasseh and Amon* (v. 10), who were among the worst kings. If God would bring the Messianic line through these, He must be a God of grace. Christ was born not to escape our sin, but to carry it away. Thus even the foreign and the dishonorable were included in His ancestry. The genealogy of Jesus further contains slaves, psalmists, prophets, kings, miserable failures and some very ordinary people we don't know much about. We look forward to Christmas by remembering God's grace as displayed in the lives of individuals. His grace is still working wonders in our lives today. No one is too sinful for Christ's blood to cleanse.

2. **God's Sovereignty Displayed in the Affairs of History.** Matthew's record of Jesus' forbears is carefully divided into three eras of history, each containing 14 names. The first runs from Abraham to David. That was to have been the era of faith, though it was marked by anything but faith. The second era extended from David through Jeconiah. That was to have been the age of royalty under God, but the history of the kings of Judah was anything but royal or godly. The third division covers the period of the captivity of God's Old Testament people, a period of unmitigated failure and misery. Matthew could have listed other descendents, but he put together the Messiah's family tree in three groups to show that all three had equal weight and importance as far as the Messiah is concerned. At the darkest moment of failure Jesus was born. He became God's perfect Man of Faith, God's Royal King, and the One Who frees all people from their captivity. "The hopes and fears of all the years Are met in thee tonight."

3. **God's Love Is Displayed in the Fullness of Time** (see Gal. 4:4). Having given the human lineage of Christ, Matthew is careful to demonstrate that Jesus cannot be accounted for by them. Identified with them, He was also separate from them. The process by which Jesus was born is stated differently in Matthew 1:16 from the process by which anyone else in the list of 42 names is born. After 39 uses of the word "beget," or "was the father" Matthew says, "Mary, by whom was born Jesus." This is a subtle difference not brought out in some translations, but it is important. The proclamation in verse 16 is climactic: no human birth, however royal, can account for Jesus; He came by a

>>> *sermon continued on following page*

APPROPRIATE HYMNS AND SONGS

O Come, O Come Emmanuel, John M. Neal/Henry S. Coffin/Thomas Helmore; Public Domain.

Prince of Peace, Kathie Hill; © 1995 Van Ness Press, Inc. (Admin. by Genevox Music Group).

Lord, Come This Christmas, Andy Park; © 1990 Mercy/Vineyard Publishing.

Joy to the World, Isaac Watts/George Frederick Handel; Public Domain.

Eternal Father, Strong to Save, William Whiting/Robert Nelson Spencer/John Bacchus Dykes; Public Domain.

direct act of God in the fullness of time. Thus we have the mystery of Incarnation—Jesus identified with us yet is unique from us.

Conclusion: Looking forward to Christmas? Perhaps this look back will help you look forward. God in grace and mercy does for us what we cannot do. Matthew 1:21 tells us why Jesus came—to save His people from their sins. The best news is that His love and grace are still active today.

Kids Talk

Show the children a large candy cane and tell them the traditional story behind it: Candy canes were reportedly developed by a Christian candymaker in Indiana who built the story of Christmas into each piece. The hardness of the candy represents the solid rock of the Christian faith. The white represents the sinlessness of Christ, and the red stripes symbolize the bloody wounds caused by his flogging. The shape of the candy is that of a shepherd's staff, representing Christ as our Good Shepherd. Turned upside down, it forms the letter "J"—for Jesus.

FOR THE BULLETIN

❀ Nero Claudius Caesar Drusus Germanicus was born on this day in A.D. 37. He became Roman Emperor at age 16, and served A.D. 54 to 68, during which time he murdered (among others) his mother, his wife, his teacher, and his second wife. When two-thirds of Rome burned, he blamed the Christians, persecuting them viciously. During his reign both Peter and Paul are thought to have been executed. His army turned against him in 68, and he fled to a friend's villa where, in great agony, he committed suicide. ❀ John Oldcastle, advisor to King Henry IV, was a knight, a politician, a soldier, a preacher, a baron, a fugitive, a martyr, and the inspiration for Shakespeare's character, Falstaff. After the death of John Wycliffe, Oldcastle sought to protect Wycliffe's preachers, the Lollards. Against him arose the Archbishop of Canterbury. Oldcastle was imprisoned in the Tower of London, tried, and condemned. He escaped, but at length was recaptured and returned to London where, on December 15, 1418, he was "hanged up by the middle in chains of iron, and consumed alive in the fire, praising the name of God so long as his life lasted." ❀ On December 15, 1629, Roger Williams, 26, married Mary Barnard, daughter of a Puritan clergyman. Two years later they sailed for the New World, seeking religious freedom, and later founded Rhode Island.

WORSHIP HELPS

Worship Theme:
As we recall the grace of God, we truly anticipate the real meaning of Christmas.

Call to Worship:
"Behold, the virgin shall be with child, and bear a Son, and they shall call His name Emmanuel," which is translated, "God with us" (Matt. 1:23).

Appropriate Scripture Reading:
Isaiah 7:14–16
John 1:1–14
Galatians 4:3–7

A Poem by Martin Luther
All praise to Thee, Eternal Lord,
Clothed in a garb of flesh and blood;
Choosing a manger for a throne,
While worlds on worlds are Thine alone.

Prayer:
O God, whose Son Jesus was born in a small town, in a tiny nation, in a harsh age, and amid the animals of a damp and smelly stable, teach us today the humility of Jesus, but impress us with His greatness. Lead us to the manger, but teach us there of Him whose comings and goings are from old, even from eternity. May we see not only the crib of a child, but the creator of the cosmos. And may we, too, be humble of heart, yet alert to the grandeur of following our Lord Jesus Christ, in whose name we pray. Amen.

Benediction:
May the blessings of the Babe of Bethlehem so fill this day that we no longer think of it as a holiday, but a holy day and a hallowed day, for Jesus' sake. Amen.

STATS, STORIES AND MORE

The Oriental Manger

In his book, *When Iron Gates Yield,* British missionary Geoffrey T. Bull tells of being seized by Communists following their takeover of China in 1949. His captors drove him day and night across frozen mountains until he despaired of life. Late one afternoon, he staggered into a small village where, after a meager supper, he was sent to feed the horses. It was very dark and very cold. He clambered down the notched ladder to find himself in pitch blackness. His boots squished in the manure and straw on the floor. The fetid smell of animals was nauseating. Geoffrey, cold, weary, lonely, and ill, begin to feel sorry for himself.

"Then as I continued to grope my way in the darkness," he later wrote, "it suddenly flashed into my mind. What's today? I thought for a moment. In traveling, the days had become a little muddled in my mind. Suddenly it came to me. 'It's Christmas Eve.' I stood suddenly still in that oriental manger. To think that my Savior was born in a place like this.

"I returned to the warm clean room which I enjoyed even as a prisoner, bowed to thankfulness and worship."

A Modern Manger

This article appeared on page 4 of the *Boston Globe* on Christmas Eve, 2000, datelined Lexington: Hundreds of singing and shivering worshipers congregated on historic Battle Green last night to turn the site of a controversy into a place for celebration. They came to sing Christmas carols and witness a live Nativity scene. Activists planned the event after town officials banned them from displaying a crèche on the historic green. The battle over the crèche "has been a blessing in disguise," said Eleanore Mannuzza of Chelmsford, who carried a candle and exuberantly sang, "Oh Come All Ye Faithful." "It brought us together," she said.

The service was led by the Rev. Tom DiLorenzo of Holy Rosary Church in Winthrop. "This isn't being done as a protest," said DiLorenzo a few hours before the event, even as he expressed outrage over the decision by the Board of Selectmen to ban the crèche. "This is being done as an act of faith."

Additional Sermons and Lesson Ideas

Celebrating Christmas
Date preached:

By Dr. Timothy Beougher

SCRIPTURE: Luke 2:17–20

INTRODUCTION: We can look back to the first Christmas celebration to gain insight on how we as 20th century believers can and should celebrate Christmas.

1. **We celebrate Christmas by telling others about Christ.** Verse 17 says: "When they had seen Him, they made widely known the saying which was told them concerning this Child."
2. **We celebrate Christmas by reflecting on its wonderful meaning.** Verses 18 & 19 tell us that everyone who heard about the birth of Christ marveled, and Mary pondered these things in her heart.
3. **We celebrate Christmas by offering praise and glory to God.** Verse 20 tells us the shepherds glorified and praised God for all they had heard and seen.

CONCLUSION: Put Christ back into your Christmas. Tell others about Him and invite them to our church Christmas services. Make time to ponder Him in your heart, and take every opportunity of praising the Christ of Bethlehem.

Wonderful Counselor
Date preached:

SCRIPTURE: Isaiah 9:6

INTRODUCTION: The football games of December and the coming bowl games remind us that no one plays football alone. Up above in the stands are coaches with binoculars, sending down advice to coaches wearing headsets on the field. Christians have a divine counselor above who sees things more clearly and sends us counsel from on high. According to the Bible, all three members of the Trinity are our counselors:

1. **God the Father Counsels Us** (Ps. 16:7). "I will bless the LORD who has given me counsel...." Also see Isaiah 28:29; Job 12:13; Psalm 32:8; Psalm 73:23; Proverbs 8:14.
2. **God the Son Counsels Us** (Is. 9:6). "Wonderful Counselor...." When Jesus promised to send *another* counselor, He was implying that He Himself also served in that role. Notice how He counseled the people of His day.
3. **God the Spirit Counsels us** (John 15:26). "When the Counselor comes, whom I will send to you from the Father, the Spirit of truth" (NIV).

CONCLUSION: We receive God's Triune counsel as we pray, study the Scriptures, and attune our hearts to Him (Ps. 119:24; Ps. 32:8). Do you need a counseling today? He is our Wonderful Counselor.

The Kneeling Christian

In our Lord's last discourse to His loved ones, just before the most wonderful of all prayers, the Master again and again held out His kingly golden scepter and said, as it were, "What is your request? It shall be granted unto you, even unto the whole of My kingdom!"

Do we believe this? We must do so if we believe our Bibles. Shall we just read over very quietly and thoughtfully one of our Lord's promises, reiterated so many times? If we had never read them before, we should open our eyes in bewilderment, for these promises are almost incredible. From the lips of any mere man they would be quite unbelievable. But it is the Lord of heaven and earth Who speaks; and He is speaking at the most solemn moment of His life. It is the eve of His death and passion. It is a farewell message. Now listen!

"Verily, verily I say unto you, he that believeth on Me, the works that I do shall he do also; and greater works than these shall he do: because I go unto the Father. And whatsoever ye shall ask in My name, that will I do, that the Father may be glorified in the Son. If ye shall ask anything in My name, that will I do" (John 14:13, 14). Now, could any words be plainer or clearer than these? Could any promise be greater or grander? Has anyone else, anywhere, at any time, ever offered so much?

How staggered those disciples must have been! Surely they could scarcely believe their own ears. But that promise is made also to you and to me.

And, lest there should be any mistake on their part, or on ours, our Lord repeats Himself a few moments afterwards. Yes, and the Holy Spirit bids St. John record those words again. "If ye abide in Me, and My words abide in you, ask whatsoever ye will, and it shall be done unto you. Herein is My Father glorified, that ye bear much fruit; and so shall ye be My disciples" (John 15:7, 8).

These words are of such grave importance, and so momentous, that the Savior of the world is not content even with a threefold utterance of them. He urges His disciples to obey His command "to ask." In fact, He tells them that one sign of their being His "friends" will be the obedience to His commands in all things (verse 14). Then He once more repeats His wishes: "Ye did not choose Me, but I chose you, and appointed you, that ye should go and bear fruit, and that your fruit should abide: that whatsoever ye shall ask the Father, in My name, He may give it you" (John 15:16).

One would think that our Lord had now made it plain enough that He wanted them to pray; that He needed their prayers, and that without prayer they could accomplish nothing. But to our intense surprise He returns again to the same subject, saying very much the same words.

"In that day ye shall ask Me nothing"—i.e., "ask Me no question" (R.V., marg.)—"Verily, verily I say unto you, if ye ask anything of the Father, He will give it you in My name. Hitherto have ye asked nothing in My name: ask, and ye shall receive, that your joy may be fulfilled" (John 16:23, 24).

Never before had our Lord laid such stress on any promise or command—never! This truly marvelous promise is given us six times over. Six times, almost in the same breath, our Savior commands us to ask whatsoever we will. This is the greatest—the most wonderful—promise ever made to man. Yet most men—Christian men—practically ignore it! Is it not so?

The exceeding greatness of the promise seems to overwhelm us. Yet we know that He is "able to do exceeding abundantly above all that we ask or think" (Phil. 3:20). So our blessed Master gives the final exhortation, before He is seized, and bound, and scourged, before His gracious lips are silenced on the cross, "Ye shall ask in My name . . . for the Father Himself loveth you" (16:25, 26). We have often spent much time in reflecting upon our Lord's seven words from the cross. And it is well we should do so. Have we ever spent one hour in meditating upon this, our Savior's sevenfold invitation to pray?

Gracious Savior, pour out upon us the fullness of the Holy Spirit, that we may indeed become Kneeling Christians. ✿

—from the anonymous classic on prayer, *The Kneeling Christian*

DECEMBER 22, 2002

From Old, Even From Everlasting   *Date preached:*

Scripture: Micah 5:1–5a, especially verse 2 But you, Bethlehem Ephrathah, though you are little among the thousands of Judah, yet out of you shall come forth to Me the One to be Ruler in Israel, whose goings forth are from of old, from everlasting."

Introduction: What if we could predict with confidence who would win the U.S. Presidential race two years from now? After the mess the polling organizations made in the last presidential election, we could make a fortune. But what if we could predict with certainty the name of the person to be elected President 700 years from now? The prophet Micah told us of a Messiah who would be born in a little town called Bethlehem, and he made his prediction 700 years in advance. Micah predicted:

1. **A Great Ruler Will Be Preceded by National Distress and Divine Judgement** (Micah 5:1). In verse 1, Jerusalem is told to mobilize her army and prepare for siege, for the Israelites were going be encompassed by enemies who would strike their king. That is exactly what happened. The people of Israel disregarded the Lord's prophets and disobeyed His precepts. A series of weak and wicked kings dragged the nation into a moral and military abyss until Judah fell to besieging Babylon. Later Israel experienced a series of humiliations—the tyranny of Antiochus, political confusion by the Hasmoneans, defeat by the Romans, and the despotism of half-insane Herod the Great, at which point Christ came. Sooner or later, our sins find us out (Num. 32:23; Prov. 14:24).

2. **The Ruler Would Be Born in Bethlehem** (Micah 5:2a). There were two Bethlehems in Israel in those days, one in the area of Zebulun, and the other near Jerusalem. The ancient name of the latter was Ephrathah (Gen. 35:19). Micah was being quite specific, and he especially noted the town's smallness. One of the most remarkable demographic trends of the past century has been the global shift to urbanization, but large cities have been around from antiquity. The first city to reach one million was Rome about 130 years before Christ. You would have thought the Messiah would have been born in Rome, Alexandria, or Jerusalem. But He came in tiny Bethlehem, and Micah

was chosen to reveal that information to us, for he was a small town prophet who ministered to small towns. We think bigger is better, but the Bible tells us to despise not the day of small things. "Little is much when God is in it; / Labor not for wealth or fame. / There's a crown, and you can win it, / When you go in Jesus' name." Edward Payson, a 19th century preacher in Portland, Maine, had but one hearer one stormy Sunday. Payson preached his sermon, however, as carefully as though the building had been thronged. Later his solitary listener called on him. "I was led to the Savior through that service," he said. "For whenever you talked about sin and salvation, I glanced around to see to whom you referred, but since there was no one there but me, I had no alternative but to lay every word to my own heart and conscience!"

3. **The Ruler Is Eternal** (Micah 5:2b). "His goings forth have been from of old, from everlasting" (KJV). Our Lord's miraculous conception in Nazareth and His birth in Bethlehem didn't mark the beginning of His existence. He once told the Jews, "Before Abraham was, I am." See John 1:1.

4. **The Messiah Will Be a Threefold Ruler**
   A. **He Is Our Shepherd** (v. 4a). See John 10:11–15.
   B. **He Is Our Security** Verse 4b in the NIV reads: "And they will live securely, for then his greatness will reach to the ends of the earth." This has millennial implications, but even now we can live securely in Him, and His greatness reaches to the ends of the earth.
   C. **He Is Our Serenity** Verse 5 tells us He is our peace—not just that He will establish peace, make peace, or impart peace. He *is* our peace. See Ephesians 2:14 and Isaiah 9:6.

>>> *sermon continued on following page*

APPROPRIATE HYMNS AND SONGS

Arise, Shine, Steven Urspringer/Jay Robinson; © 1983 Priesthood Publications.

Of the Father's Love Begotten, Aurelius C. Prudentius/John Mason Neale/Henry W. Baker; Public Domain.

O Thou Joyful, O Thou Wonderful, Johannes D. Falk; Public Domain.

Jesus, Name Above All Names, Naida Hearn; © 1974, 1978 Scripture in Song (Admin. by Integrity Music, Inc.).

One Small Child, David Meece; © 1971 Word Music, Inc.

Conclusion: Seven hundred years before His birth, the little town of Bethlehem was chosen as the town of His nativity. Still now, 2,000 years later, we celebrate the birth of Him whose goings forth have been of old, even from everlasting. And His greatness reaches to the ends of the earth. Does it reach into your heart?

O little town of Bethlehem, how still we see thee lie!
Above thy deep and dreamless sleep the silent stars go by.
Yet in thy dark streets shineth the everlasting Light;
The hopes and fears of all the years are met in thee tonight.

FOR THE BULLETIN

✽ Innocent I began his pontificate on December 22, 401. ✽ On December 22, 1216, Pope Honorius III officially approved the Order of Preachers (the Dominicans), founded by St. Dominic. This order produced many European intellectual leaders during the Middle Ages, and sent many Spanish-speaking missionaries to America during the colonial era. ✽ On December 22, 1800, William Carey witnessed his first conversions after seven years laboring in India. Four Hindus came to faith in Christ at Serampore. ✽ As a child John Hunt often sat by the fire, engrossed in his father's tales of military adventure. As a boy, he labored at the plow. At 16, he nearly died of "brain fever." Recovering, he found the Lord in a Methodist Chapel. He later married Hanna Summers, and on December 22, 1838, they arrived on the Fiji islands as missionaries. During their years there, much of Fiji was transformed, causing one historian to call Fiji a "jewel in the missionary diadem."

Kids Talk

If possible, situate an easy chair by a Christmas tree on stage. Have the children gather around you as you read Luke 2:1–24 from the King James Version. It is even more meaningful against the backdrop of soft sounds of traditional Christmas carols from a keyboard.

Worship Theme:
The Babe of Bethlehem is the eternal Messiah whose comings and goings have been from old, even from everlasting.

Call to Worship:
Come and adore Him, born the King of Angels! Oh, come, let us adore Him!

Responsive Reading:

Leader: For unto us a Child is born, Unto us a Son is given; And the government will be upon His shoulder. And His name will be called Wonderful, Counselor, Mighty God, Everlasting Father, Prince of Peace.

People: Of the increase of His government and peace There will be no end, Upon the throne of David and over His kingdom, To order it and establish it with judgment and justice From that time forward, even forever.

Leader: "But you, Bethlehem Ephrathah, Though you are little among the thousands of Judah, Yet out of you shall come forth to Me The One to be Ruler in Israel, Whose goings forth are from of old, From everlasting."

People: Jesus was born in Bethlehem of Judea in the days of Herod the king.

Leader: And when (Herod) had gathered all the chief priests and scribes of the people together, he inquired of them where the Christ was to be born.

All: So they said to him, "In Bethlehem of Judea, for thus it is written by the prophet: 'But you, Bethlehem, in the land of Judah, Are not the least among the rulers of Judah; For out of you shall come a Ruler Who will shepherd My people Israel.' "

Taken from Isaiah 9:6–7; Micah 5:3; Matthew 2:1, 4–6.

STATS, STORIES AND MORE

Be Sure Your Sins Will Find You Out

The *Wall Street Journal* carried an article about people who accidentally jostle their cell phones and make calls unawares. One man was engaged in a very graphic, sexual conversation with his buddies when he hit a button that automatically called his mother, who overheard the whole thing. Another man accidentally called his wife while he was involved with another woman. The Bible warns that God is always listening, always watching, and that our sins will find us out.

No Man's Land

This story has been told in a variety of ways, but this is the researched version that appeared in newspapers nationwide on December 25, 1994, from the Associated Press, dateline London.

Eighty years ago, on the first Christmas Day of World War I, British and German troops put down their guns and celebrated peacefully together in the no-man's land between the trenches. The war, briefly, came to a halt.

Pvt. Oswald Tilley of the London Rifle Brigade wrote to his parents: "Just you think that while you were eating your turkey etc. I was out talking and shaking hands with the very men I had been trying to kill a few hours before!! It was astounding."

Both armies had received lots of comforts from home and felt generous and well-disposed toward their enemies in the first winter of the war, before the vast battles of attrition began in 1915, eventually claiming 10 million lives.

All along the line that Christmas Day, soldiers found their enemies were much like them and began asking why they should be trying to kill each other.

The generals were shocked. High Command diaries and statements express anxiety that if that sort of thing spread it could sap the troops' will to fight.

The soldiers in khaki and gray sang carols to each other, exchanged gifts of tobacco, jam, sausage, chocolate and liquor, traded names and addresses and played soccer between the shell holes and barbed wire. They even paid mutual trench visits.

This day is called "the most famous truce in military history" by British television producer Malcolm Brown and researcher Shirley Seaton in their book *Christmas Truce*, published in 1984.

Additional Sermons and Lesson Ideas

The Original Christmas Gift

Date preached:

SCRIPTURE READING: John 3:16

INTRODUCTION: Many people think Christmas gift-giving had its start when the Magi brought gifts to the Christchild, but the original Christmas gift came even earlier. It was Christ Himself. "For God so loved the world that He gave His only son." Romans 6:23 says, "The gift of God is eternal life through Jesus Christ." The very letters of the word *Gift* explain this to us.

1. **G Is for Gospel.** Though we have all sinned, God loved us so much He became a man to die and rise again for us.
2. **I Is for I** must receive this gift for myself, making Christ my own personal Lord and Savior.
3. **F Is for Forgiveness.** When I receive the gospel, the blood of Christ is applied to my soul, and my sins are forgiven.
4. **T Is for Transformation.** God begins at that point to make me into a different person, into a person pleasing to Him.

CONCLUSION: A gift only becomes ours when we receive it.

The Way It Was

Date preached:

By Dr. Melvin Worthington

SCRIPTURE: Matthew 1:18–25

INTRODUCTION: Wondrous truth surrounds Christmas. Long before Jesus was born, history was rushing toward Bethlehem, fulfilling Isaiah's promise regarding a virgin (Isa. 7:14), and Micah's prediction about the Messiah (Micah 5:2).

1. **The Partners** (v. 18). Matthew gives us the names of two humble youths of Nazareth, Mary and Joseph.
2. **The Problem** (v. 18). "Before they came together, she was found with child...."
3. **The Pronouncement** (vv. 18–23). After Joseph had anguished over the problem, which doubtlessly drove him first to despair than to the Lord, the angel of God gave him the wondrous explanation.
4. **The Peace** (vv. 24–25). Joseph responded to the message with faith and obedience. What wonderful news! Let us rejoice and be glad, for this is the way it was when Jesus was born.

CONCLUSION: Partners in any enterprise who respond to problems by trusting and obeying God find peace in any storm.

DECEMBER 29, 2002

SUGGESTED SERMON

Formula for Faithfulness

Date preached:

By Dr. Melvin Worthington

Scripture: Daniel 1:1–21, especially verses 8–17 But Daniel made up his mind not to defile himself by eating the food and wine given to them by the king. He asked the chief official for permission to eat other things instead. Now God had given the chief official great respect for Daniel. But he was alarmed by Daniel's suggestion. "My lord the king has ordered that you eat this food and wine," he said. "If you become pale and thin compared to the other youths your age, I am afraid the king will have me beheaded for neglecting my duties."

Daniel talked it over with the attendant who had been appointed by the chief official to look after Daniel, Hananiah, Mishael, and Azariah. "Test us for ten days on a diet of vegetables and water," Daniel said. "At the end of the ten days, see how we look compared to the other young men who are eating the king's rich food. Then you can decide whether or not to let us continue eating our diet." So the attendant agreed to Daniel's suggestion and tested them for ten days. At the end of the ten days, Daniel and his three friends looked healthier and better nourished than the young men who had been eating the food assigned by the king. So after that, the attendant fed them only vegetables instead of the rich foods and wines. God gave these four young men an unusual aptitude for learning the literature and science of the time. And God gave Daniel special ability in understanding the meanings of visions and dreams.

Introduction: Most of us are busy making our New Year's resolutions, and for many of us, they involve food. Or better put—staying away from food. In that, we have a great hero in the prophet Daniel, who, as a young man, made some resolutions in chapter one of his book to which he stayed faithful all the days of his life. New Year's resolutions only work for people who understand and practice faithfulness, and faithfulness exemplified Daniel's entire life, in things both large and small (Dan. 6:4).

1. **The Providence of Sovereignty** (vv. 1:1–2, 9, 17). Faithfulness requires that we understand that the providence of God is continually at work in the life of every believer. Here we see God's sovereignty in: *The Defeated People* (vv. 1, 2a). Divine providence allowed Nebuchadnezzar to besiege Jerusalem and defeat king Jehoiakim. It is interesting that the Bible says "And the Lord gave Jehoiakim into his hands..." (v. 2a) *The Desecrated Place* (v. 2b). Nebuchadnezzar had also desecrated the house of God, removing part of the vessels from the house of God to the land of Shinar to the house of his god. *The Deported*

Person (vv. 3–4). Under the watchful eye of divine providence, Daniel was taken captive to Babylon as a teenager. He did not waste his time criticizing or complaining about his terrible circumstances, for he rested in the providence of the living God. Never once wavering, he was aware that the superintending hand of the Almighty was in full control. His faithfulness was founded upon confidence in the providential dealing of Jehovah. God still controls all. Trust His providence. Take His pathway. Triumph in His power.

2. **The Pressure of Society** (vv. 3–7). Faithfulness requires that Christians withstand the pressure brought to bear by the society in which they live. Shortly after his arrival in Babylon as a captive, Daniel faced tremendous pressure from the pagan society, both in the rigorous training to which he was subjected and with the royal table with which he was tempted. Society exerts constant pressure on Christians. Faithful resistance must be maintained if we expect to display a positive and powerful witness. Faithful allegiance must be given to the Lord and His law. Disobedience and defection mean disaster. Daniel's faithfulness was challenged by the pressures of the Babylonian society, but he prevailed.

3. **The Power of Steadfastness** (vv. 8–16). Faithfulness requires that Christians resolve in their hearts that they will not disobey God. *Daniel's Resolution* (v. 8a): When faced with the forbidden food, Daniel purposed in his heart that he would not defile himself with the king's dainties. *Daniel's Request* (v. 8b): He asked the prince of the eunuchs that he not be required to eat the king's meat. *Daniel's Reasoning* (vv. 9–15): Daniel presented his case, and the royal

>>> *sermon continued on following page*

APPROPRIATE HYMNS AND SONGS

Another Year is Dawning, Frances R. Havergal/Samuel Wesley; Public Domain.

Savior, Like a Shepherd Lead Us, Dorothy A. Thrupp/William B. Bradbury; Public Domain.

Day by Day, Carolina Sandell Berg/Oscar Ahnfelt/Andrew Skoog; Public Domain.

Hear, O Lord, Dori Howard/Tom Howard; © 1982 Maranatha! Music.

I Hope In You, Craig Musseau; © 1990 Mercy/Vineyard Publishing (Admin. by Music Services).

eunuch agreed. *Daniel's Relief* (vs.16): As a result, Melzar took away the king's portion of meat and wine and gave him a vegetarian diet. Nothing short of a disciplined, dedicated and determined heart will enable one to obey God rather than man regardless of the consequences. We must purpose in our hearts to wholly follow the Lord. Daniel's faithfulness was finalized in a heart with purpose.

4. **The Placement of Servants** (vv. 17–21). Faithfulness allows God to strategically determine the placement of His servants, and Daniel spent the rest of his life in high office, overseeing nations, as God's man in a unique place for about 80 years. Those who faithfully adhere to the Word of God will be strategically placed for service.

Conclusion: Faithfulness focuses on a special place of service, which only the Lord can give. When God places a man or woman in a specific place of service it is because that person has been divinely taught, trained, tested and tempered. The Sovereign's school equips His servants for effective employment in His service.

FOR THE BULLETIN

❀ On December 29, 1170, Thomas Becket, Archbishop of Canterbury, was murdered in his own cathedral by overzealous agents of King Henry II who later did penance by having himself flogged over Becket's tomb. ❀ December 29, 1499, marks the death of Katherine von Bora, wife of Martin Luther. ❀ Robert Boyle, the "father of modern chemistry," is remembered as the founder of the Royal Society. On December 29, 1640, at age 13, Boyle was converted to Christ during a terrific thunder storm at night. He remained a devout Christian and a supporter of missions all his life. ❀ When Medical student William Savage Pitts learned of a congregation in Bradford, Iowa, that needed a location and building for their services, he offered to write a song about the project, subsequently penning the words to "The Church in the Wildwood." Inspired by his song, the church mustered its resources, purchased the land, and built their little brown church in the vale, which was completed and dedicated on December 29, 1864. ❀ During the Christmas holidays of 1876, hymnist Philip Bliss visited family in Pennsylvania. On December 29, 1876, they boarded the Pacific Express in Buffalo to return to Chicago. About 8 p.m. in a blinding snowstorm as the train crossed a ravine, the wooden trestle collapsed. The cars plunged 75 feet into the icy river and caught fire. Over a hundred people perished in the wreck, among them — Philip Bliss and his family. He was 38.

Worship Theme:
God's people must remain faithful.

Call to Worship:
It is good to give thanks to the LORD, and to sing praises to Your name, O Most High; to declare Your lovingkindness in the morning, and Your faithfulness every night (Ps. 92:1–2).

Appropriate Scripture Readings:
Proverbs 28:18–20; Matthew 24:45–51; 1 Timothy 1:12–17

Hymn Story: "Great is Thy Faithfulness"
The hymn "Great is Thy Faithfulness" was written by Thomas Chisholm, who was born in a log cabin in Kentucky. He was converted in early-adulthood by evangelist H. C. Morrison. Chisholm's health was unstable, and he alternated between bouts of illness and gainful employment in which he did everything from journalism to insurance to evangelistic work. Through all the ups and downs, he discovered new blessings from God every morning. Lamentations 3:22–24 became precious to him, and he wrote this hymn after 30 years of serving Christ. It was relatively unknown until popularized around the world by George Beverly Shea and the choirs at the Billy Graham Crusades, especially hitting a high note at the famous 1954 Harringay Crusade in England.

Kids Talk

Ask the children to define "New Year's Resolution." Ask them if any of them have made any resolutions for the coming year, and, if so, what they are. Suggest some good resolutions: To be honest at school; to come to church every Sunday; to read their Bible each day. Have a prayer for the children for the coming year.

STATS, STORIES AND MORE

Someone Once Said:
"New Year's Resolutions are like friends. They are easier to make than to keep." —*Anonymous*
"A New Year's Resolution usually goes in one year and out the next."
—*Anonymous*

From Matthew Henry
"When God's people are in Babylon they need take special care that they partake not of her sins. Those who would excel in wisdom and piety, must learn betimes to keep the body under. Daniel avoided defiling himself with sin; and we should more fear that than any outward trouble. It is easier to keep temptation at a distance, than to resist it when near."
—*Matthew Henry*

The Fresh Start
In 1995, Glenna Salsbury wrote a book entitled, *The Art of the Fresh Start: How to Make and Keep Your New Year's Resolutions for a Lifetime.* Daniel never read that book, but he knew something about purposing in his heart and keeping promises to himself—and to his God.

From Vance Havner:
According to Vance Havner, Daniel faced three tests in Babylon:
- The table of Nebuchadnezzar (Dan. 1).
- The feast of Belshazzar (Dan. 5).
- The decree of Darius (Dan. 6).

Rotten Within
After a violent storm one night, a large tree, which over the years had become a stately giant, was found lying across the pathway in a park. Nothing but a splintered stump was left. Closer examination showed that is was rotten at the core because thousands of tiny insects had eaten away at its heart. The weakness of that tree was not brought on by the sudden storm; it began the very moment the first insect nested within its bark. With the Holy Spirit's help, let's be very careful to guard our purity.

—from *Our Daily Bread.*

Additional Sermons and Lesson Ideas

Trees Walking

Date preached:

SCRIPTURE: Mark 8:24

INTRODUCTION: The Bible compares God's people with trees. Three Old Testament passages help us understand this analogy:

1. **The Meditating Tree** (Ps. 1:1–3). David had perhaps been meditating on Joshua 1:8, turning the verse into a vivid picture.
2. **The Trusting Tree** (Jer. 17:7–8). As we meditation on God's Word, we learn to trust Him as we should (Rom. 10:17).
3. **The Fruitful Tree** (Ps. 92:12–15). "The noble and beautiful palm tree affords an agreeable shade: its fruit makes a great part of the diet of the East, the stones of which are ground for the camels; the leaves are made into couches, baskets, etc.; its boughs, into fences; the fibers of the boughs, into ropes, and the rigging of small vessels; its sap, into arrack; and its wood serves for lighter buildings and fire wood" (from the *New Treasury of Scripture Knowledge*).

CONCLUSION: As we respond to the Lord's message and ministry we become "oaks of righteousness, a planting of the LORD for the display of his splendor" (Isa. 61:3 NIV).

Have A Hopeful New Year!

Date preached:

By Drew Wilkerson

SCRIPTURE: Lamentations 3:18–23

INTRODUCTION: For many people this has been a discouraging year. The writer of Lamentations reminds us of four wonderful truths that fill each day—and year—with hope.

1. **Truth #1—Through the Lord's Mercies.** Also see 1 John 4:10. We cannot "outlove Him", and we cannot do anything that will keep Him from loving us.
2. **Truth #2—We are not Consumed.** 1 John 4:10 goes on to say, " . . . but He loved us and sent His Son as an atoning sacrifice for our sins." When hopelessness comes, we need not be consumed by it. God's Son forgives and heals.
3. **Truth #3—His Compassions Fail Not.** The word compassion means, "to have deep sympathy." God is a Heavenly Father who wants our best, and every day He provides new hope and a fresh start.
4. **Truth #4—Great Is Thy Faithfulness.** Regardless of our emotional state, God is consistent and faithful.

CONCLUSION: Perhaps Lamentations 3:22–23 is the tonic you need for the beginning of a New Year.

WEDDING CEREMONY

Leaving, Cleaving, and Weaving

Dear friends, we are together in this sweet and sacred hour to witness the uniting of _____ and _____ in the enduring bonds of Christian marriage. This happiest and holiest of human relationships was first celebrated in the quiet gardens of Eden, in the springtime of world history. God saw that it was not good for man to live alone, and so He created woman and gave her to him to be his companion, his wife. The Lord said: "For this cause shall a man leave father and mother and shall cleave unto his wife. And they two shall be one flesh."

This first description of marriage gives us three words for the establishing of a home. The first is leaving. *For this reason a man will leave his father and mother. . . .* When a man and a woman establish a new home, there is a sense in which they leave their old ones. They don't leave in terms of love or communication. But they leave in terms of authority and priority. The most important human relationship for you now is the one you're establishing today, in this place and before these witnesses. The primary relationship in your life shifts from the parental to the spousal, from mother and father to husband and wife.

The second idea in Genesis 2:24 is cleaving. *For this reason a man will leave his father and mother and be united, shall cleave, to his wife. . . .* The word "cleave" here means to stick like glue, to be devoted, committed to each other. Every marriage goes through difficult periods and challenging times. It's easy for love to grow lukewarm, then cold. Disillusionment can descend on a home like a Smokey Mountain fog. That's why you have to remember that divorce is never an option, that the vows you are taking before God are holy, binding, and permanent. You are today deciding to stick to one another like glue, through thick and thin, through good and bad.

We know not what the encircling years will bring, nor how life and labor will unfold before you. But whatever the passing seasons hold, you must always remember to keep your poise, guard your purity, find your place, and fulfill your purpose. *Do everything without complaining or arguing, so that you may become blameless and pure, children of God without fault in a crooked and depraved generation, in which you shine like stars in the universe.*

But that leads to a third concept in Genesis 2:24: Weaving. The verse goes on to say that the man and the woman who leave their parents, cleave to one another, should then become as one. They should weave their lives together. Marriage requires developing common interests, common hobbies, good communication, time together, frequent dating, and growing love. A wedding takes twenty minutes to perform. A friendship takes a lifetime to perfect.

Be completely humble and gentle; be patient, bearing with one another in love. Make every effort to keep the unity of the Spirit in the bond of peace.

And in your marriage, put off falsehood and speak truthfully to one another. In your anger, do not sin. Do not let the sun go down while you are still angry, and do not give the devil a foothold. Do not let any unwholesome talk come out of your mouths, but only what is helpful for building each other up according to your needs.

In your marriage, rid yourselves of all bitterness, rage and anger, brawling and slander, along with every form of malice. But be kind and compassionate to one another, forgiving each other, just as in Christ God forgave you.

In three words, a godly marriage requires leaving, cleaving, and weaving.

If you then, _____ and _____, having freely and deliberately and prayerfully chosen each other as partners for life, will you please unite your right hands and repeat after me:

In taking the woman I hold by the right hand to be my wedded wife, before God and these witnesses I promise to love her, to honor her in this relationship; and leaving all others to be in all things a true and faithful husband as long as we both shall live.

In taking the man I hold by the right hand to be my wedded husband, before God and these witnesses I promise to love him, to honor him in this relationship; and leaving all others to be in all things a true and faithful wife as long as we both shall live.

Then you are each given to the other for richer or poorer, for better or worse, in sickness and in health by the grace of the Lord Jesus Christ.

WEDDING CEREMONY

The 23rd Psalm

Dear friends, we are assembled here this afternoon to unite _____
and _____ in marriage. The establishment of marriage and the
ordination of the home is found within the pages of Scripture; and between the
covers of that same Bible we also find every other good word fitting us for holy
matrimony.

The 23rd Psalm is the portion to which I turn today, for it provides a good
theme-song for this couple, its every phrase and figure of speech having implications of hope for the family being established today.

"The Lord is my Shepherd; I shall not want. He maketh me to lie down in
green pastures: he leadeth me beside the still waters. He restoreth my soul: he
leadeth me in the paths of righteousness for his name's sake. Yea, though I walk
through the valley of the shadow of death, I will fear no evil: for thou art with
me; thy rod and thy staff they comfort me. Thou preparest a table before me in
the presence of mine enemies: thou anointest my head with oil; my cup runneth
over. Surely goodness and mercy shall follow me all the days of my life: and I
will dwell in the house of the LORD forever" (KJV).

When two people like _____ and _____, both
committed to Jesus Christ, say, "The Good Shepherd is My Shepherd," and
when both these people then become united in Christian marriage, then the
pronoun of the entire Psalm changes from *my* to *our*:

The Lord is our shepherd: We shall not want. . . .

In other words, they are thereby saying: We know that our Shepherd will provide for the needs of our home. And our Shepherd will feed us in the green pastures of His word. He will lead us by the still waters of His Spirit. And He will
restore us day by day, giving us fresh supplies of love, patience, optimism, and
understanding each new morning of each passing day.

And that's not all; such a couple says: Our Shepherd will give us wisdom in
the decisions and dilemmas we face from time to time. He will lead us in the
right paths for His name's sake.

Not only so, but we know that even during dark days of sickness and stress, disappointment, poverty, and death, the Great Shepherd of the sheep will never leave us or forsake us. He will be with us, and we will fear no evil.

Furthermore, day by day he will provide food for our children and clothes for our bodies and a roof for our head. He will prepare a table before us, making our cups overflow.

Atop all these, there's a final word, for the psalmist ends his poem in a great and glorious affirmation which we can paraphrase like this: Surely goodness and mercy shall follow you all the days of your lives, through all the seasons of your marriage; and you shall dwell in the presence of the Lord forever.

If you have freely and deliberately chosen each other as partners in this pastoral relationship, in token thereof, will you please join your right hands and repeat after me:

In taking this woman to be my wedded wife before God and these witnesses, I promise to love her, to honor her and cherish her in this relationship, and leaving all others, cleave only unto her, in all things a true and faithful husband, as long as we both shall live.

In taking this man to be my wedded husband before God and these witnesses, I promise to love him, to honor him and cherish him in this relationship, and leaving all others, cleave only unto him, in all things a true and faithful wife, as long as we both shall live.

Then you are each given to the other for richer or poorer, for better or worse, in sickness and in health, till death shall you part.

WEDDING CEREMONY

The Fruit of the Spirit

We have today assembled to witness the highest normalization of the deepest kind of friendship, the uniting of _____ and _____ in the bond of marriage. Just as Jehovah joined Adam and Eve in the effulgence of Eden during the days of Genesis, so He is present here tonight, ordaining and presiding over this wedding.

He has designed your marriage, _____ and _____, to be permanent, lasting as long as you both shall live. The Lord doesn't permit divorce, save in the most extreme cases of betrayal and sin. He still means, *"till death shall you part . . ."* and *"for richer or poorer, for better or worse, in sickness and in health."* Marriage is an enduring institution, though not to be endured, but enjoyed for a lifetime.

Adam and Eve almost destroyed their marriage because of fruit which was forbidden, but yours can be enriched by fruit which is forever—the fruit of the Spirit.

The apostle Paul, in the fifth chapter of the New Testament Book of Galatians, wrote: *"The fruit of the Spirit is love, joy, peace, patience, kindness, goodness, faithfulness, gentleness, and self-control."* These nine attitudes, cultivated by the Holy Spirit, will garrison the gates of your house through all the days of your lives.

First, there is love. Love isn't a fleeting feeling into which you have fallen, nor an emotion out of which you can tumble. It is a decision—a choice to care more for your partner than for yourself. It is the attitude of putting the other first.

Joy, the next attitude, is the unexpected pleasure we feel when we choose to put the other first. It is the laughter of love.

Next comes peace, the quiet glow of a laughing fire in the hearth of your home. It's the awareness that no one on God's earth enjoys a greater blessing than you—namely, the privilege of living in the same house with your two best friends—your Savior and your spouse. Peace is the contentment of love.

Patience is the ability to remain calm when the other grows angry. It's the willingness to nurture when you'd rather nag, and to smile when you'd rather scold, scald, and scheme. It's the acceptance of your partner's weaknesses and limitations, knowing well that your spouse is also married to an imperfect mate. Patience is love in slow-motion.

Kindness is nothing more nor less than good manners—treating the other with dignity. It is the elegance of love.

Goodness implies moral purity. It's the absence of rot and ruin in your relationship. It is temptation resisted, or failing that, of sin confessed. It's the holiness of love.

Faithfulness is the greatest ability of all—dependability. Can _____ trust you with her heart, _____? Can he trust you with his hopes, _____ ? Faithfulness is the absence of the fear of betrayal. It is the loyalty of love.

Gentleness, the next virtue, is softness of voice, twinkle of eye, and lightness of step. It's a hug and sometimes a shrug. It's a rose in the vase, a candle by the plate, a card on the pillow. It's the lift of love.

Self-control, the final virtue in Paul's list, is love maturing. It's the discipline of daily discipleship which ties all the other virtues together. These character qualities, after all, can only be acquired by living a life totally yielded to Jesus Christ, and totally filled with His Spirit. This list of happy ingredients is called, for this reason, the fruit of the Spirit.

This simply means that the Spirit-filled husband and wife will be loving, joyful, peaceful, patient, kind, good, faithful, gentle, and self-controlled. In essence, Christ Himself will be living through you, and you will be growing in His image.

That alone makes marriage meaningful, and a home happy.

If you then have thus been led by the Holy Spirit to take one another as life-partners, and if this marriage is, from the beginning, to be committed to Jesus Christ, will you please join your right hands for the exchanging of your vows and repeat after me:

In taking the woman I hold by the right hand to be my wedded wife, before God and these witnesses I promise to love her, to honor her and cherish her in this relationship, and leaving all others, cleave only unto her, in all things a true and faithful husband, as long as we both shall live.

In taking the man I hold by the right hand to be my wedded husband, before God and these witnesses I promise to love him, to honor him and cherish him in this relationship, and leaving all others, cleave only unto him, in all things a true and faithful wife, as long as we both shall live.

Then you are each given to the other for richer or poorer, for better or worse, in sickness and in health, till death shall you part.

FUNERAL MESSAGE

He Knows the Way

Scripture: Mark 7:37

Introduction: This has been a very hard week for us. We have tears and sorrow, and our hearts are breaking. But even today, we can fix our eyes on Jesus, the author and finisher of our faith.

1. **"He Knows the Way He Taketh."** Today I want to remind you of the words of an old hymn that says:

> *In heavenly love abiding, no change my heart shall fear,*
> *and safe is such confiding for nothing changes here.*
> *The storm may rage without me, my heart may low be laid,*
> *But God is round about me, and can I be dismayed.*

> *Wherever He may lead me, no want shall turn me back.*
> *My Shepherd is before me, and nothing can I lack.*
> *His wisdom ever waketh; His sight is never dim.*
> *He knows the way He taketh, and I will walk with Him.*

   Let that phrase, "He knows the way He taketh," flash into your mind like an electric light. God knows what He is doing. He knows what He's about. He doesn't make mistakes, especially of this magnitude. He has purposes of which we're not always privy.

2. **He Does All Things Well.** (Mark 7:37): "And they were astonished beyond measure, saying, 'He has done all things well.'" We don't always understand His means or His methods, but we know He does all things well. His ways are not our ways and His thoughts are not our thoughts, but He does all things well. He allows winds to blow and storms to rage. Sorrows and tears befall us, and our ways may wind through darkness and difficulty. But as for God, His ways are perfect. He works all things together for good. The Bible

says, "Our times are in His hands." A. W. Tozer once wrote, "To the child of God, there is no such thing as accident. He travels an appointed way. Accidents may indeed appear to befall him and misfortune stalk his way, but these evils will be so in appearance only and will seem evils only because we cannot read the secret script of God's hidden providence and so cannot discover the ends at which He aims. . . . The man of true faith may live in the absolute assurance that his steps are ordered by the Lord. For him, misfortune is outside the bounds of possibility. He cannot be torn from this earth one hour ahead of the time which God has appointed, and he cannot be detained on earth on moment after God is done with him here." He does all things well, or as Charles Spurgeon once put it, "When we can not trace His hand, we can trust His heart."

3. **He Gives Grace When We Wonder Why.** God does not always answer our "why" questions, but He does understand our asking them.

- Moses asked: *Lord, why have you brought trouble to this people?*
- Gideon: *Why then has all this happened to us?*
- Naomi said: *I went out full, and the Lord has brought me home again empty. Why?*
- Nehemiah: *Why is the house of God forsaken?*
- Job: *Why have you set me as your target?* In fact, there are over 300 questions in the Book of Job, most of them unanswered.
- David: *Lord, why do you cast off my soul? Why do You hide Your face from me?*
- Jeremiah: *Why is my pain perpetual and my wound incurable?*

But the greatest "why" in the Bible was uttered by the Lord Jesus Christ on the cross when He said, "My God, My God, why have you forsaken me?" And there is something about that "why" that swallows up all the others.

Because Jesus gave Himself on the cross, we can trust Him to have answers to all our other "whys".

Vance Havner: *You need never ask "Why?" because Calvary covers it all. When before the throne we stand in Him complete, all the riddles that puzzle us here will fall into place and we shall know in fulfillment what we now believe in faith—that all things work together for good in His eternal purpose. No longer will we cry "My God,*

>>> *sermon continued on following page*

why?" Instead, "alas" will become "Alleluia," all question marks will be straightened into exclamation points, sorrow will change to singing, and pain will be lost in praise.

Conclusion: Until then, we live by promises, not by explanations. We just trust the One who knows the way He taketh, who does all things well, and who understands our "whys." I don't have a lot of answers, but I do know this: the death of a Christian isn't as tragic a thing to God as it is to us. To us it is separation and sorrow. To God it's

- A promotion
- A release from the burdens of earth
- Early furlough from the battle zone
- Relocation to a better climate
- Instant transport to the celestial city
- To depart and be with Christ, which is far better
- To be absent from the body but present with the Lord

I don't know why tragedy, sadness, and death crowd into our lives, but I know that we can trust Jesus with them. He does all things well. He always has and He always will, and He is our strength today.

FUNERAL MESSAGE

Christ's Words of Comfort

Scripture: John 14:1–6

Introduction: In times of sorrow and distress, we instinctively turn to the Bible, and very often to this passage. It has dried more tears, strengthened more hearts, and graced more funerals than perhaps any other passage excluding Psalm 23. Jesus spoke these words in the Upper Room on the eve of His crucifixion. His intention was to comfort the troubled hearts of His disciples, for the last verse of John 13 was a very troubling prediction to Peter: "Will you lay down your life for My sake? Most assuredly, I say to you, the rooster shall not crow till you have denied Me three times." We are frail, fallible human beings, and we're often filled with confusion, shame, guilt, or sorrow. Jesus knows. In His very next words, He gave reassurance.

1. **The Peace Jesus Provides—John 14:1—**"Let not your heart be troubled; you believe in God, believe also in me." He is telling us that we can take charge of our hearts. We can take control of our emotions and our attitudes. He is commanding us to "let not our hearts be troubled." How can we endure trials without being troubled? We must trust Him with those things we don't understand. We must "believe in God, believe also in Me." As we do so, He pours peace into our troubled hearts (see John 14:27).

2. **The Place Jesus Prepares—John 14:1–4—**He is here promising us a home in heaven. The old versions say that Jesus is preparing for us a mansion. Some of the newer translations use another word, but don't you think the smallest dwelling spot in heaven will be far greater than the finest mansion on earth? I still like that old word "mansion." Furthermore, Christ here promises to return to earth, to come back for us, a promise that Paul amplifies in 1 Thessalonians 4:13–18.

3. **The Path Jesus Prescribes—John 14:5–6—**The last two verses of this paragraph warn us that every road doesn't lead to heaven. There's only one way, one road, one plan of salvation. Peter later put it this way: "Nor is there salvation in any other, for there is no other name under heaven given among men by which we must be saved" (Acts 4:12).

Conclusion: Today we need the peace that Jesus provides. We're eager for the place that Jesus is preparing. And we need to make sure we're on the path that Jesus prescribed.

FUNERAL MESSAGE

The Way of the Pilgrim

Scripture: Psalm 84:5: "Blessed is the man whose strength is in You, whose heart is set on pilgrimage."

Introduction: Christians in earlier days often referred to life as a pilgrimage. The prefix, *Pil* is a Latin preposition meaning *through*. The root word *grim* is from an old Latin word meaning *land*. A pilgrim is someone traveling through a foreign land, a wayfarer. That is the biblical definition of a Christian. John Bunyan, writing from his prison cell in Bedford, England, devoted an entire book to the pilgrim lifestyle—*Pilgrim's Progress*. Many of our old hymns speak of the Christian life as a pilgrimage.

> *While we walk the pilgrim pathway*
> *Clouds will overspread the sky*
> *But when traveling days are over,*
> *Not a shadow, not a sign.*

Another song says:

> *This world is not my home, I'm just a passing through . . .*

The old-time preachers spoke of life as a pilgrimage. North Carolina evangelist Vance Havner once said, "We aren't citizens of earth going to heaven; we're citizens of heaven passing through the world."

In Genesis 47, when Pharaoh asked the patriarch Jacob how old he was, Jacob replied, "The days of the years of my pilgrimage are one hundred thirty years."

Psalm 119:19 in the *Living Bible* says: "I am but a pilgrim here on earth; how I need a map—and your commands are my chart and guide."

Peter told us to live as pilgrims and strangers in the world, abstaining from sinful desires which war against your soul.

And the writer of Hebrews 11 said:

"By faith Abraham obeyed when he was called to go out to the place which he would receive as an inheritance. And he went out, not knowing where he was going. By faith he dwelt in the land of promise as in a foreign country, dwelling in tents with Isaac and Jacob, the heirs with him of the same promise, for he waited for the city which has foundations, whose builder and maker is God. . . .

"These all died in faith, not having received the promises, but having seen them afar off were assured of them, embraced them and confessed that they were strangers and pilgrims on the earth. For those who say such things declare plainly that they seek a homeland. And truly if they had called to mind that country from which they had come out, they would have had opportunity to return. But now they desire a better, that is, a heavenly country. Therefore God is not ashamed to be called their God, for He has prepared a city for them."

But the verse that I want to come back to is the one I quoted at the beginning— Psm 84:5: "Blessed are those whose strength is in you, who have set their hearts on pilgrimage."

This passage tells us five things about pilgrims:

1. **A Pilgrim's Pathway Is Happy.** The word "blessed" means "happy, fortunate, to be envied and congratulated."

2. **The Pilgrim's Strength Is in God.** Verse 5 tells us that a pilgrim's strength is in God, and verse 7 tells us that pilgrims "go from strength to strength." Like the writer of Psalm 46, he says, "God is my refuge and strength, a very present help in trouble."

3. **The Pilgrim's Heart Is Set.** *Blessed is the man whose strength is in You, whose heart is set on pilgrimage.* He has decided to follow Jesus, no turning back. He has put his hand to the plow, no looking back. He has turned his heart to the future, no going back.

4. **The Pilgrim's Route Is Difficult.** The next verse, Psalm 84:6, says that the pilgrim's route winds through the "Valley of Baca," a Hebrew word meaning "weeping." But read on: "As they pass through the Valley of Baca, they make it a spring. . . . They go from strength to strength." Their pathway is both appointed and anointed, and they have a transforming effect as they pass through this world.

>>> *sermon continued on following page*

5. **The Pilgrim's Destination Is Glorious**—Look again at verse 7: "They go from strength to strength; each one appears before God in Zion." There's an old song that says:

> *I am a poor wayfaring stranger*
> *While traveling through this world below,*
> *Yet there's no sickness, toil or danger*
> *In that bright world to which I go.*
> *I'm going there to see my father;*
> *I'm going there no more to roam.*
> *I am just going over Jordan;*
> *I am just going over home.*

Conclusion: Francis and Edith Schaeffer set out as missionaries to Switzerland, where they founded a study center for European students searching for truth. They called it "L'Abri," a French word meaning "Shelter." Through their hospitality at L'Abri and through their books and seminars, the Schaeffers helped thousands of young people find Christ.

Then, during a 1978 visit to Mayo Clinic in Rochester, Minnesota, Francis was diagnosed with an advanced case of lymphoma and was told he had only six to eight weeks to live. His cancer went into remission twice, and his life was extended five more years, during which he ministered on both sides of the Atlantic with unusual power.

Nearing death, he said, "By God's grace, I have been able to do more in these last five years than in all the years before I had cancer." He continued taking his treatments, praying for healing, and speaking quietly for the Lord; but it became clear he was dying.

As was his custom, he met this final challenge by turning to the Scriptures, and the Lord gave him this passage, Psalm 84:5–7: "Blessed is the man whose strength is in You, whose heart is set on pilgrimage. As they pass through the Valley of Baca [Valley of Weeping], they make it a spring; the rain also covers it with pools. They go from strength to strength; each one appears before God in Zion."

Those words became a constant comfort to Francis. The Lord gave him strength. His valley of weeping became a spring from which others found the Lord. And finally, early on May 15, 1984, he appeared before God in Zion.

Special Services Registry

The forms on the following pages are designed to be duplicated and used repeatedly as needed. Most copy machines will allow you to enlarge them to fill a full page if desired. Since they also are included in the CD-ROM in the back of the book, you may use that digital file to customize the forms to fit your specific needs.

Sermons Preached

Date	Text	Title/Subject

Sermons Preached

Date	Text	Title/Subject

Marriages Log

Date	Bride	Groom

Funerals Log

Date	Name of Deceased	Scripture Used

Baptisms / Confirmations

Date	Name	Notes

Baby Dedication Registration

Infant's Name: _____

Significance of Given Names: _____

Date of Birth: _____

Parents' Names: _____

_____

Siblings: _____

_____

_____

_____

Maternal Grandparents: _____

Paternal Grandparents: _____

Life Verse: _____

Date of Dedication: _____

Wedding Registration

Date of Wedding: _____

Location of Wedding: _____

Bride: _____

        Religious Affiliation: _____

        Bride's Parents: _____

Groom: _____

        Religious Affiliation: _____

        Groom's Parents: _____

Ceremony to be Planned by Minister: _____ by Couple: _____

Other Minister(s) Assisting: _____

Maid/Matron of Honor: _____

Best Man: _____

Wedding Planner: _____

Date of Rehearsal: _____

Reception Open to All Wedding Guests: _____ By Invitation Only: _____

Location of Reception: _____

Wedding Photos to be Taken: _____ During Ceremony
                              _____ After Ceremony

Date of Counseling: _____

Date of Registration: _____

Funeral Registration

Name of Deceased: _____

Age: _____

Religious Affiliation: _____

Survivors:

    Spouse: _____
    Parents: _____
    Children: _____
    Siblings: _____
    Grandchildren: _____

Date of Death: _____

Time and Place of Visitation: _____

Date of Funeral or Memorial Service: _____

Funeral Home Responsible: _____

Location of Funeral or Memorial Service: _____

Scripture Used: _____ Hymns Used: _____
                                                _____

Eulogy by: _____

Other Minister(s) Assisting: _____

Pallbearers: _____

Date of Interment: _____ Place of Interment: _____

Graveside Service?: _____ Yes _____ No

Subject Index

Scripture Index